W9-ADI-873

GIOVANNI MARIA BONONCINI

GIOVANNI MARIA BONONCINI OF MODENA

A Chapter in Baroque Instrumental Music

WILLIAM KLENZ

Durham, North Carolina DUKE UNIVERSITY PRESS *1962*

LIBRARY OF CONGRESS CATALOGUE CARD NUMBER 62-20213

CAMBRIDGE UNIVERSITY PRESS, LONDON N.W. 1, ENGLAND

THIS BOOK IS PUBLISHED WITH THE
ASSISTANCE OF A GRANT TO THE
DUKE UNIVERSITY PRESS BY
THE FORD FOUNDATION.

PRINTED IN THE UNITED STATES OF AMERICA
BY THE SEEMAN PRINTERY, DURHAM, N. C.

PREFACE

This book is the consequence of the curiosity of a string player regarding the origins and traditions of his craft. The search led inevitably, of course, to Italy—to Bologna, and finally to Modena, where enough traces of the intense personality of Giovanni Maria Bononcini were visible to afford a glimpse of the man through the haze of prevailing biographical confusion. When seen against the local background, his historical importance was at once apparent, marking as it does the confluence of French and Italian elements in secular chamber music and a new level of contrapuntal force in instrumental church music.

The music speaks for itself. It is, like its composer, marked by distinction, refinement, force, and occasional audacity. The tedious job of transcription of some nine collections of sonatas (of which perhaps a third are contained in this volume) was constantly lightened by a sense of discovery.

I hope the account may not seem too circumstantial, and will feel well served if it contributes in any way to more reasonably conceived performances of the music of the whole period.

I am, of course, indebted to many helping hands, known and unknown—far too many to properly acknowledge, thank, or implicate here. To Mrs. Sang Ei C. Kim credit must go for the prodigious task of preparing the music for reproduction; likewise, to the staff of the Duke University Press for their patience and resourcefulness.

The original research of which this book is a partial result was supported by grants from the American Council of Learned Societies and the Research Council of Duke University, of which grateful acknowledgment is made here.

WILLIAM KLENZ

June, 1962

TABLE OF CONTENTS

GIOVANNI MARIA BONONCINI

CHAPTER I. GIOVANNI MARIA BONONCINI: *VITA*

Giovanni Maria Bononcini was born on the twenty-second or twenty-third day of September, 1642, at Montecorone (*presso Zocca*), Modena.[1] The son of Lucio Bononcini and his wife, Lucia, he was baptized Giovanni Maria on September 23.[2] He is thus a true child of the latter half of the seventeenth century, stylized by a name derived from figures of the Christian hierarchy. Such Christian names were then in vogue among the middle class, having supplanted such classical names as Claudio, Orazio, and even the Lucio of Bononcino's own father. They reflect the atmosphere of the Counter Reformation and the appeal of popular evangelical aspects of Catholicism. Further, they represent social and religious currents which were formative forces in Bononcini's life and career. The arts were invoked as principal agents of propaganda by the coalition of Church and State in the service of which Bononcini's life was to be spent. His published works are for the greater part specifically designated as *da chiesa* (for church) or *da camera* (for chamber or court).

Of Bononcini's youth and training we know little. It is assumed that he came at an early age from the outlying district of Montecorone to Modena,[3] then newly elevated to the status of a provincial capital. Modena had become, some forty years before, the seat of the governing family, d'Este, after their forced removal from the original family seat in Ferrara.

In Modena, it seems likely that Bononcini would have been a pupil of D. Marco Uccellini.[4] Uccellini was one of the best violinists of the day and held the positions of *Capo degl' Instromentisti del Serenissimo Signore Duca di Modena* between 1642 and 1662.[5] In any case, young Bononcini could

1. Evarista Pancaldi and Gino Roncaglia, *Maestri del Duomo di Modena VII: Giovanni Maria Bononcini,* Vol. IV of *Studi e Documenti della Reale Deputazione di Storia Patria per l'Emilia e Romagna* (Vols. III-V of Series VIII, Modena, 1939-1941), p. 136. (These several chapters—Chapter V, *D. Marco Uccellini;* VI, *Padre Mario Agatea;* VII, *G. M. Bononcini;* and VIII, *Giuseppe Colombi*—will be referred to as Pancaldi-Roncaglia, *MDM V,* etc.)

See also Luigi Francesco Valdrighi, *Musurgiana* No. 8, *I Bonocini da Modena* (Modena: G. T. Vicenzi e Nipoti, 1882), p. 6 n. 2. Valdrighi, who probably misread "8" for "6" in Bononcini's death notice (1678), did however surmise correctly: "forse . . . nelle vicine montagne di Monteombraro, Montecorone o circostanti, dove il cognome Bononcini e communissimo." (Hereinafter referred to as Valdrighi, *Musurgiana* No. 8.)

2. Pancaldi-Roncaglia, *MDM VII,* p. 136.

3. *Ibid.*

4. *Ibid.*

5. Pancaldi-Roncaglia, *MDM V,* p. 27.

hardly have escaped Uccellini's influence in so compact a social and professional milieu. This supposition receives additional support if we consider that Bononcini's best professional prospects were to occupy the same or a similar post. It is quite possible (and more probable than not) that Bononcini was in professional contact with Uccellini as a student and colleague from the time he gained competence as an instrumentalist. Because of his obvious talents, this contact might reasonably have begun by Bononcini's seventeenth or eighteenth year.

In any event, a certain sign of independence and professional status may be observed in the fact that on February 19, 1662, at the age of nineteen, Bononcini married Anna Maria Prezza.[6] Of this marriage there were born eight children, only two of whom—Giovanni and Antonio—survived infancy.[7]

These brothers became the two "Bononcinis" of European reputation. One, the operatic rival of Handel in London, was impaled on an epigram of Byrom[8] (often attributed to Pope). The other, working in Vienna, was one of the host of musicians who were the principal cultural export of Italy during the eighteenth century. Their fame has obscured that of their father and created the prevalent confusion regarding the lives and works of all three members of the family.

Whatever Giovanni Maria's economic situation at the time of his marriage, it was not destined to improve much in the sixteen remaining years of his life. Then, as now, artists, employed as creators of propaganda or "guarantees of immortality," were kept tame by hand-feeding. It is to be feared that the resounding titles Bononcini held as court and church musician offered more of glory than material reward.[9] Giovanni, his son, wrote (at age thirteen) in the dedication of his op. III[10] to his teacher, Gio. Paolo Colonna of Bologna:

6. Pancaldi-Roncaglia, *MDM VII*, p. 137.

7. *Ibid.* See also Evarista Pancaldi, "Su la famiglia dei Bononcini" (*Atti e memorie di R. Deputazione di Storia Patria per le provincie modenesi*, Series VII, 1929), VI, 13.

8. John Byrom, "Epigram on the Feuds Between Handel and Bononcini," *Miscellaneous Poems* (Manchester, 1773), pp. 343 f.

> Some say, compar'd to Bononcini,
> That Mynheer Handel's but a Ninny;
> Others aver, that he to Handel
> Is scarcely fit to hold a candle;
> Strange all this Difference should be
> 'Twixt Tweedle-dum and Tweedle-dee!

9. Pancaldi-Roncaglia, *MDM VII*, p. 140.

10. Giovanni Bononcini, *Sinfonie a 5, 6, 7, e 8 Instromenti . . . Da . . . Opera Terza* (Bologna: Giacomo Monti, 1683), quoted in Claudio Sartori, "Bibliografia della Musica Strumentale Italiana Stampate in Italia fino al 1700," *Biblioteca di Bibliografia Italiana XXIII* (Florence, 1952), p. 518. (Hereinafter referred to as Sartori, *BMI*.)

From my parents I had that much of life which sufficed to make me known to misery, while they [by] dying, abandoned me, yet a babe in arms, to poverty.[11]

With respect to G. M. Bononcini's training in theoretical aspects of music, especially in counterpoint, we are on more certain ground than with regard to his formation as a violinist. In the practical manual on music theory and counterpoint, *Il Musico Prattico,* which forms his op. VIII, Bononcini pays tribute to one of his teachers of counterpoint:

Should one wish to make a canon, which, each time it starts over, begins a tone away from the [preceding] beginning, he should consider that [example] which is prefaced to the first part of this book by Padre D. Agostino Bendinelli, *Lucchese, Canonico Regolare, Lateranense,* to whom Music serves only as the ornament of many other virtues, but [he] is so excellent in this that there are few today who rival him, and I myself can bear testimony in recognition of his affectionate and well-founded teaching [whence I have] all the best which I have learned of this profession.[12]

The relationship seems to have been one of mutual respect, as Bendinelli appropriately provides a canon with a laudatory text for the prefatory apparatus of his pupil's book. Bendinelli is, then, at least partly responsible for the refinement of Bononcini's taste and his technical skill in the higher aspects of counterpoint and canon. The reappraisal and systematic application of the classic polyphonic science of the sixteenth century, which itself had been (and remained) an official aesthetic symbol of the Counter Reformation, is a general feature of the evolution of instrumental music of the middle years of the seventeenth century. Bononcini's music clearly relates him to this movement while his treatise on counterpoint, *Il Musico Prattico,* places him squarely at the center of this development.

By 1671, and probably earlier, Giovanni Maria Bononcini seems sufficiently established in professional capacities and (which is the same thing) well-enough established at the Este court to request an appointment to succeed Giovanni Mazzi as violinist at the Cathedral of Modena.[13] The *Maestro di Cappella,* Padre Mario Agatea, reported that all of the candi-

11. Ibid. "Da i Genitori hebbi quel tanto di vita, come basto per produrmi alle miserie, mentr'essi, morendo, m'abbandonarono Fanciullo ancora in braccio alla pouerta."

12. "Volendo ancora fare un Canone, che ogni volta, che si torna da capo si posta alzare un grado lontano dal principio, si consideri quello posto di sopra nella prima parte del Padre D. Agostino Bendinelli Lucchese Canonico Regolare Lateranense, a cui se bene la Musica serue solamente per ornamento di molt'altri virtu, e pero anche in questa cosi eccellente, che al giorno d' hoggi, per mio credere, ha pochi, da suoi amoreuoli, e ben fondati onsegnamenti tutto il meglio, che ho appreso di questa professione." Giovanni Maria Bononcini, *Il Musico Prattico* (Bologna: Monti, 1673), p. 108. See also p. 169 *infra.*

13. Valdrighi, *Musurgiana* No. 8, p. 39.

dates examined were qualified. Bononcini, who had the recommendation of the Duchess d'Este (the actual ruler, as Regent for her son, the minor, Francesco II), was accepted by the Chapter and—the posts being apparently connected—"for her own service."[14] This implies that Bononcini became, or was confirmed in his situation as, a court musician of the *Concerto degli Strumenti della Serenissima Altezza di Modena.*

The most consequential developments of his professional life occurred in 1673 with the events leading up to his appointment to the post of *Maestro di Cappella* at the Cathedral of Modena. Bononcini showed here every evidence of professional confidence and determination to succeed to the position for which he felt qualified. Further, he demonstrated considerable aplomb in the management of court figures in his well-planned campaign.

On October 11, 1673, he requested of the Chapter of Canons of the Duomo their consideration for the post of *Maestro di Cappella* in the following terms:

Illustrious and Revered Gentlemen:

Gio. Mª Bononcini, humble and devoted servant ... has for years indefatigably applied himself to the Art of composing Music to render himself one day capable of [fulfilling] this post and able to perform especially at the Cathedral, and in the service, consequently, of Yʳ. Highness. Now, having with the aid of God succeeded in showing some signs of achievement with several works, already published, especially in the last [op. VIII, *Il Musico Prattico*] which is dedicated to ... the Emperor, showing some ability in this profession; and relying, above all, on Yʳ. Highness's benignity, which obtained three years ago the position of violinist, to follow with that of *Maestro di Cappella* (only in the event that Padre Fra Mario [Agatea] ... be permitted to depart and not otherwise), reverently and with anticipation begs Yʳ. Ill. Highnesses to do the honor, promising to serve and obey with greatest application and diligent concern corresponding to Yʳ. charge ... which I will receive as a signal favor. *Quam Deus,* October 11, 1673.[15]

14. *Ibid.*, p. 40. See also Gino Roncaglia, *La Cappella Musicale del Duomo di Modena,* Vol. V. of *Historiae Musicae Cultores Biblioteca* (Florence, 1957) (hereinafter referred to as Roncaglia, *CDM*), p. 130.

15. Ill^{mi} et Rev^{mi} Sig^{ri}:

"Havendo Gio. Mª Bononcini Modense humil^{mo} et div^{mo} Ser^{tore} delle SS^{e} VV. Ill^{me} et Rev^{me} attese. ed applicato indefessamente per degli anni all'Arte di comporre Musica per rendersi un giorno capace di qualche posto a poterla per esercitare, specialmente nella Cathedrale, et in servigio per conseguenza delle SS^{e} VV. Ill^{me}. Hora che coll'aiuto di Diogli e riuscito di ridurse a segno di valere con diverse sue opere, date gia alle stampe, e coll'ultima in particulare che ha dedicato alla Maestà dell'Imperatore a farsi conoscere per di qualche abilità nella professione; e sperando sopra tutto della benignità delle SS^{e} VV. Ill^{me} come ottenne tre anni sono il posto di Violinista, cosi di conseguire quello di M^{tro} di Cappella (venendo pero il caso, che il Padre Fr. Mario, dell'Oratore sempre stimato ed osservato, per quel degno Virtuoso, che veramente egli e, sere licenziasse, e non in altro modo) riverente-

Bononcini also prepared the ground with his patrons, the Duchess Laure and Francesco II d'Este, whose recommendations would, in the circumstances, be definitive. On October 18, 1673, Bononcini wrote to the Duchess requesting her "most benign recommendation to the Chapter of Canons ... to whom he has already presented a memorandum."[16] At the same time he approached the young Duke, Francesco II:

... again begging the great humanity of Y^{r}. Highness to deign to honor me equally with the other two who have also implored Y^{r}. protection, since the Chapter will elect him who wins the competition and is most capable for the post. Y^{r}. Highness will do an act of true justice which the petitioner will receive as a signal grace....[17]

The Duchess again supported Bononcini's claims, as we may see from the transactions of the Chapter dated November 18, 1673:

The Archbishop reports that Marchese Pij was commissioned by the Serenissima Madonna [the Duchess] to recommend Bononzini [*sic*] with the warmest and most solicitous recommendations of her Highness, to the Chapter as *Maestro di Cappella* of this Cathedral, showing [them] his memorandum to Her Highness, and reporting in like manner that this had the consent of His Highness [the Duke]....

The matter was put to a vote using gold and silver balls and "when collected, all the balls were gold, whereby the proposal passed."[18]

The Duke at first supported Bononcini's competitor, Giuseppe Colombi, but retracted in the face of his mother's recommendation of Bononcini and

mente per tanto ed anticipatemente applica le SS. VV. Ill^{me} a fargliene l'honore adesso per all'hora promettendo di servirle ed obbedirle con tutta la maggiore applicazione dilig^{za} premura, in corrispondezza del Suo dovere, e dell'ardentissima brama che ha sempre havuto e ne ha, che io ricevera per segnalatissima grazia. *Quam Deus.* il 11 Ott^{re} 1673." Cited in Pancaldi-Roncaglia, *MDM VII,* p. 133.

16. "Potendo essere che Padro F. Mario Maestro di Cappella vada in breve altrove, Gio. Maria Bononcini hum^{o} servo di V. A. S. la supplica di Sua benignissima raccomandazione al Capitolo del SS. Canonici ai quali ha gia presentato memoriale...." Quoted in Pancaldi-Roncaglia, *MDM VII,* p. 134, and Roncaglia, *CDM,* p. 138.

17. "... riverentiss^{mo} hora di nuove supplica la somma umanita dell'A. V. a degnarsi di egualm^{te} honorarlo con gli altri due, che per lo stesso effetto hanno anch'eglino implorato l'altiss^{ma} protezione di Lei, perche d^{o} Capitolo faccia elezione di quello che più al concorso ed alla prova riuscira migliore, e capace del d^{o} posto che come V. A. fara un atto di vera guisto, cosi l'Orat^{e} le ricevera per segnalatissima grazia...." Quoted in Pancaldi-Roncaglia, *MDM VII,* p. 135. See also Valdrighi, *Musurgiana No. 8,* p. 40.

18. "Riferi il S. Arcipe che il S. Marchese Pij per parte della Ser^{ma} Madonna gl' havea commesso il raccomandare caldam^{te} e con comma premura di S. A. al Capitolo il Bononzini p. M^{ro} di Capella [*sic*] di q^{ta} Cat^{le} esibendo il di lui memoriale dato a d^{o} S. A. e parimenti rifferi havere havuto l'assenso di Mons. Illmo p. detto Bononzini; attese le quali propositi si diede il partito seg^{o}: A chi delle SS. loro Ill^{me} e Rev^{me} par e piace d'ellegere p. M^{ro} di Capella di q^{ta} Cated^{le} il S. Gio. Mª Bononcini, caso che il P. Mario moderno M^{ro} di Capella si licenzii, come si suppone, ne in altro modo, ed adesso p. alhora di la palla in Oro. et a chi no in arg^{to}. Date e raccolte le palle furono tutte in Oro, onde il partito ottenne." Quoted in Pancaldi-Roncaglia, *MDM VII,* p. 135, and Roncaglia, *CDM,* p. 140.

the *fait accompli.* This episode provides our most intimate glimpse into the courtly *ambiance* in which Bononcini worked and sets forth the tone and atmosphere of the situation. The event itself, as noted by Pancaldi and Roncaglia, is not without human interest and humor:

On the afternoon of the same day ("after dinner") the *Acts of the Chapter* relate a curious event. Here is the account:

"S. Tomasi reports that his Serene Highness, the Duke, had, the preceding morning, charged him with recommending S. Gioseffo Colombi to the Chapter as *Maestro di Cappella* of the Cathedral, and on coming to the church to deliver it, [he] found that the Chapter had appointed Bononzini as recommended by Her Highness. Returning to his Highness and relating the event, he received no other reply from His Highness than that he had recommended, not commanded."[19]

The situation was possibly made more piquant by the fact that Bononcini appears to have been subordinate to Colombi: Colombi was at that time *Capo degli Strumentisti* (Chief of Intsrumentalists), of which Bononcini was a *Suonatore* (player).

Colombi was, moreover, the violin teacher of the Duke, as shown by the dedication of his op. V,[20] and thus in close contact with the nominal ruler. He was to have his day in 1678 when he succeeded, with the support of the Duke, to the position of *Maestro di Cappella* at Bononcini's death.

As for a *prova* (competition) or a third candidate for the post, it appears there was neither, despite Bononcini's apprehensions or hopes. The "old system"—influence, prestige, and party—had worked once again. This time, however, it was for the best: we can see from today's vantage point that Bononcini was certainly the better choice. This is certainly true as regards his qualifications as a composer. His work is more consequential in structure and fabric than Colombi's, whose style was—all in all—lighter and more obviously instrumental.

In 1672, beginning with the title page of op. VI, Bononcini used the title

19. Senonche nel pomeriggio ["il doppo pranzo"] del medessimo giorno gli Atti Capitolari (G. 23) ci danno notizia uno curioso avvenimento. Eccone la narrazione: "Riferi il S. Tomasi che il Ser^{ma} S. Duca la matt^{a} preced^{e} l'havea imposto il raccomandare il S. Gioseffo Colombi al Capitolo per M^{ro} di Capella della Cated^{le}, e che venuto in Duomo p. servirlo, havendo inteso essere statto Bononzini raccomandata da Madamma Ser^{ma} essere ritornato a S. A. et haverli dato parte del seguito, ne havere poscia havuto altra riposta da S. A. se non che questo l'havea raccomandato, non comandato." Quoted in Pancaldi-Roncaglia, *MDM VII*, p. 138. See also Valdrighi, *Musurgiana* No. 8, p. 40, and Roncaglia, *CDM*, p. 140.

20. "... dell'A. V. S. l'hauer sortito l'honore d'auanzare la di lei destra nata a gli Scetri à trattare pacificamente l'arco sonoro...." ("...I have the honor to train the hand of Y^{r}. Highness, born to the scepter, to peacefully guide the sounding bow..."). Quoted in Sartori *BMI*, p. 552.

Accademico Filarmonica,[21] referring, of course, to the celebrated Accademia Filarmonica of Bologna, and all of his subsequent works bear this title. Padre Martini, in his manuscript history of the Accademia, does not mention him. Nor has any documentary evidence of the date and circumstances of his election to the Accademia been reported by the modern researchers Gaspari, Catelani,[22] Pancaldi, Roncaglia, or by its official historian, Nestore Morini.[23]

There can be little doubt of Bononcini's right to this title. Otherwise, he would not have dared to publish in Bologna itself eight works (his opp. VI-XIII) using the designation. It is likely that the theoretical treatise, *Il Musico Prattico,* earned him this distinction. We do know that the treatise was *gia compito, ed in pronto per mandarsi alle Stampe*[24] (ready for publication) before 1671 according to Bononcini's own statement in the preface of his op. VI. *Il Musico Prattico* may have circulated in manuscript before publication. Certainly its contents, based on the classic contrapuntal science of the preceding century, conformed to the practical teaching and aesthetic precepts current at the *Accademia,* where the treatise may well have been used as a text.

In 1674 Bononcini sought to alleviate his economic situation by approaching the *Signori Conservatori della Città di Modena* with regard to the vacant post and emoluments of the *Maestro di Cappella* of the votive chapel, the perquisite of "others of his predecessors."[25] Again Colombi appears as his rival, and this time, presumably because he had applied previously, was given the post.[26]

Like those of any artist, Bononcini's critical faculties were sharpened essentially for the purposes of self-development, but became inevitably applied to the world at large. In turn, he received his own share of criticism and resentful attack from less well-endowed colleagues. Direct competition with Colombi may have precipitated the two men's differences, but Bononcini's honest eagerness for recognition and his consciousness of his own worth must have aroused the ill-will of others. In any case, we

21. Pancaldi-Roncaglia *MDM VII,* p. 141, and Roncaglia *CDM,* p. 148.
22. Pancaldi-Roncaglia, *MDM VII,* p. 144.
23. Nestore Morini, *La R. Accademia Filarmonica di Bologna,* (Bologna: L. Capelli, 1930).
24. Sartori, *BMI,* p. 464.
25. Ill^{mi}SSig^{ri} 1674 il 14 Dic^{bre}
"Gio. Mª Bononcini, Cittadino Modanese, M^{tro} di Cappella del Duomo, e riverentiss^{mo} Servi^{re} dell' SS^{rie} V.V. Ill^{me} colla brama da lui havuta fin quando entro nel posto sud^{o} di potere insieme godere al solito degli altri sui antecess^{re} dell'honore piu che dell'emolum^{to} di M^{ro} di Cap^{a} delle SS^{rie} V.V. Ill^{me} nella Santis^{ma} Madonna del Voto essendone hora la vacanza," quoted in Pancaldi-Roncaglia, *MDM VII*, p. 140, and Roncaglia, *CDM,* p. 143-144.
26. *Ibid.*

owe to Bononcini's righteous indignation some account of the criticisms made concerning the demonstrations of contrapuntal virtuosity, viz., the canons which "decorate" his op. III,[27] including a "puzzle" canon with the motto, *Caecus non iudicat de colore* (The blind are no judges of color), which contains the key to its solution. (Cf. Plate I.)

Plate I

Obbligo à 4. *Caecus non judicat de colore.*

The motto, a translation of a line from Chaucer's *Troilus and Cressida* plays on the word "color" in the sense of note values, *color temporis.*

These canons apparently evoked critical reaction to which Bononcini felt constrained to reply. In the dedication of his op. IV he strikes out at

> ...the censure by critics, sharply made under the motto, *Caecus non iudicat di colore,* applied to one of my Canons...mischievously believed and publicly asserted not to be mine... [and] should it come to cases, they would oblige by naming the true authors....[28]

27. Sartori, *BMI,* pp. 454-456.

28. "...censure de' Critici, i quali fatti forti sul motto, *Caecus non iudicat,* etc., sottoposto ad uno de' medemi Canoni hauendo malamente creduto, ed assertiuamente publicato non essere miei, potranno più, che da qual si sia altro, da V.A. Illustrissima medema, che hà hauuta la bontà e sofferenza di vedermi talhora operare, rimanere, e disingannati, e distolti da

It is interesting to note that the criticism is not based on technical grounds, but is, rather, an accusation of plagiarism. Apparently this attack occurred before the publication of op. IV, for Bononcini felt it necessary to make a public reply in a *Discorso Musicale... in defense of his Third Opus... judged not [to be] his....*[29]

Critical concepts in the seventeenth century were more completely oriented to technique (in music, formulated in contrapuntal terms) than they have become since the nineteenth century and the intervention of the Romantic point of view and its emphasis on personal genius. Also, the attitude of the seventeenth-century mind was increasingly directed toward scientific inquiry into quantitative causal relationships, an attitude which has characterized subsequent European thought. The entire tenor of the *Discorso*—the professional carping, the technical refutation (not without its appeal to lay curiosity)—is possibly the best reflection, in a single document, of the intellectual climate surrounding Bononcini. Its sound critical opinions and technical observations, couched in a mordant and forthright style, are perhaps the clearest indication—apart from the qualities of his music—of his own intense personality, visible through the ramifications of seventeenth-century epistolary style.[30]

The records of the Chapter of the Cathedral of Modena give us little information about Bononcini's activity in the five years of his tenure as *Maestro di Cappella,*[31] except for routine entries such as that regarding the tuning of the organ on May 30, 1674.[32] In 1675 an incident of friction occurred between Bononcini and one Ippolito Bellini, a violinist at the Duomo who had been strongly recommended by the Duke.[33] A measure of Bononcini's security and good relations with the Chapter is visible in the fact that an emissary was sent to the Duke claiming Bellini was "ignorant, incapable" [and had] "used the *Maestro di Cappella* badly,"[34] and the man was apparently dismissed.

In the last two years of his life, 1677 and 1678, Bononcini saw the be-

---

cosi fallace, & erronea opinione, si come essere pregati (se mai le cadesse in taglio) che, se pure ursurpati dette Canoni, com'essi vogliono, si compiacciono di accennarne nominatamente i proprj Autori...." Quoted in Sartori, *BMI,* p. 464.

29. *Discorso Musicale di Gio. Maria Bononcini Sopra una Composizione a 3 datagli per aggiungervi il Basso; et in difesa della 3ª sua Opera uscita gia dalle Stampe, e giudicata non di lui, ma tolta e rubata in buona parte da altri Autori.* Quoted in Valdrighi, *Musurgiana No. 8,* p. 41; See also Pancaldi-Roncaglia, *MDM VII,* p. 142, and Roncaglia, *CDM,* p. 146.

30. Valdrighi, *Musurgiana No. 8,* pp. 8 ff. (For the text of the *Discorso Musicale,* see appendix A.)

31. Pancaldi-Roncaglia, *MDM VII,* p. 138.

32. *Ibid.*

33. *Ibid.,* p. 139, also Roncaglia, *CDM,* p. 143.

34. "... questo sonatore esser ignorante, inabile e trattar male col M^ro^ di Cappella." *Ibid.*

ginning of what—had he lived longer—would have become more than local success. His works were reprinted: op. VII by Gardano in Venice (1677?) and opp. VI and VII by Monti in Bologna (1677) at the instigation and enterprise of Marino Silvani. In the dedication of the second edition of op. VII Silvani describes these works as "dalla voracità de' virtuosi assorbite" (devoured by the voracity of virtuosi). Opus VI he describes as "more worthy of admiration than praise" (*tacio il lodar quest'Opera, mentre e più degna d'ammiratione, che di lode: il nome Solo dell'Autore l'inalza alle Stelle.*) An edition of *Il Musico Prattico* was published in Venice in 1678 by Giuseppe Sala, and a second Bolognese edition was brought out by Monti in 1688, for which Silvani, the entrepreneur, wrote, in the dedication:

> Sacked, no less by Time than by the avidity of the connoisseurs, the rich and pompous statue of *Il Musico Prattico* of the Great Bononcini, leaves the world of Harmony deprived of the keenest intelligence which Heaven holds in its Band.[35]

There are further testimonies of the spread of Bononcini's reputation despite a rapid change in taste after 1690. A German translation of the second part of *Il Musico Prattico* appeared in Stuttgart in 1701,[36] and English editions of his Sonatas appeared in 1700(?), 1705(?), and *ca.* 1720.[37] Johann Gottfried Walther in his *Musikalisches Lexicon* of 1732 also gives some indication of Bononcini's current reputation by the extent of the article devoted to him and his books—two columns in length—which is considerably longer than most entries.

On June 29, 1677, eleven days after the birth of Antonio Maria, the younger of Bononcini's two composer-sons, Anna Maria Bononcini died.[38] In October of the same year Bononcini married Barbara Agnese Tosatti, the sister of the curate of San Pietro. Pancaldi-Roncaglia suggest that this marriage was undertaken to "normalizzare l'andamento della sua famiglia" (stabilize the life of his family). The wisdom and success of this action—if so brought about—is attested by the development of Bononcini's two older

35. "Sacheggiata non men dal Tempo, che della avidità de gl'Intendenti la Ricca e Pomposa Statua del Musico Prattico del Gran Bononcini, lascio (privo) il Mondo armonico della più Soave Intelligenza, ch'avesse il Ciel del Concerto." Cited in Giovanni Maria Bononcini, *Il Musico Prattico* (2d. ed.; Bologna: Monti, 1678). See also Roncaglia, *CDM*, p. 150.

36. Johann Gottfried Walther, "Bononcini," *Musikalisches Lexicon oder musikalische Bibliothek*, 1732 (Kassel and Basel: Bärenreiter, 1953). [Hereinafter referred to as Walther *Lexicon.*]

37. William C. Smith, *Bibliography of Musical Works Published by John Walsh* (London: Oxford University Press, 1948), pp. 56, 44, 69.

38. Pancaldi-Roncaglia, *MDM VII*, p. 137, and Roncaglia, *CDM*, p. 141.

sons into two of the most important composers of their generation. For, within little more than a year, on the eighteenth of November, 1678, Giovanni Maria Bononcini died, leaving the two sons and yet another, Giovanni Maria, born a few hours before his death, to an uncertain future.[39]

39. Roncaglia, *CDM,* p. 141.
Some light is shed on the question of who assumed material responsibility for the education of Bononcini's sons in the dedication of op. II, *Concerti da Camera* . . . 1685 to Count Alessandro Sanvitali by the elder son, Giovanni: ". . . and no less is it needful [owing] that I present this second [work] to Your Excellency whom, for just as many reasons, I should implore as my Maecenas. The intelligence and friendship with which your Excellency honors this profession . . . [among others] are reasons, although compressed into so short a time, that enlarge the abundance of proofs of the obligation of this present gift." Cited in Sartori, *BMI,* p. 517. (See also chap. vi n. 32.)

Chapter II. THE PROFESSIONAL SPHERE

The events of G. M. Bononcini's life clearly indicate that his professional activity was centered at the court and the Cathedral in Modena. While it is true that his works were published in Bologna and in Venice, accounts which associate him with positions in Bologna arise from the confusion of biographical details of G. M. Bononcini's life with those of his son, Giovanni. G. M. Bononcini himself deserves to be regarded as the head of an independent tradition, a tradition with its own distinct features arising from local circumstances, rather than a mere subsidiary branch of the "Bolognese School." Actually Modena had a continuous and homogenous violin-composer tradition represented in the persons and works of Uccellini, Bononcini's teacher, Bononcini himself, and Colombi, Bononcini's successor as *Maestro di Cappella.* This "school" antedates the comparable developments in Bologna, which can be said to begin with the appointment of Cazzati as *Maestro di Cappella* at San Petronio in 1657.

A principal factor contributing to the Modenese tradition is, of course, the presence of the Este court, which provided a professional *ambiance* which embraced a cultivated audience and insured the continuity of a responsible patronage. The social ritual of the court required elegant and austere dance music which would bear comparison with the current French models. Further, an educated, aristocratic audience exacted technical skill and refinement from composer and performer alike for both church and court. The Bolognese circumstances, including the large church of San Petronio, on the other hand, required a massive and impressive, but less intricate, style. To provide themselves with an equivalent of the court atmosphere, its occasions and its exacting audience, the Bolognese musicians and aristocracy joined forces and formed the Accademia Filarmonica.

In 1683, after his removal to Modena from Bologna, G. B. Vitali compared the two circumstances in the dedication of his op. VIII (dedicated to Cesare Ignatio d'Este; printed in Modena by Gasparo Ferri in 1683):

... What else can I do, in putting in print some of my feeble Musical [efforts], after having performed them in this most erudite country, with applause from the *virtuosi* beyond any merit of mine, and far from the sharp teeth of the Zoïli and of the Aristarchi . . . than to consecrate them to Yr. Serene Highness?[1]

The social complex of which Giovanni Maria Bononcini was a part was the product of the hierarchical socio-political order of seventeenth-century Catholic countries. The philosophy and practical administration evolved by the Counter Reformation had as their objective the restoration of the Catholic ideal, a feudal world order with clear lines of secular and ecclesiastical authority. A central feature of this order was court life—the point of contact for the elect, the Princes of State and Church—where the affairs of dependent society were decided and arranged. We have already seen how this combination of secular and ecclesiastical authority operated to affect the course of Bononcini's life.[2]

In so formalized a society the arts become official expressions. The graphic arts become didactic or propagandistic, while the dynamic arts—especially music—become ritualistic and function to regulate the forms of social intercourse by control of time, space, and social symbol. The ballet is the expression of the dynamic arts in the secular, courtly sphere, while the symbolic choreography of church ritual is the ecclesiastical form. In these circumstances art is not primarily the means of personal expression except in terms of individual mastery and refinement of technique, and Bononcini's artistic production must be regarded as the articulation of functional, ritual uses of music required by the court to which he was bound by patronage.

At the head of this social organism was the Este family, led by the hereditary feudal dukes of Modena and Reggio, and originally, of Ferrara. However, in 1597 at the death of Alfonso II (remembered as the benefactor of Tasso) the main and legitimate line of the family became extinct, and the traditional seat of the Este, Ferrara, was annexed as Papal property. The Papacy refused to recognize Cesare (1598-1628), the heir presumptive, as Duke of Ferrara, but continued to acknowledge his title as Duke of Modena and Reggio. Fearing excommunication, Cesare abandoned Fer-

1. "Hor che altro poteuo io fare, nel dare alle stampe alcune mie debolezze Musicale, dopo hauerle fatte sentire in questa eruditissima patria, con plauso de' virtuosi sopra ogni mio merito, acciò, lungi dal dente mordace de' Zoïli, e degli Aristarchi, a beneficio de' posteri si eternassero, se non dedicarle, e consecrarle a V. A. S.?" Cited in Sartori, *BMI,* p. 509. This dedication, discounting its calculated adulation, must in some measure reflect contemporary feeling about the two situations, Modena and Bologna. The term "questa eruditissima patria" was not entirely idle flattery, while "Zoïli" and "Aristarchi" are good cover names for the two Bolognese Academies Vitali lists in his title. Or perhaps "Aristarchi" is a thin disguise for the faction of Arresti, whose attacks had displaced Vitali's teacher, Cazzati, a decade before. See p. 48 *infra.*

2. See p. 3 *supra.*

rara and removed to Modena, taking with him most of the family archives and museum—the basis of the present rich Estense library. The establishment of the Este Court at Modena raised the status of the Emilian town to that of a provincial capital, and must have had the effect of attracting the likely and ambitious from the vicinity to seek their fortunes. Bononcini's own migration from the village of Montecorone was almost certainly a typical consequence.

The circumstances which surround the fortunes of the Este family at Modena in the middle years of the century are those that create the milieu of which Bononcini's work is a part. In 1629 Francesco I (succeeding Alfonso III, who abdicated into religious orders after a year of reign) came to power. Francesco appears to have been a figure of some consequence and perception. Traditionally, the Este family had been allied with the occupying Spanish. Francesco I, however, aligned the Este forces with the invading French in the hope of recovering Ferrara from the Papacy. He also began the construction of the Este Palace in Modena, the present home of the great library. Continuing family tradition and inherited taste, he also extended patronage to men of art and letters—among others, to Fulvio Testi.

The short reign of Alfonso IV (1658-1662), who continued the French alliance, was followed by that of his son, Francesco II (1662-1694), to whom, nominally at least, Bononcini was most directly responsible. Born in 1660, Francesco II reigned under the Regency of his mother, the dowager Laure d'Este. Laure d'Este (who was Bononcini's real protector) was the niece of Mazarin, and her marriage in 1655 to Alfonso IV had been in the interests of the alliance with France. Her regency was apparently marked by good, quiet government and some rise in the position—if not the fortunes—of the Este family. Her daughter, Maria Beatrice, married the Duke of York, who later became James II of England, and was thus a link between Italy and the Catholic-Absolutist aspirations of the Stuarts.[3]

3. Thus the cultural forces which caused the original remodeling of the Chapel Royal by Charles II to resemble that of Louis XIV (with its "Twenty-four Violins") were reinforced by direct political contact with Italy. These same contacts may be responsible for Purcell's knowledge of the "Most Famed Italian Masters" who were the avowed models for his production of "Sonnatas" in 1683 and 1694 for the Chapel Royal. After all, the mere presence of a member of the family famous for its taste and patronage would in itself have been a direct stimulus. Nor is it unthinkable that Maria brought, or had sent, the current Modenese production.

The actual resemblance between the styles of Bononcini and Purcell—especially their preoccupation with the sustained contrapuntal fabric—deserves notice. Doubtless the two men had much in common as personalities: their uncompromising approach to technical mastery, their pleasure in the canon, etc. While it is extremely possible that some of Bononcini's work was known to Purcell, it is probably safer to say that "like situations produce like results." In any

Laure d'Este—the niece of that Mazarin who, with Richelieu, was the author of the policy which enabled Louis XIV to say "L'Etat, c'est moi!"—was undoubtedly fulfilling the destiny arranged for her by diplomacy as well as following her own convictions and talents. It is a matter of history that the mutual intellectual and cultural exchange with the French court at the period was lively. While Italian theatrical art was in vogue in France until the death of Mazarin in 1611, the French ballet was the model for Europe in both theatrical and social dancing. With the ballet came the style and technique of the dance music which was evolving in the earlier milieu of the *Vingt-quatre Violons du Roi* and later in the ballets of Lully.

Laure's son, Francesco II, remained essentially under her domination and, at his majority, turned over much of the affairs of government to his brother Cesare and his uncle, Rinaldo. He did, however, undertake the reorganization of the library, exhibiting his interest in the arts.

Some idea of the extent of the musical establishment moved from Ferrara to Modena by the Este family may be gained from the list of musical instruments, books, etc., sent with the shipment of December 18, 1600.[4] The list mentions no fewer than nine organs, six viols of various types, a harp, *cornetti,* and other instruments and music books, totaling some forty-odd items.[5] On arrival, on January 21, 1601, these are described as being in bad condition from mistreatment and inadequate care. The treasure succumbs to the vicissitudes of neglectful storage, and in 1625-1626, another inventory has the following notice appended:

> ...(the instruments) except for such instruments...which are in various hands ...and some *viole da Gamba* and two harps...are reasonably preserved; the others are ruined...so that if it be credible, what once brought beauty to the eye and satisfaction to the ear now brings the feeling of greatest sadness to those who behold them.[6]

Some fifty years later, at the height of Bononcini's career (about 1676),

---

event, the traffic in cultural materials, as an adjunct to that in political ideology, demonstrates how completely the contrapuntal church sonata was the artistic symbol of the milieu we are describing.

4. Luigi Francesco Valdrighi, *Musurgiana* No. 19, *Capelle, Concerti e Musiche di Casa d'Este* (Modena: G. T. Vincenzi e Nipoti, 1884), p. 59. [Hereinafter referred to as Valdrighi *Musurgiana* No. 19.]

5. *Ibid.*, p. 61.

6. "... (eccettuandone quelli stromenti che e scritto di sopra essere in mano di diversi) gli altri stomenti sopranotati del Ser. Sig. Duca; delli quali, eccetto alcune viole da Gamba et dui Arpi, che sono ragionevolmente conservate, altri sono rovinati et disfatti del tutto, come li 4 Cassoni grandi; altri stroppiati et marciti dalla pioggia che vi e caduta dentro, et quasi tutti manche voli delle sue parti, che si come e credibile che una volta progressero vaghezza a l'occhio et satisfactione all'orecchio, al presente muoveno sense di grandissima compassione in chi li mira." *Ibid.*, p. 70.

an inventory of *cembali* and *spinetti* belonging to the Duke included twenty items of various sizes and qualities ranging from "buonissimo" and "pretioso" to "mediocre." Certain instruments are specified "per camera" or "teatro," and others "per teatro e Accademia."[7]

In the course of the seventeenth century the ascendancy of the violin was gradually manifest so that the varied instrumental heritage from the end of the Renaissance gave way to the homogeneous string body of the Baroque century. The *Vingt-quatre Violons* of Louis XIV was the most famous of similar groups maintained by courts all over Europe.[8] The Este court was no exception, and the list of significant violinist-composers who served in Modena is long and distinguished. G. M. Bononcini was not alone: Uccellini, Colombi, G. Bononcini, Gio. Batt. Vitali, and Tomaso Antonio Vitali also served in Modena as court musicians in one capacity or another.[9]

The various designations of their positions—"del Concerto di S.A.S.," "Capo degli Strumentisti di S.A.S.," "Maestro di Cappella di S.A.S.," "Vice Maestro di Cappella di S.A.S."—suggest that the uses of both secular (chamber and dance) music and sacred (chapel) music were served by essentially the same performers. Certainly all the composers mentioned above functioned as composers of both church and chamber music, as any list of their published works will show.[10] The positions may well have been as much honorary as functional. Their resonant titles cover many a title page, and, like the dedications bristling with academic conceits, they serve to assert—on paper at least—the dependence of the artist upon the central figures of the hierarchical world we have described.

The size of the musical forces of the "Concerto," the court orchestra at Modena, is not possible to determine. Doubtless it varied with the importance of the function, on occasion emulating in numbers the French model of the *Vingt-quatre Violons,* although in general Italian ensembles do not seem to have been so large. Bononcini wrote in the French manner ("Stil Francese") "à 4" and "à 5," but whether these parts were doubled in the French fashion is not clear from documentary evidence. The exist-

7. *Ibid.*

8. Eric Schenk, *Osservazioni sulla Scuola instrumentale modenese nel Seicento* ("Atti e Memorie della Accademia di Scienze, Lettere e Arti di Modena," Series V; Modena, 1952), Vol. X. On page 7, without giving the source, Schenk states that by 1630 the group at Modena was known as "Violini di Sua Altezza."

9. Apart from those listed, there is evidence that attempts were made to gain the services of Legrenzi (Schenk, *op. cit.,* p. 12) and even Corelli himself (Valdrighi, *Musurgiana* No. 19, p. 72).

10. Pancaldi-Roncaglia, *MDM VII,* p. 140.

ing manuscripts at Modena[11] may well have been the parts used by the players. They exist in single copies only, which suggests that one, or at most, two players, to a part was usual. The variability of the size of the group of performers is clearly suggested by the prevalence of *ad libitum* parts in the work of Uccellini, Colombi, Bononcini, and Vitali, where the directions "a 2, 3, & 4 se piace" are also frequently encountered.

Of the practices at the Cathedral in Modena, we have more precise evidence. When Uccellini became *Maestro di Cappella* at the Cathedral in 1647 there were—in addition to six singers—one violinist, one organist, and one *suonatore da violone*.[12]

In 1690, at the time of the reformation of the *Cappella* of the Cathedral under Bononcini's successor, Colombi,[13] there were—in addition to the *Maestro di Cappella*—four singers, a *Violino Primo* and *Violino Secondo,* a *Suonatore da Violone,* and an organist. These, then, were the usual forces: one player to a part for ordinary occasions whatever the practice on special occasions, when more players may have been added. That this group—a first and a second violin, a *violone* (or violoncello),[14] and the organ—seems to have been usual in most churches is clear from the great preponderance of *sonate da chiesa* for that combination and the crystallization of this norm in the remainder of the century. At San Petronio in Bologna the combination of a vast late-Gothic church (far larger than Modena's Romanesque Duomo) and a large number of enthusiastic amateurs and quasi-professional string players to form the *ripieno* eventually produced—in the 1680's with Torelli—the *concerto grosso* of which the professionals of the *cappella* form the *concertino.*

11. These do not appear to be in Bononcini's hand, but may be the work of a professional copyist—a usual member of such establishments—since works by Vitali written after Bononcini's death are to be found in the same hand.

12. Pancaldi-Roncaglia, *MDM V,* p. 29.

13. Pancaldi-Roncaglia, *MDM VII,* p. 209.

14. The *violone,* the bass of the viol family, appears to have survived the century as a normal ensemble bass despite the increasing use of the violoncello, which is the true bass of the violin family. It is possible that the terms were, in practice, more nearly interchangeable than the title pages suggest. Corelli's op. V (Rome, 1700) prescribes *Violino e Violone o Cembalo* (Sartori, *BMI,* p. 611). The Antwerp, 1692, edition of Corelli's op. IV prescribes *Doi Violini, Violoncello, e Cembalo* (Sartori *op. cit.,* p. 571), whereas the Rome, 1694, edition (Sartori, p. 580) has parts for violins I & II and *Violone ò Cimbalo.* In Bononcini's own works *Violone* is prescribed on all printed title pages. However the printed part books of op. XII (1678) are marked *Violoncello* and the MS. part in Bologna bears the characteristic variant *Violoncino.* He occasionally requires the low BB♭, which the 'cello does not today encompass, although according to Mersenne's tuning (1636) g, d, F, BB♭, it did.

Chapter III. TEACHERS AND COLLEAGUES

MARCO UCCELLINI came to Modena in 1641.[1] In court and church positions he served the same mission to the Modonese tradition as did Maurizio Cazzati sixteen years later in Bologna. Uccellini brought together in his performance and composition the different currents that made up the Venetian-Lombard school or violin tradition.

The two contributory stylistic streams were (1) the severe, massive, harmonically saturated and quasi-contrapuntal manner of the Venetians, and (2) the florid manner of a virtuoso order based upon cursive ornament and instrumental device—the *affetti.* This style of composition and performance is derived from the manner of such violinist-composers as Biagio Marini,[2] Carlo Farina, and G. B. Fontana,[3] and is the analogue of the decorative devices of the virtuoso singer, namely, the *gorgia.* Uccellini was, in this respect, one of the outstanding *virtuosi* of the day, for he explored *tessiture* and devices which were only later in general use.

These two contributory streams—structural and decorative—are visible in typical forms in Uccellini's style. In addition, he seems to have acquired precisely the style of the dance music—French as well as Italian—in use in Northern Italian courts during his varied experiences as a young performer. Further, he appears to have absorbed the dramatic and expressive possibilities of the new concerted Roman manner of Carissimi. Another aspect of his instrumental culture is his acquaintance with devices usually considered a specialty of trans-Alpine, German instrumentalists—the *scordatura* and its concomitant, double-stop playing[4]—as well as the use of imitations of natural sounds,[5] popular songs,[6] and imitations of other instruments.[7]

1. Pancaldi-Roncaglia, *MDM V,* p. 27, and Roncaglia *CDM,* p. 114.

2. D. J. Iselin, *Biagio Marini* (Basle, 1930).

3. Schering, *GMB.* Examples 182, 183, and 184 illustrate the contrast of the two styles exactly.

4. These devices, regarded as more typically German, were not so much unknown in Italy as unappreciated. The addition of harmonic possibilities was offset by prejudice to the tone quality and the "vocal" attributes of the instrument, always prized by the Italians with their sensitivity to natural beauty.

5. As in the sonata "Le nozze delle Galline col Cucu" in his op. III, *Aria Nona* (1642). Cited in Pancaldi-Roncaglia, *MDM V,* p. 28. See also Sartori, *BMI,* pp. 379 ff.

6. Uccellini, "Caporal Simon," *Sonate Correnti et Arie,* op. IV, no. 12 (Venice, 1645). Given by Torchi, *AMI VII,* p. 293. See also Sartori, *BMI,* p. 399.

7. "La Tromba," *Sonate over Canzoni da farsi a violino solo,* op. V, no. 14 (Venice, 1649). See Sartori, *BMI,* p. 405.

This extramusical "gadgetry" is balanced by a kind of supramusical demonstration of dexterity which takes the form of demonstrations of contrapuntal virtuosity in the "trick" or puzzle canons that form a kind of decorative appendix to Uccellini's op. IX. Puzzle canons were also included by Bononcini in his opp. II and V.[8] Instrumental canons of various kinds—known also as "artificii musicali"—remain a typical Modenese feature and are to be found also in the works of G. B. Vitali, specifically in op. XIII,[9] written after he had been for some years in Modena. Similarly, Domenico Gabrielli—another musician who moved from Bologna to Modena—composes (*ca.* 1690) a sonata in canon for two cellos.[10] Even in the work of a composer only briefly associated with Modena the instrumental canons appear: G. B. Bassani includes two such canons in his op. I of 1677,[11] which was probably written with an eye toward a post in Modena.

G. M. Bononcini himself makes limited use of the purely instrumental virtuosity and manneristic elements of Uccellini's style (which tend to disappear from Uccellini's own works under the influence of the cultivated Modenese audience and the general change in taste toward a more severe manner). These, including the technique of the *scordatura,* are confined to the *Arie, Correnti,* and *Sarabande* of his op. IV (a 2, *Violino e Violone*) and are appropriate in these duet chamber pieces written for himself and his amateur patron, Obizzo Guidoni who—according to the dedication—played "the *violone* with more than ordinary agility and mastery" (*Suonande con non ordinaria agilità e maestria il violone*).

Bononcini excludes completely the "imitations" of various kinds, as well as folk elements, from his style, doubtless because of the degree of cultivation of his audience. He also leaves to his compatriot, Colombi, and successor, Vitali, the exploitation of the periodic variation forms such as the *ciaccona,* the *passacaglia,* etc. No such forms appear in his works, and there are surprisingly few in Uccellini's, considering his background.

Uccellini also established a distinctive use of the instrumental "aria" or "arietta" as part of Modenese tradition. In mid-seventeenth-century instrumental practice the term "aria" meant, in general, the application of a

8. Such items met the needs of the seventeenth-century mind in its search for contacts with the world of discovery and science. This search took the form of seeking out and collecting "breaks" or apparent accidents in the natural order. It is this preoccupation with the irregular that names the period, and which we recognize today as a necessary part of scientific investigation.

9. Gio. Battista Vitali, *Artifici Musicali* (Modena, 1689). See Sartori, *BMI,* p. 553.

10. The ultimate examples of this practice in chamber music are, of course, those of J. S. Bach in the *Musical Offering* and the *Art of Fugue.*

11 G. B. Bassani, *Balletti, Correnti, Gighe, e Sarabande . . . di . . . dedicata al Eustachio Soldati Proueditore dell' Altezza Serenissima di Modena . . .* (Bologna, 1677). See Sartori, *BMI,* p. 484.

dance stylization or a variation principle to an established tune or bass, usually of popular or traditional origin, such as the *ciaccona,* the *ruggieri, folía,* etc. In his op. III Uccellini used the designation "aria" to apply to a *ciaccona* and a *bergamasca.* The "Caporal Simon" of his op. IV is also a variation piece on a popular tune. In later works, however, Uccellini used the term "aria" to apply to a simple two-part strophic form—non-imitative and tuneful—stylized in the French manner, and usually in common meter. In no other single form does Bononcini's usage so much resemble that of Uccellini. This detail seems sufficient to confirm the possibility of a teacher-pupil relationship between the two. Bononcini's op. XII[12] consists of twelve such *arie* alternating with twelve *correnti* and represents the climax of this form as used by the Modenese.

Uccellini proved himself to be a progressive individual with an eye—or an ear—for the significance of current developments: he rejected the term "canzona" almost completely, using it only once on the title page of op. V,[13] but avoiding it in the *Tavola.* Otherwise he used "sonata" or, as in op. IX, "sinfonia."[14] By "sonata" he means, of course, to convey the concept expressed by Dario Castello in what is possibly the most revealing single contemporary title: his *Sonate Concertate in Stil Moderno* of 1621 and 1629.[15] Bononcini follows Uccellini's practice, and the term "canzona" disappears from Modenese usage although it persists in other places until the end of the century and later.[16]

Uccellini left Modena in 1665 to go to the court of Parma. Whether motivated by ambition (he seems to have been very much concerned with material well-being),[17] or disturbed by invidious attacks such as later beset Bononcini is not clear. However, in Bononcini's twenty-third year the opportunities of this formative association ceased. In any case it is likely that Bononcini had, by this time, gone his own way, for his op. I was published the following year.

Of Agostino Bendinelli, whom Bononcini praises as his preceptor in counterpoint in *Il Musico Prattico,* we can ascertain little beyond the fact

12. Bononcini, *Arie e Correnti a Tre . . . da . . . Opera duedecima* (Bologna: Monti, 1678).

13. Uccellini, *Sonate Over Canzoni da farsi,* op. V (Venice: Vincenti, 1649). See Sartori, *BMI,* p. 405.

14. Uccellini, *Sinfonici Concerti Brievi e Facili* (Venice: Gardano, 1667). See Sartori, *BMI,* p. 443.

15. Venice: Gardano, 1629. See Sartori, *BMI,* p. 337.

16. Purcell used it in 1683 and 1694 to apply to the principal fugal movements of his (church) "Sonnatas," showing precise knowledge of their derivation. J. S. Bach also entitled an organ fugue "Canzona."

17. Pancaldi-Roncaglia, *MDM V,* p. 35, and Roncaglia, *CDM,* p. 123.

that he was a clergyman domiciled in Modena. In 1671 Giacomo Monti published in Bologna the *Psalmi Vespertini ternis à 4, 5 voci ad organum concinendi* (presumably) by Bendinelli.[18] According to Bononcini's statement (see footnote 12, Chapter I), he considered Bendinelli his principal formative influence in the science of counterpoint. While Bononcini would have received from Uccellini much of a practical nature directly oriented to the day-by-day business of providing the music required in their professional situations, the theoretical background and organization demonstrated by the text of *Il Musico Prattico* show the effects of more systematic training. It seems unlikely that Uccellini, the practical musician, would have been the agent who acquainted Bononcini with the long list of theorists reaching back to Prosdocimus di Beldemandis, whom Bononcini includes in his list of authorities. It is far more probable that this knowledge came from the scholarly cleric, Bendinelli, "to whom music served only as an ornament of many other virtues."

The precise point at which Bononcini mentions Bendinelli in *Il Musico Prattico* is of considerable significance: "...should one wish to make a canon which begins each time a tone away from the [preceding] beginning...", etc.[19] The artifice here described is, of course, a contrapuntal disposition of the diatonic sequence. The sequence itself is the life-blood of the serious Baroque concerted instrumental manner, the "Italian" instrumental style. Articulated by motivic contrapuntal interplay, it usually implies or is supported by sequential dominant harmonies. It is the most powerful single device for the creation of climactic and cadential sense and constitutes a principal means of development. Its centripetal harmonic and motivic force is among the strongest devices available to the Baroque composer, and its systematic use distinguishes the style of the later Baroque composers from the earlier empirical manner. The history of the Baroque sonata, especially that of the *sonata da chiesa,* is that of the conquest of this device. The clearest evidence of its power is that, by providing the material (sequences) for the episodes of fugal structures, it permits the sustained and climactic development of the self-contained fugue as distinct from the earlier *ricercare* and *canzona.*

Bononcini uses the contrapuntal disposition of the sequence with a sure hand beginning in his op. I (BI: 1, bars 15-18, 43-53),[20] and it is pre-

18. Eitner, *QL,* art. "Bendinelli."

19. Bononcini, *Il Musico Prattico,* p. 108. See chap. i n. 12.

20. Henceforward all references to Bononcini's works will be made in the following abbreviated form: BI: 1 = Bononcini, op. I, no. 1. All works thus referred to will be found in the musical supplement to this work.

cisely the development of this feature which distinguishes Bononcini's work from that of his predecessors and less systematic contemporaries. His evident conscious power of synthesis and his consequential application of this and other contrapuntal materials he doubtless owes to the systematic training of Bendinelli.

Padre Maria Agatea, Bononcini's predecessor as *Maestro di Cappella* at the Duomo in Modena, was an Augustinian friar attached to the Modenese court from 1649 on. Agatea, a singer, succeeded Uccellini in 1665 as *Maestro di Cappella.*[21] In March of 1671 Bononcini competed for and obtained the post of violinist at the Cathedral and thereby came into contact with Agatea in his twenty-ninth year if not—as is probable—earlier.

In 1673 Agatea resigned his post—possibly because of some kind of pressure from his order—and went to Bologna, with the result that Bononcini succeeded to his position. The relationships between the two men seem to have been good: Bononcini was very explicit in his letter to the Chapter dated October 11, 1673, requesting their consideration for the position only on the condition that Agatea himself resigned. (See footnote 15, Chapter I.) Agatea did, however, remain associated with the Este court as a musician and cleric, and apparently traveled between Bologna and Modena frequently, if we may judge by the passport given him by Francesco II.[22] He appears to have returned to Modena in a clerical capacity for special (musical?) occasions. His output as a composer is negligible, consisting of a few cantatas for solo voice and *basso continuo.* He is also represented in a collection of motets printed in Bologna by Monti in 1670.

Agatea's importance to Bononcini lies in the link with Bologna which he provided. This fact assumes more importance when we consider that between 1673 and 1678 Bononcini does not seem to have written any concerted vocal church works, which as *Maestro di Cappella* he might have been expected to produce.[23]

What, then, was the repertoire of liturgical vocal and concerted items at the Duomo during Bononcini's tenure? Bononcini may have relied on the great volume of published productions of the Bolognese which appeared between 1650 and 1680.

21. Pancaldi-Roncaglia, *MDM VI,* pp. 15-17, and Roncaglia, *CDM,* p. 129.

22. Pancaldi-Roncaglia, *MDM VI,* p. 20, and Roncaglia, *CDM,* p. 132.

23. It is of course possible that such works existed and are lost but—given Bononcini's contemporary reputation—it seems unlikely that they would have escaped all notice. Nor do such works by Colombi—*Maestro di Capella* from 1678-1694—exist.

A letter from Agatea to Lodovico Taglianini, archivist to Francesco II, implies that Agatea borrowed materials from the ducal library while he was *Maestro di Cappella*.[24] The present library is curiously lacking in concerted vocal church works of the period, e.g., from the time of Cazzati's large output in Bologna beginning *ca.* 1657 until G. B. Vitali's op. VI—which was dedicated to Francesco II—was published in 1686.[25]

This source of supply at hand seems a possible, although somewhat remarkable, explanation of the fact that Bononcini did not at once embark upon church vocal writing in 1673. It is interesting to note that his few secular vocal works are from this period. Further, it seems likely that we should have had such church works from his pen, possibly including works in the oratorio form which were to have their great vogue during the 1680's, had he lived longer. It is impossible to say to what extent Agatea influenced Bononcini as a composer, but Bononcini doubtless acquired practical experience and contact with vocal writing during his years as violinist at the Duomo, under Agatea as *Maestro di Cappella*.

Bononcini had, as we have seen, in the person of Giuseppe Colombi, an industrious and persistent competitor.[26] Colombi was born in Modena in 1635 and remained there until his death in 1694.

We have no specific evidence regarding Colombi's training. Since he does not seem to have left Modena, he may, like Bononcini, have studied under Uccellini. Certainly there is nothing in Colombi's style or subsequent output to contradict this. His compositions show his possession of the complete technique of the day, including all of the technical and formal elements we have noted in the style of Uccellini. In any case—like Bononcini—Colombi could hardly have escaped Uccellini's influence. Unlike Bononcini however, Colombi produced a large body of music of a purely virtuoso nature, including *ricercare, partite,* and *toccate* for violin alone, many of which are clearly practice material and studies. This corpus of no fewer than twenty-three manuscript volumes, now in the Biblioteca Estense, provides a perspective of the technical disciplines and violin training of the second half of the seventeenth century at Modena, one of its recognized

24. Pancaldi-Roncaglia, *MDM VI,* p. 19, and Roncaglia, *CDM, loc. cit.*

25. Vitali, *Salmi Concertati a due, tre, quattro e cinque Voci* (Bologna: Giacomo Monti, 1686).

26. Bononcini, though ill, was not yet dead when Colombi approached the Chapter about his position. See Pancaldi-Roncaglia, *MDM VIII,* p. 205, and Roncaglia, *CDM,* p. 159.

centers.[27] The fact that these manuscripts are in the Estense Library suggests that they may have been intended for the recreation and instruction of Colombi's pupil, Duke Francesco II himself. Some, of very considerable difficulty, may have been for Colombi's own use.[28]

Colombi became *Capo degli Strumentisti* at the Este court either in 1654 (when he would have been but nineteen)[29] or, more probably and according to Pancaldi-Roncaglia, in 1673,[30] after becoming "violinist" in 1671.[31] In 1674 he became *Sotto Maestro di Cappella.*[32] He held this post, in addition to that of *Maestro di Cappella* at the Duomo after Bononcini's death in 1678, until his own death in 1694.

Colombi's appointment as *Maestro di Cappella* at the Cathedral was attended by much of the same kind of coming and going between various members of the Este family and the Cathedral Chapter as had surrounded Bononcini's appointment five years before. This time, however, the Duke Francesco was successful in getting his teacher accepted by the Chapter.[33]

Bononcini, seven years younger than Colombi, may have had contact with him in 1670—if not earlier—but he did serve under him in the court orchestra, the "Concerto," after 1673. The work of the two men, heirs of the same traditions, working in the same circumstances, show fundamental differences in manner which can only be the result of essential differences in personality. Both wrote in all of the current forms of *sonata da camera*

27. This reputation persisted until the end of the century and attracted G. B. Senaillé to study with Antonio Tomaso Vitali, the son of G. B. Vitali. See also Valdrighi, *Musurgiana* No. 19, p. 78.

28. Colombi was primarily a practical musician whose works include a "Ciaccona" and a "Toccata"—obviously exercises—for basso (cello) solo. This suggests that, in addition to being a violinist, he also played the cello. These pieces may have been written for his own autodidactic purposes. However, it is possible that they were written in emulation of Domenico Gabrielli, the "Minghain' del Viulunzell'," who came to Modena as chamber player to the Duke, 1688-1689. Gabrielli had doubtless visited Modena previously, and when failing health forced him to abandon a successful career as an opera composer he sought the protection of the Este court. Gabrielli himself left seven *Ricercare* for cello solo and three sonatas (one in canon for two cellos) which are among the earliest monuments for the instrument and further testimony to the high level of performance current at Modena. In this connection, see W. Klenz, "Les Origines du Violoncelle, Instrument Soliste," *Le Conservatoire*: Bulletin du Conservatoire Nationale, Paris, Nov., 1952.

29. Colombi, *MGG.*

30. Pancaldi-Roncaglia, *MDM VIII,* p. 206, and Roncaglia, *CDM,* p. 160.

31. Colombi first uses the title "Capo degli Instrumentisti del Serenissima di Modena" in the title of his op. II, "Da Giuseppe Colombi, Capo degl'Instrumentisti del Serenissimo di Modana. Opera Seconda . . ." (Bologna: Giacomo Monti, 1673). Cited in Sartori, *BMI,* p. 467. He does not use it in his op. I (1668). Had he been appointed fourteen years before, this would seem disingenuous. Moreover, Uccellini—although he had left Modena at this time—used the same title as late as 1668 in an Antwerp edition of his op. VII.

32. Pancaldi-Roncaglia, *MDM VIII,* p. 206. Also see Associazione dei Musicologi Italiani: Pubblicazione, *Catalogo . . . Citta di Modena, R. Biblioteca Estense,* Serie VIII, comp. Pio Lodi (Parma, Officina Grafica Fresching). Hereinafter referred to as *Cat. Estense.*

33. Pancaldi-Roncaglia, *MDM VIII,* pp. 207-208, and Roncaglia, CDM, pp. 159-160.

and *sonata da chiesa.* Colombi, however, following his practical bent, also developed in variation pieces and dance forms for violin alone, the virtuoso and popular elements which Bononcini ignored. The learned "scientific" and contrapuntal aspect is most clearly manifested in the canons appended to Bononcini's works, and was also a constant factor in his creative process. No such canons appear in Colombi's manuscript or printed works, and his counterpoint is considerably inferior to Bononcini's, being less supple, less persistent, and of less clear outline; at once "thicker" and less strong.

These differences in manner and especially Colombi's neglect of the canon lead one to suspect that Colombi may have been one of the "Tongues" Bononcini refers to in the "Letter to the Reader" of his op. III—"these [works] I beg you to defend against those Tongues which, either from envy or mischievousness, may unjustly calumniate them."[34]—or one of the "critics" of his *Discorso.* Bononcini's spirited sally regarding the puzzle canon *Caecus non iudicat de colore* may be aimed at Colombi as *caecus,* at least in the matter of the canon. It is not likely that Colombi's "carpenter's counterpoint" escaped Bononcini's criticism. Colombi's dedication and "Letter to the Reader" of his op. IV[35] of 1676 may be a reply to Bononcini. Heavy with academic conceit, classical allusion, and references to natural history, it makes a nice distinction between the royal birds—the heraldic Estense Eagle and Swan—of the dedication to Francesco II and those served up to the commonalty in the letter, the dove (*Colombo*) and the hawk.

Perhaps nothing suggests the difference in temperament of the two men as clearly as Colombi's line in the same letter: "Diverse uses and licenses constitute special rules."[36] Bononcini, in the letter "al Benigno Lettore" of op. III, says the same thing, but very differently:

> . . . do not marvel should you find the counterpoint not to be in all and in everything according to the rules and precepts pertaining to that Art, since I have attempted nothing but to delight the ear in the variety of sonatas, fugues and diverse imitations, breaking and weaving of the figures which convey to the ear (at least according to my thinking) a more lively Harmony. . . .[37]

Colombi's blunt assertion shows his acceptance of "licenze" as a practical matter and a solution to immediate situations. Bononcini's apology is couched in terms of artistic purpose and intent.[38]

34. ". . . la quale ti prego a difendere da quelle Lingue, che, ò per inuidia, ò per malignità potessero ingiustamente calunniarlo." Cited in Sartori, *BMI,* p. 455.

35. *Sonate a Due Violine* . . . Di . . . Opera Quarta (Bologna: Giacomo Monti, 1676). Cited in Sartori, *BMI,* p. 481.

36. *Ibid.* ". . . Gli usi diuersi à varie licenze danno regole particolari."

37. The complete text is given on p. 74 *infra,* chap. vii. See also Sartori, *BMI,* p. 455.

38. Colombi seems to have had what present-day psychiatry would call a compulsion

On the basis of external evidence Colombi would seem to have been of somewhat less education than Bononcini. His handwriting and musical calligraphy in the manuscripts at Modena are far from elegant. It is also a matter of indifference whether *Adagio* becomes *Agadio* or *Agaddio.* The prose style of his dedications (if it be his style), despite the formal roulades of Baroque "Academese," also give the impression of a blunter personality than Bononcini's.

In addition to the twenty-odd manuscript volumes in the Biblioteca Estense, Colombi's published works consist of five *opere*:

Sinfonie Da Camera Brandi, e Corrente alla Francese ... Da ... Opera Prima. In Bologna. M.DC.LXVIII. ...

La Lira Armonica, Sinfonie ... Da ... Opera Seconda. In Bologna, per Giacomo Monti, 1673. ...

Balletti, Correnti, Gighe, Sarabande ... Da ... Opera Terza. In Bologna per Giacomo Monti. 1674. ...

Sonate a Due Violine ... Di ... Opera Quarta. In Bologna per Giacomo Monti. 1676. ...

Sonate da Camera a Tre Strumenti ... Da ... Opera Quinta. In Bologna, per Giacomo Monti. 1689. ...

Mute evidence of Colombi's influence and ascendancy with the Duke, which lasted all the composer's life, is to be seen in the fact that copies of opp. II, III, and IV are in the Estense Library (all dedicated to Francesco II), magnificently bound in parchment-covered boards stamped in gold with the arms of the Este family.

Colombi's music reveals a robust natural talent without interest in originality; it is "performers' music," well-made, sure of effect and based on good formulae. His counterpoint, as we have said, does not equal that of Bononcini: the parts are less independent, and the motivic development is not so felicitous. Nor does he have the spontaneous quality of Uccellini; his hard-won "gloria" shows signs of the struggle. In its

---

regarding work and idleness. In no fewer than three of his five printed prefaces and dedications (see Colombi, opp. III, IV, and V) he managed to bring up the subject—using in each case the same term, *ozio* (idleness):

> ... Publico adunque queste mie imperfettioni, non per esser applaudito, ma per esser conosciuto non otioso. ... Cited in Sartori, *BMI,* p. 476.
>
> Pretese l'Arco mio meglio di quello di Domitiano ferendo l'ozio col saetar l'oblio. ... Cited in Sartori, *BMI,* p. 481.
>
> "... ed in quei breui momenti che un'ozio nobile sà rubare al genio vigilantissimo. ..." Cited in Sartori, *BMI,* p. 552.

Do we see here a compensation for Colombi's unconscious realization of his lesser talent? It would not be difficult to read into the line "... Publico adunque queste mie imperfettioni, non per esser applaudito, ma per esser conosciuto non otioso ..." of op. III (1674) a reproach of Bononcini's self-assured attitude and willingness to make public demonstration (shown in the latter's dealings with the Cathedral Chapter and in the *Discorso*).

externals at least, he assimilates, as a professional necessity, the French style, but he remains more closely oriented to the popular Italian manner. This is clearly illustrated in the *arie* of his op. I which are not of the French type, based on the highly ornamented *Air de Cour,* as with the *arie* of Uccellini and Bononcini. Rather, they are straightforward (C; [Moderate]) or bouncy Italian tunes (3/4 or 3/2: *Presto*) much like and constituting hardly any development of their prototypes to be found in such a work as Caroso's *Nobilità di Dame* of 1605.

Colombi's melodic invention lacks savor, and he has a fatal insensibility to the melodic principle of turning back after a leap. This elementary rule of good writing is a cardinal principle of the older contrapuntal practice. Discipline in the science should have corrected or mitigated this fault.

His harmonic movement is also limited and monotonous in comparison to that of Bononcini and his taste for the closed, harmonic variation forms reinforces this failing. One of the clearest demonstrations of the differences in Bononcini's and Colombi's styles is found in the use of so-called cross-relations. This manifestation of "tonal play," a combination of harmonic security and contrapuntal energy, is exploited at every turn by Bononcini, who takes obvious delight in the freshness and piquancy it gives, while Colombi uses it far less.

While it is possible to account for Bononcini's style entirely in terms of his training by Uccellini and Bendinelli, the association of Bononcini and Colombi (on whatever basis) could not have been without its effects on the younger man. Colombi, after all, remained a favorite of the Duke and *Capo del Concerto* at court. Thus, if in no other way, he controlled to a certain extent some of the circumstances of Bononcini's development.

Of all of G. M. Bononcini's contemporaries, the one who resembles and approaches him most closely in style and technical development is Giovanni Battista Vitali. (Both published their op. I in 1666.) More cosmopolitan than Bononcini, Vitali seems in certain ways to have "completed" Bononcini's work at Modena.[39]

Giovanni Battista Vitali came to Modena as *Vice Maestro di Cappella* about 1682,[40] some five years after Bononcini's death. However, certain features of his subsequent works link the two men. Vitali was of Cre-

39. It should be noted that Bononcini was more productive, composing fourteen *opere* in twelve years (1666-78), while Vitali published an equal number in a period three times as long.

40. See the title page of Vitali's op. VII, cited in Sartori, *BMI,* p. 502.

monese origin and had been *Suonatore di violone di brazzo* at San Petronio in Bologna. He declares himself to be a pupil of Maurizio Cazzati in his op. I,[41] and, indeed, Vitali's early style has much in common with Cazzati's. Vitali was also *Accademico Filaschese* and, after 1666, a member of the Accademia Filarmonica,[42] where he would have known Bononcini. In any case he was certainly acquainted with Bononcini's works published in Bologna, including the contrapuntal treatise, *Il Musico Prattico.* The circumstances and reasons for Vitali's leaving Bologna are not apparent. Possibly he was attracted by the vacancy left by Bononcini at the Modenese court, since it was clear by this time that Vitali would not succeed Cazzati as *Maestro di Cappella* at San Petronio; Colonna had followed in the post in 1674. We have already observed Vitali's professed sentiments on the two situations, Modena and Bologna,[43] and whatever he found them actually to be, he remained in Modena as *Vice Maestro di Cappella* until 1684[44] and as *Maestro di Cappella* "dell'Altezza Serenissima del Sig. Duca di Modena" until his death in 1692.

Vitali's compositions written after his removal to Modena are of considerable interest. His first work published in Modena is op. VII,[45] a set of variation pieces. It is significant that no such items appear in Vitali's work before this time. It is possible that op. VII was written to suit the tastes of the Duke, which—it will be remembered—were developed by Colombi, in whose manuscript works such forms figure largely, and who was at that time *Capo degli Strumentisti.*

Vitali had, of course, composed dance music in the French manner before coming to Modena.[46] At the Este court, however, he had further occasion to do so and, as we have seen, more than usual reason to follow changes in French modes. That he did this is clear from the dances of his op. XI,[47] significantly (see p. 23 *supra*)—dedicated to the sister of Francesco II, Beatrice d'Este Stuarda Regina della Gran Bretagna—and op.

41. *Correnti, e Balletti Da Camera . . . da . . . Opera Prima* (Bologna: Mario Siluano, 1666). See Sartori, *BMI,* p. 434.

42. Sartori, *BMI,* p. 434.

43. See the dedication to Vitali's op. VIII (chap. ii n. 1).

44. Vitali. op. XI, *Varie Sonate alla Francese & all' Itagliana . . . Da . . . Opera Undecima* (Modena: Gio. Gasparo Ferri, 1684). This is the first of Vitali's works to carry the title "Maestro di Capella dell'Altezza Serenissima del Sig. Duca di Modona." See Sartori, *BMI,* p. 512.

45. Vitali, *Varie Partite Del Passemezo, Ciaccona, Capricii, e Passagalli . . . Da . . . Opera Settima* (Modena: Gasparo Ferri, 1682). See Sartori, *BMI,* p. 502.

46. Vitali, Balletti, *Correnti alla Francese, Gagliarde e Brando per Ballare . . . Di . . . Opera Terza* (Bologna: Giacomo Monti, 1692). See Sartori, *BMI,* p. 442.

47. Vitali, *Balli in stile Francese . . . Da . . . Opera Duodecima* (Modena: Antonio Vitaliani, 1685). See Sartori, *BMI,* p. 522.

XIV,[48] which contain some of the earliest *menuets* and *bourrées* (borea). These dances, varieties and developments of *branles* (including the *branle á mener* which becomes the *menuet*) begin their existence as chamber music here. Had he lived, Bononcini would doubtless have followed the vogue and produced such dances.

Vitali, in the "Artifici Musicali" of his op. XIII,[49] carries Bononcini's preoccupation with the canon and its devices to its logical consequence:

Kind Reader,

He does not deserve the name of musician who does not know how to treat in any fashion the more profound secrets of the Art. Thus I, especially desiring to be useful, have published this, my small work, including various Canons, double Counterpoints, and Curious inventions to serve as models to Teachers who can [thus] perfect their Scholars, if they have true information. Even though some, of little skill, have dared to say that the knowledge of these Canons was not necessary, I have talked with many of the profession who, to tell the truth, have not known how to give me the faintest glimmer [of this], yet they are deceived, because now I have observed [canons] in the ... compositions of ... virtuosi, who weave Notes together, hoping to render their names immortal, devoting laborious pains to this, judging that without it they cannot succeed to the true title of perfect composer, the Canon being the true test of Counterpoint. I have observed many included in Masses and other compositions in many Italian chapels of such art that they have amazed me. Also in Rome, where flourish the most distinguished men of this Science, they are much esteemed. Receive then in good part this Impression of these, some of which are open [clear], others artificial and provided with enigmatic mottos which, on reflection, will provide the explanation; and others to be reversed, and in contrary motion; and, finally, some which will not yield to Criticism, but to study. ...[50]

48. Vitali, *Sonate da Camera a Tre ... di ... Opera Decimaquarta* (Modena: Christoforo Canobi, 1692).

49. Vitali, *Artifici Musicali ne Quali si Contengono Canoni in Diverse Maniere, Contrapunti Dopii, Inuentioni Curiose, Capritii e Sonate Di ... Opera Decimaterza* (Modena: Eridi Cassiani Stampatori Episcopali, 1689). See Sartori, *BMI,* p. 553, and Smith College Archives, no. 14 Northampton, 1959, for an edition of entire opus.

50. Amico Lettore,

"Non merita il nome di Musico chi non sà maneggiare in qual siuoglia modo gli arcani più profondi dell'Arte. Perciò desiderando io di particolarmente giouare, hò dato in luce questa mia operetta inserta con varij Canoni, Contrapunti dopij, e Curiose inuentioni, acciò serua di motiuo à Maestri, che possano perfettionare i loro Scolari, quando però n'habbino la vera notitia; se bene alcuni poco pratici hanno osato dire non essere necessaria la cognitione di questi Canoni, hauendone io più volte hauuto discorso con molti della professione, che per verità non mene hanno saputo dare un minimo barlume, e pure s'ingannano, per che nè hò osseruato sparsi in varie compositioni d'huomini i più virtuosi, che mai intreceiassero Note, che bramando rendere il nome loro immortale, si diedero à queste laboriose fatiche, stimando senza queste non poter côseguire il nome di perfetto compositore, per essere i Canoni realmente il vero esame del Contrapunto, hauendone osseruato varij inserti in Messe, et in altre compositioni, cosi artificiosi in molte Capelle d'Italia, che mi hanno reso stupore: Anzi in Roma, oue fioriscono gli huomini più insigni di questa Scienza, sono à questi di non ordinaria stima. Riceui adunque di buon animo l'Impressione di questi, alcuni de quali sono suelati, altri artificiosi, et osseruati con motti enigmatici, à quali riflettendo haurai la dichiaratione, ed

The work contains no fewer than sixty items including canons of all descriptions, although Vitali avoids some of the complexities and archaisms of notation such as the mensural meter signatures retained by Bononcini. Vitali's prefatory letter and dedication describe the spirit in which they were undertaken and their significance, which we have noted earlier.

This demonstration of contrapuntal virtuosity, of which there is no earlier example in Vitali's printed works, is an ultimate expression of the same "academic" and scientific attitude which informs Bononcini's treatise. Although this tendency was[51]—and is—often ascribed to influences from Rome, Bononcini's book had had, in its twenty years, no small part in developing that sentiment and its formulation in teaching and practice. In Rome itself, the copy of *Il Musico Prattico* belonging to the Accademia Santa Cecilia is marked *ad usum Niccolo Jomelli.*[52]

altri don l'intelligenza de rouersi, e contrarij, e finalmente d'alcuni non già con la Critica, ma con lo studio, che si richiede. Viui felice." See Sartori, *BMI*, p. 554. One wonders if "among those of little skill" (*poco practici homo osato dire non essere necessario*) we can perceive Colombi, who was at that time *Capo del Concerto.*

51. By Vitali himself (n. 50). Also we may recall in this connection Bendinelli's title, *Canonico Lateranense.*

52. Pancaldi-Roncaglia, *MDM VII*, p. 147, and Roncaglia, *CDM*, p. 151.

Chapter IV. BOLOGNA, THE *ACCADEMIE;* CAZZATI AND COLONNA

Beginning with the 1672 edition of his *Sonate da Chiesa a due Violini,*[1] Bononcini uses the title *Accademico Filarmonica,* referring, of course, to the Accademia Filarmonica at Bologna. All his subsequent publications bear this designation, yet the extant records of that organization do not show when or under what conditions he was elected.[2] We may infer that this occurred between the publication of op. V in 1671 and op. VI in 1672, since the title does not appear on op. V, but is used for op. VI.

The regulations of the *Accademia* permitted, under certain conditions, the aggregation of professionals working in other places than Bologna, designating them as "forestieri."[3] These conditions (limited activity) may have prevented Bononcini's name from appearing in the written proceedings and business of the *Accademia.* Had his proposition and election been acted upon in open meeting, it is possible that either the action went unrecorded or that the record has been lost.

Bononcini's op. VI may have been the basis for his election. It bears certain marks of "academicism" and shows specific deference to church style in conception and execution. As he observes in the appended "Letter to the Reader," it is directly related to the treatise *Il Musico Prattico.* The tonalities of the various sonatas are designated in terms of modes, and the subjects of the fugal movements show certain "antiquarian" features, notably the severe subjects with repeated notes in the old Venetian "canzona" manner.[4]

Bononcini's preface, complete with canon,[5] goes to some length to insist in technical language upon his (and the performers') orthodoxy:

1. Bononcini, *Sonate da chiesa a due Violini ... Opera Sesta* (Venice: Gardano, 1672). See Pancaldi-Roncaglia, *MDM VII,* p. 144.

2. *Ibid.,* pp. 10-11.

3. Nestore Morini, *La R. Accademia Filarmonica di Bologna* (Bologna: L. Capelli, 1930), p. 6.

4. It is not unthinkable, also, that Bononcini was already considering the possibility of becoming *Maestro di Cappella* at Modena in this, his first and only production devoted entirely to church sonatas.

5. There follows a Canon for six voices divided into three parts, each one of which contains another at the unison. (*Segue un* Canon *à sei voci diuiso in trè parti e ciascheduna d'esse ne contienne un'altra all'unisono.*) Sartori, *BMI,* p. 466. The canon is sufficiently complicated to be offered as proof of virtuosity in this department (although the curious heterophonic doubling of the parts, even though at six voices, is hardly "classic").

To THE READER. Herewith, O courteous reader, the Sixth of my labors, in which the subjects or imitations are varied, the syncopes and fugues are broken, the figures are transposed to other tones than where they belong, from which will be derived only a confused and harsh harmony unless as in other earlier Compositions good precepts are observed. I mention this because nowadays there are some of so little intelligence of the Art, that when they sing or play they always wish, with their ill-ordered and indiscreet caprices of Bow or Voice, to alter and deform the Compositions (however carefully made) so that the Authors have become obliged to ask these singers and players to sing and play things simply as they are written. This does not include certain graces, which although not given the refinement of Counterpoint, are however apposite, and when well employed bring out their inimitable devices and singular dispositions, which not only do not detract but on the contrary, ornament and add beauty to the Compositions, bringing great praise to themselves, providing delight, *gusto* and admiration to the auditors and even to the above-mentioned Authors. In this work you will find (besides the way of weaving the Consonances and Dissonances, and diverse indications of *Tempo* which are used in the *stile concertato*) that I have named the Modes (*Tuoni*) in an unusual way, this because it is set out in my "Trattato di Musica" [op. VIII, *Il Musico Prattico*] which I have already promised to you, and which although completed—it remains only to send it to the press—I wish to delay in the execution until I see the opportunity to let it be published. Oblige me with your usual grace, while I hope to give you other things, which you may not expect, or believe could come from my hands, "e viui felice."[6]

It is remarkable that, if this work was prepared for Bologna, it was actually published in Venice, but other considerations may be at work here.

In addition, as we have suggested, the reputation of Bononcini's then unpublished treatise on counterpoint, *Il Musico Prattico,* may have been

6. "AL LETTORE. ECcoti, ò cortese lettore, La Sesta mia fatica, in cui, se si varieranno i soggetti, ò le imitazzioni, si romperanno le sincope, ò le fughe, ò si trasporteranno le figure fuor delle corde, oue sono collocate, non potrà deriuarne, se non concento aspro, e confuso; sicome in altre Composizioni ancora fatte coll'osseruanza dè buoni precetti. Dicoti tutto ciò, perche oggidì vi sono alcuni cosi poco intelligenti di quest'Arte, che ò cantando, ò sonando vogliono sempre cò loro sregolati, & indiscreti capricci d'Arco, ò di Voce, alterare, anzi deformare le Composizioni (quantunque fatte con tutto studio & applicazione) in modo che gli Autori sono arriuati à douer pregare gli medemi Cantanti, e Sonatori, acciò si contentino di dire, è di fare le cose schiettamente e puramente come per appunto stanno. Non entrano già in questo numero certuni soggetti di garbo, che sebene non dotati di finezza di Contrapunto, sanno però cosi bene à tempo, & aggiustatamente far spiccare i loro inarriuabili artifici, e singolari disposizioni, che nô solamente non punto tolgono, ma anzi aggiungono fregio, e vaghezza à Componimenti, riportando gran lode à se stessi, & arrecando insieme sommo diletto, gusto, & ammirazione à chiunque gli stà à sentire, & à medesimi e sudeti Autori. In questa mia fatica ritrouerai (oltre il modo di contessere le Consonanze, è Dissonanze, e diuersi inditij del Tempo, che nello stile concertato si può praticare) che hò nominati gli Tuoni fuor dell'uso, comune, e ciò perche questo particolare nel mio Trattato di Musica, che già ti hò promesso, è 'l quale sebene è compito, ne resta più che di metterlo sotto'l Torchio, vò però differirne l'esecuzione sino à tanto che io conosca l'opportunità di lasciarlo uscire alla luce. Compiacciati fauorirmi del tuo solito aggradimento mentre spero donarti altra cosa, che da me non aspetti, e forse credi, che dalle mie mani non possa venirti, e viui felice." Cited in Sartori, *BMI,* p. 466.

the reason for his election. His presentation of contrapuntal science would have conformed directly to the express purposes of the *Accademia,* and it may well have been used there as a manual as it was in other places.[7]

We have no further evidence of Bononcini's continuing relationship to the Accademia Filarmonica. His duties in Modena cannot have offered him much opportunity for frequent visits, although it seems possible that he may have visited Bologna at least occasionally in connection with the publication of his works.

Bologna, the scene of the Accademia Filarmonica, presented an aspect differing from that of Bononcini's *patria,* Modena, as we have already had occasion to notice (p. 15 *supra*) in the dedication of G. B. Vitali's op. VIII. Bologna was a papal fief without court or truly hereditary or feudal nobility headed by a *principe* in whom spiritual and civil responsibility resided. This function, essential to absolutist and Counter-Reformation[8] political philosophy, was fulfilled by an appointed council composed of influential individuals (*Senatori*) and by which Bologna was governed.[9]

The Accademia Filarmonica was a body somewhat analogous to this, a professional organization which cultivated members of Bolognese aristocracy and the professional church musicians of the town devised to provide circumstances for musical activity beyond the ordinary routine of church services and civic ceremonies. In the absence of true court life it was necessary to invent the combination of social and professional conditions which would supply the ritual occasions that were the basis of Baroque musical usage. The Accademia Filarmonica was originally formed in 1666,[10] in the house of a Bolognese nobleman, Count Vicenzo Maria Carrati, by a group of fifty of the leading professional musicians of the town's churches. These included—to mention only those whose names have, for one reason or another, survived—Agostino Fillipuzzi, Giulio Cesare Ar[r]esti, Gio. Paolo Colonna, Gio. Benvenuti, Pietro Degli Antonii, Gio. Batt. Vitali, and Giuseppe Felice Tosi.[11]

7. See p. 32 n. 52, *supra.*

8. Vitali's prefaces to op. VIII and op. XIII imply his conviction of the propriety of this order to artistic production. See Sartori, *BMI,* pp. 509 and 553. Also, Smith College Archives, Number XIV (Northampton, 1959).

9. This municipal body had its own musical organization (brasses) for ceremonial purposes, but lacking a continuing tradition of taste its patronage was not itself productive of a style. However, the massive style appropriate to official occasions may have an echo (as it did in Venice) in the church style at S. Petronio. The presence also of the virtuoso brass players necessary to the "state" style may have led directly to the *tromba* concertos and sonatas of Cazzati and Torelli.

10. The year of publication of G. M. Bononcini's op. I as well as the op. I of G. B. Vitali.

11. Nestore Morini, *La R. Accademia Filarmonica di Bologna,* pp. 1-3.

The following year the activities of the Accademia were extended beyond the house of Count Carrati to the celebration of a Solemn Mass in honor of the patron saint of the Accademia, Saint Anthony of Padua. This became a yearly function[12] and a central point of the Academy's activity[13] carried out in turn at various Bolognese churches. The occasion was marked by music composed by the *Accademici Compositori* and performed by the *Accademici Cantori e Sonatori* and celebrated with fireworks and illuminations.[14] The Academy also undertook social functions, providing for mutual assistance, death dues, and funeral observances.[15]

The organization of the Accademia Filarmonica was originally based on the general features of earlier, but moribund,[16] Bolognese literary *Accademie* such as the Accademia Floridi, and the Accademia Filaschisi.[17] The professional nature of the body, however, caused it to develop along more dynamic practical lines, accounting for its long life, reputation, and influence.

The reasons for this vitality are found in the character of Bologna itself. Bologna was a university town[18] containing both law and medical faculties. It was also a mercantile center with developed commercial and social organizations including numerous lay religious auxiliaries or confraternities.[19] The relatively large concentration of a lettered class was an atmosphere favorable to the cultivation of violin and chamber music as a means of social exchange. This is evident from the spate of chamber music published in Bologna from *ca.* 1660 on.[20] It was the large group of *dilettanti* that

12. This is a specific example of a "manufactured" ritualistic occasion. The Solemn Mass replaced the yearly celebration of a ruler's Saint's-Day (or Name Day) usual in such circumstances as Modena.

13. Nestore Morini, *op. cit.*, chap. i.

14. *Ibid.*

15. *Ibid.*, p. 6.

16. Although Vitali was to continue to use the title *Accademico Filaschisi* until 1684 (op. XI) and after his removal to Modena.

17. Michele Maylender, *Storia delle Accademie d'Italia* (Bologna: L. Capelli, 1926), VI, 29 and 395 respectively.

18. A university chair of music theory dating back to 1420 was first occupied by the Salamancan, B. Ramo Pareja. See *ibid.*, p. 377.

19. The Confraternities also supported "intramural" musical organizations and *Maestri di Cappella.* (Maylender, *loc. cit.*) These did not—and for the same reasons that the functional music of the *Signoria* did not—so much produce style as they served the useful function of dissemination of the production of higher professional echelons. This popularization had, of course, its consequences in the vogue for the concerted church music in the subsequent decades.

20. The richness of the violinistic atmosphere of Bologna may be judged by the fact that it was sought—with the unerring instinct of genius—by the young Corelli *ca.* 1666. His principal early studies took place in Bologna, and he was admitted to the Accademia Filarmonica in 1670, the year of his departure for Rome. The Bolognese violin tradition is the basis of the instrumental aspects of his style. See Mario Rinaldi, *Arcangelo Corelli* (Milano, 1953), p. 32.
Corelli was later (1685) the center of an academic quarrel involving members of the Accademia Filarmonica. This is the celebrated altercation involving Corelli and Gio. Paolo

provided the *ripieni* of the *concerto grosso*[21] that evolved in San Petronio in the next decade.

The character of the Accademia Filarmonica crystallized in 1689-1690 with the adoption of its constitution, a codification of anterior "*dichiarazioni Accademiche.*"[22] The constitution provided for:

the annual observance in honor of San Antonio di Padova,

the arrangements for mutual assistance, both spiritual and temporal,

the election of officers—a *Principe* chosen from among the *Accademici Compositori* assisted by *Consiglieri* appointed from other ranks along with *Censori,* whose function was the technical surveillance and evaluation of works produced at "classes" of the Accademia—and other technical assistants,

the conditions and qualifications of membership,

the arrangements of meetings, and

the conduct of the *Esercizi e Conferenze* [the technical "classes"] of the *Accademia.*[23]

The atmosphere and workings of the Accademia Filarmonica are perhaps best conveyed by the *Memorandum to Signori Compositori of the Accademia Filarmonica.*[24] (A very similar set of *Ricordi* was addressed to the *cantori* and *suonatori.*) This little volume, handed to the newly elected *Accademici,* strikingly resembles a set of present-day bylaws:

I Everyone aggregated to our *Accademia* as Composer is urged to recite each day a Pater Noster and an Ave Maria to the patron saint of the *Accademia* [St. Anthony of Padua].

II Once consigned to the *Principe,* and judged by the aggregation, the [qualifying] composition [submitted] must be preserved in the Archives in perpetuity, and may on no account be removed....

III All are required to attend and co-operate at the annual function, the Solemnities in celebration of St. Anthony of Padua....

IV All are required to pray for the souls of defunct brother *Accademici.*...

V All are required to pay the treasurer each year one *lira* and four *soldi* for use as alms....

Colonna concerning the passage of fifths in Corelli's op. II (*ibid.,* pp. 108 ff.). The acrimonious correspondence—which is no credit to Corelli—reveals the atmosphere of technical and theoretical conservatism, not to say perfectionism, of the *Accademia* which Corelli had left fifteen years before. (*Ibid.,* p. 424).

21. By the end of the century a *ripieno* of one hundred players was not unheard of. Franz Giegling, *Giuseppe Torelli* (Basel: Bärenreiter, 1949).

22. Nestore Morini, *La R. Accademia Filarmonica di Bologna,* p. 22.

23. *Ibid.,* pp. 22-27.

24. *Ricordi per li Signori Compositori dell'Accademia di Signori Filarmonica* (Bologna: Eridi d'Antonio Pisarri, 1689).

VI On being summoned by note or by voice by order of the *Principe* to meet with the *Accademia,* he must not fail to show so that the number of deciding opinions may be as great as possible....

VII When called to any office in the *Accademia* [he] must discharge it exactly in the interests of our group....

VIII Should he wish to propose a candidate for election...he may do so only in the manner prescribed in our Constitution and *Dichiarationi Accademiche....*

IX He shall be present at the *Accademia* on Thursdays to practice *virtuosamente.* Absences, with just cause and recognized necessity, are to be arranged beforehand with the *Sig. Principe,* and if continued, he shall be excluded from the *Accademia....* Anyone may, at his pleasure, bring a composition to be heard and tried and discussed as he desires. However, in the interests of the continuation and conservation of these exercises, such compositions should be considered appropriate for such an audience. It is his duty to ask for the favor of their *virtù* (abilities) of the singers and players with every sign of respect, and shall respond with all courtesy, reciprocating received favors. For, in so civil and decorous congress as is ours, all [mutual] respect is due. Thus, any who dare to banter, mock, or make personal jests at any function whatever of the *Accademia* shall be at once excluded....

X He shall not introduce into the *Accademia* anyone who is not an *Accademico,*...for the purpose of hearing the performance or making himself heard as singer, player or composer, without first having obtained the permission of the *Principe,* whom he should afterwards thank.

XI On leaving the *Accademia* before [the meeting is] finished...he must do so at the pleasure of the *Principe* and must leave alone, without taking anyone with him, so that that which is going forward may not be disturbed.

XII In addition he stands ready to conserve...and advance...the public regard...of the *Accademia*...

XIII ...He shall agree to the punctilious observance of these Memoranda (*Ricordi*) and items.

These memoranda were published after Bononcini's death, yet they reflect much of the Academy's earlier character since they are a consolidation of earlier regulations.

The significance of Bononcini's membership in the Accademia Filarmonica is that he was thus recognized as one of the leading musicians of the day. It means that, despite his residence in Modena, he was considered part of this most energetic and advanced group whose traditions in classic church music persisted until the end of the next century and brought even young Mozart into its orbit.

Bononcini's works, beginning with op. III, were all published and republished in Bologna for the use of the violin-playing public of the town (and to the economic advantage of the publishers). That his works were popular is shown by the existence of the reprints as well as the contents of the prefaces appended to these reprints. For example, the preface to the reprint edition of op. VII (1677) states: "These *correnti,* which, barely printed ... were devoured by the voracity of the *Virtuosi.*"[25]

Bononcini's treatise on counterpoint, *Il Musico Prattico,* op. VIII of 1673, was brought out in 1688 in a second Bolognese edition by the astute musical entrepreneur, Marino Silvani, as well as in a Venetian edition by Gardano in 1678, the year of Bononcini's death. Like the Accademia itself, *Il Musico Prattico* was dedicated to the "classicizing" attitude toward the sixteenth-century polyphonic science, and it may have been used there as a manual as it was at other *accademie.*[26] This classicizing attitude, the professed object of the Accademia Filarmonica, was inherent in the intellectual climate of the original organization, and was insisted upon in the regulations of the Academy:

> Let it be established in the first place that he who shall be admitted to the order of Composer and *Maestro di Musica* resident in Bologna shall for at least an entire year—as provided by the Statutes of the *Accademia*—have performed various of his Compositions at various of the Thursday meetings, or other sessions, so that the acting *Principe,* the two *Censori,* and the other *Maestri* may judge of his ability and his possession of the Rules of Counterpoint necessary for composition in the True Ecclesiastical style.
>
> In the second place he must present himself three times to the body of the *Maestri dell'Accademia* to show his ability in various tests.[27]

The Accademia Filarmonica represents a single specific example of the social configuration given to intellectual life in the seventeenth century—the academy. Its function was to give ritualistic form to intellectual exchange and to determine and maintain the ordained place of such activity within the established social order. Such *accademie* were rife in Italy, and

25. "Le presenti correnti ... che appena stampati furon per la loro esquisitezza dall' voracita de' Virtuosi assorbiti...."

26. See p. 32 n. 52.

27. *Leggi presentate dall'Accademia de Filarmonici* (Bologna, 1773), pp. 3-4.

"Viene per tanto stabilito in primo luogo, che chi deve essere ammesso nell'ordine de' Compositori, e Maestri di Musica residente in Bologna, debba per un'Anno intiero almeno, come vien preferito dagli Statuti dell'Accademia aver fatte sentire diverse due Composizioni in vari Esercizi de' Giovedi, o altra giornata, affinche il Principe pro tempore, i due Censori, e gli altri Maestri possano rilevare la sua abilita, e il suo possesso delle Regole di Contrapunto necessarie per il comporre nel verro stile Ecclesiastico.

"In secondo luogo dovranno presentarsi per tre volte ai Maestri dell'Accademia radunati, per dar saggio del loro valore in diversi sperimenti."

whether devoted to literary,[28] historical, scientific, or artistic matters, provided the point of contact for constituted authority and intellectual endeavor.

There had been in Bologna prior to the founding of the Accademia Filarmonica three *accademie* devoted to music: the Accademia Floridi, the Accademia dei Filomusi, and the Accademia Filaschici.[29] These followed the earlier literary academies (the *Floridi* was actually a descendant of one) in the use of the elaborate "Arcadian" formulae. The members used neo-Hellenic, "pastoral" academic names[30] and built up an atmosphere heavily laden with classical allusion.

The guiding spirit of *I Floridi* had been the colorful personality of Adriano Banchieri, the Bolognese organist and composer. *Il Dissonante,* his academic name in both the Accademia Floridi and the Accademia Filomusi, expressed his energetic and constructively critical spirit. The Accademia Floridi was really a resuscitation by Banchieri in 1615,[31] of the first Bolognese literary academy (also called "Floridi") dating from 1537 and, in its new guise, oriented to music as well as to art and letters.

The Accademia dei Filomusi was founded in 1622 by D. Girolamo Giaccobi, *Maestro di Cappella* at San Petronio. It was dedicated, from the first, to the study of theoretical and practical music.[32] The third musical *accademia,* the Accademia dei Filaschici, was formed in 1633 by Brunnetti and Bernacchi, also *Maestri di Cappella.*[33]

A glimpse of the proceedings at a meeting of the Accademia dei Filaschisi is given in a published account of the discourse on the origins of the *sampogna* given by *Il Dissonante* [Adriano Banchieri] on November 14, 1625.[34] The ritualistic nature of the affair is evident from the printed

28. Vernon Lee, "The Arcadian Academy," *Studies in the Eighteenth Century in Italy* (London, 1907), p. 15.

29. Michele Maylender, *Storia delle Accademie d'Italia,* pp. 29, 435, and 395.

30. Itself a ritualistic formula of the first order. This was the practice of the "Arcadian" academy, the *Aborigeni* in Rome, which served as a model for numerous "colonies" in other cities. The *Aborigeni* counted among its members Corelli, who was known as *Arcomelo Arimanteo.* See Vernon Lee, *op. cit.,* pp. 36 and 40; and Mario Rinaldi, *Arcangelo Corelli,* p. 428.

31. Michele Maylender, *Storia delle Accademie d'Italia,* pp. 29-30.

32. *Ibid.,* pp. 435-436.

33. *Ibid.,* p. 395. Some members of this academy seem to have gone over to the Accademia Filarmonica after its foundation in 1666, as did G. B. Vitali. Vitali, however, continued to use the title *Accademico Filaschese* until 1685 (his op. XI).

Significantly, Cazzati is not included among the members of the Accademia Filarmonica, although he called himself, after 1659, *Accademico Eccitato,* which refers to another academy in Bergamo.

34. *La Sampogna Musicale* di D. Adriano Banchieri, Academico Filomuso il Dissonante, Rappresentatà sotto il dì 14 Nouembre 1625, nel Virtuoso Ridotto delli Signori ACADEMICI FILOMVSI DI BOLOGNA. Dedicata Al maturo Giuditio del Reverendiss, Padre, IL PADRE

version, especially in the use of instrumental and vocal music to give the occasion form. On page 4 we read: *Doppo un Ripieno di varije diversi stromenti musicali, il Dissonante Accademico Filomuso intraprende.* (After a *Ripieno* [here to be understood as a piece, sonata, in massive style suitable for an introduction] by various and diverse musical instruments, *Il Dissonante Accademico Filomuso* begins [his discourse].)

Next is the text of Banchieri's introductory remarks to the discourse on the *sampogna* (*canne rusticali* = shepherd's pipes) which is to follow: *Doppo alcune sonate e concerti di voci e stromenti, il Discorso seguita.* (After several sonatas and concerted [pieces] for voices and instruments, the Discourse continues.)

Then follows the discussion itself, on the nature and invention of the *sampogna,* heavily larded with references to antique literature and the Bible.

This is followed by a *Ripieno di Voci, e Stromenti in Applauso Musicale gli Accademici Filomusi al Dissonante Concertanto* (*Ripieno* for voices and instruments as Musical Applause [by] the *Accademici Filomusi* to *il Dissonante*) and the text of the *Applauso Musicale.* Page 8 is a *Racconto De Musici Poeti e Scrittori* (the authorities to whom Banchieri's Discourse makes reference):

A

Aristotile Musico [!]
Accademici Filomusi
Accademico Dissonante
Agostino Mascardi Scrittore

C

Cassiodoro Scrittore

D

Dauidde Musico

F

Franchino Musico

G

Guido Aretino Musico
Giuseppe Zarlino Musico
Girolamo Giacobbi Musico
Gio. Battista Marino Musico & Poeta
Giobbe Scrittore

H

Horatio Flacco Poeta
Horatio Tigrini Musico

I

Iuballe Musico

L

Lattantio Firmiano Scrittore

M

Marco Iulio Cicerone Scrittore

D. ANGIOLO MARIA CANTONI, Abbate, e Vicario Generale Apostolico Olivetano. DIO CONSERVI. In Bologna. Appresso Girolamo Mascheroni. . . .

As advertised, the music was published in Venice in *Il Virtuoso Ritrovo Academico,* op. XLIX (Venice: Bartholomeo Magni, 1626). See Sartori, *BMI,* pp. 306-307.

P

Pan Musico
Pietro Pontio Musico
Polidoro Vuglio Scrittore
Platone Scrittore

S

Socrate Scrittore

V

Virgilio Poeta

IL FINE

This list of authorities with its mixture of Renaissance and Antique figures (Zarlino, *Musico,* cheek by jowl with Pan, *Musico,* and David!) clearly shows the "classicizing" attitude toward antiquity and the century just preceding.

Another work of Banchieri, not strictly "academic" but of practical import, is his *Conclusioni nel suono dell' Organo,*[35] a manual for church organists which shows the effects of academicism and is a foretaste of the practical doctrines of the Accademia Filarmonica itself. Banchieri shows his awareness of the "canonization" of sixteenth-century classicism in an interesting way. Incidentally directing the attention of organists to their obligations to Saint Cecilia, he refers to the celebrated painting by Raphael. (Raphael was to painting what Palestrina was to music: the artist whose work embodied the attitudes and aesthetic policies adopted by the Council of Trent.) Banchieri wrote:

> Copies of this marvelous canvas [i.e., the *Saint Cecilia* of Raphael, 1513] are to be found in various places, and one in particular, that by Guido Reni[36] . . . another such has been painted in the new cloister of Saint Michele in Bosco by the hand of Alessandro Albini, pupil of Lodovico Caracci, both Bolognese. . . .[37]

In addition to signifying a regularly constituted body, the term "accademia" came to refer to a social gathering at which literary or musical entertainment was provided. As was usual in the courts, including those of the Este family at Modena and Queen Christina at Rome, intellectual and artistic expression were turned to propagandistic ends. Entertainments were offered to visiting notables in which literary and musical performances were designed to support the established social order.[38] The term "ac-

35. Adriano Banchieri, *Conclusioni nel suono dell' Organo* (Bologna: Heredi di Gio. Rossi, 1609).

36. "La copia di questa stupenda Pala e sparsa in diversi Luoghi e in particolare una di Guido Reni . . . un altra simile viene effigata nel Chiostro novello di S. Michele in Bosco per mano di Alessandro Albini discepolo di Lodovico Caracci amendui Bolognese. . . ."

37. Reni, a Bolognese contemporary of Banchieri, whose school is perhaps the counterpart in painting to that of Bononcini, Cazzati, and Corelli in music.

38. One such performance was the *Accademia Per Musica Fatta nel Real Palazzo Della Maesta della Regina Christina Per Festiggiare l'Assonzione al Trono Di Giacomo Secondo Re D'Inghilterra. In occasione della solenne Ambasiciata mandata da sua Maesta Britannica alla Santita di Nostro Signore Innocenzo XI Versi Alexandro Guidi Accademico Reale . . .*

cademia" was also used to describe the works performed on such occasions, and in the 1680's, if not earlier, cantatas and oratorios were called "accademie."[39]

Academic activity was intermittently pursued at the court in Modena[40] and was, of course, essentially of this "occasional" order as shown by the following examples of academic compositions by Vitali:

Per l'Accademia sopra la nascita di S. A. S. (Francesco II): *Coronata d'applausi.*

Per l'Accademia della Regina d'Inghilterra (3 maggio 1685): *Donde avvien che tutt'ebro.*[41]

When not the ritualistic adjunct of notable events, the *accademie* at the Modenese court seem to have been literary events or debates with a prescribed "subject" on which the incidental cantata was a lyric commentary, as shown by these examples of academic cantatas by G. B. Vitali still in the Estense Library:

Problema. Se l'Aquila Estense sia più gloriosa nel promovere l'armi, o nel proteggere le lettere: *Datevi pace o dotti.*

Accademia sopra il problema: se il mondo migliori o peggiori: *Cessate o begli ingegni.*

Accademia: Qual ferisce più la lingua o la spada; *Qual di musiche note.*[42]

The subjects reflect the absolutist philosophy and atmosphere, being carefully chosen to avoid political implications or inferences.

Sporadic academic activity was established in Modena early in the seventeenth century by Alfonso d'Este[43] in 1609 and again in 1618. The literary figures involved were Fulvio Testi and Tassoni. However, little continuity is visible, and no *accademia* independent of court life seems to have emerged. Thus, as we might expect, Modenese academic activity would appear to have been less dynamic than that of Bologna. There was no necessity in Modena

(Rome: Reu. Cam. Apost., 1687), cited in Mario Rinaldi, *Arcangelo Corelli,* p. 130. An allegorical concerted work was apparently performed with characters including Londra, Tamigi, Fama, Genio Dominante, Genio Rubelle, and a chorus "of a hundred musicians" to celebrate the accession in 1685 of James II, whose queen, it will be recalled, was Maria Beatrice d'Este.

39. Vitali, *Due Accademie ossia Cantate per Voce di Basso e Violini, Cat. Est.,* p. 140. Another Vitali example is found on page 190 while examples of the use of the term by other composers are to be found on page 189.

40. Valdrighi, *Musurgiana* No. 19, p. 70.

41. *Cat. Est.,* pp. 270-271. This work also celebrated in Modena the accession of Maria Beatrice d'Este as Queen of England, consort of James II.

42. *Cat. Est.,* p. 271.

43. Michele Maylender, *Storia delle Accademie d'Italia,* p. 52.

to invent ritualistic forms in the actual presence of functional ones, while the more liberal uses of the Bolognese *accademie,* with an elected *Principe,* would have received little encouragement in the absolutist atmosphere of Modena.

We have no specific evidence connecting Bononcini with academic activity in Modena, although it seems likely that his vocal works, the *Cantate* of op. X[44] (on texts full of academic classicism) and op. XIII[45] were for such functions, as were the only works in this form by Vitali. Bononcini's "Madrigali," op. XI,[46] also show academic mannerisms. As laudatory offerings to Leopold I, they are a musical reflection of absolutism.

Bononcini's *Dramma per Camera,* op. XIV,[47] is another such blend of academicism and absolutism. If it is not the subject of an actual academic occasion, it is an extension of the intention and technique of the academic "occasional" work.[48]

By the mid-seventeenth century the empirical methods which had created the instrumental style of the early years of the century had given way to a process of assimilation and codification, the classicizing ("classifying") tendency observed in the activities of the *accademie.* The conscious intention of this process, to maintain continuity and identification with the past, was inherent in and received support from the official cultural agents—churchly and secular—as consonant with the general aims and methods of the Counter Reformation. The results are to be seen in the selective organization of materials and forms which tend constantly toward satisfying an ever-increasing taste for more powerful affective devices.[49]

In many situations a critical phase of the struggle to reconcile old theory and new practice was emphasized, if not precipitated, by the presence of a foreign artist whose experience united several traditions into a style of

44. Bononcini, *Cantate per Camera A Voce Sola* ... Da ... Opera Decima (Bologna: Giacomo Monti, 1677).

45. Bononcini, *Cantate per Camera A Voce Sola* ... Opera Decimaterza ... (Monti, 1678).

46. Bononcini, *Partitura di Madrigali a Cinque Voci Sopra i dodici Tuoni, o Modi del Canto Figurato* ... (Bologna: Giacomo Monti, 1678).

47. Bononcini, *I Primi Voli dell'Aquila Austriaca dal Soglio Imperiale alla Gloria, Dramma per Camera di D. Valentino Carli, Posto in Musica da Gio. Maria Bononcini Modanese, Accademico Filarmonico, del Concerto del Seres. Sig. Duca Francesco II e Maestro di Capella della Cattedrale di Modena* ... (Modena: Demetrio Degni, 1677), cited in Gino Roncaglia, "Giuseppe Colombi e la vita musicale modenese durante il Regno Francesco II d'Este," *Atti e memorie della Accademia di Scienze, Lettere e Arti di Modena* (Modena, 1952), X, Series V, 47.

48. These works have counterparts in the various occasional works of Purcell, including the several "Birthday Odes" written between 1680 and 1688 for James II's Queen, Mary of Modena.

49. Demonstrated by larger aggregations of players, (*concerti* of one hundred or more in Bologna and Rome), the orchestral style of Lully in Paris, larger forms, and the constantly increasing integration of tonality.

greater universality which influenced and challenged or overcame local practice.

Lully was one such catalytic individual, and we have previously described Marco Uccellini at Modena as a co-ordinator of traditions and compared him with Cazzati.

Maurizio Cazzati came to Bologna in 1657 as *Maestro di Cappella* at San Petronio. Like Uccellini, he had had varied experience as *Maestro di Cappella* at a number of North Italian churches and courts.[50] He seems never to have become part of the academic scene[51] in Bologna.[52] The Accademia Filarmonica incorporated other musicians from San Petronio, including Cazzati's pupil, G. B. Vitali, and his enemy, G. C. Arresti, organist at San Petronio. By 1666 a properly "academic" quarrel over technical matters (counterpoint) had been going on publicly in print between Arresti and Cazzati for at least two years.[53] Thus the Accademia Filarmonica itself may have been formed as a reaction to Cazzati's presence.

The appointment of Cazzati, like that of Uccellini, Bononcini, and Colombi, marks a high point of the invasion of church positions by essentially instrumental, i.e., violin, composers. With Cazzati, the size of the instrumental complement at San Petronio was increased and the ground laid for the definitive subsequent evolution of the church sonata and the concerto.

Like Uccellini, Cazzati had a varied background which brought together many elements of violin culture. From his work in general, his principal antecedents appear to be of the Venetian order.[54] Cazzati's treat-

50. 1641, Mantua; 1647, Bozzolo; 1650, Accademia delle Morte, Ferarra; 1653, S. Maria Maggiore, Bergamo.

51. Although he styles himself *Accademico Eccitato,* this title refers to the *Accademia* of that name in Bergamo of which Legrenzi was also a member.

52. His elevation as *Maestro di Cappella* over the heads of native Bolognese may have aroused resentment, as did his personality.

53. Maurizio Cazzati, *Risposta alle Oppositioni fatte del Signor Giulio Cesare Arresti* (Bologna: Heredi del Dozza, 1663).

54. The Venetian manner finds a direct historical consequence at this epoch in the work of Legrenzi, a Bergamese who remained essentially within the Venetian sphere and is outside the scope of this study. (He actually follows Cazzati at S. Maria Maggiore in Bergamo.) Of finer workmanship and less overtly "affective" than Cazzati, Legrenzi's work does show the same general tendencies toward "classification" of materials. His manner is marked by the use of repeated note formulae—a continuing echo of the style of the Gabrielis—harmonic stability, and the general severity of the Venetian instrumental diction.

His four collections of sonatas

Sonate ... di ... Libro Primo. Opera Seconda. (Venice: Gardano, MDCLV).
Suonate ... Del ... Opera Quarta. (Venice: Gioseppe Sala, MDCLXXXII). [reprint?]
Sonate Del ... Libro Terzo, Opera Ottava (Bologna: Giacomo Monti, MDCLXXI).
La Cetra ... Da ... Libro Quarto Di Sonate ... Opera Decima (Venice: Gardano, MDCLXXIII).

See Sartori, *BMI,* pp. 419, 504, 461, and 473 respectively.

were almost certainly known to Bononcini, although they cannot now be found in the Estense Collection. Opus VIII was reprinted in 1671 at Bologna by Monti, Bononcini's own

ment of elements of ornamentation is in keeping with his taste for the practical and effective, and he relies on the heavy, measured cadential formulae of the Venetians[55] instead of the ephemeral, cursive *affetti* of the school of Marini. Like Uccellini, Cazzati incorporates some popular and foreign materials. These gradually disappear from his style and do not figure in the work of the next, "classic," generation.

In general Cazzati's talent may be described as selective rather than original. His considerable powers of organization, synthesis, and reduction to effective formula, however, may be considered as a kind of originality. The virtues of Cazzati's style and his specific contribution to the Bolognese manner[56] are clarity and conciseness, practicality and effectiveness. His schematic formal procedure is marked by calculated and systematic use of well-differentiated, efficient, and highly stylized formulae.

It is tempting to ascribe the development of Cazzati's church style in the direction of clarity and definition of outline to the accoustical properties and demands of the vast late-Gothic (fifteenth-century) nave of San Petronio.[57] However, the immediacy of his success with the Bolognese public suggests that he was possessed of an easily accessible, effective style before he took the position at San Petronio.[58] Thus it would seem that Cazzati was gifted with a quality denied his academic adversaries, his taste and gift for pleasing the public.

Whether or not he was academically acceptable, Cazzati's professional influence must have been enormous. His published works of all kinds

---

publisher. Legrenzi is represented in the Estense by two operas: *Eteocle e Polinice* and *Germanico sul Reno* (See *Cat. Estense,* pp. 126-127). The latter is accompanied by a libretto dated 1677, published in Reggio, for the Ducal Theatre of Modena. *Germanico* was dedicated to Francesco II.

Legrenzi had also been expected to follow Uccellini at Modena, as is clear from Legrenzi's letter dated 1665 to the Duke Francesco II (Schenck, *Osservazione,* p. 12). See also La Mara, *Musikerbriefe aus fünf Jahrhunderten, Erster band* (Leipzig: Breitkopf and Härtel, 1886), p. 112. He seems to have remained in contact with Modena as his later operas were performed there. La Mara, *op. cit.,* p. 114, reports another letter written to the Duke on Feb. 24, 1689.

55. See (in musical supplement) Cazzati's op. XXXV, "La Casala," and op. VIII, "La Vertua." These cadential formulae, expanded and in various harmonic treatments, including pedal, are prototypes for passage work of the later Bolognese Concerto (Torelli), the *perfiidia.* See Franz Giegling, *Giuseppe Torelli,* p. 27, and Walther, *Lexicon,* p. 472. This feature can be properly said to enter the Bolognese manner here.

56. It may be worth noting that it is impossible to "contribute" to an unreceptive public, and it was these virtues which recommended him to the Chapter at San Petronio, who were, after all, interested in the effectiveness, not to say "stylishness," of their services.

57. Just as it has always been held that the style of the Gabrielis derived from the architectural peculiarities of San Marco.

58. F. Vatielli, *Arte e Vita Musicale a Bologna* (Bologna: Nicola Zanichelli, 1927), I, 159. Vatielli says, without giving a source:

"Di qui venuto a Bologna nel 1657 e fatte sentire sue musiche nella chiesa di S. Salvatore, avava riscosso tale ammirazione e tanto plauso da tutti, che i fabbricieri di S. Petronio, giubilato il vecchio maestro Alberto Bertelli, lo avevano eletto a direttore della loro Cappella."

go to fifty-five opus numbers published and republished in Bologna, Venice, and Antwerp. Moreover, his publishers were the most significant of the day: Gardano, Monti, Silvani, Phalese, and Potter.[59] The prestige, also, of the Basilica of San Petronio, one of the largest churches in Italy, would have insured their dissemination.

It is hard to determine how directly Bononcini was influenced by Cazzati. There can be no question that Bononcini knew the music of Cazzati and, as theorist and academician, followed the quarrel between Cazzati and Arresti. Although no music by Cazzati is now found in the Estense Collection, its very popularity and practicality may account for its absence today. Lacking Bononcini's own choral production, and given the circumstances, Cazzati's concerted Psalms, Hymns, Vespers, and other liturgical works are the logical repertoire for the period of Bononcini's tenure at the Duomo in Modena. Moreover, Agatea, Bononcini's predecessor as *Maestro di Cappella,* was acquainted with Cazzati[60] and continued to serve the Este Court for special musical occasions even after his departure from Modena in 1674.

That the copies used at the Duomo may have been borrowed from the Ducal library (and ultimately worn out) is suggested by Agatea's letter to the Ducal Archivist. (See p. 25 n. 24 *supra.*)

It is difficult to single out any specific stylistic trait which could prove Cazzati's direct influence on Bononcini, since Cazzati's principal virtues embody the eventual stylistic trends of the decades 1660-1680. However, the general tendency of Bononcini's church style, although natively more refined and expansive than Cazzati's, is likewise in the direction of concentration and classification of affective means which is Cazzati's contribution. Whether it is the result of a specific influence or simply represents a general evolution of the musical *lingua franca,* this is most visible in Bononcini's last *sonata da chiesa,* published in the collection of sonatas compiled by Marino Silvani in 1680.[61]

Cazzati's contrapuntal failings were attacked by the native Bolognese, G. C. Arresti, one of the original academicians of the Accademia Filarmonica.[62]

59. *Ibid.,* p. 251.
60. The latter dedicated a work to him.
61. See Sartori, *BMI,* p. 495; also supplement.
62. The weakness of Cazzati's counterpoint (most noticeable even to modern ears) is an insensitivity to the succession of perfect intervals. Cazzati's printed reply was the *Risposta Alle Oppositioni Fatte del Signor Giulio Cesare Arresti Nella Lettera al Lettore posta nell' Opera Sua Musicale* (Bologna: Heredi del Dozza, 1663) 47 pp., and its "Postoscritto," another 25 pages. In a prefatory letter to the reader Cazzati reveals himself as the practical musician

In printed polemics, the *Maestro di Cappella* and the organist of San Petronio indulged in undignified, if academic, recriminations. The exchange is interesting since, by quoting precept and example, they show the "sea changes" wrought in contrapuntal practice by the intervention of the harmonic saturation and the *basso continuo.*

Despite the respectability of his references and the unimpeachability of his authorities, Cazzati went—or was baited to go—too far, and the affair was judged a scandal. The native Bolognese *Maestri di Musica* had, if such was their intention, the pleasure of seeing him dismissed as *Maestro di Cappella* in 1673.[63]

Cazzati was followed at San Petronio by Gio. Paolo Colonna, a Bolognese who had studied there with Fillipuzzi before studying with Benevoli and Carrissimi in Rome. Colonna embodied and continued the combination of Bolognese and Roman traditions; the Roman "Colossal" style[64] and the "literary" manner of Carrissimi[65] as well as the Bolognese instrumental manner.

---

and anti-academic. He says:

"Know therefore . . . that the rules of Music are not Divine precepts, but human opinions, and vary as one may see from printed [music] and many virtuosi, who have appeared [in print] have not committed errors, since it is necessary to see if the[ir] Compositions please. If they please, one may say they are made by the rules, and those which do not please, even though made in observation of all the rules, are not good because they do not please, since Music is made to give pleasure not to displease."

In chapter iv, p. 20, Cazzati replies to Arresti's criticism ("One may not proceed from the octave to the unison") by referring to the Dialogo of Galileo, p. 71, Pietro Aron (Libro II, Cap. 14) and gives examples from Ignatio Donati, Stefano Bernardi, Bernardo Corsi, and Cipriano de Rore. Then he proceeds to give an example of this fault from Arresti's own work. Chap. viii answers Arresti's criticism of Cazzati's fifths:

"*On the Percussione in the situation where there are two perfect fifths, a most notable error.* To this eighth Chapter I reply that I know very well that the first documents given by the Preceptors agree that one may not use the aforementioned pair of fifths, and I myself have always prohibited the use of pairs of fifths and octaves to my students, knowing very well that all the authors prohibit them. However, all things seek their distinction, and consequently the authority of a *Maestro* is differentiated from the duty of a *Scolare,* for if two fifths are made by a *Maestro,* inadvertently or voluntarily, one cannot attribute to him a notable error, there being many compositions by distinguished men in which there are pairs of fifths. And, if I have written pairs of fifths I declare that I have not done so inadvertently, but because I expressly wished to. . . ."

He continues and gives examples (Sabatini, Rigati, Gastoldi) which he says "are . . . classics and the authors [are] approved, which means that the example of any one of which should suffice to stop the mouth, bites, and slaps, of whosoever. . . ." On page 41 Cazzati quotes a passage of no fewer than four successive fifths from Arresti.

Cazzati's transgressions are, indeed, numerous. A most striking example of no fewer than six fifths is found in the *Corrente Italiana detta la Palcotta* of his op. 50, bar 27:

V1	a″	g″	f″	e″	d″	c″	d″
V2	d″	c″	b′	a′	g′	f′♯	b′
BC	F				A		G

Although the dissonant sixths and sevenths and the two diminished fifths play their part, the passage is certainly daring and irregular.

63. *MGG,* art. "Cazzati."

64. I.e., that of Benevoli.

65. Colonna, *Motetti sacri a voce sola con due violini . . . Di . . . Opera 2a* (Bologna: Giacomo Monti, 1681). See *Cat. Est.,* p. 27.

The nature of the relationship between G. M. Bononcini and Colonna is not known; Colonna was almost certainly as much influenced as influential. We do know that Colonna kept a highly regarded music school in his house, and it was here that Bononcini's son, Giovanni, received his early training.[66] It seems unlikely that Bononcini's widow would have allowed this had not Bononcini himself had a good opinion of Colonna.

66. From the letter of Gio. Bononcini to Colonna (La Mara, *Musikerbriefe aus fünf Jahrhunderten,* p. 119) it seems that young Bononcini may also have had responsibilities there.

Chapter V. EDITIONS

Opus I of Giovanni Maria Bononcini was published in 1666 as:

PRIMI FRUTTI / DEL GIARDINO MUSICALE / A due Violini / DI GIO: MARIA BONONCINI / Dedicati ALL' ILLmo. D. GIULIO TESTI / Cauagliero dell'habito di S. Iago, e Marchese / Di Touano, e Caula / (device) / IN VENETIA MDCLSVI Apresso Francesco Magni detto Gardano A /

Copies of the three part books (Violin 1, Violin 2, Basso Continuo) are preserved at Bologna,[1] in the Library of the Liceo,[2] and in the library of the Accademia Filarmonica.[3] Opus I consists of twelve sonatas,[4] a dance sequence in the French manner; *Brando Gavotta Corente* [sic] and four *arie* followed by four *corrente* in Italian style. These are listed in a *Tavola*:

Sonata Prima	4	Brando Prima	42
Sonata Seconda	7	2.3. parte	
Sonata Terza	11	Gauotta	
Sonata Quarta	14	Sua Corente	4
Sonata quinta	17	Aria prima	45
Sonata Sesta	20	Aria Seconda	46
Sonata Settima	24	Aria Terza	47
Sonata Ottaua	27	Aria quarta	48
Sonata Nona	30	Prima Corente	49
Sonata Decima	33	Seconda Corente	50
Sonata Undecima	36	Terza Corente	51
Sonata Duodecima	39	Quarta Corente	52

IL FINE

Opus II was published in 1667 as:

...SONATE / DA CAMERA, E DA BALLO / A 1.2.3. è 4. / Dedicate / ALL'ALTEZZA SERENISSIMA / DEL SIGNOR PRINCIPE / RINALDO D'ESTE / DA GIO: MARIA BONONCINI / Opera Seconda. / (device) IN VENETIA MDCLXVII. Apresso Francesco Magni Gardano A /

The three part books (V. 1, V. 2, and *Spinetto Violone*) are preserved at Bologna; Acc. Fil.[5] The contents, *sonate da camera e da ballo,* consist of

1. Sartori, *BMI,* p. 437.

2. Bologna, Biblioteca Comunale anessa al Conservatorio di Musica "G. B. Martini," (*olim* Liceo Musicale). Hereinafter "Bologna; Liceo."

3. Hereinafter "Bologna; Acc. Fil."

4. The sonatas are of the contrapuntal church order, containing no dance movements.

5. Sartori, *BMI,* p. 441.

thirty-seven items of dance music of various kinds and in varying sequences listed in a *Tavola*:

No.	Title	Page
1	Allemana	3
2	Sarabanda	
3	Gigha	4
4	Gigha	5
5	Corente	
6	Gigha	6
7	Gigha	7
8	Gigha	8
9	Allemana	9
10	Corente	10
11	Balletto	11
12	Corente	12
13	Balletto	13
14	Corente	14
15	Corente	15
16	Corente	16
17	Corente	17
18	Corente	18
19	Corente	19
20	Corente	20
21	Corente	21
22	Corente	22
23	Corente	23
24	Corente	24
25	Corente	25
26	Corente	26
27	Brando in stil francese	27
28	Corente	29
29	Corente	
30	Brando in stil francese à 4	30
31	Corente	32
32	Corente	
33	Corente	33
34	Corente	
35	Corente	34
36	Corente	
37	Aria Discordia Concors. à 4	35

Opus III was published in 1669 as:

VARII FIORI / DEL GIARDINO MUSICALE, / Ouero Sonate da Camera a 2.3. e 4. col suo Basso continuo, / & aggiunta d'alcuni Canoni studiosi, & osseruati. / OPERA TERZA / DI GIO. MARIA BONONCINI MODONESE / DEDICATA / ALL'ILLUSTRISS. SIG. CONTE / BARTOLOMEO SCAPINELLI / (device) / Canon a 2592. Voci dopo un mezo sospiro dall'una all'altra diuise in 648. Chori, / e volendo uscir fuori dell'ordine Musicale, cioè di far valer la Massima più di / quello, che nella Musica hà il suo termine, si può procedere in infinito. / Segno del tempo perfetto, / della prolazione perfetta, e / del modo maggior perfetto. / (staff and notes) / In Bologna, per Giacomo Monti. 1669. Con licenza de' Superiori. /

The five part books are preserved as follows:

> Bologna; Liceo (V.1, V.2, Violone e B.C.) London; Br. Mus. (V.2, Alto Viola, Violone)[6]

Thus, while neither set is complete, the whole opus is extant. The contents, called *Sonate da Camera,* are nineteen pieces of dance music of various types and ten canons, or sonatas in canon, as given in the *Tavola*:

6. *Ibid.,* p. 454.

1 2 3 4 Gighe a 2. Violino, e Violone
5 6 7 Gighe a 4.
8 Allemanda a 4.
9 Corente a 4.
10 Allemanda a 4.
11 Corente a 4.
12 13 Allemande a 4.
14 Corente a 4.
15 Allemanda a 4.
16 Sonata da Camera a 4.
17 Sonata da Camera a 3.
18 19 Brando, e Corrente in stil Francese a 4.

Canoni studiosi, et osseruati.

20 Sonata a due Violini in Canon all'Unissono, col suo Basso Continuo.
21 Canon a quattro Soprani, ò Contralti all' Unissono.
22 Canon a 8. Voci all'Unissono, & all'ottaua bassa, dopo un sospiro dall'una all' altra.
23 Canon a 12. Voci all'Unissono.
24 Sonata a due Violini in Canon alla terza bassa per mouimenti contrarij, col suo Basso Continuo.
25 Canon a due Voci alla quinta bassa, con l'osseruazione de gli effeti del Punto.
26 27 Canoni a due Voci all'Unissono, sotto diuersi segni.
28 Canon a 3. Voci, sotto varij segni, *Qui potest capere capiat.*
29 Sonata a due Violini in Canon alla riversa, ma naturalmente, col suo Basso Continuo.
30 Sonata a due Violini in contrapunto doppio all'ottaua bassa, col suo Basso Continuo.[7]

Opus IV was published in 1671 as:

... Arie, Correnti, Sarabande, Gighe, / & Allemande / A Violino, e Violone, ouer Spinetta, con alcune intauolate / per diuerse accordature / COMPOSTE / DA GIO. MARIA BONONCINI / Del Concerto de gli Strumenti / Dell'Altezza Serenissima di Modana / OPERA QUARTA. / DEDICATA / ALL'ILLUSTRISSIMO SIG. / OBIZZO GUIDONI. / (device) / Canone à quattro voci. Canto Primo, e Secondo all'unisono. / (Staff, notation and text) / In Bologna, per Giacomo Monti. 1671. Con licenza de' Superiori. /

The two part books are preserved as follows:

Bologna; Liceo (Violino and Violone o Spinetta) London; Br. Mus. (Violino and Violone o Spinetta)[8]

The contents, *allemande, arie, correnti, sarabande,* and *gighe* in various orders, total twenty-seven items identified by titles taken from the names of Bolognese (?) families and are given in a *Tavola* as follows:

7. *Ibid.*, p. 456.
8. *Ibid.*, p. 464.

Aria in stil Francese, detta l'Anghisciola. Carte 3
Corrente in stil Francese, detta la Molza. 3
Aria in stil Francese, detta la Palauicina. 4
Corrente in stil Francese, detta la Strozza. 4
Sarabanda in stil Francese. 5
Corrente in stil Francese, detta la Barbiera. 5
Aria, detta la Pozza. 6
Corrente, detta la Montanara. 7
Sarabanda. 7
Aria, detta la Fontana. 8
Corrente, detta la Nigrella. 9
Sarabanda. Carte 9
Giga, detta la Cimicella. 10
Sarabanda. 10
Corrente, detta la Buffalina. 11
Giga, detta la Marsiana. 12
Sarabanda. 13
Corrente, detta la Gherardina. 13
Allemanda, detta la Fogliana. 14
Corrente, detta la Pegolotta. 15
Allemanda, detta la Magnanina. 16
Sarabanda. 17
Corrente, detta la Caporiaga. 17
Corrente, detta la Brusciata. 18
Corrente, detta la Casteluetra. 19
Allemanda, detta la Guelfa. 20
Corrente, detta l'Incognita. 21

IL FINE[9]

The pieces in intavolature—Nos. 24, 25, 26, and 27—begin on page 18 of the "Violino" with the following note as preface:

> The following sonatas are not printed with the notes placed together in a single staff, as they are written, for want of the requisite symbols. However, should you wish to perform them the more easily you may rewrite them as above, which will make it easier to the eye.[10]

Actually the "intavolature" consists of printing the double stops in score, i.e., on two staves.

With regard to the *scordature,* No. 24 is for normal tuning, No. 25 is c, e, a, c′, and Nos. 26 and 27 are both for b-flat, d, a, d′, evidence that they form a pair, *allemanda* and *corrente.*

Opus IV was reprinted by G. Monti in 1674, probably at the instigation of Marino Silvani, who wrote and signed the dedication to Pietro Garutti, a different individual from that of Bononcini's original dedication of 1671:

> ...Arie, Correnti, Sarabande, Gighe, / & Allemande / A Violino, e Violone, ouer Spinetta, con alcune intauolate / per diuerse accordature / COMPOSTE / DA GIO. MARIA BONONCINI / Maestro di Capella del Duomo di Modona / OPERA QUARTA. / DEDICATA / Al Molto Reuerendo Padre il Padre / D. PIETRO GARUTTI / MONACO CELESTINO /(device) / Canone à quattro

9. *Ibid.*

10. "Non sono stampate le seguente suonate, intavolate colle note l'una contro l'altra in una rigata sola, come si scrivono, per mancanza di Carateri a proposito; ma volendole praticare con facilita maggiore si podranno rescrivere nel modo si sopra accennato, che cosi riusciranno più commode all'occhio."

voci. Canto Primo e Secondo all'unisono.... In Bolona, per Giacome Monti. 1674. Con licenza de' Superiori. /

Copies of the part books are conserved at Bologna; Liceo. The contents remain unaltered from the earlier edition.[11]

Opus V was also published in 1671 by Monti in Bologna as:

...SINFONIA, ALLEMANDE, / CORRENTI, E SARABANDE / A 5. e 6. col suo Basso Continuo; / Et aggiunta d'una Sinfonia à quattro, che si può suonare ancora al / contrario riuoltando le parti, e cambiando il Soprano in Basso, / l'Alto in Tenore, il Tenore in Alto, & in Soprano il Basso. / OPERA QUINTA. / DI GIO. MARIA BONONCINI. / Del Concerto de gli Strumenti. / DELL'ALTEZZA SERENISSIMA DI MODANA. / DEDICATA / Al Molt'Illustre Sig. il Signore / GIACOMO LODIVICO / ARIGONI. / (device) / In Bologna per Giacomo Monti. 1671. Con licenza de Superiori. A /

The six part books have survived as follows:

Bologna; Liceo (V. 1, V. 2, Alto Viola, Tenor Viola, Violone, B.C.)
London; Br. Mus. (V. 1, V. 2, Alto Viola, Tenor Viola)[12]

The contents are a *Sinfonia a 5*, seven suites of *allemande-corrente-sarabande* and two of *corrente-sarabande* with a final *sinfonia a 4* which can be played "by reversing the parts." The books include a table[13] preceded by these instructions from the author:

If the following compositions are not played precisely as they are written, they will not result in a harmony gratifying to the ear, by reason of the weaving of the themes and other things they contain.[14]

Sinfonia à 5. per introduzione. Carte	3	Sarabanda à 5. Carte	12
Allemanda à 5.	4	Corrente à 5.	13
Corrente à 5.	4	Sarabanda à 5.	13
Sarabanda à 5.	5	Allemanda à 5.	14
Allemanda à 5.	6	Corrente à 5.	14
Corrente à 5.	6	Sarabanda à 5.	15
Sarabanda à 5.	7	Allemanda à 6.	16
Allemanda à 5.	8	Corrente à 6.	16
Corrente à 5.	8	Sarabanda à 6.	17
Sarabanda à 5.	9	Allemanda à 6.	18
Allemanda à 5.	10	Corrente à 6.	19
Corrente à 5.	10	Sarabanda à 6.	19
Sarabanda à 5.	11	Sinfonia à 5 [*sic*]	20
Corrente à 5.	12	FINIS.	

11. Sartori, *BMI*, p. 475.
12. *Ibid.*, p. 465.
13. *Ibid.*
14. "Se le seguenti Composizioni non si suoneranno giusto come appunto stanno, non recheranno grata armonia all'udito, per l'intreccio de i Soggetti, e d'altre cose, che in esse si trouano."

On page 20 of the Basso Continuo, the author provides the following note:

> *Sinfonia a quattro,* which can also be played "al contrario" by reversing the parts, and changing the Soprano to Bass, the Alto to Tenor, the Tenor to Alto, and the Bass to Soprano. Be advised that when the parts are reversed the rests do not change; the *Diesis* is changed to *B molle* [flat] and the *B molle* to *Diesis.* In this Composition the subjects are not merely the result of having been inverted, but even of having been reversed as will be shown on another occasion.[15]

The Basso Continuo ad Libitum is written out twice (or rather, two basses are supplied); on page 20 as *B. C. Ad Libitum* and on page 21 as *B. C. Ad Libitum per la sudetta sinfonia al contrario.*

On page 22 of the Basso Continuo the following note precedes a four-part contrapuntal study (*Cantilena*) (SATB):

> There are those who desire that any *Cantilena* might be reversed in the manner described above, and produce good harmony. How false this is the example below demonstrates.[16]

At the middle of the same page, the same composition inverted *al contrario* is followed by:

> Should I desire that in inversion the counterpoint remain free of error, not only must I have a good knowledge of fugue by inversion and reversion, but also of other particular details.[17]

Opus VI was published in 1672 by Gardano of Venice as:

> Sonate da Chiesa a due Violini, Opera Sesta di Gio. Maria Bononcini. Del Concerto de gli Strumenti dell'Altezza Serenissima di Modano et Accademico Filharmonica. Dedicata All'Illmo. et Revmo. Sig. Conte Giulio Camillo Campori. In Venetia, 1672. Appresso Francesco Magni detto Gardano.[18]

Of the three part books (V. 1, V. 2, B. C.) the B. C., without title page, is reported to be in Bologna; Liceo by Sartori, who also reports that a complete copy listed in the catalogue of the Bologna Accademia Filarmonica is at present untraceable.[19] The contents are twelve church sonatas.

15. "Sinfonia a quattro, che si puo suonare al contrario riuoltando le parti e cambiando il Soprano in Basso, l'Alto in Tenore, il Tenore in Alto, & in Soprano il Basso; s'auuerta, che nel riuoltar le parti le pause non si mutano; il Diesis si cangia in *B molle* & il *B molle* in *Diesis.* In questa Composizione i Soggetti non solo riescono nel riuoltar le parti contrarie, me exiamdio riuersati, come per altra occasione si dimostrera."

16. "Alcuni vogliono che ogni sorte di Cantilena si possa riuoltare cambiandosi le parti nel modo sudetto, e che no riesca buona armonia; il che quanto sia falso l'infrascritto esempio lo dimostra."

17. "Mi volendo che nel riuoltar le parti il contrapunto da gl. errori, non solo bisogna havere buona cognizione della fuga contrario, e riuersa, ma eziandio d'altre osseruazione particolari."

18. Pancaldi-Roncaglia, *MDM VII,* p. 144.

19. Sartori, *BMI,* p. 466.

In 1677, probably at the instance of Mario Silvani, who signed the second dedication, Monti reprinted Opus VI as:

...SUONATE / A DUE VIOLINI / con il Basso Continuo per l'Organo / DI GIO. MARIA BONONCINI / Maestro di Capella nella Cattedrale di Modana, & Accademico / Filarmonico di Bologna. / OPERA SESTA / Al Molt' Illustre Sig. il Signor / ANTONIO MARIA PADOVANI. / (device) / IN BOLOGNA MDCLXXVII. / Per Giacomo Monti. Con licenza de' Superiori.[20]

Of the three part books of this edition Sartori reports a complete set (V. 1, V. 2, *Organo*) in Bologna; Liceo, and at Münster; Archiv und Bibliothek des Bistums. The contents are unchanged from the 1672 edition.

There may have been an English edition of BVI published about 1720. In the *Bibliography of Musical Works Published by John Walsh*[21] William C. Smith lists as item #604, p. 169, "Bononcini's Sonatas for 2 Violins and a Bass; not identified. Date Unknown." As "Illustration 27" he gives a facsimile of Walsh's *Catalogue of English and Italian Musick* (*ca.* 1721) which lists, in addition to "Bononcini's *Aires*" (op. XII), "Bononcini's sonatas" without opus number. That this may have been Opus VI is a reasonable deduction since it is the only work exclusively devoted to sonatas (*da chiesa*) as distinct from *arie,* etc., (*da camera*); also, it is the only opus of Bononcini that contains the word "sonata" in its title. But the question must remain open, for no copy seems to have survived.

Opus VII appears to have been published[22] in Bologna by Monti in 1673 as:

Ariette, Correnti, Gighe, Allemande, e Sarabande: le quali possono suonarsi a Violino solo; a due, Violino e Violone; a tre, due Violini e Violone; e a quattro, due Violini, Viola e Violone. Opera Settima di Gio. Maria Bononcini del Concerto de gl'Istrumenti dell'Altezza Serenissima di Modona e Accademico Filarmonico di Bologna. Dedicato all'Illmo. Sig. Marchese Giuseppe Orsi. In Bologna per Giacomo Monti. 1673.[23]

No parts seem to have survived of the edition.

In 1677 Monti, at the instance of Silvani, who signed the (re-)dedication, republished Opus VII as:

...ARIETTE, CORRENTI, GIGHE, / ALLEMANDE, E SARABANDE, / Le quali ponno suonarsi à Violino solo; A due Violino, e Violone / A trè due

20. *Ibid.*, p. 485.
21. London, Oxford University Press, 1948.
22. Sartori, *BMI,* p. 472.
23. Pancaldi-Roncaglia, *MDM VII,* pp. 145-146.

Violini, e Violone, & à quattro, due Violini / Viola, e Violone. /./ OPERA SETTIMA / DI GIO. MARIA BONONCINI / Maestro di Capella nella Cattedrale di Modona, & Accademico / Filarmonico di Bologna. / *Al Molto Illustre, e Molto Reuerendo Sig.* / D. GIO. BATTISTA / DIAMANTI. (device) / In Bologna, per Giacomo Monti. 1677. Con licenza de' Superiori. A /[24]

A complete set of this edition is preserved at Bologna; Liceo.[25] It contains *sonate da camera,* i.e., suites of dance movements. There is no *Tavola,* but the volume contains:

Arietta	pag. 3	Gigha	pag. 9
Corrente	3	Arietta	10
Arietta	4	Sarabanda	11
Corrente	5	Corrente	11
Arietta	5	Arietta	11
Sarabanda	6	Corrente	12
Corrente	6	Corrente	12
Gigha	7	Allemanda	13
Sarabanda	8	Corrente	14
Corrente	8	Allemanda	14
Arietta	9	Arietta	15
Sarabanda	9	Sarabanda	16

Also in 1677 Gardano in Venice published, without dedication, an edition[26] of op. VII as:

ARIETTE, CORRENTI, / GIGHE, ALLEMANDE, E SARABANDE, / Le quali ponno suonarsi à Violino Solo, A due, Violino / e Violone, A 3, due violini, è Violone, & à / 4, due Violini Viola e Violone. / DI GIO. MARIA BONONCINI. / Opera Settima / (device) / IN VENETIA 1677. Stampa del Gardano.

The parts (V. 1, V. 2, *Viola, Violone o Spinetta*) are at Bologna; Liceo (X-263). This edition contains no table of contents; however, it corresponds exactly with the contents listed for the Monti edition of 1677.

Opus VIII was published in 1673 as:

MUSICO PRATTICO / Che breuemente dimostra / Il modo di giungere alla perfetta cognizione di tutte quelle / cose, che concorrono alla composizione de i Canti, e / di cio ch'all'Arte del Contrapunto si ricerca. / OPERA OTTAVA / DI GIO. MARIA BONONCINI MODANESE / Del Concerto de gli Strumenti / DELL'ALTEZZA SERENISSIMA DI MODANA, / Et Accademico Filarmonico di Bologna. / ALLA SACRA CESAREA MAESTA' / Del sempre

24. Sartori, *BMI,* p. 486.
25. *Ibid.,* p. 487.
26. Not listed by Sartori.

Augusto / LEOPOLDO PRIMO / IMPERATORE. / (device) Bologna per Giacomo Monti. 1673. Con licenza de' Superiori.

This work was reprinted in Venice in 1678 by Giuseppe Sala and in 1688 in Bologna by Monti. The latter edition, with a change in dedication, reads: *All'Illustrissimo et Eccellentissimo Sig. il Sig. Federico De Franchi, nob. Genovese.* This reprinting was probably also undertaken at the instance of Silvani, who again signed the rededication.[27]

A German translation of part II was published in 1701 in Stuttgart by Paul Treu as:

Johannis Mariae Bononcini ... Musicus Practicus, Welcher in Kurze weiset die Art, wie man zu vollkommener Erkanntnis ... was di Kunst des Contra-Puncts erfordert, gelangen kan.[28]

Opus IX was published in 1675 by Monti in Bologna as:

... TRATTENIMENTI / MUSICALI / A trè, & à quattro Stromenti, / OPERA NONA / DI GIO MARIA BONONCINI / Accademico Filarmonico di Bologna; del Concerto / del Serenissimo Sig. Duca Francesco Secondo, e / Maestro di Capella della Cattedrale di Modana. / DEDICATA *All'Altezza Serenissima del Sig. Principe* / LUIGI D'ESTE. / (device) / IN BOLOGA [*sic*] B / Per Giacomo Monti. 1675. Con licenza de' Superiori. /

The four part books (V. 1, V. 2, *Violone,* and *B. C.;* the *Canto Viola* and *Alto Viola* parts for the *sonate à quattro* are included in the V. 2 and *B. C.* books respectively) are preserved in the Biblioteca Estense, Modena,[29] and the Violin II and Basso Continuo at Bologna; Liceo.[30] The contents are five church sonatas and fourteen chamber sonatas (dance movements) given in a table:

Suonate da Chiesa à trè Istormenti [*sic*]

Sonata Prima.	Carte 5	Allemanda Prima.	15
Sonata Seconda.	7	Corrente Prima.	16
Sonata Terza	9	Allemanda Seconda.	17
Sonata Quarta.	11	Corrente Seconda.	18
Sonata Quinta.	13	Allemanda Terza.	19
		Corrente Terza	Carte 20
Suonata da Camera à trè		Allemanda Quarta	21
Istromenti		Corrente Quarta	22

27. Pancaldi-Roncaglia, *MDM VII,* p. 147.
28. Johann Gottfried Walther, *Lexicon,* art. "Bononcini."
29. *Cat. Estense,* no. Mus. Fill.
30. Sartori, *BMI,* p. 479.

IL FINE.[31]

Opus X was published in 1677 as:

CANTATE PER CAMERA / A VOCE SOLA. LIBRO PRIMO / CONSECRATO / ALL'ALTEZZA SERENISSIMA / DI FRANCESCO SECONDO D'ESTE / DUCA DI MODANA, REGGIO, &C. / DA GIO. MARIA BONONCINI / Del Concerto del S. A. Serenissima; Maestro di Capella della Cattedrale, & Accademico Filarmonico. / OPERA DECIMA. / (device) / In Bologna per Giacomo Monti. 1677. Con licenza di Superiori.

Opus XI was published in 1678 as:

PARTITURA DE MADRIGALI / A CINQUE VOCI / Sopra i dodici Tuoni, o Modi del Canto Figurato, / LIBRO PRIMO, OPERA UNDECIMA / DI GIO. MARIA BONONCINI MODANESE / Accademico Filarmonico, del Concerto del Serenissimo Signor Duca Francesco II / E Maestro di Capella della Cattedrale di Modana. / ALLA SACRA CESAREA MAESTA' / DEL SEMPRE AUGUSTO / LEOPOLDO PRIMO / IMPERATORE. / In Bologna, per Giacomo Monti. 1678. Con licenza de' Superiori. / Canone à / dieci voci. (staff and notes)

Opus XII was published in 1678 by Monti in Bologna as:

...ARIE E CORRENTI / A trè, due Violini e Violone / CONSECRATE / All'Illustrissimo, et Eccellentissimo Signore / CO. ALESSANDRO / SANVITALI / Conte de Fontanellato, e Marchese di Belforte. / DA GIO. MARIA BONONCINI / Del Concerto dell'Altessa Sereniss. di Modona, Maestro di / Cappella della Cattedrale, & Accademico Filarmonico. / OPERA DUODECIMA. / (device) / IN BOLOGNA. MDCLXXVIII. C / Per Giacomo Monti. Con licenza de' Superiori.

The three part books (V. 1, V. 2, Violoncello)[32] are preserved (as F113) at the Biblioteca Estense, Modena, and (the violoncello part) at Bologna; Liceo. The contents consist of a series of alternate *arie* and *correnti* arranged in twelve pairs; the only exceptions being items nineteen (*aria*) and twenty-two (*sarabanda*).

Opus XII was published *ca.* 1700 in London by J. Walsh and J. Hare as:

31. *Ibid.*, p. 480.

32. This is the first use of the modern term for the cello in Bononcini's titles. The MS. in Modena incidentally bears the alternative *Violoncino*: other bass parts are designated as *Violone*.

Bononcini's *Aires in 3 Parts* Violin I, Violin II, and "Through Bass for the Harpsichord," as Almands, Corrants, Preludes, Gavotts, Sarabands, and Jiggs. With a Through Bass for the Harpsichord. London. Printed and sold by I. Walsh Musicall Instrument maker in Ordinary to his Majesty at the Golden Harp & Hoboy in Catherine Street, near Somersett house in the Strand, and I Hare Musicall Instrument maker at the Golden Viol in St. Pauls Church Yard and at his Shop in Freeman's Yard near the Royal Exchang [*sic*] in Cornhill. Pr. 3ˢ.[33]

This was reprinted as late as *ca.* 1720.[34] In 1705 the same opus was brought out as:

Bononcini's *Aires for two Flutes and a Bass or two Flutes without a Bass* the Aires Consisting of Allemands, Sarabands, Corants, Preludes, Gavots, and Jiggs with a Through Bass for the Harpsichord or Bass Violin. Fairly Engraven. London. Printed for I. Walsh, Serv. to her Ma. at the Harp and Hoboy in Katherine Street near Somerset House in the Strand, and I Hare at the Golden Viol in St. Pauls Church yard and at his Shop in Freeman's yard near the Royal Exchange.[35]

The 1700 edition for violins undertook considerable rearrangement in the matter of sequence of items and also changed more than a few titles.[36] The 1705 edition for flutes undertakes the same changes in title with but one change in order. However, to accommodate the register of the flute, certain transpositions of key are made. The following table collates the two English and the original Italian edition.[37]

Monti, 1678			W. H. 1700 (1720)			W. H. 2 1705		
No.	Name	Key	No.	Name	Key	No.	Name	Key
1	Aria	d	1	Allemand	d	1	Allemand	d
2	Corrente	d	2	Corrente	d	2	Corrant	d
3	Aria	a	3	Slow Aire	a	3	Aire	d

33. W. Barclay Squire, *Catalogue of Printed Music . . . in the British Museum* (London, 1912), I, 174. See also William C. Smith, *Bibliography of Musical Works Published by John Walsh* (London: Oxford University Press, 1948), pp. 56, 44, 69.

34. William C. Smith, *op. cit.*

35. These editions may have been undertaken to make capital of the growing reputation of the younger Bononcini, Giovanni, who was acquiring the continental fame which eventually brought him to London and into competition with Handel about 1720. Walsh's editions, it will be noted, give the composer's name simply as "Bononcini" without prefacing a Christian name. This is the first of many instances which contributed to the confusion regarding the lives and works of all three members of the family.

36. The original titles—simply, *Arie* and *Correnti*—may have been changed in the interests of diversity; however, the changes are not merely arbitrary. Instead they show a certain consistency which independently bears out our premises in regard to the function and mutual relationships of company dances and the *aria.* The *arie* here become further designated as *Allemands, Gavotts,* or *Preludes,* and several of the *Correnti* are called *Sarabandes.*

37. The original sequence of movements (Monti, 1678) has been retained or restored in all cases. Thus the discrepancies in the sequence of numbers will show the changes in order of the later editions which tend to group items by tonality.

4	Corrente	a	4	Corrante	a	4	Corrant	d
5	Aria	e	5	Gavott	e	5	Gavott	g
6	Corrente	e	6	Saraband	e	6	Saraband	g
7	Aria	e	7	Prelude	e	7	Prelude	g
8	Corrente	e	8	Corrente	e	8	Corrant	g
9	Aria	C	12	Allemande	C	9	Allemand	F
10	Corrente	C	13	Saraband	C	10	Saraband	F
11	Aria	F	14	Allemande	F	11	Allemand	F
12	Corrente	F	15	Sarabande	F	12	Saraband	F
13	Aria	Bb	16	Prelude	Bb	13	Prelude	F
14	Corrente	Bb	22	Corrente	Bb	14	Corrant	C
15	Aria	Bb	21	Allemande	Bb	15	Allemand	C
16	Corrente	Bb	17	Corrente	Bb	16	Corrant	C
17	Aria	e	9	Gavott	e	17	Gavott	g
18	Corrente	e	10	Saraband	e	18	Saraband	g
19	Aria	e	11	Aire	e	19	Aire	g
20	Aria	F	19	Allemande	F	20	Allemand	G
21	Corrente	Bb	18	Aire	Bb	22	Corrant	C
22	Sarabanda	Bb	20	Corrente	Bb	21	Aire	C
23	Aria	c	23	Prelude	c	23	Prelude	e
24	Corrente	c	24	Gigha	c	24	Iigga	e

Opus XIII was published in 1678 by Giacomo Monti in Bologna as:

CANTATE PER CAMERA / A VOCE SOLA / LIBRO SECONDO / CONSECRATO / ALL'ILLUSTRISS. ET ECCELLENTISS. SIG. IL SIG. CONTE / SCIPIONE ROSSI / Marchese di S. Secondo &c. / DA GIO. MARIA BONONCINI / Del Concerto dell'Altezza Sereniss. di Modana, Maestro di Capella della / Cattedrale, & Accademico Filarmonico. / OPERA DECIMATERZA. / (device) In Bologna, per Giacomo Monti. 1678. Con Licenza de' Superiori.

Opus XIV was published in Modena in 1677 by Demetrio Degni as:

I primi Voli dell'Aquila Austriaca del Soglio Imperiale alla Gloria. Dramma da Camera di D. Valentino Carli. Posto in Musica da Gio. Maria Bononcini Modanese. Accademico Filarmonico; Del Concerto del Seren. Sig. Duca Francesco II e Maestro di Capella della Cattedrale di Modana. Alla Sacra Cesarea Maestá del Sempre Augusto Leopoldo Primo Imperatore. In Modana, per Demetrio Degni. 1677. Con licenza de' Superiori.[38]

In 1680, two years after Bononcini's death, an isolated sonata for two

38. Gino Roncaglia, "Giuseppe Colombi e la vita musicale . . . modenese durante il Regno Francesco II d'Este," *Atti e memorie della Accademia di Scienza Lettere e Arti di Modena* (Modena, 1952), X, Series V, 47.

violins and organ in church style appeared as "Sonata Settima" in a collection[39] brought out by Marino Silvani and printed by Monti as:

...SCIELTA / DELLE SUONATE / A due Violini, con il Basso Continuo / per l'Organo, / RACCOLTE / Da diuersi Eccelenti Autori. / Al Molto Illustre Signore il Signore / GIOVANNI / PAULI. / (device) In Bologna per Giacomo Monti. 1680. Con licenza de' Superiori. /

A set of the parts is preserved in Bologna; Liceo.

39. This interesting collection also contains sonatas by G. B. Bassani, Andrea Grossi, P. degli Antonii, and Alessandro Stradella. Three anonymous sonatas by Romans and a Venetian (N. N. Romano and N. N. Venetiano) are intriguing. They may be the work of amateurs who, by reason of social position (clerical?), could not be associated with the publication of music.

Incidentally, this is the only work in which any mechanical discrepancy exists among the several instrumental parts. Some four bars have, of necessity, been the subject of reconstruction in the supplement.

CHAPTER VI. DEDICATIONS

The several dedications which preface the editions of Bononcini's works are items of considerable interest. They are expressions of various dimensions of social structure and, as such, constitute social documents. The seventeenth-century dedication was a literary reflection of the system of patronage under which artists then worked. In addition to formulating the quasi-feudal relationship between patron and artist—a feature cultivated by the Counter Reformation—the dedication also served as a polemic device wherein the artist could publicly reply to critics, express aesthetic theory, or indulge in criticism of others with the moral, social, and political protection of an eminent or powerful patron.

The language of these dedications is, of course, that of the *accademia,* the agency in which the relationship between intellectual, artistic, and political life was formulated. It is against the background of the academy that these prefaces must be read. The Marinisms, the play on words, and the mythological beasts which inhabit their pages are the seventeenth-century equivalents of the clichés of technological language which characterize much official and scholarly writing even today.

The general and gradual intensification of the abject formulae (the "feudal" terms in which the artist "cast himself at the feet" of constituted authority) was a natural result of the constant use of these threadbare expressions.[1] However, the extravagance of the formulae also gives evidence of the growing interior strains on the machinery of the Counter Reformation and absolutism and the mounting artificiality imposed upon life by this philosophy.[2]

Considerable interest attaches to the personages to whom Bononcini dedicates his works. Three (opp. II, IX, X) are dedicated to members of the Este family—Rinaldo, Luigi, and Francesco II, respectively—and two are dedicated to the Emperor Leopold I. The remaining dedications are directed to persons of consequence who, like both Francesco II and Leopold,

1. To be mercilessly lampooned by Benedetto Marcello in *Il Teatro Alla Moda* of 1720.

2. A suggestion of the growing activity of censorship is seen in the ominous formula found at the end of Bononcini's op. X: "PROTESTA. Auuerta al Lettore, che le parole Fato, Destino, Dio, Adorare, Deitá, Sacerdote, Omnipotente, sono scherzi di penna poetica, non sentimenti di abuso Catholico." And, at the end of op. XIII: "Auuerta il Lettore, che le parole immortale, Fato, Destino, Dio Deitá, e simile, sono scherzi di penna poetica e che dove si tratta di Roma, s'intende quando si ritrouaua soggetta alla Gentilitá."

were actual amateurs or *dilettanti* practicing music as part of social and intellectual life.

Opus I, *Primi Frutti del Giardino Musicale* (Venetia: Gardano, 1666) is dedicated to Giulio Testi, whom Bononcini describes as "son of that Fulvio whose brow is crowned with the sublime laurels of Pindar..." (*figlio di quel Fulvio, che del più sublime Alloro di Pindar s'e coronato la fronte...*). During the early part of the seventeenth century Fulvio Testi was, along with Tassoni, a great literary figure of the Este court and had come with the family on their removal from Ferarra. Giulio Testi is described as *Cavagliero dell'habito di S. Iago, e Marchese Di Tovano, e Caula.*

Opus II, *Sonate da Camera e da Ballo*... (Venetia: Gardano, 1667) is dedicated to Signor Principe Rinaldo d'Este, the uncle of Francesco II. Rinaldo—who later became Cardinal—was given much of the responsibility of rule at Francesco's majority and, renouncing orders, succeeded to power upon Francesco's death.

The dedication plays upon the conceits of "motion" and "music" proper to *sonate da ballo.* It is a good specimen of an official courtly gesture lightly touched with academic classicism as may be seen from the following:

The Muses and the Graces always move in conjunction. Of the former Your Highness is the Patron, of the latter the source. Thus, in sending to the printer certain of my musical compositions for Playing and Dancing I am, perforce, obliged to send them in homage to Your Highness, you who are the true Apollo, of whom every virtue learns its consonance. By your gracious acceptance give them life and, as the Trumpet of Your Fame excites the harmony of the Lyre, from the regulated movements of Your Prudence they will learn the true rules by which they should be set in motion. Condone my Ambition, or my daring, since I—to raise my base works—must support them on Your Patronage; to show them in public it is wise to place them under the protection of a Great Prince, and with entreaties that You may benignly accept them, I, with profound reverence, humbly bow. Your Serene Highness' most Humble, most Devoted servant Gio. Maria Bononcini.[3]

3. "LE Muse, e le Grazie vanno sempre congionte, Di quelle l'Altezza Vostr, n'è Promotrice, di queste il fonte. Perciò douendo io rimettere alle stampe alcune mie composizioni musicali di Suoni, e Balli, forza è, che le riporti in ossequio apprendono le consonanze. Si degni in tanto gradirle, e darli spirito, quando che le Trombe della sua fama eccitaranno l'armonia nelle Cetre, e dalli moti ben regolati della sua Prudenza, apprenderà la vere regole, che dourà spiccarsi alle mosse. Condoni in tanto alla mis Ambizione questo ardire mentre m'auuiso che per solleuare questa mia bassa opera mi bisognaua appoggiarla al patrocinio del Altezza. V., per farla comparire alla luce esser saggio conseglio collocarla sotto l'ombra s'un Principe Serenissimo, e con supplicarla del suo benigno gradimento con profonda riuerenza umilimente me l'inchino. Di V. Altezza Serenissima Humilissima, Deuotissimo, seruitore Gio. Maria Bononcini." Quoted in Sartori, *BMI,* pp. 440-441.

Opus III, *Varii Fiori del Giardino Musicale* (Bologna: Monti, 1669) is dedicated *All'Illustriss. Sig. Conte Bartolemeo Scapinelli.* Bononcini plays on the emblem of his patron's house in typical Marinesque fashion:

> ... I offer them, then, the more gladly, since borne aloft on the pinions of your Eagle will they not sublimely approach that starry Lyre of Heaven in which the harmonious courses of the Spheres so luminously resound? ...[4]

Scapinelli appears to have been in some sense a patron of Bononcini from the closing sentence:

> ... Receive with favor ... this small gift as proof of the immensity of my devotion; and absolve me of the debt which I owe for the valued consideration shown me by your House....[5]

The prefatory materials of this opus include, as was common in the seventeenth century, a commendatory sonnet in praise of the author's *Giardino di varij fiori musicale* (... Garden of various musical flowers) by Gratio Sartigli:

> With what prodigious flowery treasures
> O erudite Gardener do you present us?
> Which by the ear refresh the mind
> With the divisions of sonorous Number.
>
> In their Variety they concord among them
> Making fugues with the buds, and with accents,
> the flowers:
> Breathing sweetness in concert
> From the zephyrs of sighs springs their freshness.
>
> There can be no more glorious miracle.
> While the Assyrian recorded his vanity in the
> Hanging Gardens
> finally uprooted by proud Time,
>
> You make a more noble amazement
> A harmonious and portable Garden
> And know how to give Eternity to its flowers.[6]

4. "... Glie l'offro adunque, e tanto più volontieri, quanto, che portata sù Vanni dell' AQUILA sua, chi sà non venghi sublimata presso quella stellante Lira del Cielo, che ne gli armoniosi rigiri delle Sfere cosi luminosamente risuona? ..." Quoted in Sartori, *BMI*, p. 455.

5. "Gradisca V.S. Illustrissima il picciol dono in argomento dell'immensa mia diuozione; ed assoluendomi dal debito, c'haurei di toccare i preggi ragguardeuoli di sua Casa...." *Ibid.*

6. "Qual prodigio di florido tesoro
Giardiniero erudito à noi presenti?
Qui per l'Udito si ricrean le menti
Ne comparti d'un Numero sonoro.

"Per Varietà concordi in frà di loro,
Fai di punti le fughe, i firo d'accenti:

Opus IV, *Arie, Correnti, Sarabande, Gighe,* & *Allemande* (Bologna: Monti, 1671) is dedicated to Sig. Obizzo Guidoni. This dedication continues the protestations and defense Bononcini made against certain *Critici* of his op. III in the "Discorso Musicale di ... Sopra una Composizione..." of 1669 or 1670. It appears from the dedication that Guidoni was a musician, a dilettante surrounded by others on whose personal reputation and taste Bononcini felt he could count for support against the critics. The paragraph, an example of the prevalent seventeenth-century use of dedications as polemic occasions, shows some of Bononcini's most characteristic expression. It resumes in similar language the subject of Bononcini's *Discorso* already quoted (see Appendix), namely, the attacks and charges of plagiarism leveled at his op. III, and requests the support and protection of Guidoni against this censure. Bononcini also refers to the treatise *Il Musico Prattico* as being "already completed and ready for the printer," pointing out that its contents should be additional evidence of his actual possession of the skill denied him by his critics.

The fact that Guidoni played *con agilità ... il Violone* accounts for the nature of these chamber works *a due*—in which, with only one other instrument, the bass would have as much scope as possible—and the virtuoso elements they contain. Bononcini is explicit in stating that this part, although published for *Violone o Spinetta,* was intended primarily for the Violone. At the head of page three of the *Violone* part we read:

> ... Si deve avvertire, che fara magliore effetto il Violone, che la Spinetta, per essere i Bassi più proprii dell'uno, che dell altra. (It should be noted that the *Violone* will make a better effect than the *Spinetta,* since the Basses are more appropriate to the one than the other.)

The second edition of op. IV (Bologna: Monti, 1674) was dedicated, not by Bononcini, who (it was assumed) "would approve without hesitation [and] with sentiments of rejoicing ...,"[7] but by the entrepreneur, Marino Silvani, to Padre Pietro Garrutti, a Celestine monk. The interest

---

Spiran soauità scritti concenti
Da l'aure de i sospir nasce il ristoso.

"Miracolo non sia più glorioso
Che 'l vano Assiro i pensil'Orti infiori,
Fasti, ch'addugge al fin tempo orgoglioso;

"Tù formi con più nobili stupori
Portätile un Giardino armonioso,
E sai donar l'Eternitade a i fiori."

Ibid. The double meaning, based on musical jargon, with which the poem is laden, is quite untranslatable, e.g., *sospiri* (sighs) are also quarter rests, *punti* (buds) may also mean notes, etc.

7. "Il Sig. Bononcini approuera senz'altro con sentimenti di giubilo, che di nuouo escano sotto il di elei Patrocinio le sue si degne Fatiche a publico diletto, e sua gloria particolare. ..."

here, apart from indicating the popularity of Bononcini's work, arises from the question of Bononcini's rights in the matter. Could the enterprising Silvani simply appropriate Bononcini's work for his own purposes? And, further, were the *publico diletto* and *gloria particolare* sufficient reward?

In the editions of 1671 (Monti) and 1674 (Monti-Silvani) of op. IV we find the only examples in Bononcini's work of a practice current and common throughout the first three quarters of the seventeenth century, that of naming with proper names individual compositions ("sonate," "canzoni," and, as in this case, also dances).[8] These, while not dedications in the sense we are considering, are of similar, social derivation.

The names are most often those of prominent families of the *ambiance* in and for which they were written or published. However, such titles might also be derived from many other sources—political, social, and literary[9]—including the names of towns or such traditional titles as *La Vecchia, L'Incognita,* etc. The titles may also refer to traditional and popular materials on which the composition is based: *La Folia, Ruggiero, La Romanesca,* songs,[10] and to names of other musicians.[11]

Sartori[12] describes the practice as of Lombard origin. As such, it is part and parcel of the violin culture whose strongest lines of influence lead us repeatedly to Northern Italy. By the mid-seventeenth century the practice was general, and it disappears in the 1670's.

The usage of naming individual compositions with proper names also appears—as seems to be the case with Bononcini's work—to have been adopted as a "public relations" device by the printers or publishers. This is clear from the letter to the reader in *Il Primo Libro delle canzoni . . . del Sig. Girolamo Frescobaldi* (*Date in Luce da Bartolomeo Grassi . . . in Roma M.DC.XXVIII*). Grassi writes:

. . . The names of the *Canzoni* have been taken from the names of many of my Patrons and friends, especially the Gentlemen of Lucca, because glorying in being a subject of the Serene Republic of Lucca, it seems the best means

8. No such titles appear in the MS.

9. Such as *Canzona detta la Bolognesa* (Carlo Farina, Lib. IV, 1628). See Sartori, *BMI,* p. 321.

10. Uccellini, "*Aria Quarta Sopra la Ciaccona . . . Aria Seconda Sopra E tanto tempo Hormai,*" etc., op. III (Venice, 1642). See Sartori, *BMI,* p. 380.

11. Uccellini, "*Sonata detta la Bonamenta,* Libro Terza, Sonata Decimaottaua." *Ibid.* This practice was also followed in French instrumental music. Cf. *Pieces de Clavecin en Concert* by Rameau, *La Forqueray,* etc., and in the suites of Couperin.

12. Claudio Sartori, *La Musique Instrumentale de la Renaissance,* ed. J. Jaquot (Paris, 1955), p. 204. "Une pratique des musiciens lombards (1582-1639), l'hommage des chansons instrumentales aux families d'une ville."

suited to my talents to testify the devotion with which I regard my country, its nobles and Virtuous men.[13]

Maurizio Cazzati in his op. L (*Varii, e Diversi Capricii*...Da Maurizio Cazzati...Opera XXXXX...in Bologna...MDCLXIX)[14] dedicates, or rather, "consecrates" the entire opus to Anna Isabella Gonzaga,[15] but goes on to give names of families to individual works. In the dedication Cazzati writes:

...my work...accompanied by several Illustrious Names which are the Glory ...of this city and the ornament of these, my *Capricci*: Each carries its proper name...as a shield against the blows of Envy and as a obeisance to conciliate the benevolence of Greatness.[16]

And, in the "Avvertimento Al Lettore:"

In the *Capricci* contained in the present work and entitled with the names of the Illustrious *Senatori* of this Noble City, the Author has observed no order except that arrived at by chance, of which he wishes to inform the Reader, so that they may not think he intends any derogation of the precedence owing to each in conformity with their antiquity, and to protest his desire to be known as the servant of all, equally.[17]

These two accounts adequately describe the significance of the practice in the time and circumstances in which Bononcini's example occurs. The list of family names in Bononcini's op. IV corresponds in some instances to that used by Cazzati (op. L and op. XVIII), Vitali ("La Molza" and "La Palavicina," op. V, 1669) and Penna (op. VII, 1673).

The practice does not seem to have been favored by the Modenese: Uccellini uses names of all kinds in his op. III of 1642 (his first work written in Modena), but in general abandons the usage after this. No such names appear in Colombi's works, and op. IV is the only case in Bononcini's

13. "...Li nomi delle Canzoni, sono cauati da i cognomi di molti miei Patroni, & amici, & particolarmente di Gentil huomeni Lucchesi, perche gloriandomi di esser suddito della Serenissima Republica di Lucca, conuiene che nel miglior modo che porta il mio talento, procuri di testificare al mondo la deuotione con la quale riuerisco la mia patria, & tanti nobili, & Virtuosi Signori...." Cited in Sartori, *BMI*, p. 328.

14. *Ibid.*, p. 449.

15. "Consagrati Al Nome immortale dell'Altezza Serenissima Di Anna Isabella Gonzaga Prencipessa di Guastalla...." *Ibid.*

16. "...le mie fatiche...accompagnato da que' Nomi Illustrissimi, che sono la gloria del Cielo di questa Città, e l'ornamento di questi miei Capricci; Ogn'uno d'essi porta il suo proprio scritto in fronte, come scudo contro i colpi del liuore, e come carattere d'honore atto à conciliarle la beneuolenza de Grandi...." *Ibid.*, pp. 449-450.

17. "NE' Capricci contenuti nella presente Opera, & intitolati da Cognomi de gl'Illustrissimi *Senatori* di questa Nobile Città, non si è osseruato dall'Autore altro ordine, che quello datoli dal caso, del che hà voluto auuertire il Lettore, accioche non si credesse, ch'egli hauesse preteso di derogare alla precedenza douuta à ciascheduno in conformità della loro entianità, mentre si protesta, e vuole essere riconosciuta egualmente per Seruitore di tutti. E viui felice." *Ibid.*, p. 450.

work. As we have said, no such titles appear in the manuscripts of Bononcini in the Biblioteca Estense, so that their use here may very well be the undertaking of the publisher Monti, probably at the suggestion of Marino Silvani, to suit the circumstances at Bologna.

Opus V, *Sinfonie, Allemande, Correnti, e Sarabande* . . . (Bologna: Monti, 1671) was dedicated to Giacomo Lodovico Arigoni, who, from Bononcini's terms of address, was a man of affairs for whom music was an avocation.

> Although your Highness devoted the larger part of your efforts to affairs which require [the] profound attention corresponding to your talents and judgment . . . your rare and virtuous gifts raise you above the greatness of any undertaking of your incumbency, and also support the genius and taste which inclines you to the peaceful diversion of Music, so closely allied to Arithmetic, of which the perfect cognition and knowledge . . . admirably illuminate the vivacity of your Spirit.[18]

The names "Giacomo" and "Arigoni" immediately raise the question of a relationship between this man and the "Giacomo Arrigoni" who in 1635[19] published *Concerti da Camera . . . da Giacomo Arrigoni Organista della Sacra Cesarea Maestà di Ferdinando II* . . . VENICE MDCXXXV.

The title page, hence the dedication, of Bononcini's op. VI in the 1672 edition by Monti has not survived[20] except as given by Pancaldi-Roncaglia.[21] The dedication is made to Sig. Conte Giulio Camillo Campori, but we lack the dedicatory letter itself. The second edition of op. VI of 1677 is, like that of op. IV, dedicated by Marino Silvani, the music dealer for whom it was published, to Antonio Maria Padovani, apparently an amateur. The second part of Silvani's dedication is fulsome of praise of Bononcini. He writes: "I will refrain from praise of this work as being more worthy of admiration than of praise: the Name alone of the Author raises it to the stars."[22]

18. "Ancorchè a V.S. per la maggior parte del tempo conuenga di spendere le sue saggie applicazioni in affari, che richiedono una profondissima attenzione corrispondente all' ingegno, e giudizio suo, ad ogni modo le sue rare, e virtuose doti la rendono cosi superiore alla grandezza di qualunque arduo negozio di sua incombenza, che può anche secondare il genio, & il gusto, con che resta inclinata à i piaceuoli diuertimenti della Musica tanto strettamente congionta all'Aritmetica, nella perfetta cognizione, & esperienza della quale ella sopra tutto fà mirabilmente spiccare la viuacità del suo spirito. . . ." *Ibid.*, p. 465.

19. *Ibid.*, p. 346.

20. *Ibid.*

21. Pancaldi-Roncaglia, *MDM VII*, p. 141.

22. *Ibid.*

The title page and dedicatory letter of the first edition of op. VII, *Ariette, Correnti, Gighe, Allemande, e Sarabande*... (Bologna: 1673) have not survived.[23] This work was dedicated to the Signor Marchese Giuseppe Orsi,[24] doubtless a member of the same Bolognese family as the Alessio Orsi to whom Bononcini's son G. B. Bononcini dedicated his op. VI in 1687.[25]

The second edition of Bononcini's op. VII[26] is dedicated (by Silvani) to Sig. Gio. Battista Diamanti. The dedicatory letter is as much an occasion to advertise Bononcini as to praise Diamanti. It shows again that Bononcini's works were popular with the *dilettanti* and *virtuosi*: "...the present *Correnti,* when hardly printed were devoured because of their exquisiteness by the voracity of the *virtuosi*" (*...le presenti Correnti, e che appena stampati, furon per la loro esquisitezza dalla voracita de' Virtuosi assorbiti...*).[27]

The first edition of Opus VIII, *Il Musico Prattico* (Bononcini's treatise on counterpoint) was dedicated to the Emperor Leopold I, *Alla Sacra Cesarea Maestà del sempre Augusto Leopoldo Primo Imperatore,* himself a good composer. There is a distinct propriety in Bononcini's dedication of his theoretical *capo lavoro* to the head of the social complex, the hierarchical chief of the secular branch of the Counter Reformation, who was also a professional colleague.[28]

The edition of op. VIII of 1688 by Monti in Bologna is dedicated to Sig. Federico De Franchi Nob. Genovese[29] by Marino Silvani, who again praises Bononcini: "...Pillaged, no less by Time than by the avidity of Connoisseurs, the richly arrayed Statue of the *Musico Prattico* leaves the World of Harmony deprived of the most gentle Intelligence of the Heavenly Harmony...."[30]

23. Sartori, *BMI,* p. 472.

24. Pancaldi-Roncaglia, *MDM VII,* p. 145.

25. *Sinfonie a Due Strumenti... Dedicate All'Illustrissimo Signor Co. Alessio Orsi Senatore di Bologna. Da... Opera Sesta.* (device). Bologna: Monti, 1687.... See Sartori, *BMI,* p. 539.

Cazzati, in op. V (Bologna, 1669), includes as number 1 a "Corrente Italiana detta l'Orsa." *Ibid.,* p. 450.

26. *Ibid.,* p. 486.

27. *Ibid.;* see chap. iv n. 25.

28. The dedication itself is a labored and formal "Academic" effusion, viz., the inevitable "E i giubila di peruenire come Musico al suo Trono Maestoso, oue quanto la Spada di Marte trionfa la Cetra d'Apollo" (Rejoice to approach as Musician his Throne of Majesty where the lyre of Apollo Triumphs beside the sword of Mars), but has no other interest.

29. Pancaldi-Roncaglia, *MDM VII,* p. 147.

30. *Ibid.*

Opus IX, *Trattenimenti Musicali* (Bologna: Monti, 1675) was dedicated to Principe Luigi d'Este. This member of the Este family is revealed in Bononcini's dedication to have been one of its military and diplomatic representatives. Bononcini writes with a certain glow of admiration. After a self-deprecatory sentence about his temerity in presenting his music to so meritorious an individual: "... since his earliest age accustomed to the proud Concert of Trumpets and Drums ... on the field of Military Glory. ..."

He points out the courtly experience of Luigi:

> ... You, who have traveled all over Germany, and seen the Courts of Vienna, Stockholm, Coppenhagen [*sic*], Monaco, Baviera[*sic*], Hanover, Disseldorf [*sic*] and others may know better than others how other noble souls, and ferocious, do not disdain to incline the ear to the gentle incantations of melody, thus savoring the explosion of bombs and the braying of warlike brasses attuned to artifice mixed with honor, and with delight, the sweet sounding Instruments.

No classical allusions or academic conceits here! The letter ends with a better-than-usual string of protests of humility, obedience, etc.

The *Cantate per Camera ... Libro Primo, op. X* (Bologna: Monti, 1677) are "consecrated" to Francesco II. These are, as the style of the dedication also shows, probably academic works. (See p. 44 *supra.*) They are prefaced by a letter dated August 9, 1676, in which Bononcini rings the changes on such evergreen images as: "... Desirous of making counterpoint of the sounds which the Trumpet of Fame causes to resound against your Name ... [and] the benign *Air* of your Highness animates this Harmony. ..."

Opus XI, *Partitura de Madrigali a Cinque Voci* ... (Bologna: Monti, 1678) is dedicated, like op. VIII, to the Emperor Leopold I. These works are praises of Leopold; we have discussed elsewhere their "academic" aspects, texts, and modes. (See p. 44 *supra.*) Bononcini describes and emphasizes in the dedicatory letter: "... my Madrigals ... which are sons of that *Musico Prattico* which I reverently dared, [some] years since, to consecrate to the Exalted name of Yr. Majesty ...."[31] He further observes that "theory not reduced to action remains sterile."

The letter seems singularly free of Marinisms and exaggerated obsequiousness and is essentially no more ingratiating than an ordinary letter of the period to a colleague, which the Emperor Leopold, himself a musician and composer, might also be considered.

Opus XII, *Arie e correnti a tre* ... (Bologna: Monti, 1678) was dedicated

31. "... miei Madrigali da Camera, che sono figli di quel Musico Prattico, che con riuerentissimo ardire, anni sono, io consecrai all'Invitissimo nome della M.V. ..."

to Sig. Co Alessandro Sanvitali, Conte di Fontanellato e Marchese di Belforte. The latter was clearly a dilettante aristocrat who "for his own pleasure performs with instrument and bow in hand" (*per suo mero diletto illustrare collo Stromento da arco alla mano*). Sanvitali was but one of the class of amateurs for whose private diversion the vast body of ensemble music which appears in this decade was being printed. Bononcini, in the dedication, turns names and titles into elegant compliments and makes puns on titles and on the name of his patron:

> ... These "Arie" then, animated by the Vitality inspired by the benignity of Yr. Excellency may hope for that longevity which their natural complexion and weakness do not allow them to pretend; and the "Correnti" also will flow more felicitously.

Sanvitali seems to have been a patron of no small consequence and connection. He was the recipient of numerous dedications.[32]

Bononcini's op. XIII, *Cantate per Camera ... Libro Secondo* (Bologna: Monti, 1678) is dedicated to Count Scipione Rossi, Marchese of San Secondo.[33] Rossi was a lutanist, as appears from Bononcini's words: "... Your Excellency ... is, of these, so gifted as to evoke admiration in those who have had the honor on some occasion of hearing [you], Theorbo or lute in hand...."[34]

The cultivation of this type of music, i.e., the *cantata* with lute, seems to have been a tradition in the Rossi family. In 1621 Sigismondo d'India dedicated *Le Musiche del ... da Cantarsi nel Chitarrone ... Libro Quarto* to Count Federico Rossi of San Secondo.[35]

32. The following, among other works, were dedicated to Sanvitali:

Lorenzo Penna, op. VIII, *Correnti Francesi a Quattro ... Applausi Nozziali* ... 1673, cited in Sartori, *BMI*, p. 470.

G. B. Vitali, op. VII, *Passemezo, Ciaccona, Capricij e Passagalli ... 1682.* Vitali describes Sanvitali as "numbering among his gifts a perfect intelligence of Harmonic proportions," *ibid.*, p. 502.

G. B. Bassani, op. V, *Sinfonie a due e tre instrumenti* ... 1683, *ibid.*, p. 506.

Giovanni Battista Bononcini, op. II, *Concerti da Camera* ... 1685, *ibid.*, p. 517.

Gio. P. Colonna, *Messe Piene a Otto Voci*.... Cf. Associazione dei Musicologi Italiani: *Pubblicazione* "Catalogo ... Serie II ... Città di Bologna. Bibl. Avv. Raimondo Ambrosini" (Parma, Officina Grafica Fresching), p. 55.

Luigi Taglietti, *Opera Prima*, 1697, cited in Sartori, BMI, p. 600. Tagletti was a Brescian Jesuit. His first works contain works for violoncello solo, relatively scarce, suggesting that Sanvitali played that instrument.

33. In 1694 Antonio Caldara dedicated his op. II to Antonio Maria Rossi, calling him "Marchese di S. Secondo Nobile Veneto." Cited in Sartori, *BMI*, p. 610.

34. "... Pure riflettando al l'eccellente Humanità, con che V. E. si degna di gratuosamente accogliere chiunque ispezie professa, ed essercita la bell'Arte di Musica (come ch'ella n'e cosi ben dotata, che rende ammirazione a chi ha l'honore di poterla tal volta sentire con la Tiorba, o Leuto alla mano)...."

35. Federico Mompellio, *Sigismondo d'India* (Ricordi, 1957), p. 48.

These *cantate* were intended for voice with lute (or, specifically, theorbo) accompaniment. Bononcini says, "...the present little work with its object of offering Your Excellency, if not a rare and longed-for pleasure, at least some curious diversion...."[36]

The use of the lute, especially the theorbo, in chamber music and church music persisted in the Bolognese-Modenese circle. It was used as part of the *continuo* at San Petronio during the development of the *concerto grosso* by Torelli; D. Gabrielli gave it a *concertante* role in arias or oratorios. Corelli prescribed it as an appropriate bass for his *sonate da camera,* and it must be regarded as an alternative or adjunct to the *Violone* or *Spinetta* in the Basso Continuo of chamber music until at least 1700.

Another instance of the classicizing attitude toward the artistic achievements of the past century shared by Bononcini is seen in the following sentence:

> ...May Yr. Excellency have the kindness, in any case, after giving them a benign glance, to consign them to the lowest place among others more worthy and conspicuous which have and retain value, as in a [picture] Gallery a certain picture of unknown authorship is as much applauded for its subject as those of a Titian and a Buonarotti are admired for their excellent and always marvelous and incomparable brush....[37]

This passage also gives some hint of Bononcini's general culture and aesthetic sensibility.

36. "...preso animo mi diedi tosto a comporre la presente Operetta, con oggetto, esperanza di ricare all'Eccellenza Vostra se non istrano, ed aspetato diletto, qualche almeno curioso divertimento...."

37. "...Habbia Vostra Eccellenza in ogni caso la bonta, dopo daragli vna benigna occhiata, di farla riporre nel più infimo luogho delle molt'altre più degne, e co' spicue, che tiene e conserua perche vaglia, come in una tal Galeria certa Pittura coperta d'Autori altretanto applaudito per le incise del suo, quanto quelle di vn Tiziano, e di vn Buonaroti, stimati per l'eccellenza del loro sempre marauiglioso ed inarriuabile Pennello...."

CHAPTER VII. LETTERS TO THE READER

Like the dedications, the several letters to the reader with which Bononcini prefaces the printed editions[1] of his works are items of considerable interest. Addressed to the ultimate patron, the public, they are couched in far more direct language than the "academese" of the dedications. They offer us suggestions, at least, of Bononcini's aesthetic intentions as well as some indications of contemporary performance practice.

The letter addressed *Al Benigno Lettore* which prefaces op. III is particularly interesting since it proposes criteria for chamber music:

> ...Herewith (O Benign Reader) the third of my musical Labors, composed as diversions for the Chamber...and thus do not marvel should you find the Counterpoint not to be in all and everything according to the rules and precepts pertaining to that Art, since I have attempted nothing but to delight the ear with the variety of the Sonatas, fugues, and diverse imitations, breaking, and weaving of the figures, which convey to the ear (at least according to my thinking) a more Lively Harmony, which I beseech you to defend against those tongues which for envy of malignity may unjustly calumniate it.
>
> For the rest, receive my Flowers kindly; for in them lives the desire to offer you Harmonic Delights of which I hope shortly to offer the taste of fruits of greater studies...e vivi felice....[2]

(This is, of course, the work to which Bononcini refers in the "Discorso"; see Appendix.)[3]

From this letter to the reader it is clear that Bononcini considers the logical and structural, i.e., contrapuntal, element, its refinement and interest, of the first importance in music destined for the cultivated auditor or per-

1. No "dedications" or "letters" appear in the MSS. in their present state, although the dedication of op. IX does exist in manuscript in the municipal archives, along with the *Discorso.*

2. Sartori, *BMI,* p. 455.

3. The *opus* contains canons of various kinds, some more curious than beautiful. It also contains *sonate da camera* not based on dance forms with some daring "lively" modulations and chromatic harmonies to which the apology for transgressions against the precepts of good counterpoint may apply. It may also extend to the acrid harmonies of the dance music in French style the work contains. In particular, Bononcini here makes use of parallel seconds in the approach to the cadence; $\begin{matrix}5 & -4 & 8\\ 4 & -3\sharp & 8,\\ V & & I\end{matrix}$ a "lively" harmony indeed, based not on contrapuntal logic but upon a secure harmonic function, as in BIII:7, bar 23 and bar 35.

forming amateur. The simple translation of dance music or merely correct counterpoint to the chamber was not enough; the mind as well as the ear must be invited and regaled. This has always been a crucial problem at any change in direction in the evolution of chamber music, and its solution, in just the terms Bononcini describes, by Haydn, Mozart, and Beethoven is the consequence of this attitude. This is also the significance of the inclusion of canons,[4] sonatas in canon (the "Canoni studiosi & osservati" of the Tavola), and such abstract items among the "diversions" (*Trattenimenti*), a practice already followed by Uccellini. The integration of these with idealized dance types within the classic *sonata da camera* is to be the achievement of Corelli.

In a note "To the Reader" preceding the table of contents of op. V, (*Sinfonia, Allemande, Correnti, e Sarabande a 5. e 6*), Bononcini insists that "if the following compositions are not played just as they are written, they will not render a grateful harmony to the ear on account of the interweaving of subjects and other things that are in them."[5]

The same sentiments inform the letter of op. VI, where they are more positively and explicitly stated:

...nowadays there are some of so little intelligence of the Art, that when they sing or play they always wish, with their ill-ordered and indiscreet caprices of Bow or Voice, to alter and deform the Compositions (however carefully made) so that the Authors have become obliged to ask these singers and players to sing and play things simply as they are written. This does not include certain graces, which, although not given the refinement of Counterpoint, are, however, apposite, and when well employed, bring out their inimitable devices and singular dispositions, which not only do not detract, but on the contrary, ornament and add beauty to the Compositions, bringing great praise to themselves, providing delight, *gusto* and admiration to the auditors and even to the above-mentioned Authors....[6]

4. The Trio in canon of the Menuet of Haydn's "Quinten" Quartet is a lineal descendant of just such pieces.

5. Bononcini's op. V contains his most heavily instrumented works, for five and six parts in the homophonic French orchestral manner, largely without imitations, suspensions and crossing of parts. In this style the compounding of independently conceived and executed ornamentation in several parts (forbidden by Lully) would have a bad effect. The instrumentation calls for Violins 1 and 2, Alto Viola, Tenor Viola, Violone, and Basso Continuo. What was meant by "Violone" is not clear. In such an ensemble the double bass (of which the Italians seem to have made more use than the French) would have been appropriate. However the cello was certainly in use, as solo works by Colombi and others, and the existence of actual instruments show. It seems unlikely that it was excluded altogether from ensemble music. The disappearance of the true "Tenor Viola" is a loss; it must have contributed greatly to the massive, gleaming sonority.

6. "...oggidi vi sono alcuni cosi poco intelligenti di quest'Arte, che ò cantando, ò sonando vogliono sempre cô loro sregolati, & indiscreti capricci d'Arco, ò di Voce, alterare, anzi deformare le Composizioni (quantunque fatte con tutto studio & applicazione) in modo che gli Autori sono arriuati à douer pregare gli medemi Cantanti, e Sonatori, acciò si contentino di

Bononcini here as clearly rejects the accretion of improvised diminutions and divisions as he does, in general, the *obbligo* variation forms which derive from it. For him the virtues of the violin family lay in its flexibility and ability to articulate a large range of rhythmic and tonal expression: no more. The purely idiomatic, colloquial, or virtuoso element did not interest him; the structure and logic of the music remained the preeminent consideration.

With these protests Bononcini takes his place in the long list of composers (Lully, Couperin, Gluck, *et al.*) who objected to excessive and inappropriate interpolation of improvised diminutions in the performance of their music.[7] The meaning of these passages depends upon the relative interpretation of the phrase "just as they are written." His strictures are directed against the indiscriminate use of "divisions" or "diminutions"[8] in which large intervals were filled up with scale and arpeggio figures, sustained tones were converted to figures and broken chords, and double stops and other instrumental tricks were added which "alter and deform the music."

He explicitly provides for the proper use of *customary* graces (*soggetti di garbo*) or embellishments which "ornament and add beauty to the compositions." That it was not customary for Italian composers of this period to indicate the usual embellishments may be shown (once again) in Roger North's statement: "The elder Itallians, in their finest cantatas have exprest no graces, as much as to say, whoever is fitt to sing this knows the common decorums."[9]

Roger North's attitudes and taste in violin playing and ornamentation

dire, è di fare le cose schiettamente e puramente come per appunto stanno. Non entrano già in questo numero certuni soggetti di garbo, che sebene non dotati di finezza di Contrapunto, sanno però cosi bene à tempo, & aggiustatamente far spiccare i loro inarriuabili artifici, e singolari disposizioni, che nô solamente non punto tolgono, ma anzi aggiungono fregio e vaghezza à Componimenti, riportando gran lode à se stessi, & arrecando insieme sommo diletto, gusto, & ammirazione à chiunque gli stà à sentire, & à medesimi e sudeti Autori." Cited in Sartori, *BMI*, p. 466.

7. Similar offense and doubt were also expressed by at least one informed contemporary at a famous, not to say notorious, example—that of the ornamented versions of Corelli's op. V brought out by Roger in Amsterdam *ca.* 1710 and imitated by Walsh in London, which claimed to represent Corelli's own gracing. Roger North, the "Musical Grammarian," decried the practice and this specific instance: "Some presumer hath published a continuall course of this sort of stuff in score with Corelli's solos, and is thereby intituled onely to a tolle for his reward. Upon the bare view of the print any one would wonder how so much vermin could creep into the works of such a master.... Judicious architects abominate anything of imbroidery upon a structure that is to appear great, and trifling about an harmonious composition is no less absurd." And "these [florid graces] are shewed as fine things neer [at] hand *solo,* but have no use or effect at a distance or in consort, and for that reason the best masters in such cases decline them and sound plain." *Roger North on Music,* ed. J. Wilson (London: Novello, 1959), p. 160.

8. Bononcini, like Uccellini in op. IX *Sinfonia Decima* (end of example), *writes out* divisions and extended ornaments; see B IV: 15 and B IV: 20.

9. *Op. cit.,* p. 160.

had been formed by Italians, among them the elder Matteis, and the singing teacher and writer on ornamentation,[10] G. F. Tosi. Nicola Matteis was a contemporary of Bononcini, and Tosi was both a contemporary (four years younger) and fellow academician of the Accademia Filarmonica of Bologna. Therefore, their precepts and practice described by North would presumably have been of a piece with those current in Bononcini's working period. Thus by "as they are written," we may infer that Bononcini meant "graced with embellishments" such as are described by Tosi and North as "usual." John Playford in his publication *An Introduction to the Skill of Music*[11] also gives a table of "Graces Proper to the Violin," which may be considered as a summary of the observed practices of Italian players.

We may also accept as "common decorums" the use of graces described by Geminiani in *The Art of Playing the Violin* (London, 1751).[12] His "Example XVIII" "contains all the ornaments of Expression, necessary to playing in good taste." His conservative attitude still reflected the taste of the Corelli generation, and the "Examples" and "Compositions" of his book, in severe style, may (for want of a comparable earlier source) be taken as a general indication of customary uses.

Of these "usual graces," some form of the almost indispensable cadential trill with *grupetti,* and anticipations of the following tone such as the heavy, measured, mannered trills written out by Uccellini (op. IX *Sinfonia Prima,* bar 33) and Cazzati (op. VIII, *La Vertua,* bar 37-38) would have been supplied by the players at such places as BI:5, bar 35 (V1), bar 45 (V1 and 2), BI:6, bar 110 (V1 and 2), BI:12, bar 58, BIX:5, bar 11 and 12. These cadential formulae would also almost certainly have been further intensified by the so-called Corelli clash, i.e., simultaneous leading tone (result of resolution of a 4-3 suspension) and the (anticipated) tonic in the last metrical unit before the final tone. This formula is written out in Bononcini's French dance music, of which it is a feature. In music for the pre-Lullian *Vingt-quatre Violons du Roi* it very considerably antedates Corelli. This configuration comes about naturally only in the ornamentation of cadences in which the upper two parts resolve in a unison, rare in Bononcini's *sonate da chiesa.* Bononcini's normal cadence (to a third between the two upper parts) is suitably graced by the *echappée*-like rise of a second from the upper tone of a diminished fifth followed by a "pathetic" fall to the (major) third

10. *Observations on the Florid Song* (London, 1743).
11. 16th edition, London: 1713, p. 90.
12. Francesco Geminiani, *The Art of Playing the Violin,* Facsimile edition ... by David Boyden (London: Oxford University Press, 1951).

b♭c	a
e	f[13] as in BI:12, bar 58—or similarly, by the rise of a fourth from the
G	F

fifth of a dominant chord followed by a fall to the third

e	a	f♯	
d	c♯	d	as in
A		D	

BI:6, bar 27-28; 53-54 (see also BIV:7, bar 14).

It should be noted, however, that Bononcini frequently approaches important cadences in such a way that the usual trill formula is inappropriate—BI:2, bar 77 (end)—or unusable—BVI:8, end; BVI:3, end; BI:12, end.

Short trills, with or without anticipations of the following tone, *grupetti,* or afterbeats offer definition and impetus at such incidental cadences in "Allegro" movements as BI:12, bar 12, last beat, V2; also BVI:12, bar 4, beat 2; bar 17, beat 2; BIV:3, bar 2, first beat; bar 5, third beat. The short trill is applicable everywhere in the two- and three-part dance music, especially at small cadences in the French types, as the French name for this ornament, *cadence,* indicates. Cf. BI:13, bar 11, beat 3, V2; BI:14, bar 7, beat 2, V1.

The simple appoggiatura from below would be appropriate in BI:9, bar 36, last note V1, and in many places in "Adagio" movements.

Transient, ephemeral graces, such as lie easily under the fingers, include "short touches of the finger and slides" and are inseparable from accentuation, as are those that arise from various synchronizations of finger and bow change. These include the *port de voix* (See Plate IV, p. 107, *infra*) and the "slur," a rapid, accented or unaccented slurred filling-up of an interval, especially of a third.[14] This grace would apply in Bononcini to BVI:5, bar 60, last beat, V1; bar 62, first beat, V2; and bar 28, second beat, V1.

North and Tosi both include as graces the delay or "retard" of one part in (descending) passages of consonant chords, with resulting suspensions. Bononcini's style in general relies heavily on the suspension as the written-out result of contrapuntal movement, the addition of yet more is not frequently possible. One situation where it seems possible and advisable is BVI:3, bar 21, V1. Long chains of suspensions in "Allegro" movements are usually ornamented by Bononcini himself (with changing tones just before resolution, etc.) to maintain the continuity of figure. However such series of quite bare suspensions in *Grave* movements as BI:6, bars 7-10; 16-19; and

13. See Roger North, *op. cit.,* p. 156.

14. North, *op. cit.,* pp. 158, 159. See also Geminiani, "Compozitione IX," *loc. cit.,* p. 46, Var. 2, etc.

89-92 and 105-111 were certainly ornamented with every suitable device of hand and bow.

Graces executed primarily with the bow include the *tremolo,* actually prescribed everywhere in Bononcini's church sonatas (see p. 130, *infra;* p. 135, *infra*). This *tremolo* (not the "agitation symbol" of subsequent operatic and orchestral music) was produced by successive pressure and release of fingers, twice or four times in a slow bow-stroke—what today we would call a *louré des doigts*—and was a way of enlivening the limited sustaining power of the short, arched, seventeenth-century bow.

The *stoccata* or stab was a sudden, heavy, fast stroke which was at once contrasted with a following smooth stroke.[15] North describes the Lullian manner (*op. cit.,* p. 185) as composed of alternate *stoccata* and *arcata* (long bow); however, the *stoccata* is described by Purcell and others as being in Italian taste. Its sound would be today indicated as "fp" (*accent filé*).[16] North also describes (*op. cit.,* p. 186) the tremolo as "now [1720] performed with a tempered stoccata," and suggests that this is an exaggeration and that the effect should be that of a "shaking stop of an organ."

The very long bow stroke or *arcata* (sostenuto) with *crescendo, diminuendo,* and *vibrato*[17]—the *messa di voce*—was a specialty of the Italians and a chief ornament of slow movements.

The natural diction of string instruments in the seventeenth and early eighteenth century in "Allegro" was *staccato,* i.e., the naturally incisive articulated stroke, whetted or stropped, not sustained, of the short, arched bow of the period. This is described by Addison:

> The sounds of our English words are commonly like those of string Musick, short and transient, which rise and perish upon a single touch; those of other languages are like the Notes of Wind Instruments sweet and swelling and lengthen'd out into a variety of Modulation.[18]

Geminiani (whose bow was, to be sure, probably longer than that usual in the 1660's and 70's) warns against the monotony of single alternate

15. "Another grace ... is the stoccata or stabb, which is a peculiar art of the hand upon instruments of the bow.... Old Sign^{r} Nicola Matteis used this manner to set off [express by contrast] a rage, and then a repentance; for after a violent *stoccata,* he entered at once with bipedelian [long] bow, as speaking no less in a passion, but of the contrary Temper." North, *op. cit.,* p. 168.

16. Was it used to emphasize the "outrageous" harmonies, "the flatt sixth before a close," described by Purcell, which precipitated so many of the full cadences of the seventeenth-century Italians and their imitators? See for example: BVI:8, bar 31, last beat; BIX:5, bar 45, last beat, V1; Sonata in *Scelta Silvani,* bar 31, beat 2, V1. Also, is this a reason for the peculiar notation in Bononcini of the V2 part (instead of) in this and similar places?

17. North, *op. cit.,* p. 164.

18. Joseph Addison, *The Spectator,* no. 135, Saturday, Aug. 4, 1711.

up and down strokes, and against "marking time with the bow" and prescribes short slurs (two sixteenths) alternating with detached strokes (*loc. cit.*, pp. 6, 9, 22, 33). The time-honored patterns, would seem to have been as well regarded then as now.

The bow was apparently used somewhat differently in music in the French style from the way in which it was used in the Italian, and the designation *alla Francese* applied to manner of performance as well as to composition. Roger North speaks (*op. cit.*, p. 221) of "lowdness . . . [and] . . . a strong snatching way of playing, to make the musick brisk and good" (cf. BIV:3; 4; 5). This seems to refer to the French way of bowing (deplored by Geminiani), which required a down bow on the first beat of each bar. In ternary meters this would require constant retaking of the bow, which, in vigorous (dance) music, could account for the "snatching." Also, North describes the use of the stab (*stoccata*) and long stroke (*arcata*), and the stab and abrupt stop (silence between long and short notes of dotted figures) in the Lullian entrée (BVII:23).

Another item was the rhythmic exaggeration of (slurred) pairs of short notes in which the first is made short and the second lengthened (as though dotted). This is known as the "Lombard figure" from the Franco-Lombard dance music,[19] in which it is a necessary grace (cf. BII:11, up beat and bar 3; and BIX [14], bar 11 and bar 23).

In keeping with the Baroque taste for the irregular, many other exaggerations seem to have been made,[20] especially at cadences. Notes written as were performed as double dotted, , etc.[21]

Double stops are prescribed by Bononcini only in BVII, for solo playing in *scordatura*. They were considered by North to be harsh in effect although considerably used by Matteis in solo playing. In well-written, contrapuntal ensemble fabric they would generally be redundant. Here as in other matters, Bononcini was at the mercy of the performer, to whom his letter is addressed.

Although a study of ornamentation in general lies beyond the scope of this book, it may be well to include an example of conjectural gracing of a few of Bononcini's full closes; see Plate II.

The reference to *Il Musico Prattico* made in the letter of op. VI is especially interesting since Bononcini writes that he "had already promised

19. Cf. Apel, *HDM* art. "Dotted Notes," III, and Sol Babitz, "A Problem of Rhythm in Baroque Music," *MQ*, Oct., 1952, pp. 533-565.

20. Cf. North, *op. cit.* p. 151.

21. Babitz, *op. cit.*

Plate II

BIX:3

(Allegro)
[Adagio]
vibrato
stoccata
rit.
sfz
rubato e rit

BVI:11

sfz
sfz
vibrato
4#3

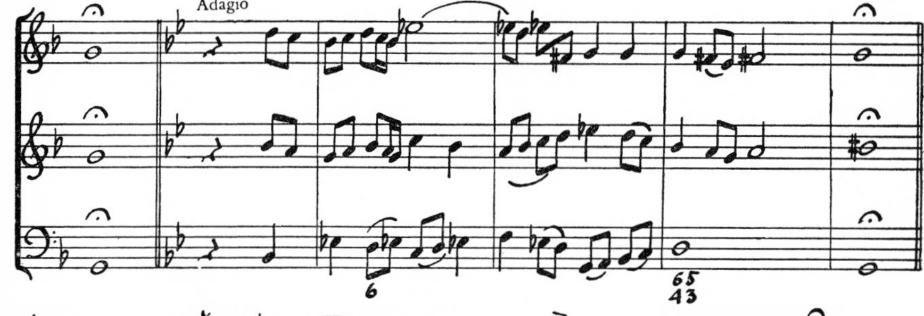
Adagio
6
65
43

vibrato
sfz
6
♭6 3
(rubato)

it." This sentence indicates that the line in the letter prefacing op. III, "I hope shortly to let you taste the fruits of further study" (*spero in breve farti gustare frutti maggiormente osservate*), may well refer to the treatise itself and that the work was written about 1669 or 1670, although not published until 1673. The letter to the reader accompanying *Il Musico Prattico* adds further evidence, for Bononcini says, "It was composed some years since to serve for my own use to facilitate the perfect acquisition of this noble profession."

He claims that he was prevailed upon by "diverse learned members of the profession" (*diversi intelligenti di questa professione*) to publish it, despite the existence of other works on practical and speculative music, including the work of Zarlino, which was noted for its clear rules and precepts. According to Bononcini, he himself did not intend to embrace everything, but rather published in the treatise only that which he considered necessary to good practice. He goes on to say that besides the text the guidance of a good teacher is necessary and closes with a characteristically mordant remark addressed to those "critici" of the "Discorso" and his "rule of thumb" colleagues:

> Do not be persuaded by certain ignoramuses that the true rules are superstitions, and that it suffices only not to make two fifths and similar folly; otherwise you will remain forever in the darkness of ignorance....

The letter addressed to the "Musico Lettore" of op. X, *Cantate a voce sola,* conveys little beyond a reiteration of the dedication and a reference to a forthcoming work, the "Madrigali" of op. XI.

In 1677 Marino Silvani published a second edition of Bononcini's op. VII which had been printed by Monti. On the last page of this edition is reproduced what must be the letter to the reader from the original edition.

> The graciousness...which you have shown my compositions, even though unpolished, has given me spirit to give you other things which may, if not in all, at least in part, be to your satisfaction. Here, then, is a little work which may be played by one, two, or three or four players (excepting two "Correnti" and two "Allemande" which must be played as indicated...).[22]

In this practice Bononcini was following earlier precedents, notably that of

22. "IL gradimento, che per tua gentilezza, o cortese Lettore, hai dimostrato de' miei Componimenti, benche rozi, m' hà data animo di donarti altra cosa, che se non in tutto, almeno in parte riesca di tua sodisfazione. Eccoti dunque un'Operetta, che potendosi suonare à uno, e due, e à tre, et à quattro (eccetuato due Correnti, e due Allemande, che obligate sono nelle conformità in esse accennate) stimo sia per riuscirti nel modo sopradetto...." Cited in Sartori, *BMI,* p. 486.

Uccellini op. IV of 1645,[23] and op. VII of 1668,[24] and Cazzati's op. XXII[25] in prescribing *ad libitum* parts.[26]

In these capital was made of the direct, non-imitative style of French dance music and, in works in imitative Italian style, of a strong harmonic organization. In general the difference between the two manners lay in the conception of French style as *two* essential parts, soprano and bass, in similar rhythmic movement with harmony supplied by middle parts. The Italian style was essentially a *trio* style, that of two equal parts in imitation over a bass,[27] a manner which dates back to the earliest Renaissance.

By combining these styles (the pieces of op. VII are largely in French manner)[28] and being careful in the use of the fourth between the two upper parts (certainly no trick for a contrapuntist of Bononcini's skill), it would be possible to produce a variety of satisfactory pieces for the various groups indicated.

The letter of op. XI, *Partiture De Madrigali A cinque Voci Sopr' i dodici Tuoni, o Modi del Canto Figurato,* is addressed, as befits an academic work, not simply to the "reader," but to professionals: "a' gl'intendente a Professori di Musica." Bononcini points out the relationship between his practice in these *Madrigali,*[29] *Compositioni da Tavolino*[30] and his theoretical treatments of such subjects as modes, imitation, etc., in various chapters of his treatise, of which he considers this work to be a demonstration "... solo per maggior esplicazione...."

There are no "letters to the reader" in the remaining works.

23. Uccellini, "*Sonate Correnti Et Arie Da Farsi* ... con diuersi Stromenti sì da Camera, come da Chiesa à duo à due, & a trè. Opera Quarta. Di ... In Venetia A Appresso Alessandro Vincenti MDCXXXXV." *Ibid.,* p. 399.

24. "Compositioni armoniche sopra il Violino e diversi altri strumenti ... Di ... Libro Settimo. (device) In Anversa, Presso i Heredi di Pietro Phalesio, al Rè David. M.DC.LXVIII." *Ibid.,* p. 449.

25. "Trattenimenti Per Camera ... A' Due Violini, e Violone, Se Piace ... Di ... Opera XXII ... In Bologna, MDCLX. Per Antonio Pisarri. ..." *Ibid.,* pp. 424-425.

26. He was following the precedent in domestic music-making by which Bach and Beethoven also arranged their works for ensembles of different sizes, and which finds its ultimate use in the multitudinous editions of *Hausmusik* for all combinations from violin and harmonium to the "add-a-part" principle, still with us.

27. This difference is specified by Vitali in op. XI, *Varie Sonate Alla Francese*: *Averta il Lettore,* "che quest'Opera ancorche composta a sei Stromenti, si puo sonare con il primo Violino solo, e Violone," and by Uccellini's op. VII where the correnti are listed, some as "a quattro strumenti in stil Francese per ballare qual si pono sonare a Violino solo," others as "a cinque strumenti al Itagliana quale si pono sonare a due Violini lasciando l'altre parti."

28. The *sarabande,* characteristically, are entirely so; the *correnti* and *arie* are of both orders.

29. As vocal works they remain outside the scope of this study.

30. I.e., madrigals sung in the old-fashioned way around a table, without keyboard Basso Continuo, rather than in the then newer concerted style with instruments.

CHAPTER VIII. THE *SONATA DA CAMERA:* FORM; ITALIAN AND FRENCH SOURCES

Bononcini's published works continue the practice of circulating as a commercial enterprise the music produced for functional uses of court and church in the form of chamber music for private diversion, a practice which had arisen in the preceding century with the invention of music printing. The courtly uses of music as "entertainment"[1] represent the original meaning of *musica da camera,* of which our term "chamber music" and its uses are an extension. Once published and in the hands of the *virtuosi* and *dilettanti* any and all music becomes, or can become in the larger sense, chamber music. The dance music was specifically referred to as *da camera;* church sonatas were certainly also so used. However, as long as the functional uses of each class also remained operative, each retained its distinct character.[2]

The originally secular character of violin music[3] is apparent from the large proportion of dance music included in the many collections of such music published by composers of the earlier seventeenth century. Dance music as "secular entertainment" is the essential and largest ingredient of the *sonata da camera* and as such it is the reflection of social life. In "extended use" as chamber music its meaning for the listener is inevitably related to its form.[4] The earliest collections also show awareness of the deficiencies of simple dance music as "diversion for the chamber," namely, the very repetitiousness of form and diction actually required for dancing. To provide the necessary variety, and to please the saturnine as well as the sanguine temperament, non-dance (*genre*) elements of several kinds—"pictur-

1. Angelo Solerti, *Musica, Ballo e Drammatica* (Firenze: R. Bemporad & Figlio, Editori, 1905), pp. 158, 172. "(1624) . . . per trattenimento di detto Ambasciatore di Francia fu cantato di musica della Cechina. . . ."

2. Bononcini's op. I, 1-12, are twelve unspecified *sonate* of church character. His op. IX, 1-5, are specifically *sonate da chiesa* included under the title *Trattenimenti Musicali* ("Musical Diversions"). The "Letter to the Reader" of BVI also shows that these *sonate da chiesa* were intended to be enjoyed for their intrinsic properties, the "breaking and weaving of figures, etc.," and not necessarily as adjuncts to church service, although their style and content were directly related to liturgical propriety.

3. Insisted upon by its detractors. See Thomas Mace, *Musick's Monument* (London, 1676), p. 236.

4. J. Ecorcheville, "auditeur sédentaire," *Vingt Suites d'Orchestre du XVII Siecle,* 2 vols. (Paris: L. Marcel Fortin, 1906), I, 45. (Hereinafter referred to as Ecorcheville, *VSO*).

esque" and "scientific" (the two ends of the axis of Baroque thought)—were frequently included.

These non-dance elements include various types of musical "mannerism":

1. Program pieces, *Battaglie*, etc., with imitations of natural sounds (cuckoos, cocks, etc.)[5]

2. Imitations of vocal models, especially the concerted madrigal and cantata

3. Pieces designed to exploit instrumental possibilities and virtuosity in closed variation forms—*partite, ciaccone,* etc., and *ricercare* (études)

4. Pieces based on contrapuntal virtuosity—canons, *ricercare, fantasie,* and *capricci.*

As integral parts of the general instrumental culture of the sixteenth and seventeenth centuries, all of these elements are well developed in the violin traditions with which Bononcini was in contact during his formative period.

Characteristically, Bononcini quite completely rejects the "mannerist," programmatic elements in favor of rigorous contrapuntal development, especially the canon (op. III: nos. 20-30). He also applies the principle of contrapuntal development to overt dance music as well as to sonatas on vocal models (BIII: 16, 17), all of which he indifferently entitles *sonate da camera.* Neither the repetitive, closed variation form nor any aspect of pure instrumental virtuosity figures in his work.

Bononcini's productive life (1666-1678) coincides with the definitive, critical period in the evolution of the "classic" *sonata da camera* out of earlier constitutent elements. This is clear from the fact that at least a nominal distinction appears between dance music (*per ballare* or *da ballo*) and chamber music (*da camera*) as in Vitali's op. III of 1667,[6] Colombi's op. I of 1668,[7] and Bononcini's op. II of 1667.[8]

5. Uccellini includes a *sinfonia,* "La Gran Battaglia," in his op. VIII of 1669 (Wasielewski I, p. 51), an *aria,* "Mariata insieme la Gallina e il Cucu" in Libro III, 1642 (Sartori, *BMI,* p. 380). The *sinfonie* of his op. IX, 1667, rely heavily upon the manner of the concerted madrigal with characteristic changes of pace and texture. The variation technique and the *ricercare* (étude) form essential parts of Colombi's style, as we have seen.

6. Sartori, *BMI,* p. 442.

7. *Ibid.,* p. 445.

8. In all of these works the indications of eventual decadence, due to separating dance usage and chamber practice, begin to appear. *Correnti da camera,* properly "fast" dances, are marked *Grave* and *Largo.* The practice of playing *correnti da camera* slowly had been growing up since (at least) 1645 when Uccellini in op. IV, *Sonate, Correnti et Arie da Farsi con diversi Stromenti* felt obliged to include a final remark: "Avertasi che tutte le Correnti di presenti libro vano [*sic*] sonate presto. . . ." Cited in Sartori, *BMI,* p. 399.

One has only to consider the differences between "concert" and dance performances of nineteenth-century waltzes to arrive at a parallel. The comparison with present-day secular music will not escape the observer. The variety of stylizations by which "popular" dance

This period also marks significant and comparable changes in dance and theatrical uses. Just as simple dance music was not sufficient to retain the attention of the *auditeur sédentaire* (listener), simple social dances were no longer adequate to maintain the interest of the spectator.[9] In this decade (the 1670's) social dancing and theatrical dancing—which had been virtually identical—part company.[10]

Bononcini's *sonate da camera* represent the highest stage of evolution of the separate elements which go to make up the "classic" *sonata da camera* (e.g., Corelli, op. II, 1685). In Bononcini's work the dance forms retain their complete character as dances while the contrapuntal "demonstrations" retain their abstract nature, an uncompromising, almost "academic" character.

However, as shown by the contents of op. III (1678), Bononcini does not amalgamate dance and non-dance materials into a single consistent "form,"[11] but instead relies for continuity upon the active traditions of the dances which comprise his *sonate da camera.* Following his natural bent as a contrapuntal virtuoso, Bononcini informs his dance movements with a highly developed contrapuntal component while the consistent grouping of dances into suites (op. V and op. XII) shows a sense of "form" or, more properly, "formality," which foreshadows the "classic" model of Corelli.

There are a number of contemporary accounts to remind us of how completely these dance traditions were common cultural property of the

---

music is converted into private diversion, and among "progressives" of the jazz world into an intellectual preoccupation (via D. Milhaud and academic counterpoint) are descendants of the same devices current in the seventeenth century.

9. Menestrier was to write in 1679: "Il est seulement à craindre que tant d'entrées de Ballets qui *ne sont plus que de simples danses* ne se ressemblent fort, & qu'on ne revienne si souvent aux Jeux, aux Zephirs, aux Amours, aux peuples de Scythie, de Lybie, & d'autres lieux, aux Cyclopes, aux Silvains, & aux Bergers, qu'a la fin si les Pantomimes ne se retablissent, on ne se degoute de ses danses figurées qui n'expriment que de beaux pas sans rien representer." Menestrier, *BAM,* p. 301. (italics added)

10. For both arts it is a "point of no return." European classic instrumental forms in "art" music have been distinguished from utilitarian (social) forms ever since. Art forms retire behind the proscenium while social forms remain "in the round." The ballet and the opera, by a process of abstraction similar to that we here observe at work in respect to chamber music, go on to produce the orchestral symphony. Chamber music itself continues its evolution along the same lines, but remains freer of theatrical convention. This separation represents the demarcation of a fundamental dimension within the European "disassociated" personality which has remained an artistically useful distinction ("classic" vs. "colloquial-popular") until our own time. Ecorcheville *VSO,* I, 35, quotes DuBos as saying in *Réflexions critiques sur la poésie,* Paris, 1719: "Il y a soixante ans le mouvement de tous les airs de ballet étaient un mouvement lent. Les danseurs pouvaient garder toute la décence possible dans leur maintien en éxécutant ces ballets dont la danse n'étaient presque pas different de celle des bals ordinaires. . . ."

11. It is interesting to speculate on what forms the *sonata de camera* might have taken at Bononcini's hands had he lived a normal life expectancy (to *ca.* 1690).

period, and thus a valid basis for community of understanding. The first account to come to mind is that of middle-class Samuel Pepys:

> May 4th (1663).—The dancing-master come, whome standing by, seeing him instructing my wife, when he had done with her, he would needs have me try the steps of a *coranto*: and what with his desire and my wife's importunity, I did begin, and then was obliged to give him entry money 10*s*. and become his scholar. The truth is, I think it is a very useful thing for any gentleman.
>
> May 16th.—After dinner comes Pembleton again and I did go up to them to practice, and did make an end of *La Duchesse* [a figured *courante* which bore this name] which I think I should, with a little pains, do very well.

Solerti has given an overwhelming documentation of the uses of dance and music in the seventeenth century Italian courtly circles.[12] The ballet even invaded the *accademia* in the form of allegorical representations, as contemporary accounts show.[13] Also, if the ballet was a vitalizing force to violin music, it appears the reverse was also true: Menestrier says: "Les violons sont aujourd'hui universellement par tout l'âme de tous les Ballets, parce que sur les violons on joue des airs de trompettes, de fluttes, de musettes & de la plupart des autres instruments."[14]

In the title of op. II Bononcini, like several contemporaries, equates dance and ballet music and the *sonata da camera*. Cazzati published in 1660 as op. XXII, *Trattenimenti per Camera d'Arie, Correnti, e Balletti*. This is, to all appearances, actual dance music—judging from the titles, a collection from some theatrical representation to which variation pieces have been added. They have little enough to recommend them beyond the simple articulation of dance formulae and "ballet" characterizations as required by the titles *Ballo dell'Ombre, Adagio, Ballo de Matacini* (a mock battle by clowns, according to Arbeau), *Ballo de Contadini*, etc.[15]

Uccellini published as op. IX *Sinfonie Concerti ... Con Brandi e Corenti alla Francese, e Balletti al Italiana giusta l'uso approvatissimo della Corte di Parma....* This includes *Brandi* "alla francese per ballare" and "balli al Italiana." These seem to have been written for the wedding festivities of Maria d'Este, who married the Duke of Parma in 1667. Uccellini went to Parma as *Maestro di Cappella* in the same year.

12. Solerti, *Musica, Ballo e Drammatica* (Firenze: R. Bemporad & Figlio, Editori, 1905).

13. Menestrier, *BAM*, p. 279; see also chap. iv n. 38.

14. Menestrier, *BAM*, p. 279.

15. Is this a collection of ballet *entrées* written for some civic affair in Bologna by the then new *Maestro di Cappella* of San Petronio? Or one of the older works for courts where Cazzati had worked before coming to Bologna? Or are they flights of fancy in imitation of published ballet music?

In 1668 Uccellini published as *Libro* VII the *Compositioni armoniche* (probably written at Modena), which contains *Corrente a quattro strumenti in stil Francese per ballare qual si pono sonare a Violin solo* and *Corrente a cinque strumenti al Itagliana, quale si pono sonare a due Violini, lasciando l'altre parti.*

In 1668 Colombi published as op. I *Sinfonie da Camera Brandi, e Corrente alla Francese, con Corrente e Arie da Camera . . . Dedicate All'Altezza Serenissima Della Sig.ra Duchessa Maria Di Parma.* Like Uccellini's op. IX, Colombi's *Sinfonie* may have been written for the wedding of Maria d'Este di Parma in 1667.

As late as 1692 G. B. Vitali at Modena composed *Sonate da Camera,* op. XIV, *per far concerto a gl'applausi de' Popoli nelle gloriose nozze di V. A. Serenissima Margharita Farnese D'Este,* to whom the work is dedicated. These dances, of types then currently popular as dances—*borea, menuet,* and *gavottes* (i.e., the "galanteries" of the French order which by then had pervaded Europe)—were almost certainly used on this occasion.

Ballet, as somewhat theatricalized social dancing, appears to have been highly cultivated at Modena. Menestrier describes a ballet presented there.[16]

> In Modena in the year 1652 the archdukes Ferdinand, Charles and Sigismond François, passing [through] with the Archduchess, sister of the Grand Duke of Tuscanny, there was performed for their reception a small *action en Musique* accompanied by Ballets in the hall of the Palace. The subject was the departure of Achilles from the Palace of Lycomedes, where he was hidden among the daughters of the Queen. The Centaur Chiron, who represents in the heavens the sign of Sagittarius and who had been charged with the education of Achilles, began the action, appearing in the Sky in the part of the Zodiac he occupies.

The dedication of Bononcini's op. II reads very much like the *scenario* of such a ballet:

> The Muses and the Graces always move in conjunction. Of the former Your Highness is the Patron, of the latter the source. . . . By your gracious acceptance [you] give them life, and as the Trumpet of your Fame excites the harmony of the Lyre, [and] gives them the regulated movements of Your Prudence, they will learn the true rules by which they should be set in motion. . . .[17]

16. Menestrier, *BAM,* p. 121. "A Modena l'an 1652. les Archiducs Ferdinand, Charles, & Sigismond Francois, passant avec l'Archiduchesse, soeur du Grand Duc de Toscane, on fit pour leur reception une petite action en Musique accompagnée de Ballets dans la Sale du Palais. Le sujet fut la sortie d'Achille du Palais de Licomède ou il étoit caché parmy les filles de la Reine. Le Centaure Chiron, qui fait dans le Ciel le signe du Sagittaire, & qui avoit eu soin de l'éducation d'Achille, fit l'ouverture de l'action paroissant dans le Ciel dans la partie due Zodiaque qu'il occupe. . . ."

17. See pp. 64-65 *supra.*

On the other hand, his op. III, on the basis of the "Letter to the Reader," was clearly written as chamber music: "Herewith ... the third of my Musical labors, composed as diversions for the chamber...." (*Ecoti ... la terza mia fatica Musicale, composta per trattenimenti da Camera....*)[18]

Opus IV is clearly indicated as chamber music, since it was intended for the actual use of Obizzo Guidoni, a dilettante player to whom it is dedicated. (See p. 66 *supra.*)

> Mie Compositioni fatte appunto; se non di espresso suo commando, per servire, e sodisfare almeno al suo genio & ammirable talento....[19]

That op. V was likewise intended as chamber music is shown by the dedication to the dilettante Giacomi Lodovico Arigoni (see p. 69 *supra*). Bononcini says: "... my new Compositions ... whose birth-cries were heard in your house...." (*....mie nuove Composizioni Musicali, nella di cui nascita alla si compiacque ... di sentire i lor primo vagiti in di lei Casa....*)[20]

The dedication of the 1677 edition of Bononcini's op. VII (see p. 70 *supra*) attests that the contents were greatly appreciated by the playing public. The "add-a-part" principle of the title and Bononcini's letter indicate that they were probably originally designed as chamber music with the optional addition of a second violin or viola part in mind.

The title of op. IX, *Trattenimenti Musicali,* points clearly toward chamber use; *trattenimenti* means "diversion" or "entertainment." The rest of the dedication indicates that Bononcini invites comparison with what Luigi d'Este, the courtier and warrior to whom op. IX is dedicated, may have heard at other courts of Europe.

The very "formality," the regularity of alternation of the *arie* and *correnti* of op. XII, while it stems directly from dance practice itself, suggests that it is probably to be considered as chamber music. A collection of dances and ballets would have been of more diversity. This formality, the kernel of the "classic" *sonata da camera,* receives further support from the dedication to the dilettante Sanvitali (see p. 72 *supra*), who "simply for his own pleasures, with a bowed instrument in hand ... [united] ... Music ... to many other virtues."

As we have indicated, whatever Bononcini's specific intention as music *da camera* (for dancing or ballet), the form-giving element resides in active

18. See p. 74 *supra.*
19. "My Compositions, made a-purpose, if not at his express command, to serve and satisfy his genius and admirable talent...."
20. Sartori, *BMI,* p. 465.

dance tradition itself, and it is to this we must turn for the formal principles we seek.

The dances of the *sonate da camera* are grouped[21] without further indication, in several traditional sequences[22] which refer to dance practice as described in contemporary dance works by F. De Lauze,[23] and in the critical theoretical work of Marin Mersenne,[24] and P. Rameau.[25] A central concept of dance usage in social dancing and ballet alike was the contrast of "group dances" (*danses de compagnie*)[26] and "couple dances."[27] This sequence serves the two ritualistic functions—political and sexual pantomime—underlying the stylized social intercourse which Baroque dancing represents.[28]

The first, the linear march and ring types together with their mutual variants serve to orient and dispose the company in the room in order of rank. Given the Baroque preoccupation with hierarchial order, the march type of *danse de compagnie* is a determining form. In the *pavane* and *allemande* and in the *entrées* of the theatrical Lullian version they represent and, indeed, dramatize the political aspect of the European personality.

21. It is the natural diversity and variation of these, all of which are valid "forms," which give the early *sonata da camera* its varied aspect. This is better understood as a "principle" than classified as a "form." This latter miscomprehension is the inevitable result of artificial dualism which seeks a mutually exclusive antithesis to the *sonata da chiesa.*

22. This is by no means usual, and only becomes a general use from this period on. Uccellini groups dances by categories (op. III, 1642, and op. IV, 1645), i.e., all *correnti* together, all *arie* together, etc., pointing to a lower degree of internal organization of sequences and to utilitarian, dance use, as even the ballet required a more explicit order.

23. F. De Lauze, *Apologie de la Danse,* trans. Joan Wildeblood (London: Frederick Muller Ltd., 1952). [Translation from the original edition of 1623.]

24. Marin Mersenne, *Harmonie Universelle contenant la théorie et la pratique de la musique* (Paris: Chez Sebastien Cramoisy, 1636). Livre Second Proposition XXIII.

25. P. Rameau, *The Dancing Master,* trans. Cyril W. Beaumont (London: C. W. Beaumont, 1931). [Translation from the original edition of 1725.]

26. Mersenne, *Harmonie Universelle.* Livre II Prop. XXIII.

27. C. Sachs, *World History of the Dance* (New York: Norton, 1937), p. 95.

28. That this ritualistic significance of dancing in social and political life was consciously exploited and is not a subsequent interpretation is clear from Sir John Davies' *Orchestra,* 1594, Stanzas F3 and F4:

F3. The various forms of dancing Love did frame
And beside these a hundred million mo';
And as he did invent he taught to shine
With goodly gesture and with comely show
Now keeping state, now humbly honouring low,
And ever for the person and the place
He taught most fit and best according grace.

F4. Since when all ceremonious mysteries
All sacred orgies and religious rites
All pomps and triumphs and solemnities
All funerals, nuptials, and like public sights,
All parliaments of peace and warlike fights,
All learned arts and every great affair
A lively shape of dancing seems to bear.

The ring and linear types hark back through centuries of evolution and assimilation to pagan ritual and its residue in Christian forms. These gained great vogue during the reign of Louis XIV. Their point of orientation, the "Sun-King," is the center of all natural religions, and the central image of the individual European psyche.

The second of the two basic functions of social dancing is served by the "closed couple dances." These are danced by independent couples, each couple forming its own center, characteristically in ternary meters, to permit turning. In Baroque use these are represented by the *courante* or *corrente,* which contain in their leaping steps elements of virtuosity. They are, further, stylized sexual pantomime and thus represent the egocentric aspects of personality.

In Bononcini's work dances are generally grouped in pairs or longer sequences properly called *suites* and organized by the formal opposition of "company" versus "couple" dances related by key. They are seldom (but occasionally, as BI:[17, 18] and BII:37, 38) specifically related (*Aria, sua Corrente*) and are then related by thematic reference.[29] These sequences follow the orders usual in actual dance music.[30]

Two general types of sequence or suite are visible in Bononcini's work. The first, ceremonially "higher" and more complete, invokes the *allemanda* or "company march dance." The second provides a lighter ritual substitute, the *aria* or *balletto* of a "lower" social significance. The *corrente,* the ubiquitous couple dance, remains constant, e.g.:

1. *Allemanda, Corrente*
2. *Aria* (*Balletto* or *Giga*), *Corrente*

The first "higher" sequence in its basic, amplified version is represented in Bononcini's work by:

Opus	*Allemanda*	*Corrente*	*Tonality**	
II	9	10	d	
III	10	11	"B♭," "g"	
	(13	14	"B♭")	
	15		"B♭"	*A-C-A*

29. Nor is the practice of Bononcini's contemporaries at this period by any means consistent. Compare Vitali, op. I, *Correnti e Balletti da camera* (1666), where the items are arranged by categories, with his op. III, where they are grouped in suites.

30. Vitali, op. III, *Balletto e Corrente . . . per ballare* and those in Ecorcheville, *VSO.*

IV	19	20	"f"	
	26	27	B♭	
VII	20	19	d	[reversed]
	22	21	d	[reversed]
IX	[6]	[7]	"g"	
	[8]	[9]	"c"	
	[10]	[11]	"d"	
	[12]	[13]	"A"	

The second sequence provides a less complete ceremonial stylization of the initial member, as an *aria* or *balletto* ("tune" or "dance-tune") implying formal "honors" by a smaller number of persons than that required by the march formula—the couple, or in the *balletto,* several couples—but not "the company."

These are represented by:

Opus	*Aria*	*Corrente*	*Tonality*	
II	37	38	"G"	*sua Corrente;* "Discordia Concors"
IV	1	2	"g"	
VII	1	2	e	
	3	4	"A"	
	17	18	B♭	
XII	1	2	"d"	
	3	4	a	
	5	6	e	
	7	8	e	
	9	10	C	
	11	12	F	
	13	14	B♭	
	15	16	B♭	
	17	18	e	
	19	—	e	*A-C-A*
	23	24	"c"	

The basic pair is frequently amplified or "decorated" by the addition of a *sarabanda* (reputedly Spanish) after, or sometimes before, the *corrente.* This occurs in Bononcini's work as follows:

*(The designations are in modern terms. Quotation marks denote "incomplete" signatures with modal implications.) See *infra,* pp. 152 ff.

Opus	*Allemanda*	*Corrente*	*Sarabande*	*Tonality*	
IV	21	23	22	B♭	
V 1 *Sinfonia*	2	3	4	"d"	
	5	6	7	B♭	
	8	9	10	"g"	
	11	12	13	"E♭"	"double" *Corrente*
		14	15	"E♭"	and *Sarabande*
	18	19	20	"c"	
	21	22	23	B♭	
	24	25	26	"F"	

The "lighter" suite, i.e., with the *aria* replacing the *allemande* (it will be noted that no *balletti* or *arie* appear in op. V, which is heavily instrumented "a 5" and uses the *allemanda* exclusively), is also ornamented by the addition of the *sarabande* as follows:

Opus	*Aria*	*Corrente*	*Sarabande*	*Tonality*
IV	7	8	9	C
	10	11	12	F
VII	5	7	6	D
	14	16	15	B♭
XII	20	21	22	B♭

The *balletto* is to be regarded as the dance equivalent of the *aria.* In the ballet, the *balletto,* or dance-song *cum aria,* was the item in which elements of pantomime and stylized exposition of argument were undertaken. In social dancing it was a stylized series of "honors" and the occasion for the gentleman to lead the lady "out" so that the couple could make their ceremonial bows to the company[31] before dancing the *corrente.* That they are of the same function and order as the aria is shown by Cazzati.[32]

These *balletti* occur in Bononcini's works as follows:

Opus	*Balletto*	*Corrente*	*Tonality*
II	11	12	"g"
	13	14	"c"

Whenever the *allemanda, aria,* or *balletto* are present, the *giga* (BII: 3, 4, 6, 7, 8, and BIII: 1, 2, 3, 4, 5, 6, 7, and BVII: 13) is left as an optional member, as in the keyboard suite of the period.[33] Bononcini, however, occasionally uses the *giga* to *replace* the *aria* as *first* in the sequence:

31. F. De Lauze, *Apologie de la Danse;* see also Fabritio Caroso, *Nobilità di Dame* (Venetia: Muschio, 1605).
32. Cazzati, op. XXX, no. 30, "*Aria overo Balletto. . . .*" Cited in Sartori, *BMI,* p. 427.
33. Bukofzer, *MBE,* p. 167.

Opus	*Giga*	*Sarabande*	*Corrente*	*Tonality*
IV	13	14	15	D
	16	17	18	e
VII	8	9	10	b

This is an interesting sidelight on the history of the *giga* which appears here as a variant stylization in compound meter of the *aria* or dance tune. Also the *arie,* like the single *gighe* of BII above, stand alone in BI.

In at least one case the *corrente* is duplicated. This is clearly a reflection of dance practice in which such a series of *correnti* and *sarabande* would be danced by a single couple:

Opus	*Aria*	*Corrente*	*Sarabande*	*Corrente*	*Tonality*
IV	3	4	5	6	"g"

As we have said, the *corrente* is the (virtually) constant factor of the suite and is rarely omitted.[34] It was the most popular couple dance of the day and since it was danced by one couple at a time, it was necessary to provide a greater number of these dances than of the "company" types. (This explains the form of Bononcini's op. XII, alternate *arie e correnti*). The fact that there are a considerable number of single *correnti* or sequences of *correnti* in Bononcini's *sonate* is some evidence that they were actually dance music. Of these the long sequence of paired (by key) *correnti* of op. II, nos. 15-26, all of the Italian order, comprises the largest group. This *opus* is the one that bears the designation *da camera e da Ballo;* "da Ballo" may apply to these *correnti,* although the contrapuntal element here is very high for simple dance music. Also, the pair of *correnti* of op. IV: 24, 25 "a due, Violino e Violone" is for the *Violino* "scordatura," a virtuoso practice, and therefore to be understood here as chamber music with a special interest for the performer.

Such groupings account for a large majority of the dance movements in Bononcini's work with the exception of some isolated numbers and the suites of *branles* in the French style represented by:

Opus I, "Brando Prima, 2.3.parte; Gavotta: sua Corrente"
Opus II, "Brando in Stil Francese"
Opus III, "Brando e Correnti in Stil Francese"
Opus IX, "Suonata a quattro in Stil Francese: Brando Gavotta Corrente Primo"

These suites are imitations of the sequences of *branles* (*brando*) which were the current vogue in social dancing at the French court during the sixties

34. As in BVII: 23 (*aria*), 24 (*sarabanda*).

(All writers agree more completely on this point and on all other details connected with the *branles* than with respect to any other dances—which may be some indication of their vogue.)

Rameau describes the *branles* precisely. Since his description tells us a great deal about this sequence and about seventeenth-century social dancing in general, it is worth quoting here:

> I believed it impossible to give a description more likely to inspire regard for the ceremonies and rules of private Balls than first to attempt some brief account of the King's Grand Ball, since it is the most important of all such functions and should serve as a model for private Balls in regard to the order of the proceedings, and the respect and politeness to be observed thereat.
>
> In the first place, none is admitted to the royal circle save Princes and Princesses of the Blood Royal, then Dukes and Peers, Duchesses, and afterwards the other Lords and Ladies of the Court according to their rank. The Ladies are seated in front, while the Lords are placed behind them....
>
> Every one being thus placed in order, when his Majesty wishes the Ball to begin he rises, and the whole company does likewise.
>
> The King takes up his position at that end of the room where the dancing is to begin, which is near the musicians. In the time of the late King [Louis XIV], the Queen danced with him, or, in her absence, the first Princess of the Blood, and placed themselves first. Then the company took up their station behind them, two by two, according to their rank. That is to say: *Monseigneur* and *Madame la Dauphine, Monsieur* and *Madame* (the wife of the King's brother), then the other Princes and Lords. The Lords stood on the left side; the Ladies on the right. Retaining this order, they made their bows in turn. Afterwards the King and Queen led the *Branle* with which all Court Balls opened, and all the Lords and Ladies followed Their Majesties, each on their own side. At the conclusion of the strain, the King and Queen went to the end of the line, then the next couple led the *Branle* in their turn, after which they took up their position behind Their Majesties. This continued until all the couples had danced and the King and the Queen were at the head again.
>
> Then they danced the *Gavotte* in the same order as the *Branle,* each couple successively retiring to the end of the line. The dance finished, they made the same bows on parting as those with which the Ball had opened.
>
> Then came the danses à deux... the *Courante* was danced after the *Branles*....[35]

By "the *Branle*" Rameau, of course, meant the suite of *branles* of which six were usual in mid-seventeenth century France. De Lauze[36] and Mersenne,[37] whose accounts agree, call them the "first Bransle," meaning a

35. P. Rameau, *The Dancing Master* (1725), trans. Cyril Beaumont (London: Beaumont, 1931), pp. 37 ff. Compare with the quotation from Sir John Davies' *Orchestra.* (See n. 28 this chap.)

36. De Lauze, *Apologie de la Danse,* pp. 135 ff.

37. Marin Mersenne, *Harmonie Universelle,* Livre II Prop. XXIII, p. 168.

branle simple, the "Bransle Gay" or second *branle,* and "the Bransle de Poitou" or third *branle*—which was also known as the *branle à mener* and is so called by Uccellini in op. IX, *Brando Primo.* (It is the source of the *menuet.*) The fourth *branle* was a "Bransle Double de Poitou," the fifth was a variant of the fourth,[38] and the sixth *branle* was the *Gavotte.*

The *Brando in stil Francese* is but a variant of the fundamental theme of Baroque dancing. The *branles* were linear and circle dances, as Rameau describes, and thus represent as a group the "company dances" to which the succession of *courantes* or other couple dances was opposed. This is the significance of the suites of *branles* (*Brando in stil Francese*) with their following *correnti* in Bononcini's work. As was usual in Italy, he habitually includes only four *branles,* omitting the variants of the *Bransle de Poitou.* Bononcini's dances correspond in all salient details of style to the comparable *branles* found in Ecorcheville *VSO* and the examples given by Mersenne[39] as well as to those to be found in the *Ballet du Roy dansé a Fontainebleau*[40] published by Ballard at Lyons in 1664, which is found in the Estense Library. Bononcini's *brandi "in stil Francese"* are, with one exception (BI: [13-15]) in the homophonic, orchestral manner of the *Vingt-quatre Violons.* Thus the French influence must be judged complete, as acknowledged.

In Bononcini's works the *brando* and associated *corrente* are represented as follows:

Opus			*Tonality*	
I	13	*BS, BG, M, G, C*	"e"	The *corrente* is marked *sua corrente* and is derived from BS. Nos. 28, 29 *correnti* in the same key.
II	27 (28, 29)	*BS, BG, M, G, C, C*	"D"	
	30 (31, 32, 33)	*BS, BG, M, G, C, C,*	"a"	Nos. 31, 32, 33 *correnti* in the same key.
III	18, 19	*BS, BG, M, G, C*	"B♭"	
IX	[14, 15, 16, 17, 18]	*BS, BG, M, G, C*	"g"	This is followed by a [19] *balletto* (g), a

38. The *menuet,* although itself a *branle,* is detached and becomes, in the "galant" eighteenth century, the principal couple dance. This concentration of attention on the "Bransle de Poitou" or "à mener" and its variants, is part of its evolution into the separate couple dance, the *menuet* and its trios.

39. Mersenne, *Harmonie Universelle,* Livre II Prop. XXIII, p. 168.

40. These are the same as the *Branles de M. Brular* given by Ecorcheville, *VSO,* II, 5 as Suite VI.

[20] *gagliarda* (B♭) and a [21] *corrente* (B♭)—i.e., the "couple" dances which followed the *branles,* in their usual order, albeit a "high" stylization.

Code

BS	*Branle simple*
BG	*Branle gai*
M	*Branle à mener* (or *menuet*)
G	*Gavotte*
C	*Corrente*

Whatever the intention—idealized or functional—of the rest of Bononcini's dances, there can be little doubt that these French *brando* sequences and their *correnti* were actually danced at a court so closely linked to France as that of Modena. The descriptions of Arbeau (1588) and De Lauze (1623) are echoed by Rameau (1725), who says: "...the *Branles* with which... all Court Balls were and are still begun...."[41] Bononcini's output coincides with the height of the period, the "dancing years" of "Le Roi Soleil," Louis XIV.

Bononcini's op. III, *Varii fiori del Giardino musicale,* contains two works specifically designated as *sonate da camera* (BIII: 16, *Sonata da Camera a quattro* and 17, *Sonata da Camera a 3*) which contain no dance elements, but are abstract forms, the principal ingredient of which is counterpoint. These are representatives of the more developed types of the instrumental *divertissement* (*sinfonie, canzone,* and *sonate*) which were included obviously for secular use in earlier books of concerted madrigals.[42]

The first, BIII: 16 "a quattro," is apparently without Basso Continuo, and, while it does not, as enthusiastic commentators would have it, make Bononcini the inventor of the classic quartet, it is, nonetheless, among the earliest extended abstract (non-dance) secular instrumental works without *continuo.* The second, BIII: 17, requires the usual complement of string parts and *continuo.*

These two *sonate* of op. III, although explicitly secular (*da camera*), contain no popular or traditional material such as the airs or basses frequent in

41. Rameau, *The Dancing Master,* p. 74.

42. Madrigali et Symphonie ... di Biagio Marini opera Seconda 1618. See Sartori, *BMI,* p. 244. Also *Il Terzo Libro di Madrigali ... concertati, con alcune Sonate accommadate per ogni sorte d'instrumenti ...* Stefano Bernardi, Opera decimaterza, 1624." See Sartori, *BMI,* p. 296.

earlier productions and germane to the concerted vocal works with which these were associated. As forms they must, like the Uccellini *Sinfonie* of op. XI which they resemble, be considered as instrumental intensifications of the concerted vocal prototypes, i.e., the concerted madrigal and cantata with which the whole classification is identified.

Within Bononcini's own output they can be compared as abstract structures only with the *sonate da chiesa* of op. VI and op. IX, and the unspecified *sonate* of op. I. The differences between Bononcini's works specifically called *sonate da chiesa* and these *sonate da camera* are of two orders, affecting, respectively, scope and stylization. They are approximately half the length of Bononcini's usual church sonatas, and in neither of the *sonate da camera* are the component sections as completely developed as they are in the *sonate da chiesa.* The homophonic sections are confined to single phrases instead of being developed into the strophe or period usual in church works. The contrapuntal sections are likewise not so completely worked out. The systematic fugal counter-exposition with parts exchanged, characteristic of such movements in the *sonata da chiesa,* is not developed here.

As regards stylization, the homophonic sections are not given the same rhythmic forms (suggestive of sententious moments of the mass) as they are in the church sonata, but seem to emulate expressive opening moments characteristic of the madrigal. The melodic cast and rhythmic vocabulary of the fugal sections do not conform to the more severe liturgical mold in either rhythmic or tonal detail. The principal figure of BIII: 16 with its "secular" interval of the major sixth and its *galant* motion, and the ascending sequences have an experimental quality. This sonata also contains Bononcini's most extreme chromatic uses (including a g-flat), which may account for the absence of a keyboard part, since the tunings in use may not have been able to accommodate the keys (B-flat minor, D-flat major, G-flat major).

Bononcini's op. I contains twelve *sonate* of unspecified function. On the general basis of their content and development they appear to be church sonatas of the kind so designated by Bononcini in op. VI and op. XI. However, two (BI: 3, 4) are written over sequential, if not genuinely *ostinato,* basses of the "Ruggiero" type, relating them to the style and technical procedures usual in variation forms and in the early cantata. They might thus be taken for chamber pieces, but are not invalidated as church works. It is under this latter classification that we shall, for formal reasons, consider the opus as a whole.

Chapter IX. THE DANCES (1): PROCESSIONAL AND COMPANY TYPES; *ALLEMANDE, BALLETTO* AND *ARIA*

As we have observed, the dances which give form to the *sonata da camera* fall into two general classes: processional company dances and closed couple dances. These are distinguished by their social function, the stylized deportment ("honors") of the one being contrasted with the expressiveness and virtuosity of the other. They are, further, distinguished by their rhythms (binary *vs.* ternary), their step patterns and spatial orientation (group-linear *vs.* couple-axial). The entire group of such dance types current in the seventeenth century constitutes a graded series illustrating all degrees of ceremonial formality, social relationships, and sizes of company. The stylistic treatment and connotations of these are a central fact of the *sonata da camera,* and may be said to constitute its "subject matter."

In descending order of ceremonial significance, the processional company dances are:

entrée, intrada — From sixteenth-century prototypes, highest stylization (fanfare, solemn, massive manner); also in theatrical and ballet version (Lully).

pavane and *passamezzo* — Sixteenth-century social stylization of slow march, hierarchic disposition of company.

allemande (*allemanda*) — Seventeenth-century social stylization of slow march, hierarchic disposition, "galant" version.

branles, (*Brando*) — Social stylization of linear and ring types and combinations—popular origins.

balletto — Formal stylization of honors.

aria, air — Low stylization, improvised "honors." The *aria* and *balletto* represent a smaller aspect of the processional function, the deportment and salutations, stylized "honors" by which the couple reaches and takes possession of the space in which they are to dance the *courante.* They may be improvised, as suggested in the *aria,* or learned, as in the *balletto.* These are the subject of careful development and explanation at the hands of Caroso, (*Nobilità di Dame,* 1605) and other dancing masters.

air, aria, vaudeville — Basic materials of all the above, no social stylization —popular elements in basic condition or in individual stylization as in the ***gigue.***

Mersenne properly describes the *allemande,* relating it to the song (*vaudeville,* thus *air* and *aria*), to the *pavane* and to the *passamezzo.*[1] From the strophic song the *allemande* inherits its periodic form; from the *pavane* its ceremonial function, binary rhythms, and massive sound. From the *passamezzo,* by way of German lute and keyboard tablatures and instrumental style, it inherits (in addition to its name) the stylistic tradition of a rich figuration. The *allemande* or *allemanda* (whose full name should be "Aria-Balletto, *galant* representative of the processional order, stylized in the florid instrumental manner of the Germans, as distinct from the homophonic French pavane") is equated with the *balletto* by Biagio Marini in op. XXII of 1665, "Balletto 4 Alemano"[2]; Cazzati in op. XXX[3] equates it with the *aria; Arie overo Balletto.* The mutual relationship of these forms is further borne out by the English edition (*ca.* 1700?) of Bononcini's op. XII. Here Bononcini's original titles, *Arie,* are changed variously to *Aires, Allemands, Gavotts* (which are a variety of *branle*), and *Preludes.* In a group thus generically related stylistic cross-references constantly appear at all levels and pass, singly and in combination, up and down the series as the several forms evolve. These stylistic details and their combinations, as realized and disseminated in the ballet and social dancing, must be regarded as the central "core of meaning" of the *sonata da camera* as abstract music. To give but a single example: the rhythmic intensification characteristic of the *entrée* (dotted notes—as in the Lullian theatrical version in *Ouvertures*) tends to be applied to all the forms of the processional group, including the *branles,* as a trademark of the fashionable *stil Francese* (*ca.* 1665 on). This is frequently the case with Bononcini, e.g., the *arie* of op. IV and *branles* [*simples*] of BII: 27, 30. This "dotted" manner eventually becomes associated with the *allemande* (the source of the traditional short "up beat") as seen in Bach and Rameau. It is found in the earlier examples in the repertoire of the *Vingt-Quatre Violons* given in Ecorcheville,[4] but is only occasional with Bononcini, as in BIX: [12], *Allemanda Quarta.*

1. Marin Mersenne, *Harmonie Universelle,* Livre II Prop. XXIII, pp. 164-165.
2. Sartori, *BMI,* p. 418.
3. *Ibid.,* p. 927.
4. Ecorcheville, *VSO,* Vol. II.

Bononcini most often treats the *allemanda* according to the manner of the pre-Lullian composers of the *Vingt-quatre Violons.* He welcomes the serious form as an opportunity for writing a closely knit contrapuntal fabric in imitative Italian style with sequences and suspensions, the *concertante* equivalent of the florid keyboard manner. When the imitative principle is not present, as in the essentially homophonic pieces called "Allemande" of op. III: 8, 10, 12, the pieces are virtually indistinguishable from *arie,* thus supporting our observations regarding their mutual relationship.

Bononcini's *allemande* are generally marked "Allegro" and even "Presto," although occasionally with slow cadences, "Adagio." This is contrary to dance practice which required a moderate tempo. This may suggest a divergence in practice between chamber and dance usage which implies the decadence of the form. Bononcini's op. V, which is based on the suite form with the *allemande* as the initial member and contains the most typical examples, also bears out our contention that the stylization implies the size of the "company," since it is for five parts. Further, the next largest group of *allemande* appears in Bononcini's op. III as nos. 8, 10, 12, 13, and 15, "a 4."

Bononcini's single *sinfonia* (BV: 1, "Sinfonia a 5 per introduzione") is an introduction to the *allemande, correnti,* and *sarabande,* all "a 5," comprising Bononcini's most heavily instrumented (i.e., "symphonic") work. It consists of an opening "Adagio" of four bars, C, followed by an "Allegro," C, in massive, saturated and quasi-contrapuntal style. In form the "Allegro" is bipartite and essentially indistinguishable from the *allemande* which follow. Its function, as its position and the title declare, is that of "introduction," and it is thus an *intrada* or *entrée,* a heavier, higher stylization of the processional form.

One connotation of the term *sinfonia* at this period seems to have been music for theatrical use. G. B. Vitali's op. II[5] carries the following advertisement: "Si stampano al presente Balletti... per ballare... Correnti per Camera e Sinphonie per Teatro, del medemo Auttore." These *sinfonie* are of precisely the same order as that by Bononcini.

Possibly Bononcini was copying the traditions of earlier publications of theatrical and ballet music in which introductory *sinfonie* are to be found, as, *Il Primo Libro delle Musiche di Lorenzo Allegri*... 1618.[6] The *Tavola* of Allegri's work begins: "Sinfonia... (per 5 strumenti e B.C.)... Primo Ballo della notte d'amore (per 6 str... danzato nelle nozze dell'A.A. Serenissimi da Paggi e Dame)," etc. Or he may have followed an example of the

5. Vitali, *Sonate A Due Violini, Opus II* (Bologna: Giacomo Monti, 1667).
6. Sartori, *BMI,* p. 243.

characteristic Florentine theatrical use: "*Intermedi di Filippo Vitali Fatti per la Commedia de gl'Accademici Inconstanti*... Firenze 1623...,"[7] which begins (*Intermedio I*) with a "Sinfonia a 5" and ends (*Intermedio VI*) with a "Sinfonia a 4."

Mersenne observes that the *allemande* was "little in use... except in *Balletts*."[8] In France its ritual function, that of distributing the company in the room, was—except for occasions of great formality—usurped by the *branles*, as contemporary dance writings show (see de Lauze). Bononcini's works in this form (see pp. 96-97 ff. *supra*) generally designated "Brando in stil Francese," follow French models implicitly, in predominantly homophonic manner, in the persistent use of the so-called Corelli clash and general absence of sequences. They show him to be a good "tunesmith" although they offer little opportunity for his most characteristic expression—counterpoint.

Fewer examples of the *allemanda* occur in works "a 3" and "a 2." These, being lighter in texture, naturally tend to employ the *aria* in this position. Mersenne describes the *Air* as:

> ... appliqué a toute sorte de Poésie que l'on chante note contre note sans mesure reglée... selon les longues et les brèves qui se trouvent dans les vers... sous laquelle sont compris... plein Chant... les Airs de Cour... les chansons à danser... & les Vaudevilles, & n'y assouvent que le seul Dessus qui parle, que l'on appelle aussi *le sujet*....[9]

Einstein and Haas arrive at much the same definition for the sixteenth-century Italian term aria, i.e., an "unstylized" popular tune, the basic material which, subject to stylization, was transformed into the socially applicable form.[10] The sixteenth century saw a brisk exchange in this kind of artistic materials between France and Italy. The incisive, "four square" dance tune or *chanson* with the "tune (*air*) on top" has always been a French speciality, traded at the Po for the Italian dramatic principle. In Paris, at the hands of the Italian musicians from Baltazar di Belgioioso to Giambattista Lulli, this combination becomes the court ballet—a high stylization indeed of the original materials—and once accomplished is recognizably "French" and "exportable." In sixteenth-century Italy the French *chanson* takes orders and becomes the ecclesiastical *canzona francese* while leading a secular life as the *aria* in the Italian *balletto*.

7. *Ibid.*, p. 291.
8. Mersenne, *Harmonie Universelle*, Livre II Prop. XXIII, p. 145.
9. *Ibid.*, II, 146.
10. Alfred Einstein, *The Italian Madrigal* (Princeton: Princeton University Press, 1949), II, 645; Robert Haas, "Die Musik des Barocks," *HBMW*, III, 43-44.

In the *balletti, arie,* and *aria alla francese* in Bononcini's work we are confronted with the results of several successive layers of mutual influence. Bononcini's *arie* are simply instrumental "intensifications" of the kind of dance song, written under French influence, of which those of the Lombard Gastoldi[11] are the best-known early examples. This style, based on dance stylization and a clipped, instrumental manner, combines French harmonic and rhythmic clarity with elements of the beloved Italian "trio" style (sequences and suspensions).

Bononcini presumably inherited this half-French, half-Italian form from Uccellini, who uses it in op. IV (1645) with the significant "Arie per sonare a violino solo: Il secondo violino e aggiunto ad libitum." It would seem that Uccellini gained acquaintance with the French style in his earlier, pre-Modenese days in northern Italian courts.[12] Certainly this style served him well at the Modenese court, then newly affiliated with France.

Bononcini's *arie* and *balletti* are uniformly in C (4/4)[13] and, given their character, are presumably at a moderate tempo. This corresponds with examples of Gastoldi as well as with the first section of Mersenne's example of the *air de cour.*

One aria, BII: 37, bears the superscription "Aria, discordia concors . . . " in the printed edition. This fragment of Horace (Ep. XII, 19) may point to the use of this item and the related "sua corrente" as part of the apparatus of a literary academy. We know that the *balletto* invaded the *accademia* itself. Banchieri uses the same *detto d'Horatio* in his *Accademia*: *La Sampogna,* and Gafurius, who is listed by Bononcini as an authority (*Musico Prattico*), uses this tag in his *De Harmonia Musicorum Instrumentorum.*

Its general currency quite apart, the phrase had a special connection with the artistic and literary undertakings of the Este family. It had served as a theme[14] for the decoration (paintings by Bellini, Mantegna, and Titian) of the *studio, Grotta* or Camerino of his Isabella D'Este (Gonzaga) at Mantua as well as that of her brother, Alfonso d'Este at Ferrara. The Neo-Hellenistic literary qualities of these paintings and of the atmosphere for which they were made is due to the direct influence of such humanists and

11. See also Alfred Einstein, *The Italian Madrigal,* II, 604. The fact that two of Gastoldi's *balletti* are preserved as Protestant church hymns is a demonstration of their origin in popular *melos* and an example of the principle of "conservation of energy" in (artistic) evolution by which things return to their sources.

12. For the Franco-Italian ballet in Lombard and Piedmontese Italy, see Federico Mompellio, *Sigismondo d'India* (Ricordi, 1957), pp. 58 ff.

13. Like many of Uccellini's, and unlike most of Colombi's. Colombi (op. I) uses 3/2 "Presto" for *arie,* dynamic "tunes" of very Italian character resembling some of what Uccellini calls "Balli Italiani" in op. XI.

14. See Edgar Wind, *The Feast of the Gods* (Cambridge, Mass., 1948) pp. 19, 61, *et passim.*

literati as Paride de Ceresara and especially Pietro Bembo. Its significance in Bononcini's works is hard to guess; it may refer to the subject of a *balletto* on some such subject, or simply allude to the somewhat "dissonant harmonies" (six-four chords and free dissonances) of the piece.

Menestrier describes clearly the function of the *aria* in Italian theatrical and ballet use:

> The Italians, to retain the manner of the ancient Choruses put *intermèdes* in their Tragedies and Comedies where the entrées of the *Ballet* are danced to the sound of voices and instruments. The *intermèdes* or choruses of *la Moglie odiata de Francesco Majorana* are of this kind. The first is for dancers who enter to the sound of various instruments and after the first *figure* they [the dancers] stop while these words are sung to which Echo replies:
>
> Sposa bella e vaga
> Onorata sposa
> Di cui l'huom s'appaga,
> Per cui l'huom riposa....[15]

Possibly the clearest demonstration of the relationship between Bononcini's *arie* and *balletti* and earlier models is afforded by the comparison of examples. (A *Balletto* of Gastoldi, a *balletto* BII: 11, and an *aria* BVII: 1 are given in Plate No. III.) The *aria* retains a basic vocal quality while the *balletto* insists upon its instrumental privileges and suggests the agility of the dancer with instrumental means, scales, leaps, etc.

The *balletto* which is a part of the "Sonata a quattro, in stil Francese" (BIX: 19), is a good demonstration of combination and transposition of stylistic elements from our "series" of processional types. It begins *Adagio,*

Plate III

Gastoldi; Balletto

15. "Les Italiens pour retenir la maniere des anciens Choeurs ont des intermedes dans leurs Tragedies & leurs Comedies où l'on danse des entrées de Ballet au son des voix & des instrumens. Les intermedes ou les choeurs de la *Moglie odiata de Francesco Majorana* sont de cette maniere. Le premier est de danseurs qui entrent au son de divers instrumens & après la premiere figure ils s'arrétant tandis que l'on chante ces paroles ausquelles l'Eco répond

> Sposa bella e vaga
> Onorata sposa
> Di cui l'huom s'appaga
> Per cui l'huom riposa...."

(*BAM*, p. 293).

BII:11 Balletto

BVII:1* Aria

(Gastoldi, cont.)

(BII:11, cont.)

(BVII:1, cont.)

*N.B. the sequences

with a “Fanfare”: (thus an *Entrée*) 𝄵 𝄾𝅘𝅥𝅮 | 𝅗𝅥. 𝄾𝅘𝅥𝅮 | 𝅗𝅥., and continues, *Allegro,* to complete—in two parallel periods—the binary form, exploiting a single motive. It is a classic symphony movement in miniature: formally, historically, and genetically a true prototype.

During the 1660's the ascendancy of French dance music was everywhere complete, as the specific designations of Uccellini, Colombi, Bononcini, and Vitali “alla Francese per ballare,” “in stil Francese,” etc., show. Bononcini's *arie* in op. IV marked “in stil Francese,” as well as others patently in the French style, are imitations of what was to the 1650's and 1660's the contemporary French vocal manner of the highly ornamented *air de cour.* In fact Bononcini copies, almost to the point of caricature (BIV: 1, 3), the conventional ornaments, especially the *port de voix* described by Mersenne.[16] The comparison of Mersenne's example (see Plate IV) with BIV: 1, 3 should be sufficient illustration.

The sixteenth-note upbeat is apt to intensify the beginning:[17] a slightly melodramatic touch which, as Lully found, was technically useful in heightening the effect of the attack.[18] These traits are to be seen in BVII: 3, 11, which—it will be remembered—are for violin solo with optional other parts (Mersenne's “le seul Dessus qui parle”). These details are also visible in the masterpieces of BXII: 5, 15 among others more in Italian *gusto.*

The “pathetic” trick of repeating—“piano”—the final cadence becomes increasingly frequently indicated in Bononcini's work, just as it becomes a mannerism for the whole period. It is a way of protracting the melodic span (based on the four-accent lines of popular verse which is very “short breathed” for instruments) without increasing its motivic content or contrapuntal weight.

Its origins may be traced to instrumentalism itself, to the improvised “tag” of accompanying lutanists and to the instrumentalism of the *chanson à danser*. In the Gastoldi *Balletti* and Bononcini's Italianate *arie* the cadences are characteristically approached by a sequence in imitative, “sham” counterpoint—a device which originally, in the vocal works, had been used to suggest instruments. This material, of lighter weight (“Fa la la, fa la la”) than the incisive opening motive, tends to gather momentum as it is spun out and requires the repetition of the cadence itself to assure a kinesthetically “balanced” close.

16. Mersenne, *Harmonie Universelle,* II, 412.

17. Compare the beginnings of Bononcini's *arie* of this order with those of Uccellini's op. IV (in) Torchi, *AMI, VII,* 199 ff.

18. See R. North, *op. cit.,* p. 185.

Plate IV

Air de M. Boesset

Mersenne H. U. p. 142

Diminution de M. Bailly

Diminution, (Port de voix)

N.B.

(Port de voix)

BIV:1, Aria in stil Francese

BIV:1

BIV:3 Aria in stil Francese

BIV:3

N B.

BXII:5 Aria

BXII:5

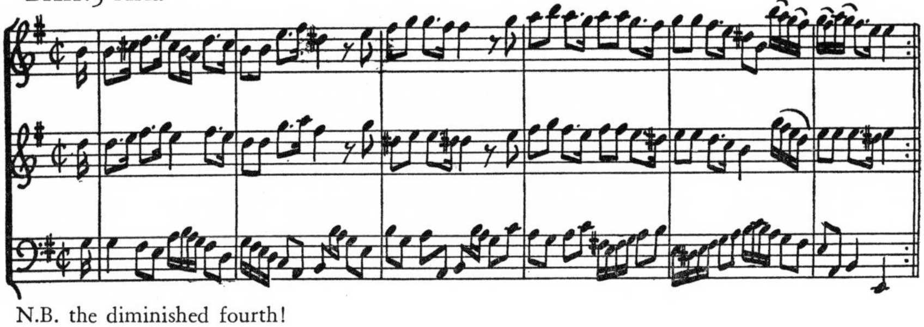

N.B. the diminished fourth!

This repetition, the echo ("piano"), is yet another minor example of the antiphonal devices which held such fascination for the Baroque era. Its origins lie in the play between instruments and voices and their spatial distributions (In the seventeenth century it was a poor theatrical representation indeed that did not have a chorus concealed in a cloud or cave)[19] and the mechanical "f," "p" imitation of this effect within a group.

The echo itself, as a device in Baroque music,[20] is of the sublest and most profound aesthetic significance. Although an expressive, even pathetic device, it falls into the category of "scientific mannerism" and is the direct illustration to the senses of the then new concepts of the nature and commensurability of time and space (Newton, Galileo) and of the similar nature of sound (Descartes, Mersenne).

As the reminder and illustration of the transitoriness of human life it is an effect of a truly "pathetic" order. It is the conscious stylization[21] of the threshold between sensate—exterior and conceptual—life and subjective experience[22] (the reflection of a new degree of disassociation of personality), which is the fundamental achievement of Baroque music.

19. H. Purcell, *Dido and Aeneas.* See also Solerti, Musica, *Ballo e Drammatica,* p. 43.

20. It corresponds exactly to the experiments in perspective and lighting of the mannerist painters and seventeenth-century scenery designers, as the ceiling of almost any stage setting or any Baroque church will show, if by no more than the representation of the scenic devices, perspectives, clouds, singing and playing *amori,* etc. Roger North, *op. cit.,* p. 218, refers it directly to space-perception. In "Of Soft and Loud" he says, "this conduceth much to the delight of musick; because it is a renewall, like life after a swooning, or as in a dance, the image goeth into the *lontaine,* and then comes up again and fills the eye. . . ."

21. John Keats completed the concept: "Heard melodies are sweet, but those unheard are sweeter. . . ."

22. As in the song in Purcell's music for *The Tempest,* "Full Fathom Five Thy Father Lies," and the celebrated passage in Monteverdi's *Orfeo* (the shepherd's announcement of Eurydice's death), where the "threshold" effect is heightened by the contrast of tonality (g *vs.* c-sharp) as well as by the exchange of instruments (*cembalo* and organ *continuo*).

CHAPTER X. THE DANCES (2): COUPLE TYPES; *CORRENTE, SARABANDA*, AND *GIGA*

Like the processional company dances, the couple dances of the sixteenth and seventeenth centuries can be arranged in a series according to their ceremonial significance. As axial couple dances their rhythms are ternary to permit the characteristic turning figures. They thus offer the formal contrast to the binary, linear march types, a contrast which is an essential aesthetic dimension in both dance itself and its "abstract" version, the *sonata da camera*. Including the more important surviving prototypes, this series (in descending order of stylization) is as follows:

gaillarde figurée	sixteenth-century prototype, highest stylization; learned sequence of virtuoso steps, leaps, etc.; "figure";
gaillarde, gagliarda	high stylization, social dancing improvised on basic step pattern with virtuoso capers, leaps, etc., combined *ad libitum;*
tordion	low social stylization; couples; repetitive step pattern; ordinary social dancing; "on the floor";
volte	virtuoso-athletic elements of *gaillard;* these sixteenth-century forms combine with the popular *corrente* and converge in the *courante* of the seventeenth century;
courante figurée, (*reglée*)	high stylization; learned sequence of steps or "figures";
courante, corrente	social dancing improvised over basic step patterns.

Underlying these, as with the processional dances, is the melodic substance, the *air,* or unstylized melodic material; Mersenne says "La courante se danse . . . par deux personnes à la fois, qu'elle fait courir souz un air mesuré [*stylized*] par le pied iambique."[1]

Of the *Gaillard* Mersenne says, "The *Gaillard* is a dance which takes its name from the *Gaillardise* which is employed in dancing it, and the liberty which permits one to go on the bias, across and along the space in the hall,

1. Mersenne, *Harmonie Universelle,* Livre II Prop. XXIII, p. 165.

either on the floor or by leaps, such as the *entrechats* and *sauts ronds*."[2]

The *gagliarda* is represented in Bononcini but once, as part of the "Sonata a quattro in stil Francese" (BIX: [20]). Together with the four examples in Vitali's op. I it must be among the last *gagliarde* written in Italy. By this time (the 1670's) the *gagliarda* had been supplanted by the *corrente* and was an "antique" used only for the ballet; thus the stylization is very "high," a *Gagliarda Figurata.* This stylization results in the great intensification of the rhythm by the "[double] dotting" which exaggerates the contrast of short and long in the characteristic anacruses.

Here the *gagliarda* has suffered the fate of all aging dances; it has become slower and involved with decorative accretions, until it is now a caricature of itself, better known for its idiosyncracies than for its fundamental character. A comparison of the original *gagliarda-gaillard* rhythms with late examples shows this clearly (see Plate V). The Bononcini, Artus, and Vitali examples represent the standard decorative intensifications made by dancer and musician alike and described in many sources, especially by Arbeau. Although Vitali retains the original metrical indication 3/2, Bononcini adopts the simple *alla breve* (₵) of the French example, bringing focus on the ornamental details at the expense of the fundamental rhythm. This bit of evidence again points out Bononcini's awareness and exact knowledge of the details of the current and recent French practices.

The *courante,* the courtly French version of the *corrente* which had been circulated during the sixteenth-century vogue for Italian dances, was the most important couple dance of the seventeenth century, replacing the *gaillard* and eventually succeeded by the *menuet.*[3] Its original character[4] as social pantomime is reinforced by contact and blending with the *gaillard* and the related dances, the *tordion* and the *volte.* As with the processional dances, the features of analogous forms and prototypes tend to be assimilated by the currently popular form.

The Italian *corrente* remained a "step" dance based on improvisation[5] over a repeated step pattern in which the legacy of older and popular couple dances, the *saltarello* and *tordion,* was kept alive. Its character is spontaneous: its history and that of its music is therefore one of variation

2. *Ibid.*

3. Thoinot Arbeau [Jehan Tabourot], *Orchesography,* trans. Cyril W. Beaumont (London: Beaumont, 1925), hereinafter referred to as *Orchesography.* Arbeau, *ca.* 1550, gives first place to the *tordion* and *gaillards;* De Lauze, 1623, begins his instruction with the *courante;* and Rameau, 1725, says "formerly instruction began with the *courante,*" but he gives first place to the minuet.

4. Arbeau, *Orchesography,* p. 108.

5. And is, therefore, not described in the dancing manuals.

and instrumentalism; assimilation from related forms, higher and lower, new and old.

In France the *courante* replaces the *gaillard-tordion* as a social dance (*danse de ville*), but not without being itself profoundly influenced. In addition to being a step dance improvised[6] to the cadence,[7] it is also cultivated as a figure dance.[8] The composed *courante*, the *courante figurée* or *reglée,* referred to by name (e.g., *La Duchesse* of Pepys' comment and Bononcini's op. IV, "La Pegolotta," etc.) was the pride of the French dancing masters and the reflection of the highly ritualistic French court. The *courante figurée* drew upon the high stylization and virtuosity of the *gaillard figurée* and also assembled in its composition other elements from the dance traditions of the time. Its character as a "composed" dance is order and formality, a blend of virtuosity and austere elegance. Its music, therefore, developed in the direction of refinement and structural logic.

Ordinary practice in social dancing seems to have been a blend of the two methods of dancing, learned figures and improvisation. The music of

6. As such it was deplored by the professional dancing masters Arbeau, De Lauze, and Rameau, and satirized by Shakespeare.

7. Mersenne says: "La Courante est la plus frequente de toutes les dances pratiquées en France, & se dance seulement par deux personnes à la fois, qu'elle fait courir souz un air mesuré par le pied iambique . . . de sorte que toute cette dance n'est qu'une course sautelante d'allées et de venues depuis la commencement iusques à la fin . . . . Son mouvement est appellé sesquialtere ou triple . . . . L'on peut néammoins luy donner telle mesure que l'on voudra." *Op. cit.,* p. 165. See also Arbeau, *Orchesography,* p. 109.

8. Mersenne, *Harmonie Universelle, op. cit.,* p. 170. ". . . une courante figuree . . . a ses pas mesurez, & ses figures particulières . . . elle a sa mesure triple, ou sesquialtère, comme les autres Courantes. . . ."

the usual *courante* tends to begin each of its two complementary periods with a suggestion of a formula ("hemiola," a learned figure) which then (in concession to the frailty of memory) gives way to sequential improvisation to the cadence (see BII: 25, BIV: 20, BVII: 2, BIX: [9]), which may also be a "hemiola" figure.

Arbeau's description[9] of the ordinary way of dancing the *gaillard,* the sixteenth-century analogue, applies also to the hybrid, half-figured, half-improvised *courante* of Bononcini's day. The *gaillard* was then (*ca.* 1550) at the same stage of evolution as was the *courante* in the mid-seventeenth century. Arbeau says:

> Those who dance the *Gaillarde* today in the towns dance it confusedly and are content with making the five steps [the "figure"] and some passages ["sequences"] without any order, and care for nothing so long as they make the cadence in time.[10]

He says (p. 108) of the *Courante* "... But young men who do not know and have never learned ... dance it according to their fancy and are content simply to keep time to the cadence; and in dancing it they turn the body, letting go of the damsel's hand." The combination of initial figure and subsequent improvisation is also the meaning of Rameau's description:

> After you have made the customary bows ... you execute a *temps de courante* [the opening *courante* figure]. Afterwards you begin the *pas de courante* [the "steps" improvised to the cadence, which have their musical counterpart in "sequences"]. Cf. BII, 25.[11]

Rameau also calls the *temps de courante* the "pas grave"; i.e., it occupies six beats (hemiola), while the *pas de courante* occupies three (iamb or trochee).

The contact between the two versions, figured and improvised, produces a "hybrid" in which French formalism and Italian spontaneity are combined. This hybrid form is the basis of the *corrente* of the late seventeenth-century *sonata da camera.*

In titles of Italian printed music the distinction between "correnti alla Francese" and "correnti all'Italiana" begins to appear in the 1630's.[12] In

9. Arbeau, *Orchesography,* p. 65.

10. This "choreographic scenario" is an explanation of Bononcini's (otherwise) astonishing instrumental abstraction of dance practice, the *corrente* BIV: 15, *La Buffalina;* 20, *La Pegolotta;* and BV: 25. The heavily stylized beginning of each section—"Adagio"—and highly ornamented (the most decorated piece in Bononcini) gives way to driving repeated patterns—"Allegro." This may refer to the ballet, i.e., to an effort to give dramatic "expression" to "simple dances." Menestrier, *BAM,* p. 122.

11. Rameau, *The Dancing Master,* p. 75.

12. B. Marini, op. VIII (1629); Pesenti, Lib. II (1630); and Pesenti, op. X (1639). See Sartori, *BMI,* pp. 338, 339, and 368, respectively.

the 1650's the distinction becomes more explicit[13] and reaches its height with the Modenese-Bolognese composers during the sixties in the atmosphere of the Francophile Este Court.[14] This coincides with the period of the highest cultivation of the *courante* in France before the invasion by the *contre-danses.* This decade embraces the youthful years of Louis XIV, who made a personal reputation for dancing the *courante.*[15] The cosmopolitan, abstract variety of *courante-corrente*—the hybrid of French and Italian forms —was making its appearance in Italian chamber music. Vitali, op. III and Colombi, op. I, list such works as "Correnti per Camera." The opposite principle is clearly visible in the work of Couperin who, in *Concerts Royaux,* 1715 (written in suite-minded, anti-sonata France for the intimate chamber music of Louis XIV) maintains the distinction and points it out by contrasting two examples: *à la Française* and *à l'Italienne.*

The differences lay in rhythmic vocabulary and structure. In Italian violin music the nature of the Italian *corrente* as a step dance, its ternary meter, predominantly iambic foot, and cadential hemiola are clearly expressed in such patterns[16] as:

Any one of the patterns may be, in Italian fashion, spun out by typical imitations and suspensions into a sequence terminated by a cadential hemiola. The melodic manner is generally smooth and conjunct, although characteristic jagged Italian "violin" motives also appear.[17] The fabric is essentially

13. *Primavera dei Vaghi Fiori Musicali* . . . di Francesco Boccella, Detto Primi . . . Ancona, 1653. See Sartori, *BMI,* p. 416. "La Cadolina, Corrente," "Le gran ballet," "La Corrant de gran ballet."

Correnti & Balletti alla Francese & all'Itagliana . . . Di Salvador Gandini . . . Opera Quarta . . . Venezia, 1655. See Sartori, *BMI,* p. 418.

14. Vitali, op. III (1667): "Corrente alla Francese per ballare."

Uccellini, op. IX (1667): "Correnti (1-6) alla Francese per ballare"; "Balli (1-15) al Italiana," which are clearly *correnti.*

Uccellini, Libro Septimo (1668): "Corrente a quattro strumenti in stil Francese per ballare"; "Correnti a cinque strumenti al Itagliana."

Colombi, op. I (1668): "Corrente alla Francese."

Cazzati, op. XXXXX (1669): "Corrente Italiana."

Bononcini, op. III (1669): "Brando e Corrente in Stil Francese."

Bononcini, op. IV (1671): "Correnti in stil Francese."

15. Rameau, *The Dancing Master,* p. 74: "Formerly the *Courante* was much in fashion . . . as it is a very solemn dance with a nobler style and grander manner than the others, is very varied in its figures, and has dignified and distinguished movements. Louis XIV, of happy memory, was pleased to prefer it."

16. These are drawn from the "Correnti Italiana detta L'Orsa," Cazzati, op. 50, which, with its twelve variations, forms a reliable compendium of *corrente* patterns.

17. These instrumentalisms are unknown in the French *courante* and, in general, constitute the difference between Italian and French style at this period.

additive and motivic. Its accents recur and mark the iambic foot; and, although trochaic designs appear, the systematic alteration of the two in the choriambics and hemiola characteristic of the French version is not carried out.

The French manner, as found in examples of the repertoire of the "Vingt-quatre violons"[18] and in explicit imitations by Italians, shows the signs of development as a figure dance with an actually "composed" series of steps. The rhythmic vocabulary is that of constantly alternating or opposed iamb and trochee, or choriambus with anacrusis  ,

which permits and invites interpretation as a higher organization, the hemiola. As a result, the hemiola and choriamb pervade the whole rhythmic fabric. The standard figures are:

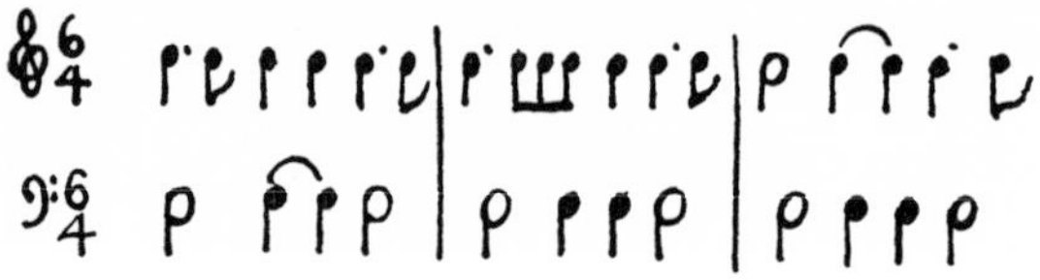

The harmony is consonant and the movement homorhythmic. The melodic line is smooth, contiguous, and undulating; the absence of melodic accent permits the continual shift and equivocation of 3/2 and 2/𝅗𝅥.[19] The principal interest (as in the *air* itself, Mersenne's "sujet," of which the dance is but a stylization)[20] is in the top part ("le seul Dessus qui parle"). The harmonic flow is even and, like the melodic curve, smooth and consonant. Dissonances are reserved as the mark of the cadence and usually appear only at the cadential hemiola. Sequential imitation, so characteristic of the Italian instrumental style, is not exploited for its climactic value; thus the two complementary periods of the form are shorter and more tightly constructed, consisting largely of direct exposition and without motivic development.

Of Bononcini's dances the *correnti* are the most numerous, constituting a large fraction of his work.[21] He employs both French and Italian types

18. Ecorcheville, *VSO,* Vol. II.

19. This shifting from binary to ternary grouping is the meaning of Mersenne's "L'on peut néanmoins luy donner telle mesure que l'on voudra." But see also BIX: 7 in $\frac{6}{8}$.

20. Mersenne says "... qu'elle fait courir souz un air mesuré par le pied iambique. . . ."

21. This fact alone is perhaps the strongest evidence that Bononcini's music was actually danced, since the actual uses of social dancing required more *correnti* than anything else Were the *sonate da camera* abstract suites, we might expect to find a more nearly equal number of *all* dances. In any case, we of today must overcome our prejudices regarding "mere" dance music by recalling that social dancing was an art at least on a par with, and even more widely practiced than, private music-making. It was certainly as highly developed technically and as demanding in terms of discipline and talent.

as well as "hybrid" forms. The extremes of his usage are found in BIV: 4, "Corrente in stil Francese 'La Strozza,' "[22] and BIV: 8, "Corrente 'La Montanara.' "[23]

These two examples serve as illustrations of the formal and rhythmic characteristics of the two types. However, the greater number of Bononcini's *correnti* are in a "hybrid" style, examples of which are called *corrente da camera* by Colombi and Vitali. These contain all degrees of combination of the satisfactory features of both styles: the contrast itself is an affective dimension."[24]

Bononcini's formula for each of the two periods of this hybrid form of *corrente da camera* embraces the following elements (usually in the following order, often repeated entirely or in part):

1. An opening in French manner (homorhythmic stereotype choriambic with anacrusis; implied hemiola, the "figure" or *temps de courante*) which lapses into
2. a motivic sequence in Italian taste in short iambic and/or trochaic imitations, the sequences articulated by climactic (cumulative sequential) harmony. The Italian device of suspension is less frequently found than usual, dissonance being reserved for the culmination in
3. a clear (explicit) hemiola, often unanimous in all parts with stereotyped suspension dissonance (4-5) or element of harmonic "color" (chromaticism) in Italian taste.

Thus, the voluble repetitiousnesss of the Italian *corrente* is tempered by the severer *courante,* and the lack of climactic quality (De Lauze's "unaffected negligence") characteristic of the French form is overcome by the spontaneous dramatic qualities of the Italian sequence (ex., BXII: 16).

These dances are "structures" of abstract, rigorously balanced design. The a-melodic manner, entirely devoid of popular elements (except in the most Italianate examples), is a mosaic of patterns arranged in a cumulative scheme which appeals to the kinesthetic memory of the auditor for its ultimate subjective meaning. However, as chamber music, refinement and distinction of conception and workmanship were also consciously cultivated values as we have seen from Bononcini's prefaces as well as from the music itself.

The two complementary periods tend to be co-ordinated by motivic unity

22. The *correnti* associated with the several "brandi in stil Francese," are, of course, in the French manner. (See table, p. 96.)
23. The latter is not specifically so designated but is "all Italiana" by implication. Bononcini nowhere uses the term "all Italiana."
24. As in B:IV, "La Pegolotta."

and harmonic contrast. In this process melodic inversion and tonal opposition (I-V, i-III) of the beginnings and endings of the sections—the common methods of the epoch—play a large part (ex., BIV: 4).

Only occasionally, as in the "Brando in stil Francese" and "sua Corrente" of BI: [13-17] and BIV: 3, 4 is a thematic relationship undertaken between the company dance (*branle*) or *aria* and the *corrente*. This is the old variation or "transformation" principle referred to by Mersenne which induces a higher organization in the suite.

Frequently and characteristically, especially in op. IX, (*Trattenimenti per Camera*), Bononcini sets aside the homophonic opening and uses the melodic and rhythmic materials of the French formula in a contrapuntal, fugal exposition (BIX: "Corrente Seconda"). This is in line with the requirements of abstract chamber music[25] as distinct from dance music.

Even in usual textures his contrapuntal skill is expressed in motivic economy, clarity, and the linear energy of the part writing. In this matter Bononcini surpasses his contemporaries—Cazzati, Uccellini, Vitali, and Colombi—and equals Corelli.

Bononcini uses for the *corrente* the meter signatures 3/4, 6/4, 3/2, 3/1.[26] In a good proportion of cases (manuscript and editions) Bononcini also, according to the waning practice of the times, prefixes the older signs of proportion, C and ¢. However, these must be regarded as vestigial rather than applicable in any absolute terms. The sources are not consistent in their use; the manuscript of op. II does not contain them nor does that of op. XII. In the London edition (c. 1700) of op. XII they are, of course, omitted entirely.

The bases of Bononcini's uses of these older mensural signs are to be found in his own presentation of the subject in *Il Musico Prattico*. As did the sixteenth-century theorists,[27] Bononcini calls C "tempo ordinario, o alla semibreve" and ¢ "tempo alla breve" saying, however, of the latter that "by the moderns it is used as the preceding, just beating so much the faster." He presents these signs in a series of combinations with modern meter signatures and says, "As for the others... for greater brevity the following general rule is followed: the lower number denotes which values make up the bar, and the upper how many of these there will be."[28]

25. See *supra* p. 74.
26. And exceptionally, 6/8, BIX: [2] (*Corrente Prima*). This piece, which exploits syncopations and contrived rhythms much in the spirit of a Beethoven *scherzo*, is not characteristic of the *corrente* as ordinarily danced, although it may have been a special, "virtuoso" number.
27. Apel, *NPM*, p. 148.
28. Bononcini, *Il Musico Prattico*, p. 11.

Thus in this respect Bononcini stands at the threshold of modern usage. Despite his precise uses of proportional mensural signs in the canons of op. III, they cannot be systematically interpreted in his instrumental music. For actual *tempo* he follows current conventions, i.e., the variable usage of the "moderns" he describes.

There are, however, certain consistencies in Bononcini's use of proportional signs. The *corrente,* explicitly or patently in the French style, are all in 6/4 or C-6/4. This practice corresponds to that of Uccellini (op. IX), from whom Bononcini probably learned the "stil Francese" as a professional matter. It does not correspond to the usage of the Cassel manuscript[29] containing the repertoire of the "Vingt-quatre Violons," which exhibits the meter signatures C-3, ¢-3 or 3. Here again we see variability in the use of the sign of proportion, which may also be contradictory among the several instrumental parts of the same *courante.*

On page 22 of *Il Musico Prattico* C-6/4 is called "super biparziente quarta," a "sextuplet of semi minims . . . ," six semi minins to the bar, three on the [down] beat, and three on the up [beat]." This meter signature applies to a great many of the hybrid *correnti.* The bar of six beats is appropriate for the hybrid *corrente-courante,* as the characteristic hemiola can then be accommodated as well as the usual five-beat final chord 𝅗𝅥 ♩♩ 𝅗𝅥 | 𝅗𝅥. 𝅗𝅥 :||:|| of each period[30] (necessary to balance the preceding hemiola and for the dancer's *posture*).

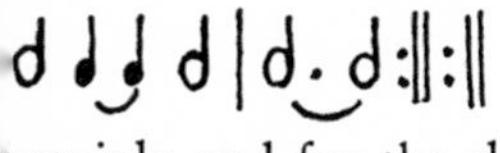

Like Vitali, however, Bononcini, in hybrid *correnti da camera,* also uses C-3/4 or 3/4—the "tripla of semi minims—*Sub-sesquiterza* in which there are three semi minims per bar, two on the [down] beat and one on the up [beat]."[31] In such cases he fairly consistently omits every other bar line[32] so that the grouping is effectively the same as in 6/4. Bononcini is "consistently inconsistent," using C-3/4 with alternate barring for overtly "Italian" *correnti* such as BIV: 8 and 6/4 for the equally "Italian" BV: 6, BVII: 18, and BXII: 24.

Occasionally the barring in the several instrumental parts is systematically opposed, especially in imitative textures where the six-beat motive overlaps for half its length (BXII: 10). In such cases each part is barred to accommo-

29. Ecorcheville, *VSO,* Vol. I.
30. This shows the true rhythm of the *corrente-courante* to be a double foot, Mersenne's *iambique redoublé,* or (in the French form) combined iambic-trochaic, the choriamb.
31. Bononcini, *op. cit.*
32. Bar line practice in general is irregular and inconsistent.

date its own rhythm. From this it is clear that Bononcini considers the bar line in its modern sense, i.e., accentual as well as metrical.[33]

A great number of Bononcini's *correnti* are given the meter signature 3/2 or C-3/2 or ₵-3/2. In *Il Musico Prattico* C-3/2 is called "Tripla Minore," "Sesquialtera minore imperfetta" in which there are three Minims per bar, two on the [down] beat and one on the up [beat]." This meter signature, 3/2, is probably to be regarded here as an injunction to a broad style—[34] "Largo"—[35] appropriate to the massive texture (five parts) of op. V, where this signature is most consistently used. Two such *correnti* (BV: 12, 16) are marked "Largo," and a third (BV: 25) alternates between "Adagio" and "Allegro." As we have seen the *corrente da camera* was frequently indicated as "Largo" or even, as in Vitali, op. III, "Grave."[36]

Special interest attaches to the hemiola. Implicit as the opening of the French *courante,* its ambivalence pervades the subsequent rhythmic fabric. As the culmination of the sequence in the Italian and "hybrid"[37] *corrente,* it is the climax of the phrase and of the period, and is the point of greatest rhythmic interest. The hemiola is often intensified by added tonal interest—i.e., dissonance, of which the preceding sequence is more than usually free. The cadential suspension formula as a readily apparent and audible detail is reserved for this place and serves as a "warning" to the (improvising) dancer (real or *sédentaire*) of the approaching cadence and its necessary *posture.*[38] A characteristic decoration, the *échappée,* often appears in this situation (BXII: 24).

33. This is an Italian trait analogous to much earlier Italian notational practice. See Apel, *NPM,* pp. 370 ff. On one occasion (op. II, No. 23) we find the following:

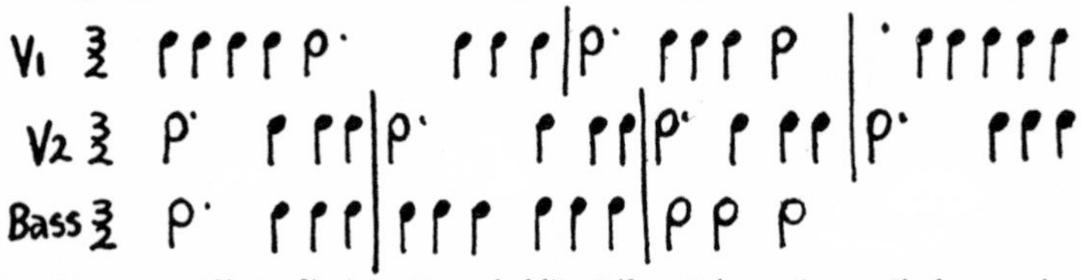

V1 3/2

V2 3/2

Bass 3/2

34. See Letter *A Gli Studiosi* in Frescobaldi's *Libro Primo*: ". . . Si deuono i principii-cominciarli adagio a dar maggior spirito e vaghezza al seguente passo & nelle Cadenze sostenerle assai prima che si incominci laltro [*sic*] passo, e nelle trippole, ò sesquialtere, se sara no maggiori, si portino adagio, se minori alquâto più allegre, se di tre simiminime, più allegre se saranno sei per quattro si dia illor [*sic*] tempo con far caminare la battuta allegra. . . ." Cited in Sartori, *BMI,* p. 296.

35. At this period "Largo" was understood as a moderate, not slow, tempo. See Purcell, Preface, *Sonnatas* (London, 1683).

36. On the other hand Cazzati, op. L, twice uses 3/1 "Presto presto" for a *giga,* and also feels obliged to use superscriptions "Presto" and "Vivace" for 3/8 and 3/16. The increasing use of such verbal qualifications of tempo is the best indication of the final disappearance of the proportional system.

37. Although in one place (BII: 25) Bononcini *begins* a *courante* with this hemiola (*Temps du Courante*), colored notation, suspension and all.

38. As might be expected, this feature—suspension within the hemiola—is far more

The cadential hemiola also becomes the occasion for the introduction of lissonant chromatic harmony in Italian taste.[39] This is a trait of the *cor-ente Italiana,* as is shown by the cadence in Cazzati's example, "La Palcotta," ›p. L. Bononcini uses it frequently, as in BII: 25.

Except in the *correnti* "in stil Francese" Bononcini frequently uses the ›lder manner of notation of the hemiola introducing black (*oscurati*) semi-›reves and minims (coloration) in accordance with his instructions on page hirteen of *Il Musico Prattico*:

> Also, you will find certain parts [written] in this manner
> Emiolia maggiore ♦ ♦ ♦
>
> Emiolia minore
> called by musicians "Emiolia" [Hemiola] and used in uneven bars.

3oth appear in BII: 25.

Another expedient which serves the same purpose (since it obviates di-'iding a note value) is his frequent practice of suppressing the bar line.

Thus there is seldom a question as to the position of the hemiola—the ›erformer is "warned" in advance of the change in accentuation and group-ng and of the advent of the cadence. Also the performance practice may vell have required a particular accentuation or bowing, which is thus pro-'ided for.

Like the *correnti,* Bononcini's *sarabande* reflect the diversity of prevailing lance traditions. As with the *corrente,* two versions of the *sarabande* were urrent. Its origins are a matter of conjecture, and its original character by all accounts) base. However, its introduction (*ca.* 1585) to Europe is hrough Spain, which accounts for its ultimate character of severe simplicity, natural foil for the gravity of the *allemande* and the frank gallantry of the 'ourante.

In mid-seventeenth century Italy the *sarabande* was danced to a quick, equential tribrach,[40] a ternary bar with all three beats marked. Bononcini ›rovides us with clear examples of this in BV: 26 (6/4 "Presto) and BIV: 22 (3/4).

sual with the Italian Bononcini than in the French *courantes* (figured or not) of the rep-rtoire of the "Vingt-quatre Violons."

39. Purcell, in W. B. Squire, "Purcell as Theorist," *SIMG,* VI, 560.

40. It is tempting and probably correct to trace this type to the Spanish occupation in Italy nd consider it as close to the popular (i.e., base and pre-courtly Spanish) prototype. Sachs, 'HD, p. 336.

In BIV: 5 we find a *Sarabanda* "in stil Francese" and the *Sarabanda,* BV: 20 ("Adagio") is of the same order. These, like other items "in stil Francese" are in imitation of the style to be found in the repertoire of the "Vingt-quatre Violons." Under the same refining influences which produced the French *courante,* the *sarabande* was cultivated as a slow dance reflecting the severity of Spanish court etiquette. No virtuosity is admitted; it was danced on the floor: "Ses pas sont composéz des tirades ou des glissades . . ."[41] to a simple repeated figure as its music shows. The internal structural tension of the *courante*—caused by varying phrase lengths and counter-rhythms—is essentially foreign to it,[42] as is any climactic quality, the metric scheme being a foregone conclusion.

Evidently the rhythm of the French *sarabande* was originally much the same as that of the Italian version. Mersenne says: "Son mouvement est Hegemeolien ♩♩♩𝅗𝅥♩" or a tribrach and a *trochée.*[43] Like the *courante* and many other patterns, the *sarabande* was subjected in France to "high stylization" (i.e., a slow tempo) and intensification (dotting) of the rhythm, ♩ ♩ ♩ | 𝅗𝅥 ♩ eventually becoming ♩ ♩. ♪ | ♩. ♪ ♩ |. The resulting accentuation brings about the alternation of iamb and *trochée:*[44] ♩ 𝅗𝅥 | 𝅗𝅥 ♩ in the reverse of the *counrante* pattern.

The greater number of Bononcini's *sarabande* are, like the *correnti,* a mixture of elements from both French and Italian types. The usual initial tribrach is contrasted with the following *trochées* and iambs. The melodic style, as written, is severe and unornamented.[45]

The harmonic manner is consonant and homorhythmic. Dissonances are reserved for cadences, as in the *correnti,* and are brought about in the same way or, occasionally, within an implied hemiola as in BIV: 22.

Bononcini's form is very constant: two equal periods or sections of four 6/4 or eight 3/4 bars (twenty-four beats) repeated. The first period is addressed to the dominant and the second to the tonic. Each pair of 3/4 bars or six beats encompasses an entire phrase whose rhythmic details tend

41. Mersenne, *Harmonie Universelle,* Livre II Prop. XXIII, p. 165.

42. Although in two dances so closely allied in function and rhythm, some hybridization is inevitable, as we shall see.

43. Mersenne, *Harmonie Universelle, loc. cit.*

44. This pattern is standard, or very nearly so, in the *sarabandes* of the Cassel MS. and remains so in the classic suite. See Ecorcheville, *VSO,* Vol. II.

45. The performance practice in respect to ornamentation (*agréments*) is not ascertainable: the part books give no sign. However, see *supra* pp. 77 ff., esp. 80.

repeat sequentially in subsequent phrases. Despite the melodic, harionic, and formal severity there is a lingering sentimentality in both the rench *sarabande*[46] and those of Bononcini's "hybrid" type.

This stems from the reiterations of the feminine cadence (which may ppear in any or all of the even-numbered trochaic bars). It is heightened y the "pathetic" trick of the repetition of the final phrase "piano," which ve have already discussed. This practice, the *petite reprise* of the French nodels (not written out but indicated by a *segno*), sometimes extends in ononcini to the whole *sarabande,* alternate phrases in "echo" (*forte* and iano), as in BV: 20. The "echo" is carried to yet another level ("forte," piano," "più piano" and "pianino") in BV: 17, a sure sign of the affective nd pathetic sentiment of these dances.

Details of the *courante,* the dominant ternary dance type, are inevitably ssimilated by the *sarabande,* most especially the cadential hemiola. By the nd of the century the confusion between the fast types of the *sarabande* nd the *courante* is complete. In England the edition (*ca.* 1700) of Bononini's op. XII calls some *courantes* "sarabandes," and the one genuine *arabanda* of the opus is called an "air."[47]

The *giga* introduces the comic element into the dance repertoire of the eventeenth century. Brought from England to Germany during the sixeenth- and early seventeenth-century vogue for English comedians at Geran courts, its character and function was that of a sartiric or parodic ehicle for a solo dancer—a clown.[48]

That it retains these characteristics and—as an improvised solo step lance—the lowest ceremonial rank until Bononcini's time is clear from epys' diary:

October 11, 1665.
"...and mighty merry we were; but especially at Mercer's [his maidservant] lancing a jigg, which she does the best I ever did see, having the most natural vay of it, and keeps time the most perfectly I ever did see."

March 2, 1669.
"We fell to dancing and continued...till two in the morning, the musick eing Greeting and another most excellent violin, and theorbo, the best in town. nd so with mighty mirth, and pleased with their dancing of jigs afterwards everal of them, and among others Betty Turner who did it mighty prettily...."

46. This is explicit in the performance directions of Lully and Couperin. See also chap. ix, . 18 *supra.*

47. See *supra* p. 61, item 22.

48. The connection between the *giga* and its descendants, the tap and clog dancing of wentieth-century vaudeville uses, is too obvious to insist upon.

The *gigue* is a late-comer to the *sonata da camera.* Bononcini's *gighe* (op. III, "Allemande, Correnti, and Gighe," 1667) appear to be among the first violin *gighe* printed in Italy. Uccellini published no works in this form. Vitali's first *gighe* appear in his op. IV, 1668, and those of Cazzati are found in op. L of 1669. In Bononcini's work[49] the *gighe* remain optional additions except for three cases where they form the initial member of the suite, and replace the *aria* or *balletto* as an alternate stylization. With these exceptions they are grouped by themselves and not paired with other dances, as in BII.

Originally (in the late sixteenth century) the rhythms of the English jig were binary[50] with dotted figures that could be interpreted by the dancer in either a grotesque or lilting character. As developed in Italy (*giga*) and France (*gigue*), two types emerge.[51] The Italian "violin" *giga*[52] is simply an alternate stylization in rapid compound meter of the form (two periods) and melodic material of the *aria, balletto,* or *allemanda.*

Thus it is an application of the old variation principle by which the several dances were derived from basic "unstylized" melodic raw material, *air* or *aria.* Its evolution from a way of dancing rather than from a fixed form is clear from early sixteenth-century English precedent.[53]

The typical rhythmic pattern (12/8) of the Italian *giga* with its "rolling" and lilting figures

is doubtless of popular origin. It may be a legacy from the old *saltarello* whose patterns survived and were transmitted in the Italian *corrente* and attain new spontaneity and "drive" in the *giga.*[54] The dynamic increment of the reiterated "rolling" figures (satisfactory instrumentalism for hand and bow) is heightened by the "arcades" of melodic and rhythmic sequence typical of other Italianate forms.

In its mid-seventeenth-century French version[55] the *gigue* is in rapid ternary (3/4), not compound, meter. The affective "dotting" of the values is also

49. As with keyboard composers.

50. Ecorcheville, *VSO,* I, 67 ff.

51. In German keyboard music all three types remain distinguishable.

52. So characteristic of the violin is the Italian *giga* that much ink has been wasted trying to derive the name from the germanic term for the instrument (*Geige*). The English considered the *giga* (when imported by them in the late seventeenth century) to be of Italian origin.

53. Jeffrey Pulver, "The Ancient Dance Forms," *Proceedings of the Musical Association* 1913-1914, p. 81, cites examples of the "Jig-Alman" in keyboard sources.

54. This ancestry is borne out by the fact that it was possible in the English editions of Bononcini's op. XII (London, *ca.* 1700?) for the final *corrente,* BXII: 24, to be retitled "Gighia" and "Jigga."

55. Ecorcheville, *VSO,* II, 154.

present here in the characteristic rhythms: 3/4 ♩. ♪ ♩ | ♩. ♪ ♩ | ♩. ♪ ♩ | 𝅗𝅥. |. The persuasive and obvious logic of sequential repetition is avoided, and the period is a simple melodic span. The melodic style is, however, very instrumental and marked by wide intervals. The spontaneous Italian "lilt" is lacking, and the manner is severe and heavier, tending toward the ardent, not to say truculent.

Bononcini offers us examples of both types. BII: 3 and 4 are both of the Italian order. BII: 6 and 7 are, although not specifically so designated, in the French manner. In BIII: 5 and 6 the form is treated contrapuntally with the four parts entering in imitation, although the bass, as usual, must also support the other entrances until its own arrives. BIII: 7 (3/4), ("Prestissimo") offers an example of a "hybrid" in which the Italianate sequential element is added to the French formula. Also, as often in the *brandi* and *corrente* "in stil Francese," the keyboard *basso continuo* is silent, the part being marked, "B.C. Tacet."

BIV: 13 (12/8) is an instance of the assimilation of the "dotted" figure of the French style by the Italian *giga*.

Chapter XI. The *Sonata da Chiesa:* Forms, Antecedents and Precedents

In the same way that the *sonata da camera* reflects the ritualistic uses of dancing and dance music in the secular atmosphere of court and social life, the history of the *sonata da chiesa* and its immediate ancestor, the instrumental *canzona,* is that of the increasing use of concerted instrumental music in Italian churches in the course of the seventeenth century.

Just as the early collections of concerted madrigals and vocal music for secular use had included instrumental works as *divertissements,*[1] so had the collections of concerted vocal church works—masses and motets—provided the instrumental works—*canzone* and *sonate*—which had become customary ornaments of the service. This development is easily traceable in the titles and contents of the numerous such collections published from the 1590's onward.

To cite only a few typical examples:

Sacrae Symphoniae, Ioannis Gabrielii . . . Senis, 7, 8, 10, 12, 14, 15 & 16, Tam vocibus, Quam Instrumentis. Editio Noua . . . *Venetiis,* Apud Angelum Gardanum, M. D. XCVII. (Sartori, *BMI,* p. 95.)

. . . *Concerti Ecclesiastici* . . . per sonare nell'Organo ò altri Instrumenti. *Con Una Canzone A Quattro. Di Aloisio Balbi Veneto . . . Libro Primo. In Venetia. Appresso Alessandro Raverii.* MDCVI. (Sartori, BMI, p. 140.)

Concerti raccolti dal Molto Reuerende *Don Francesco Lucino* . . . di diuersi Eccellenti Autori . . . con una Messa, due Magnificat, le Letanie della Beata Vergine, e dodeci Canzoni per sonare . . . *In Milano,* Appresso Filippo Lomazzo, 1617. . . . (Sartori, *BMI,* p. 231.)

Primo Libro Delle Messe E Motetti Concertato Con Basso E Due Tenori Nell'-Organo. Opera XXXXII. *Di D. Adriano Banchieri Abate Olivetano* . . . In Venetia, Appresso Alessandro Vincenti. M D C XX. . . . (Sartori, *BMI,* p. 268. The "Tavola delle Messe" lists three masses, three motets and a *sonata*—"Due Violini e Trombone sopra l'aria del Gran Duca.")

Messe, Magnificat et Motetti Concertati e correnti Falsi Bordoni con Gloria Patri e Canzon Francese . . . *Di Francesco Bellazzi* . . . Opera Ottaua . . . *Canto* . . . Primo Choro. *Stampa Del Gardano. In Venetia* M.DC.XXVIII. Appresso Bartolomeo Magni. . . . (Sartori, *BMI,* p. 319.)

1. Biagio Marini, "Madrigali et Symfonie. . . ." The *Tavola* contains three examples; see Sartori, *BMI,* p. 244.

Canto Primo, O Tenore Cinque Messe A Due Voci, Accommodate in modo, che da ogni sorte di voce diuersamente possono esser cantate; con li suoi auertimenti. Et Vniti due *Motetti* à Voce Sola per tutte le parti . . . Con Otto Sonate per gl'Instrumenti, Bassi, & Soprani . . . *Di Tomaso Cecchino Veronese. Opera Vigesima Terza . . . In Venetia,* Appresso Alessandro Vincenti. MDCXXVIII. (Sartori, *BMI,* p. 323.)

Also, collections of organ works for church use—versets and responses, etc. —contain *canzone francese* "per concerto," such as:

Di Gio. Maria Trabaci . . . Il Secondo Libro de Ricercate, & altri varij Capricci, Con Cento Versi sopra li Otto finali Ecclesiastici per rispondere in tutti i Diuini Officji . . . *In Napoli,* Nella Stamparia di Gio: Giacomo Carlino. 1615. (Sartori, *BMI,* p. 208, which lists in the Tavola, among numerous items, a *Canzone Francesa* [*sic*] "per concerto de Violini, o Viole ad Arco.")

Collections devoted entirely to concerted *canzone francese,* presumably for church use, are also frequent. For example:

. . . Di Tarquinio Merula Cremonese *Il Primo Libro Delle Canzoni* A Quattro voci per sonare Con ogni sorte de strumenti Musicali Con Il Basso Generale. Aggiuntoui due Alemane, & una Corrente . . . Stampa Del Gardano In Venetia M DC XV. Appresso Bartholomeo Magni.

Just as the ubiquitous printed tracts and sermons of the period represented an aspect of "serious" literature, the *canzona* and *sonata da chiesa,* removed from functional use, become by extension "serious" chamber music. These collections were also certainly used in this fashion as chamber music for the pleasure of performers.

The liturgical uses of instrumental music, both for the organ (alternating with, or replacing, the choir) and concerted (for highly developed musical items, entries, exits, etc.), are shown in such works as Adriano Banchieri's practical manual for church organists, *L'Organo Suonarino,* which went through seven editions and revisions from 1605 to 1638. The first edition[2] contains organ versions of many liturgical items, including those of the ordinary of the mass: *Kyrie, Credo,* etc. The *Tavola* also lists motets and hymns as well as *suonate.* The *suonate* given in "spartiture a Quattro" (i.e., for either concerted or organ solo use) are further variously classified as "Fugue," "Concerto Enarmonico," and "In Aria Francese" and also as

2. *L'Organo Suonarino Di Adriano Banchieri Bolognese.* Entro il quale si pratica quanto occorrer suole à gli Suonatori d'Organo, per alternar Corista à gli Canti fermi in tutte le feste, & solennità dell'anno . . . Nel Primo si concerta la Santa Messa, nel Secondo gli Salmi Vesperini, nel Terzo gli Hinni, nel Quarto gli Magnificat, et nel Quinto le Sacre Lodi di Maria Vergine, Insieme vinti Suonate in spartitura . . . *Opera Terza Decima* . . . In Venetia appresso Ricciardo Amadino. 1605. See Sartori, *BMI,* pp. 129-130.

"Ingresso d'un ripieno," "In Dialogo," and "Capriccio." In the fourth section, devoted to the *Magnificat,* the *Tavola* includes *capricci* (per 2 str.) and two *ripieni* (per 4 str.) "per Deo Gratias."

These are the items to which Banchieri has reference in his treatise on the organ, *Conclusioni nel suono dell' organo,* p. 20, where he says: "Of the *Magnificat* play the first and last verses, . . . and after the said canticle there is played a *canzona francese* or motet, as preferred" (*Del Magnificat tocca il primo, e ultimo verso . . . & dopo il detto cantico suonarsi una francese overo motteto come più piace.*)

Banchieri further describes the uses of the organ in the service, uses which increasingly extend to the *concertante* instrumental body as the century progresses and which have their ultimate expression in the *concertante* mass. He says:

Ninth Conclusion Explained

Regarding the Mass sung in alternation with the organ on the *canto fermo*. . . On all feasts and Sundays of the year the Organ is played in Church . . . and here we shall treat of that which the organist should play in the Mass on the prescribed *Canto fermo.*

On all Sundays of the year, after tierce an Antiphon is sung as an Introit which begins *Asperges me Domine,* and when it is finished and repeated, the Introit [itself] is sung, to which, when the versicle *Sicut erat* a *ripieno* is played which serves as a reiteration of the Introit alternating with the Choir five responses to the Kyrie and Christe briefly.

The Gloria is intoned by the Priest with which alternation is made.

When the Epistle has been sung a *ripieno* or a *fugha* is played at [one's] discretion.

When the Alleluia and its verse have been sung one responds with the second Alleluia.

Regarding the Credo we will speak later in another place.

When the priest has sung *Oremus,* one plays until the prayers are over.

For the Sanctus one plays twice briefly.

For the Elevation [of the Host] one plays gravely, to induce devotion.

After the Pax Domini one plays a moment of [for?] the Agnus Dei.

When the second Agnus Dei has been sung by the Choir one plays a [*canzona*] *francese* or *aria Musicale.*

Special Notice

On Holy Thursday when the *Gloria in excelsis* has been intoned, a *ripieno allegro* is played, together with the bells.

On Holy Saturday when the Gloria has been intoned one responds as above. One does not play after the Epistle nor is the Credo sung. For the offertory and Sanctus one plays as has already been described, and similarly for the Elevation (there is no Agnus Dei).

After the Pax Domini one plays until the priest has finished communion.

Afterward the response attached to the Mass is sung by the Choir and one plays after the psalm *Laudate Domini omnes Gentes.*

For the canticle, *Magnificat,* one plays responses in the eighth tone, and at the end a *francescina allegra* [small *canzona*] and *Ite Missa est.*

The Credo of the Mass should be sung by everyone together for the greater devotion of the faithful . . . however, it is sung alternately with the organ at such times as when the organ & Organist respond with voices or when the choir is small in number when, while the Organ is played a Clerk reads the versicle in an understandable voice, notice that at the *Et Incarnatus est* one plays for the choir to sing it, for the genuflection.[3]

In addition to the evidence supplied by chapter records[4] which describe instrumental bodies retained by large churches, Banchieri's own remarks show that the organist was expected to do both solo and improvisational playing and also to form part of the *concerto* (which, it would seem, was gaining in importance).[5] Banchieri says:

There remains at the end the *Basso seguente* (which is so much in use). But by this we do not wish to mean that it is a thing easily done; many Organists of today succeed excellently in concerted playing, but persuaded by this vain-glory or being competent in ensemble, do not care to further exert themselves in *fantasia* [improvisation?] and *Spartiture* [score reading]. . . .[6]

An interesting collection of church music, both vocal and instrumental, which shows very specific uses of instrumental forms is *Choro Apparato Musicale Di Messa, Canzoni, Motetti, & Letanie della Beata Vergine.*[7] The *Tavola* shows:

3. Banchieri, *Conclusioni,* pp. 22-23; see Appendix "B" for complete Italian text.

4. Pancaldi-Roncaglia, *MDM VIII,* p. 209.

5. The publication of such works as *Del Sonare Sopra 'L Basso Con Tutti Li Stromenti* . . . E dell'uso loro nel Conserto . . . Agostino Agazzari . . . Siena Appresso Domenico Falcini . . . Anno 1607 (see Sartori, *BMI,* p. 146) shows the importance of this aspect of the training and activity of the church organist.

6. "Resta per ultimo il Basso seguente (il quale tanto e in vso) Ma cosi non fosse egli vero, per essere cosa facile da praticarsi, molti Organisti al giorno d'hoggi riescono eccellenti nel concerto, ma vinti da tale vanagloria di essere sicuri i concerto, non curano più d'affaticarsi in fantasia, & spartiture. . . ." Banchieri, *Conclusioni,* p. 24.

7. Opera Quinta. D'Amante Franzoni Servita . . . Libro Primo . . . In Venetia, Appresso Ricelardo Amadino. 1613. See Sartori, *BMI,* p. 188.

Motetti a otto.

Duo Seraphim 15
Cantantibus Organis 16
Concerto a cinque da suonarsi con quattro Tromboni cioè Tre Bassi, un Tenore, & il Soprano sempre canta. (Sancta Maria). 17
Catharine Virgo a otto. 18
Letanie della Beata Vergine a otto. 20[8]

Similarly, the publication of Milanuzzi's *Armonia Sacra Di Concerti, Messa & Canzoni*[9] shows specific uses of concerted *canzoni* and *concerti* for designated positions in the service. The *Tavola* lists:

Concerto A 5.	Per l'Introito.	1
Messa Liquide perle Amor A 5.		2
Canzon A 5. detta la Zorzi.	Per l'Epistola. (per 6 strum.: 2 violini, viola, ten. basso e organo)	5
Concerto A 5.	Per l'Offertorio.	10
Concerto à due Canti, ò Tenori.	Per l'Eleuatione.	12
Canzon A 5. detta la Riatelli.	Per il Post Comunio (per 6 strum.)	14
Canzon A 2. alla Bastarda	Per il Trôbone, e Violino Per il Deo Gratias. (a pag. 16: La Guaralda di P. A. Mariani. Per Violino, Trombone e B. per l'Org.)[10]	16

Frescobaldi's celebrated and unquestionably influential publication, *Fiori Musicali Di Diverse Compositioni,*[11] is also such a collection and includes *toccate* "avanti la Messa" and a *Tocata Cromaticá* "per le levetation [of the Host]," organ settings of mass movements, Kyrie and Christe, and *canzone* "Dopo la Pistola" and "Dopo il post Comune." There is evidence[12] that the Gradual, Alleluia, and Offertory were often replaced by instrumental *sonate.* That the Credo was sometimes not sung but read to the accompaniment of instrumental music (organ improvisation?) is clear from Banchieri's instructions.

8. *Ibid.*
9. *Ibid.*, p. 281.
10. *Ibid.*, p. 282.
11. . . . Toccate, Kirie, Canzoni Capricci E Recercari in Partitura A Quattro Utili Per Sonatori Autore Girolamo Frescobaldi Organista Di S. Pietro Di Roma. Opera Duodecima . . . In Venetia, Appresso Alessandro Vincenti. MDCXXXV. See Sartori, *BMI,* p. 344.
12. Reviewed by P. Wagner, "Die Konzertierende Messe in Bologna," *Festschrift . . . H. Kretschmar* (Leipzig, 1918), p. 165.

The original position of the concerted fugal *canzona* in the service was following the Epistle ("Dopo la Pistola") associated with the musical high point of the mass, the Gradual (antiphon). This was, in the Baroque period, often a concerted motet[13] for which the *canzona* served as prelude or, when singers were not present, as replacement.

However, as the cited examples show, *canzone* and *sonate* were also used in other ritual positions and functions to articulate the form of services—vespers, offices, and litanies—as well as in the mass itself. These uses are notably in the function of entries[14] or Introit (*Intrada-Ripieno*),[15] and exits, "Dopo il Post Communio" and (*Ripieno*) "per il Deo Gratias."[16] Also the expressive type of toccata incorporating suspensions (*ligature*), chromaticisms, (*durezze*), and moving basses, as well as such overtly affective elements as "tremolo" and "echo"[17] (used for the meditative moment of the Elevation of the Host), originally for the organ, became a function of the concertante group.[18]

The typical stylizations of these musical functions—*ripieno* and *toccata*—are thus assimilated to the basic *canzona*[19] elements. The result is a composite form, a sequence of functional liturgical items in which the same contrasts and opposition of form, style, sonorities, and rhythms which articu-

13. Otto Ursprung, "Die Katholische Kirchenmusik," *HBMW,* IX, 300.

14. The parallel ritual functions served by the *entrée, balletto, allemande,* and *aria* of the *sonata da camera.*

15. See Ursprung, "Die Katholische Kirchenmusik," *HBMW,* IX, 300. See also Cazzati's *Mass,* op. XXIV and Perti's (16) *Sinfonie,* which are specifically called "Sinfonia da suonarsi avante la Messa" and "Sinfonia avanti il Chirie." And see "Archivio di S. Petronio," *Bolletino del Assoziazione dei Musicologi Italiani,* comp. Alfredo Bonora (Bologna: Zerbini and Fresching, 1913).

16. See Banchieri, *Conclusioni,* as well as the quotation given on page 126 of this chapter.

17. These two effects, both based on tectonic spatiality, are of course typically Baroque "pathetic" items. The "artificial" echo is known to the sonata from the onset, being used as a device in the celebrated "Sonata pian e forte" of Gabrieli. The tremolo (with suspensions) is an attempt to imitate in smaller space the shimmering effects of the play of harmony in a resonant cavity, such as that of Saint Mark's in Venice. They are the musical counterpart of the innumerable "perspective" ceilings of Jesuit churches.

The tremolo—an effect of the bow (see article "Tremolo" in Walther's *Lexicon* and p. 79 *supra*) produced by rearticulating the tone within the bow stroke—was one of the traditional *affetti* of the early Italian violin school, e.g., that of Biagio Marini. Its dramatic possibilities were realized by Monteverdi (with whom Marini had been associated at Mantua) in *Il Combattimento di Tancredi e Clorinda.* Its appearance here is but one of the details of the penetration of the church style by overtly affective instrumentalism which gains momentum throughout the century.

18. Gabrieli, *op. cit.* See also Sartori, *BMI,* p. 97, and Frescobaldi, *Fiori Musicali,* p. 9 and Gio. Battista Riccio, *Il Terzo Libro Delle Divine Lodi Musicali* (Venetia: Gardano, 1620) as cited in Sartori, *BMI,* p. 260, where we find *canzone* "in Ecco" and "con il Tremolo," and even "in Ecco con il Tremolo."

19. The designations *canzona* and *sonata* were interchangeably used, but in terms of its complete evolution these characteristic accretions to the *canzona* must be regarded as the basis of the distinction. This is clearly seen in later uses as, for example, Purcell, who uses the term *canzona* to designate the fugal sections of his "Sonnatas."

late secular ritual in the *sonata da camera* are at the service of liturgical ritual in the *sonata da chiesa*.[20] In general aesthetic terms, the schematic treatment of affective and sententious elements, usually invoking powerful means of contrast, is a truly Baroque feature. The typical tendency to ornament and emphasize the cadential "joints," the points of contact of the larger formal elements, first by improvised and then by standardized ornament (irregular outline, tectonic tension) is of course part of the very growth process of the Baroque style itself.

These ritualistic and affective additions to the concerted *canzona* become usual in the 1630's. Their position and nature show their origins to lie in the functional *ripieno* (homophonic manner) and in the expressive *toccata* (*tremolo,* suspensions, and "moving" bass). They are frequent in both organ and concerted works of Frescobaldi and in so typical a work as Tarquino Merula's *Canzone,* Libro II (1639). They are, significantly, less frequent in Merula's earlier *Canzone,* Libro I (1615). By the 1630's the *canzona,* built up in motet fashion on the principles of variation and parody typical of the last decades of the sixteenth century, revealed a strong tendency to devolve, in the *sonata da chiesa,*[21] into forms of fewer, larger sections.

The typical form of the mid-seventeenth-century (Merula) *canzona* "proto-sonata" may be schematically represented as A*, B, x, A, A*, with "A" and "B" as the original *canzona* elements and "x" representing the expressive *toccata* or *ripieno.* And, where

"A" is a worked-out fugal movement in fast binary (C 4/4) meter, usually in traditional and instrumentally effective dactylic and anapestic figures;

"B" is a fugal, imitative, or homophonic (or alternately, imitative and homophonic) movement in ternary meter (3/2) which exhibits traditional iambic and trochaic figures;[22]

20. Questions as to the precise uses of the various component elements in a service inevitably arise. Were the various sections of the *sonate* played piecemeal as functional music? The several movements, together with a few organ responses, would serve for the functions of a low (spoken) mass in which brevity was a virtue. In this way the musical component of the mass could be furnished by three instrumentalists without singers. Also the concerted mass distributes the several elements in this fashion (see Cazzati, op. 24). Or was an entire sonata performed as the Gradual item as a prelude or substitute for a motet, and in other places in the services? This would indicate a long service. The inconsistencies of usage with regard to length of movements, cadences, etc., offer no satisfactory clues; it seems probable that usage was adapted to the size and importance of the occasion.

21. However the multi-section (Flick-Kanzone, "Quilt Canzona") principle does not disappear. Frescobaldi fluctuates between the two types and Corelli includes a "patchwork" or "quilt" canzona in his *sonate da chiesa* of op. III (no. 12).

22. These, with their variants, have been related to the *gaillard* and even to the *courante* just as the rhythms of "A" have been traced—with perhaps more reason—to the original stylization of the *chanson* as a *pavane.* However, it would be more proper to refer the resemblances to the general principles of composition, rhythmic stylization, variation, parody, and contrast generally prevalent in the entire period in both church works (including the mass

"x" is an "expressive/affective" prelude or interlude (*intrada ripieno* or *toccata*), homophonic, or with *tremolo,* suspensions, etc.;

"A*" is a (shorter) recapitulation of "A," the asterisk denoting (as in subsequent schematic representations) thematic relationship or (as here) identity.[23]

Cazzati, whose works illustrate in form and title the definitive transition from *canzona* to *sonata,* uses such affective *toccata* and *ripieno* elements freely. Like Frescobaldi in organ *canzone,* he frequently introduces the opening fugal movement by a *ripieno* "Intrada" in homophonic, monumental "lapidary" *conductus* style. He often includes, like Merula, an expressive section in sententious harmony and the "echo" itself is found even within the "canzona" ("A") movements.

The variety of Cazzati's formal disposition of these elements also suggests his transitional, not to say, experimental position. In op. VIII he uses, in the *canzona* "La Galeazza," the sequence x*, A*, B, A. In the sonatas of op. XVIII he uses A*, x, B* ("La Ferdinanda") and x, A, B, x, A ("La Rosetta"). In op. XXXV, sonata "La Casala" (see supplement), Cazzati combines structural and affective elements in a more plastic way, using the athematic *tremolo,* echo, and the sequential *perfidia*[24] in conjunction to bring to an effective close what had begun as a *canzona* "A" movement, a powerful device used by both Bononcini and Purcell.

It is also in the work of Cazzati (as both vocal and instrumental composer) that we may, perhaps, best observe the stylization of the various sections of the *canzona* "proto-sonata" and the mutual interaction of their liturgical implications, which is the source of their meaning. Cazzati begins his *concertante* Mass, op. XXIV[25] with a *Sinfonia,* clearly an instrumental *ripieno-intrada-introito,* which lends its rhythmic coloration to the *tutti* opening of the following Kyrie. The *Sinfonia* is in the precise form (a [I], a [V], b [—I]) of its counterpart in many a sonata or *canzona;* for example, Cazzati's own "La Malvasia" of op. XXXV (see supplement). The Kyrie itself (see supplement), fugal, with a short initial *ripieno,* were it reduced to instruments,[26] would be indistinguishable from one of Cazzati's own comparable *canzona* ("A") movements.

---

itself) and dance music. The contrast of binary and ternary meters was also inherent in the Italian popular vocal forms, which are the equivalents of the French *chanson.*

23. This *ritornello*-like recapitulation is a typical feature of the mid-century *canzona* "proto-sonata," possibly related to liturgical requirements. (Is it for the "Deo Gratias" which is traditionally an echo of the "Kyrie"?) It is not a feature of the Gabrieli *canzone,* nor does it appear in Corelli's *sonate da chiesa.* However, see the article "Canzone" in the Walther *Lexicon.*

24. *Messa, e Salmi a tre voci . . . con violini . . .,* op. XXIV.

25. As is also the case in Bach's B-Minor Mass.

26. See Banchieri's description, pp. 125-126 *supra.*

The instrumental *ritornello* (played between Kyrie-Christe-Kyrie) exhibits all the characteristics of the affective *toccata* (homophonic basis, contrapuntal formulae, suspensions, etc.) which we have seen to be typical of such a section ("x") of the *canzona* "proto-sonata." The choral Christe illustrates the basic features of rhythmic contrast we have already mentioned as being fundamental to the formal disposition and methods of composition of the period. It is set in 3/2, in a rhythmic vocabulary which places it in precisely the same relationship to the preceding Kyrie as the ternary ("B") section of the typical mid-century *canzona* stands in relation to the opening fugue ("A").

The *tremolo,* characteristic of the affective *toccata* designed to inspire meditation at the moment of the Elevation of the Host, is used in the setting (*tutti*) of the ideologically related liturgical text from the Credo—"Et Incarnatus est...." This is stylized as a moment of choral recitative[27] in block harmony to which the resemblance of the *tremolo* is obvious.[28] These examples could be multiplied at length with cases drawn from many vocal works—motets, *concerti Sacri,* etc.,[29] as well as masses[30]—of the period. It must suffice here to set forth and illustrate the principle of transference of significance and aesthetic symbol in the stylistic syntax and formal arrangement of the *sonata da chiesa.*

27. See quotation from Banchieri's *Conclusioni,* n. 3, this chapter, and exx. (Cazzati, Colonna) in supplement.

28. See Cazzati, "La Casala," in supplement.

29. The "cross reference" between the sonata and the mass is inherent from the beginnings of the *concertante* style itself. The *concertante* Mass of Gio. Gabrieli (1597) (See P. Wagner, *Geschichte der Messe* [Leipzig, 1913], p. 413) already contains in its opening the affective elements which are to be developed in the *sonata da chiesa*: sententious opening motivic figure, "echo" and imitation, florid passage to the cadence.

30. See G. P. Colonna's *Missa Prima* (*incipits*) in supplement and J. S. Bach, *Mass in B-Minor.*

Chapter XII. The *Sonate da Chiesa* of G. M. Bononcini

1. FORM

Bononcini's *sonate da chiesa* are contained in his op. I, *Prima Fruitti del Giardino Musicali,*[1] op. VI, *Sonate da Chiesa a due Violini,* and op. IX, *Trattenimenti Musicali* (specifically called "sonate da Chiesa").

Bononcini describes his *sonate da chiesa* of op. VI as an "explication" of his treatise on counterpoint. The continued application during the seventeenth century of contrapuntal science to instrumental idiom had as a result the more extended development of thematic materials, so that the sonata, consisting of fewer and longer movements, transcended the anticlimactic sectionalism of its ancestor, the *canzona.* The assimilation of a variety of contrasting expressive elements also made possible a more complete and convincing artistic entity which went on to embrace the element of instrumental virtuosity and overt expressiveness (*affetti*).

Bononcini's disposition of formal elements shows him to be less experimental than Cazzati. He based his procedure on the outline of the *canzona*–"proto-sonata" characteristic of the Merula epoch and shows a tendency to vary and shorten that five section model—A, B, x, A, A*—in the direction of what is regarded as the "classical" model of Corelli: x, A, x, B.

Schematically represented, Bononcini's formal disposition of the elements we have described in chapter XI is as follows:[2]

Opus I						Tonality
1	A*,	B,	x,	A*		"G" (—)
2	A*,	B,	A,	A*		"G" (—)
3	A,	B,	A,	A		"G" (—)
4	A*,	B,	x,	A*		C (—)
5	A*,	x*,	B*,	x,	A*	F (1♭)
6	x,	A*,	B,	x,	A*	"d" (—)
7	A,	B,	x,	A		"g" (1♭)
8	A*,	B*,	x,	A		"g" (1♭)
9	A,	x,	B,			"B♭" (1♭)

1. The *sonate* of op. I are not specifically thus designated but, like those of Purcell, must be so regarded on the basis of internal evidence.
2. For key to symbols, see *supra,* pp. 130-131, n. p. 92, and p. 152 *infra.*

10	A*,	B,	x,	A,	A*	"E♭" (1♭)
11	A*,	B,	x,	A,	A*	C (—)
12	A*,	x,	A*			F (1♭)

Opus VI						Tonality
1	A,	B,	x,	A		"C" (—) "del Undecimo Tuono nelle sue corde naturale"
2	A,	B,	x,	A		"F" (1♭) "del Duodecimo Tuono una quinta più basso"
3	x,	A,	B,	x,	A	"B♭" (2♭) "del Undecimo Tuono, un Tuono più basso"
4	A,	B,	x,	A		"D" (2♯) "del Undecimo Tuono, un Tuono più alto"
5	A*,	B*,	x,	A		"A" (2♯) "del Ottavo Tuono, un Tuono più alto"
6	A,	B,	x,	A		e (1♯) "del Decimo Tuono una quarta più basso"
7	A*,	B,	x,	A*		b (2♯) "del Nono Tuono un Tuono più alto"
8	A,	B,	x,	A		"G" (—) "del Ottava Tuono nelle sue corde naturale"
9	A,	B,	x,	A		"d" (—) "del Primo Tuono nelle sue corde naturale"
10	A,	B,	x,	A		"c" (2♭) "del Primo Tuono un Tuono più basso"
11	A,	B,	x,	A		"g" (1♭) "del Secondo Tuono una quarta più alto"
12	A*,	B*,	x,	A		"E♭" (2♭) "del Duodecimo Tuono una terza più alto"[3]

While the *sonate* of these two *opere,* I and VI, show consistency of arrangement on the *canzona-sonata* prototype model, the five *sonate da chiesa* of op. IX exhibit considerably more variety in the distribution of principal elements:

Opus IX					Tonality
1	x,	B,	x,	A	"a" (—)
2	A,	B,	x,	A	"d" (—)
3	A,	x,	B		C (—)
4	x,	B,	x,	A	"E♭" (2♭)
5	x,	B,	A		"c" (2♭)

3. The designation of tonality according to the system of eight church modes (as amplified to twelve during the sixteenth century in such works as Glareanus' *Dodecachordon* and Zarlino's *Istitutioni Harmoniche*) carries out Bononcini's explanation of the system in *Il Musico Prattico* (pp. 121 ff.), of which op. VI was intended as "explication." See *infra* pp. 151-152 ff.

The form in general "tightens"; the ritornello-like "A*" disappears, as does the principle of thematic reference among movements occasionally found in the earlier works. The expressive and sententious homophonic (*intrada-conductus*) elements, "x," are developed into larger independent movements, i.e., complete aáb forms. These homophonic elements are also appended to the fugal *canzona* sections as cadential features, "decorations" of architectonic divisions where their sonorous possibilities and tonal richness (chromaticism) are a welcome means of bringing the fugue to an impressive close. Occasionally, on the other hand, the properly homophonic materials of these ("x") sections are subject to imitative motivic development.[4] This is a natural tendency for Bononcini, the contrapuntal virtuoso. Also, the penetration of this very section of the *sonata da chiesa* is testimony to the increasing force of systematic contrapuntal procedure in instrumental music which we have had occasion to observe in the basic development of the epoch.

Bononcini's last (?) *sonata da chiesa* (B-flat), which appears in the collection of Marino Silvani of 1680,[5] reverts to the earlier model—A*, B, x, A*—complete with thematic identity of first and last sections. Affective devices, including *tremolo,* invade the *canzona* element (A*) and are exploited for cadential, climactic values (as in op. IX).

In only one instance does Bononcini make systematic use of the variation principle (germane, although optional in practice, to the *canzona*). In BI:5 he unites four of the five movements of a sonata by the higher internal organization of the thematic transformation, A*, x*, B*, x, A*. As in the *sonata da camera,* Bononcini in his *sonate da chiesa,* rejects the variation forms as a general practice,[6] and this sonata represents in Bononcini's work the tradition of the systematic variation or "transformation" principle. Elsewhere (except in the relationship between "A" and "A*" movements which illustrates the principle of reprise or *ritornello,* rather than that of variation), the thematic materials of the several sections are usually diverse, freely derived from traditional stylizations and contrasts, and are complementary rather than cumulative in effect.

In the exceptional case, BI: 5, the bass of the initial ("A*") movement is, in a variant, used for the upper parts of the following ("x") movement (bars 29 ff.). The relationship is, appropriately, ***not*** explicit, as the two movements

4. BIX: 1, 2, 5.

5. *Scelta Della Suonate, A due Violini, con il Basso Continuo per l'Organo, Raccolte De diuersi Eccelenti Autori. . . .* In Bologna per Giacomo Monti. 1680. It may be an earlier work, see n. p. 62.

6. Although BI: 3 has *ostinato* passages.

are *canzona* and non-*canzona* elements, respectively. In the third movement (B*, bars 46 ff.) the essential thematic material and the complete working-out of the *concertante* violin parts undergo transformation into ternary meter over a new bass to become the second *canzona* element ("B"). The fourth movement is a non-*canzona* element ("x") and is (properly) not thematically related to the preceding. The final section ("A*") is a typical reprise where the material appears essentially in its original condition to form a close.

Bononcini's procedure in respect to the composition of the principal movements (*canzona;* "A") of his *sonate da chiesa* shows considerable variety in the application of its traditional contrapuntal elements. The treatment of contrapuntal devices (of which exchange between the upper two parts is the most common) varies in formal results between movements that may be properly called "fugal" in conception (as in BVI: 6, bars 66-94) and those best described as "through composed" (as in BI: 2, bars 49-69). In highly developed examples (such as BI: 2 and BVI: 6) Bononcini achieves, within the Italian "trio" style, a synthesis of the essential elements of the true instrumental fugue, including consequential uses of imitation (real and tonal) in a systematic exposition and counter-exposition. He demonstrates as well the plastic, climactic use of sequential episodes[7] based on motivic fragmentation, canon, *stretto,* dominant cycle, and pedal, features which distinguish the fugue from the more schematic *canzona* and the less dynamic *ricercare.*

The details of the treatment of these features in BVI: 6, bars 66 ff. (see also BI: 5, bars 1-26) will serve to illustrate Bononcini's general procedure in such movements:

Bar	
66-69	exposition
70-72	canon in *stretto* (pedal)
72-75	counter-exposition (parts exchanged)
75-85	sequential episode
86-88	recapitulation of original exposition
88-91	sequential episode; *stretto*
92-94	"Adagio" closing imitations; suspension, cadential formula.

Such movements are, of course, the consequence of application of systematic contrapuntal procedures, economy and consistency of material. They represent the style of evolution of the Church *canzona* as strict, "serious,"

7. See p. 23 *supra* regarding Bendinelli.

"learned" music beyond the reproach of secularism and, despite organic and expressive increments upon the earlier severity, suitable for ritual use.

Opus IX represents a considerable advance in scope and technique over op. VI. The balance of formal elements is more precise and assured and the individual movements are more concise and cosequential and less discursive. In addition to the Basso Continuo, a separate (string) bass part ("Violone") is provided, which moves with considerable rhythmic independence, forming a kind of heterophony with the *continuo*. This means that the bass participates in the fugal treatment with consequences for both form and syntax.

In such movements as BIX: 1, bars 60 ff., Bononcini approaches even more closely the self-contained fugue. Here the keyboard part is a *basso seguente,* so that the fugal entrances are genuine and the true bass entrance (for the string-bass) is a *concertante* imitation of the same importance and extent as those of the violin parts.

Bononcini's contrapuntal resources permit him to extend these "canzona" movements to an average length of some twenty-four bars (Allegro 4/4). This dimension places him midway between the stage of development achieved by Cazzati (eighteen to twenty bars) and that normal with Corelli (thirty bars).

Bononcini's natural contrapuntal predisposition and discipline are expressed in the relative economy and "concentric" quality of these ("A") movements. A sure sense of increasing tension and climactic sense (often lacking or interrupted in his contemporaries and predecessors) brought about by the knowing use of sequence and *stretto* and animates the closing moments of the movement.

The close of fugal movements themselves show, above all, the calculated effort to bring the movement to an effective, well-marked close at a high point of contrapuntal and harmonic interest. This trait—together with its concomitant, the plastic, climactic sense—is a distinguishing feature of the later Baroque manner[8] in contrast to the relatively "desultory" and "disappointing" closes of earlier decades.

These cadences are of two general types. The first type is accomplished, as in BI: 2, bars 17-21 ("A") and bars 77-79 ("A*"), and BVI: 6, bars 92-94 ("Adagio"), by brief development of a thematic fragment in *stretto,* canon, or free imitation of considerable ingenuity over a clear cadential formula in the *continuo*. The harmonic rhythm and the actual tempo is at this point

8. Bononcini's style identifies his work as being of the middle Baroque epoch, but the full realization of this climactic feature was denied him by his early death.

characteristically slower than that of the preceding fabric (as in BVI: 6, "Adagio").

The second order of cadence formula, illustrated by BVI: 6, bars 21-25 ("Adagio") and BIX: 1, bars 80-85 ("Adagio e tremolo"), is brought about by a half close (V) or close (I) approached by dominant sequence and at once amplified or balanced by a sententious phrase[9] in which thematic processes are abandoned in favor of the overtly affective materials—the chromaticism, suspensions, *tremolo,* etc.—of the expressive *toccata* ("x") type of movement. These, especially the *tremolo,* tend to play an increasingly large part in the fabric of "A" and "A*" movements; though rare in op. I, it becomes usual and more extended later.

These cadential moments are of considerable harmonic asperity and complexity.[10] The taste for chromaticism shows itself at such cadential places in the alterations of the subdominant function[11] (the "flat sixth before a close" described by Purcell as an earmark of the Italian manner), as well as in intensifications of the dominant. These frequently involve successive chromatic tones cross-relations and tritones (see n. 50, p. 149, also BI: 8), for all of which Bononcini, like Purcell, appears to have had a developed taste. This desire for harmonic intensity goes so far as to combine dominant and subdominant elements in the chord of the diminished seventh[12] as the climactic member.[13]

The cadence in BI: 2, bars 66-69, is also of an affective order; its parallel scales over a pedal resemble a brief, vestigial *perfidia.* This detail, a kind

9. E.g., the freely treated "parallel" sevenths of BIX: 1, bar 82.

10. The resemblance of these cadences in position and rhythmic and tonal distribution to the sententious, aphoristic settings in block style (see Palestrina, *Missa, Inviolata* and *Missa Beata Virgine* [Libro Secondo] and *Missa Ut, Re, Mi, Fa, Sol, La* [Libro Terzo] and Cazzati's op. XXIV of *Et Incarnatus est* and *et Homo Factus est* is too striking to be ignored. Are they an instrumental version of the *ripieno per il genuflessione* customary at this point in the mass, as described by Banchieri, or a suggestive element in an unsung, private mass? See BIX: 5, bar 45, where the text *Et Incarnatus . . .* or *homo factus est* would fit exactly.

11. Visible in BI: 9, bar 35; BVI: 5, bar 28, and BVI: 6, bar 89.

12. As in Bononcini's last *sonata da chiesa* included in the 1680 collection of Silvani-Monti, bar 31.

13. Bononcini, however, despite his taste for penultimate dissonance, rarely (BI: 1, bar 58, and BI: 9, bar 60 and bar 62 being the only instances noted) prescribes the so-called Corelli clash (simultaneous leading tone and anticipation) in church sonatas (although it was within the power and up to the taste of any player to bring it about by free ornamentation; see pp. 77 ff. *supra.*); however, it is everywhere visible in his dance music, the *sonate da camera.* Its significance there is in its presence in French sources; it is frequent in the dance music of the composers for the "Vingt-quatre Violons" (Ecorcheville, *VSO,* Vol. II). Corelli, to whom the device is carelessly attributed, likewise rarely prescribes it in church sonatas but uses it (more sparingly than Bononcini) in *sonate da camera.* Cazzati, ever mindful of effect, writes it in church sonatas of op. XXXV ("La Gonzaga"), and in variants elsewhere.

of measured cadenza in consistent note values, was a favorite of Cazzati (see p. 45 *supra.*) and was to figure in the Torelli concerto.

Another variant of the affective cadence is characteristic of movements based on subjects *à la cornetto* or *à la tromba.* (See BVI: 11, and BVI: 4.) Here the thematic material is reduced by melodic fragmentation virtually to a hocket (idiomatic for the wind instruments to which such subjects refer), which articulates a clear harmonic progression. These hocket-like cadences show signs ("f," "p") of having been executed "in echo" or in *diminuendo* (they all "fall")[14] and may have been intended for a particular liturgical situation where a resounding close was not in order. Or, they may simply represent a reaction to the heavy suspension-laden or trilled cadences which had after all been doing duty since the beginning of the century.

In two cases, BI: 9 and 12, the movement of this general category ("A") is divided by an internal cadence into a bipartite structure. This formal procedure, interesting in view of the later development of the sonata, has a possible precedent in the *capriccio.* Cazzati, in his op. L, "per camera e per chiesa," applies the term *capriccio* to just such a two-part form. The cadences, internal and final (both on the tonic), show the extremely rare instances of Bononcini's use of purely ornamental broken chords (possibly also a legacy from the *capriccio*). But even these small "flourishes," casual in effect, are animated by the imitative principle which maintains the rhythmic interest until the last beat.

The traditional melodic material (subject) of the Venetian *canzona* of the 1590's was characteristically "severe" and "instrumental," based on lively dactylic-anapestic figures with repeated notes suitable for either violins or *cornetti.* This tradition is basic to the *canzona* "proto-sonata." It is respected by Bononcini in many instances, especially in op. VI (BVI: 1, 2, 5), where, in keeping with his explicit title—"Sonate da Chiesa"—and academic intent, he would naturally conform to convention.

In addition to being traditional, the stylization of the melodic material *á la cornetto* (or, properly, *á la tromba*) of Bononcini's op. VI may well be an echo of the uses of the *tromba* in concerted works by Cazzati (as are those of Torelli later) at San Petronio in Bologna. In fact, the use of the *tromba* is a feature of the Bolognese manner itself. Cazzati's op. XXXV bears the title "Sonate a 2, 3, 4 ... con alguni per tromba," and a note in the text says that the *tromba* parts may be played on the violin.[15]

14. BVI: 10. See Praetorius, *Syntagma Musicum* (Wolfenbüttel, 1618), Tomus III, p. 16.

15. Cazzati employs the *tromba* as a *concertante* instrument in alternation with the strings, in effect using the same antiphonal devices and stylizations (and for the same acoustical reasons) which Gabrieli had used in San Marco with *cornetti.* Thus the recrudescence

Despite the forces of tradition, the interaction of instrumental manner and vocal idiom[16] (see p. 133 *supra*) greatly extended the vocabulary of stylized melodic materials and syntactical treatment appropriate for development in the *canzona* and *sonata da chiesa*. This was a natural result of their continual association in *stile concertante* and *canto figurato*.[17] (See Chapter XI, nn. 26, 30, and 31.)

In addition to the mass itself, the *concerto ecclesiastico* and especially the motet with its literary component are the immediate points of contact. Thematic materials—fugal subjects—of vocal derivation are characteristically more cursive and anacrustic in outline than the traditional schematic and thetic Venetian instrumental *canzona* subject. The gradual change from thetic to anacrustic design is a feature of the later phases of the Baroque manner.[18]

A clear example of the interaction between vocal and instrumental idiom is to be seen in the motets for church use by Bononcini's contemporary and distinguished colleague, Colonna.[19] Specifically dedicated to Francesco II d'Este and intended for the same milieu in which Bononcini himself had been working, they may be safely considered to embody current stylistic trends.[20]

---

of the *cornetto-cum-tromba* manner in the string style of the 1670's and 1680's (see Corelli and Purcell) is a kind of "doublet" whereby the original stylization is reinforced in a later evolution. The *cornetto* itself was not yet silent. Bononcini's distinguished colleague, Pietro Degli Antonii—one of the original members of the Accademia Filarmonica in Bologna—was a *cornetto* "*concertista.*" As late as 1680 Marino Silvani included in his collection (along with the last sonata of Bononcini) a sonata by Giovanni Francalanza, "Cornetto nella Steccata di Parma," which, although indicated for two violins, is obviously for the wind instruments. Also see p. 35 n. 9.

16. It was not by any means the unilateral influence of instrument upon voice as often described, but rather a mutual exchange of qualities. The progressive intensification of tonal and rhythmic means which affected both was the result of an underlying esthetic premise, the reflection and artistic expression of the same preoccupation with increasingly precise quantitative measurements which led in another way to the invention of calculus by both Newton and Leibniz. The natural superiority of instruments over voices in rhythmic articulation and pitch definition (and subsequent decay of the art of singing) make the ascendancy of the Baroque instrumental style more apparent than it was in reality. As here, instrumental vocabulary was continually enriched from the conceptual resources of the *canto figurato*, "*genere rappresentativo*," as well as from its self-contained "scientific mannerism."

17. Walther, *Lexicon*, p. 135.

18. It has as a counterpart the change from the principle of graphic design whereby the principal subjects are contained in the area of the painting, to that whereby the outline of the subject is interrupted by that of the painting and the point of perspective lies outside it. See Wölfflin on Baroque art, in H. Wölfflin, *Principles of Art History* (New York, 1932), pp. 124-132 ff. Also, Focillon, "espace limite" and "espace milieu" in Henry Focillon, *Vie des Formes* (Paris, 1947), pp. 38-40 and ff.

19. *Motetti sacri a voce sola con due violini All' Altezza Serenissima di Francesco Secondo, Duca di Modona* . . . di Gio. Paolo Colonna. Maestro di Capella in S. Petronio di Bologna, et Accademico . . . Filarmonico . . . Opera 2a . . . In Bologna per Giacomo Monti, 1681.

20. See supplement, "Ad Novum c[o]eli jubar" and its *ritornello*.

As well as using thematic materials of a melodic order comparable to those found in such vocal works, Bononcini adopts—in BI: 4, 12 and BVI: 4—the structural procedure *à risposta* whereby the two *concertante* violin parts begin, not in imitation at the fifth, but by alternation at the unison, with each part presenting the material *solo* over the bass before turning to more consequential imitation and *fugato* (which latter then has the effect of *stretto*). Such movements, with relatively long solo passages, have a more lyric than dynamic effect, suggesting concerted vocal models rather than purely instrumental prototypes. The most accessible formal precedent[21] is, significantly enough, the *Canzon Francese à quattro, a risposta* of Lodovico Viadana's *Cento Concerti Ecclesiastici,*[22] where it is the only purely instrumental work of the opus.

Perhaps the most complete interpenetration of the fugal *canzona* form and expressive, quasi-vocal materials occurs in BVI: 5, bars 1-29. Here the classically lachrymose subject (descending chromatics and suspensions) is worked out in a formally, very representative ("A") fugal movement marked "Largo," rather than the usual "Allegro."

The opposite tendency, by which the vocabulary and formal dimensions of these fugal movements are enriched and extended by idiomatic instrumental device, is visible in Bononcini's sonata included in Silvani's collection, "Scelta delle Sonate" of 1680. The jagged falling sequences of broken sixths of the first ("A") movement, bars 1-24, and the development of the *tremolo* in broken fourths of the *Grave* ("x"), bars 68-80, are but the most apparent of such items.

The *ritornello* type of fugal movement ("A*") resumes, of course, the thematic materials of its prototype, the *canzona* ("A") movement itself, although only briefly without development and climactic sense. Although occasionally exhibiting new counterpoint, it has the effect of uniting the entire sonata.[23] The derivation of this structural member of the sonata is (see p. 131 *supra*) the *canzona* itself. It tends to disappear in the 1670's and forms no part of Corelli's work.

The final bars of Bononcini's "Sonata" in Silvani's collection of 1680 (see supplement) show a synthesis of this *ritornello* ("A*") and the sententious "affective" close (harmony, "tremolo," suspensions) as well as the short closing "canon" typical of contrapuntal cadences. If it is Bononcini's

21. Riemann, *Old Chamber Music* (London: Augener, n.d.), Book I, p. 19.

22. *Cento Concerti Ecclesiastici . . . Opera Duodecima . . .* Venice 1602 (see Sartori *BMI,* p. 115).

23. Walther, *Lexicon;* art. "Canzona."

last church sonata, it might logically be expected to employ at its final cadence all of the most powerful devices of its predecessors.

Bononcini's practices in respect to the movements ("B") of the *sonata da chiesa* cast in ternary meters, the "tripla" and its variants, which derive from the *canzona* prototype, show the same combination of traditional and assimilated materials we have seen in the "corner" movements ("A" and "A*").

Although it might appear in any position in the *canzona,* this ternary movement—sometimes derived by variation or parody—usually occupies a central place between the fugal movements whose (normally) binary meter offered more dynamic contrapuntal possibilities. Bononcini adopts a conservative pattern in the placing of this movement. Only twice (BI: 9 and BIX: 3) does the "tripla" end the sonata, and it is omitted only in BI: 12. In only three instances (BIX: 1, 4, 5) does it appear as the first of the integral *canzona* elements, as occasionally with Merula and Cazzati and also with Corelli.

In the *canzona* the "tripla" movements presented two possibilities of contrast to the fugal movements in binary meter to which it was opposed: rhythmic (ternary *vs.* binary) and textural (homophonic *vs.* contrapuntal). Although the homophonic setting offers the most complete contrast, a polyphonic-fugal stylization was by no means unusual, and both might appear in an extended or "patchwork" (*Flick*) *canzona.*

Bononcini shows a natural preference for the contrapuntal manner and, in the *sonata da camera,* where the same tradition of metric restylization which informed the *canzona* was operative, accedes only rarely to the variation principle (cf. BI: 5 and BVI: 5). Of the traditional approaches to this movement the homophonic variety may be seen in BVI: 6, bar 27 and BI: 9, bar 50. Bononcini shows a strong tendency to include a canon in these movements. BI: 6 is expressly marked "canon" and in BI: 7 there is just the sort of sequential canon as that by Bendinelli;[24] cf. *supra* p. 23 and *infra* p. 169.

The enlivenment of the latter and middle portions of the ternary movement by motivic interest, i.e., with real or "sham" counterpoint, and a contrast in tempo ("Adagio," "Allegro"), texture, and sonority was normal usage in the *canzone* of the Merula epoch and with Cazzati. It remains so with Bononcini, and by his period this practice is reinforced by parallel developments in the *concertante* combination of voices and violins in the

24. This specialty also has a Modenese precedent in Uccellini's op. IX, "Sinfonia, no. 4," which exists in a modern edition in the series *Hausmusik* (Vienna: 1952).

motet (see BI: 7 and BVI: 8). The *concertante* vocal style is indeed never very far from the severe fabric of Bononcini's *sonate da chiesa,* free as they are of arrant instrumentalism.

The fugal variety of ternary movement (*tripla*) is to be seen in BIX: 1, bar 12, complete with the devices we have observed in the binary ("A") sections—including a typical sententious, non-thematic close. Bononcini's "Sonata" in Silvani's collection of 1680 offers another example (bar 33). Likewise BI: 2 affords an illustration of the through-composed *fugato concertante* in trio style on a severe "Venetian" subject "all'antico," with its repeated notes *á la cornetto* (or *tromba*). Possibly the most highly developed example of the fugal ternary movement—and also of the transformation principle to which Bononcini but rarely adheres—is the single "variation" sonata, BI: 5. Here with the slightest of changes Bononcini effects the rhythmical permutation from C to 3/2 of the entire fugue ("A"; see p. 136 *supra*).

The movements in ternary meters ("B") show in their meter signatures—occasionally written in combination with older, proportional symbols—the same vestigial uses which mark the analogous situations in the *sonata da camera,* namely the proportional relationship between the units of binary movements (*allemande* and *aria*) and the ternary dances (*courantes*) (see p. 116 *supra*). In op. I they are in all cases the traditional 3/2 or C 3/2 "tripla"[25] with hemiola, usual in the *canzona* of the earlier part of the century,[26] and the stylistic derivation from traditional treatments is likewise obvious.[27]

However, beginning in op. VI the meter signatures show greater variety and are also based on smaller units, quarters and eighths (3/1, 3/2, 3/4, 6/4, 9/4, 3/8)[28] and, in compound meters, even eights and sixteenths (6/8, 9/8, 12/8, 9/16, 12/16). These signatures (rather remarkable for the 1670's) are doubtless the result of Bononcini's speculative theoretical bent,[29] the same trait which produced the mensuration canons of op. III and the theoretical work, *Il Musico Prattico*. Here (pp. 10-13 and 20-22) he makes a systematic

25. Bononcini, *Il Musico Prattico,* pp. 10-13 and 20-22.

26. Although qualifying indications—"Presto," "Largo," and "Adagio"—show changing practice as well as the increase of the affective, "expressive" element.

27. The notation of hemiola in black (among white) notes is another indication of the force of tradition.

28. 3/8 is already in use by the progressive Cazzati in op. XVIII, "La Rosetta" (1656). These meters show the influence of association with vocal forms, since in note values requiring beams and flags the distribution of the text may be shown most accurately. This may be the beginning of the transition by which slow movements (with vocal antecedents) of eighteenth-century classical works were written with eighths as basic units.

29. Those of op. VI have an "experimental" look while those of op. IX are standard for the remainder of the century.

exposition of the gamut of meter signatures, which is clearly a point of juncture between older and modern practice in nomenclature and usage.[30]

The movements in compound meters are "modernisms" not only in respect to their meter signature. They show the effects of interaction with expressive, pictorial, non-*canzona* elements from the concerted vocal style "con violini." The effects of this interaction here parallel those observed in the binary fugal movements ("A") acting upon melodic contour and rhythmic stylization, symbol, and syntax. Here, as there, the thetic principle is exchanged for anacrustic design and schematic arrangement for cursive development.

An example drawn from the same source previously referred to—Colonna's *Mottetti* (see p. 140 *supra*)—will illustrate the particulars of symbolic and suggestive literary setting and the transfer to instrumental idiom. Two examples, showing the characteristic "exultant" texts typical of Jesuit inspirational effusions, one from the motet already cited, "Ad Novum Coeli Jubar," and another from "O Sidera," can be compared to BVI: 5, bar 30 and to BIX: 5, bar 14 (see supplement). Likewise, the assimilation of increased instrumental means is visible in such a remarkable movement (in 12/16) as that of BVI: 3. The conquest of a more flexible technique makes possible the extended sequences which, together with the dominantic harmonic principle, lend cumulative force to the gentle lyricism of such movements.

From a formal point of view these movements are, of course, the logical consequence, or, better, the Baroque manifestation, of the venerable principle of proportional increment (2-3-4; 6/8, 12/8) in the composition of large forms, including the mass and the motet.[31] Bononcini's knowledge of these antecedents is clear from their use in his mensuration canons, and the aesthetic requirements of diversity and contrast within the fixed range of symbolic stylistic materials demanded by the sonata informs their use here.[32]

30. The general shift in usual units from halves-quarters to quarters-eighths was really accomplished during Bononcini's lifetime. One has only to turn the pages of Merula and Cazzati and then those of Corelli to recognize Bononcini's middle position. The comparison of Bononcini's theoretical presentation of the subject and that of Lorenzo Penna in *Li Primi Albori Musicali* . . . (Bologna, 1684), shows the same thing.

31. This principle was still operative in Bononcini's day, being visible in Cazzati's *concertante* mass, op. XXIV and in that of Colonna, op. VIII (see supplement). In fact the habitual stylization and the "triumphant" parts of the *Gloria* may well not be without bearing in the *sonata da chiesa,* and certainly contribute to the suggestive power—the subjective "meaning" and symbolism of these movements.

32. It is certainly incorrect to designate these movements as *gigues,* although in the later decadence and hybridization of *sonate da chiesa* and *da camera* this becomes the practice. The resemblance is superficial and, in Bononcini, contradicted by the constant use of hemiola (foreign to the *gigue*) and the lack of midway cadence. On the other hand, it is true that Bononcini's interest in these compound meters may have been stimulated by the *giga,* of which his examples in op. II (1667) are among the first printed in Italy.

The type of movement ("x") we have described (p. 130) as being of liturgical but of non-*canzona* origin occurs in two characteristic positions in Bononcini's *sonate da chiesa* and presents two functionally derived sets of general stylistic characteristics.[33] The first of these, which appears in the *canzona*-"proto-sonata" of the 1630's, represents the assimilation by the *canzona* of the slow, expressive type of *toccata* liturgically used for the Elevation of the Host. A favorite stylization of this section with Tarquinio Merula and Cazzati—and after them, Bononcini—is by the use of the idiomatic affective *tremolo* in conjunction with suspensions and generally sententious harmony[34] in a free homophonic period in 4/4. The *tremolo* is the equivalent in musical terms of the deliberate blurring or "feathering" of outline and luminous effects of Baroque painting and architecture. Amorphous, a-melodic, without motivic detail, it conveyed the rarefied atmosphere of the central mystery of the mass.[35] An example of such a movement in its characteristic position just following the "tripla" ("B") and in its simplest traditional stylization is found in BI: 4, bar 55, marked "Adagio, tremolo"; BVI: 3 affords another illustration.

Another stylization of this movement is as the expressive *toccata, ricercare,* or *fantasia* of simple (not to say stereotyped) counterpoint in long tones with many dissonant suspensions (*ligature*), "harsh" (sententious) harmony (*durezze*), moving basses, and chromaticism.[36] Bononcini's use of these traditional means can be seen in BI: 12, bar 43.

The combination of these two stylizations within a single movement is seen in Bononcini's sonata in Silvani's 1680 collection, bar 65 "Grave," and in BI: 9, bar 37.[37]

The second general class of such movements used as foils to the *canzona* elements proper is as an opening *ripieno* or *intrada* (see p. 131 *supra*), a slow homophonic introduction in monumental "lapidary" style in binary meter 4/4. This is not found in Merula. However, it is not unusual with the enterprising Cazzati, infrequent with Bononcini,[38] and usual with Corelli.

These movements embody the musical-liturgical function of the *ripieno*-

33. In most instances so commingled as to make a separate schematic designation impractical.

34. These movements in Bononcini not infrequently begin or end in other keys than the tonic, in dominant or third relation to it.

35. We have referred (p. 138 n.) to the *tremolo* as an effort to heighten spatial effect and its relation to key words of the mass, usually set in choral recitative, the choral equivalent.

36. G. Frescobaldi, "Fiori Musicali" (see *Tavola* as cited in Sartori, *BMI,* p. 345).

37. See also op. VI, 9, bar 58, in *Die Italienische Trio Sonate,* ed. E. Schenk (Arno Verlag, 1954).

38. It occurs in Bononcini five times, three of them in op. IX.

intrada.[39] They are essentially homophonic (*conductus* style) and in the march-like *pavane* rhythm— 𝅗𝅥 ♩ ♩ | 𝅗𝅥 𝅗𝅥 "Adagio"—which is often intensified by dotting (e.g., ♩. ♪ ♩ ♩, and later, ♩ ♫ ♩ ♩, etc.).[40] The full range of pathetic effects—harmonic, tectonic, and rhythmic materials (especially "French" dotted figures, the intensifying effect of which we have had occasion to discuss in connection with the *allemande*)—is invoked by Bononcini to make these *intrada-introit* movements the musical symbols of inevitable circumstance they are.[41] A highly developed example of such a movement, complete with dotted figures (intensification of the tremolo), "driving" harmonies (suspensions),[42] and echo effects may be seen in BI: 8, bar 42.

These movements tend strongly to be strophic, consisting of parallel phrases (*strophe, antistrophe*) in contrasting aspects of tonality[43] (dominant or third relationship) as in BVI: 3, bar 1. In their most developed forms they are complete aáb forms, a miniature *strophe, antistrophe,* and *epode,* as is the case in BI: 6, bar 1.[44]

This type of introductory movement is frequently transposed from its logical position at the beginning of the sonata and used as an introduction to any of the *canzona* elements. It also tends to replace or combine with the tremolo movement following the *tripla,* and its form is sometimes imposed upon the homophonic stylization of the *tripla* itself. Also, as we have seen

39. Cf. page 135 this chapter and page 129 n. 14, chap. viii.

40. The resemblance between such movements and the opening of the "Sinfonia per Introduzione" of BV which we have described as an *intrada* (p. 101, chap. viii) is as obvious as the identity of musical and formal function is patent.

41. Identity of purposes (Church and State) leads to similarity of means, hence the resultant resemblance to the Lullian *overture.*

42. Cf. Henry Purcell, *Dido and Aeneas*: "But ere we this perform . . . and *drive* 'em back to court."

43. This device in *ripieno* style was not unknown to the preceding century. It is used by Palestrina in the eight-part motets of his *Libro Terzo* of 1575: *Veni Sancto Spiritus* (opening) and *Ave Regina coelorum* (*et pro nobis ff.*). It may be regarded as another "spatial" device, an echo of the antiphonal style back of the *canzona* and current in the monumental "Roman" manner.

44. The propriety of this form in this ritual situation (*intrada, introit, ingresso*) is worth notice, given its classical historical origins. It may be conscious, knowing use, and even a historical reconstruction of classic forms of Greek choral verse (and its concomitant spatial—left to right, right to left—movement) under the influence or observation of "classicizing" academic literary discussion. The forms appear in Italian as part of the apparatus and vocabulary of the literary followers of Cardinal Bembo, and come into English usage as follows: "Strophe". . . . In Greek choral poetry: a series of lines forming a system the metrical structure of which is repeated in a following system called the antistrophe . . . 1605. "Antistrophe. . . . The returning movement, from left to right in Greek choruses . . . 1671." J. G. Walther (*Lexicon,* 1723) gives a comparable definition. "Epode. . . . The part of a lyric song which follows the strophe and antistrophe . . . 1671" (*Oxford Universal Dictionary* [Oxford, 1955]).

(p. 138 *supra.* regarding cadences), the impressive properties of its materials (massive homophonic, sententious harmonic manner) recommend their use in shortened form as a solution to the aesthetic problem of the climactic, cadential moments of fugal movements, (BI: 7, bar 86).[45]

Inevitably, in response to the mounting taste for the overtly affective, which is the basic outline of Baroque aesthetic development, the affective devices, including the *tremolo,* begin (with Cazzati) to invade the *canzona* movements themselves, resulting in passages of great effect but of little truly contrapuntal consequence, as in BVI: 12, bar 78. However, Bononcini's *sonate da chiesa* embody the clearest differentiation between traditional and assimilated elements consistent with their variety and the changing stylizations of the epoch. They reflect the still vital, plastic tradition of the mid-Baroque *sonata da chiesa* before its reduction to formula, corruption with secular elements, and decadence in the last quarter of the century.

2. STYLE

i. *Melody*

The melodic vocabulary of the contrapuntal ("A" "B," *canzona*) movements of Bononcini's *sonate da chiesa* is, like that of all instrumental composers of the seventeenth century, an extension of the figuration which had been grafted on the classic contrapuntal style of the preceding epoch. Originally proposed as methodical diminution of vocal parts for the benefit of instrumentalists and virtuoso singers, the practice seems to have been well established by the 1530's, as shown by the astonishing collection of formulae offered by such a writer as Ganassi.[46]

Ganassi, op. cit. p. 104, #109.

45. See n. 10, this chapter.

46. Sylvestro Ganassi, *Opera Intitulata Fontegara Laquale insegna a sonare di flauto con tutta l'arte opportuna a esso instrumento massime il diminuire il quale sara utile ad ogni instrumento di fiato et corde: et ancora a chi si dileta di canto . . .* ("Fontegara, which teaches to play the flute with all the art pertaining thereto. Especially [the art of] diminution which will be useful to any instrument, string or wind as well as to those who delight in singing . . ."), Venice, 1535. New ed. by Hildemarie Peter (Berlin, 1956).

A principal use of this ornamental technique was in the transcription–paraphrase of madrigals and especially of the French chanson, the *canzon francese,* the ancestor of the *sonata da chiesa.*[47] In the course of the seventeenth century, and by Bononcini's time, these formulae, no longer cursiv but crystallized and amplified by usage, constituted normal instrumenta diction and became themselves the subject of contrapuntal treatment.[4] These patterns as adapted to the violin consist of all degrees of organizatior of passing tones, changing tones, *cambiata* figures, "spinning out" of figures etc., necessary to maintain instrumental activity, especially in Allegro movements.[49] By their motivic character they invite fragmentation and sequential repetition which results in the homogeneity of the thematic subjec matter and the stereotyped "filling" and sequential patterns which are the basis of the style.

A stage of the process of adaptation of this figuration to the violin is itself visible within Bononcini's work. The melodic contour of themes and passages of BI tend to be in conjunct melodic motion with occasional large

47. The characteristics of this melodic manner, including the descending sequential *coloratura,* hocket-like exchanges as well as the beloved "trio" style (two equal *concertante* parts over a free bass) are visible very early, as in the *caccia* of the Italian Ars Nova, to which some of Bononcini's movements in canon (e.g., BI: 6, bar 56) bear a startling generic resemblance. They are also to be observed in concerted madrigals for two tenors of Monteverde, e.g., the *ciaccona, "Torna Zefiro."*

48. This is yet another illustration of a principle of stylistic evolution (visible at points of stylistic change in all arts and periods) where in a "Baroque" phase the accretion of cursive, informal ornament overburdens the "classic" form and then itself undergoes "classification" and becomes the basis of the new style.

49. Being already "diminutions" they are not properly the subject of the further *extempore* diminution, to which Bononcini objects in his "Letter to the Reader" of op. VI: cf. p. 75 *supra.*

eaps, which give the instrument scope. Increasingly in BVI and BIX, and o a definitive degree in the "Sonata" in Silvani's collection, the melodic-nstrumental formula makes use of sequences of large leaps (sixths) in the agged contours typical of the Italian violin style of the late seventeenth entury.

ii. *Tonality*

Bononcini's personal melodic manner is marked by what appears to us today to be a taste for arbitrary transient inflections of melodic fragments or motives. These challenge or cause fluctuation of vhat we now refer to as "key." The result is the presence of many "cross-elations" and tonal contradictions at short notice (BI: 1, bars 1, 2 and ff. BI: , bars 11 & 12, etc.; BVI: 4, bar 19, etc.) that contribute to the vivacity of his tyle.[50] However, his taste for tonal piquancy quite apart, the apparent in-onsistency is a natural consequence of the tonal system in which he thought nd worked.

In *Il Musico Prattico* he sets forth the current solmization system based n the Guidonian hexachords, their mutation and dovetailing, which directs he singer's attention to the local position of the semitones, but does not stablish tonality by the regularity of the fifth and octave.[51]

Bononcini,[52] like Zarlino,[53] classifies intervals not only by their size, ut by the internal arrangement of tones and semitones, by "species."[54]

Bononcini's concepts of tonality were, by his own statements,[55] based n the twelve modes (two on each tone except B) set forth by Zarlino.[56] Bononcini makes an exposition of his tonal system as a series of *Tuoni* modes or tones).

A *Tuono* is nothing more nor less than a form [i.e., disposition or arrangement] r quality of harmony which is to be found in each of the seven species of the

50. In the discussion of intervals in *Il Musico Prattico,* p. 48, he observes: "The semitone the condiment of music . . . and is the cause of the diversity of musical intervals arising om the variety of positions they occupy in the different [interval] species." For Bononcini interval species" was a matter of internal arrangement of whole and half tones, not the over-ll size.

51. As observed by Willi Apel, HDM, art. "Hexachord," this system "produces the scale ithout at the same time [expressing] a preference for tonality."

52. *Op. cit.,* p. 48.

53. *Istitutioni Harmoniche,* pt. III, chap. viii.

54. I.e., he recognizes one "species" of second, and of major third, of diminished fifth nd tritone, two "species" of minor third, and major seventh, three "species" of perfect urth, four of perfect fifth, three of major sixth and of minor sixth, five "species" of minor venth, and seven "species" of octave.

55. *Op. cit.,* p. 121.

56. *Istitutioni Harmoniche,* pt. IV, chap. iii.

octave, modulated by those species of fifth and fourth which correspond to its form. It is called *Tuono* from the verb *Intonare* and is properly that of [refers to] the *Canto Fermo* [plain chant] as distinct from the [*canto*] *figurato* [polyphonic music], of which the *Tuono* is called *Modo* from the verb *Modulare* so that the *modi* are nothing but diverse *modulazione* & *armonie.* [i.e., divers modulations and arrangements of the octave]. The letters of the musical alphabet are six, which form the octave from which arise the *tuoni* or *modi.* They are D, E, F, G, A, C, omitting B, because it does not have, naturally, a perfect fifth or fourth. Each of the letters contain two *Tuoni,* one called authentic, the other plagal.... The authentic [mode] has its octave divided as may be seen in fig. 1, and in the plagal [mode] the octave is divided as in fig. 2

Fig. 1		D	a	d
Fig. 2	A	D	a	

The variety of the aforementioned *Tuoni* arises from the different species of fifth and fourth added together.[57]

Then follows a table of the twelve *Tuoni*:

		fifth (species)	fourth (species)
1 auth.	Dad	1st	1st
2 plag.	ADa	"	"
3 auth.	Ebe	2nd	2nd
4 plag.	BEe	"	"
5 auth.	Fcf	3d	3d
6 plag.	CFc	"	"
7 auth.	Gdg	4th	1st
8 plag.	DGd	"	"
9 auth.	Aea	1st	2nd
10 plag.	EAe	"	"
11 auth.	cgc	4th	3d
12 plag.	Gcg	"	"

Bononcini then (Chapter XVI) provides a series of short *duos* (two-part compositions in imitation) which illustrate the modes and their "regular" cadences. He says further:

There is no difference between an authentic mode and its plagal except that the authentic rises a fourth above the plagal and the plagal descends a fourth below the authentic. The authentic has the property of ascending and the plagal of descending. The authentic (according to some) is vivacious in nature and the plagal sad, but this is not observed in the *stile concertato.*

The rule about ascending in the authentic *Tuono* and descending in the plagal *Tuono* is arbitrary, but in observing it one proceeds in accordance with their nature.

57. *Op. cit.,* p. 122.

The regular cadences of the one [authentic] and the other [plagal] *Tuono* re made from and by means of the fifth; from and by means of the fourth. rregular cadences are made on any other tone.

The six (odd-numbered) examples in the authentic modes have themes hat rise and quickly take possession of the fifth and octave above the final, nake conspicuous use of the upper tetrachord and of the fifth degree in both arts in the formation of the final cadence. The six (even-numbered) xamples in plagal modes have themes whose initial motion is *downward,* hat show a reluctance to rise above the fifth degree. In the formation of the inal cadence the fourth degree figures prominently.

Internal cadences in the d modes are made on the fifth and third (g♯, a; , f), in the E modes on the third only (f♯, g), in the F modes on the third g♯, a). In the G and A modes internal cadences are made on the fifth c♯, d; f, e), and in the C modes internal cadences are made on the fifth f♯, g).

Unlike the modes of plain chant and the scales formed by the mutation f hexachords, these *tuoni* of the *canto figurato* are based on the related ontrast of octave, fifth, and fourth and represent a midway point between he ecclesiastical modes and modern concepts of tonality (i.e., a key defined y a tonic and two dominants).

In his theoretical writings and in his music Bononcini represents a final tage in the evolution from a contrapuntal technique based on interval and node toward a harmonically saturated tonal counterpoint based equally on nterval and tonal function[58]—the tendency toward stronger and stronger ffective means which we have had occasion to mention earlier (p. 00 *upra*).

In *Il Musico Prattico* (pp. 137, 138) Bononcini says "The *Tuoni* ordinarily ised by composers are seven." He lists:

The first [D auth.] in its normal place [**D**EFG*A*BC**D**]
The second [D plag.] a fourth higher [*D*EF**G**AB♭C*D*]
The ninth [A auth.] a fifth lower [**D**EFG*A*B♭C**D**]

58. A degree of awareness of tonal rather than intervalic relationship is expressed by ononcini's long-lived contemporary, Roger North (*op. cit.,* p. 224), writing somewhat later, n his discussion of the forbidden succession of perfect intervals. Speaking of "Our teachers n print" he writes, "But 5ths & 8ths they say may not [be used consecutively] because they re so lucious and sweet as must be tempered with thirds and sixths to prevent cloying . . . han which reason I think few more impertinent have bin met with." North's objection to onsecutive fifths between the bass and an upper part is that "they carry you out of the key, nd that makes the worst of discord when ill done as here: d/g c♯/f♯. The second note nstead of sounding in the scale of G becomes a Key note itself and so remote from G as to ave his 5th in C♯ (a ♭5th [!] to G) which brings into mind the 3rd, that is A♯, and a vorse noise cannot be made."

The tenth [A plag.] in its normal place [*E*FG**A**BCD*E*]
The eleventh [C auth.] an octave below [**C**DEF*G*AB**C**]
The twelfth [C plag.] a fifth below [*C*DE**F**GAB♭*C*]

The ninth *Tuono* [a auth. transposed down a fifth] serves in place of the seventh [G. auth.].[59] The tenth [a plag. in its normal place, E*A*E, with F♯, according to Bononcini's practice although not specified here] serves in place of the third [e auth.] and fourth [e plag.]. The eleventh [C auth.] serves in place of the fifth, and the twelfth [c plag. down a fifth] in place of the sixth [F plag.].

The substitution of the eleventh and twelfth (C) modes for the tonally unsatisfactory fifth and sixth (F) modes, and the substitution of the tenth (a) mode for the tonally recalcitrant e modes are steps toward modern major and minor scale and tonality.[60]

Of these modes Bononcini says, "The third and fourth modes are not used because at more than two or three parts they are not practical for lack of a perfect fifth on the tone B in the regular cadence of this mode."[61] This omission indicates the recognition of a real dominant function. Also, "the fifth and sixth modes are not used because they are too harsh on account of the tritone found between their final, F, and this B [i.e., lack of subdominant], and finally, the seventh is omitted as being almost the same as the eighth."

Il Musico Prattico also gives instruction (p. 159) in recognition of transposed modes by the accidentals following the clef. One flat represents for Bononcini not a single "key signature" but the transposition of a mode (1,2,3,4,6,8,10) a fourth upwards, or (7,9,11,12) a fifth downwards. Two flats indicate the transposition of a mode a tone downwards, and three flats the transposition of a mode a minor third upwards. A sharp at the clef signifies the transposition of a mode (5,7,9,11,12) a fourth down or a fifth

59. This seems strange as it replaces a "major" mode with a "minor" one; however Bononcini says elsewhere (*op. cit.*, p. 147) that "the seventh mode [G auth.] is omitted because it is nearly identical with the eighth." The second mode a fourth higher also produces the same row of tones.

60. This was accomplished before the end of the century. Purcell, writing in Playford's publication, *An Introduction to the Skill of Musick* (London, 1694), p. 123, says, "There are but two Keys in Musick, (viz) a *Flat* and a *Sharp;* not in relationship to the place where the *First* or *Last Note,* in a piece of Musick stands, but the *Thirds* above that *Note.* To distinguish your Key accordingly, you must examine whether the *Third* be *Sharp* or *Flat,* therefore the first *Keys* for a Learner to Compose in ought to be the two Natural *Keys,* which are, *A r* and *C faut,* the first the lesser, and the last the Greater *Third;* from these, all the other are formed, by adding either *Flats* or *Sharps.* When this is well digested, you must proceed to Know what other *Closes* are proper to each Key.

"To a *flat Key,* the Principal is the Key itself, the next in Dignity the *Fifth* above, and after that the *Third* and *Seventh* above.... To a *sharp Key,* the *Key* itself first, the *Fifth* above, and, instead of the *Third* and *Seventh* (which are not so proper in a *sharp* Key,) the *Sixth* and *Second* above."

61. *Op. cit.*, p. 147.

upwards; two sharps, upward transposition by a tone, and three sharps the transposition by a minor third downward. He also refers to other current, less explicit uses, saying, "however, the aforementioned signs (sharps and flats) will then be found placed through the composition on the tones where they should have been put in the first place."

A feature of Bononcini's tonal system is his retention of the plagal modes. His interest here lay in the fact that tonal imitation as he understood it was accomplished by using the plagal mode to answer subjects in the authentic mode and vice versa. He says (*Il Musico Prattico,* p. 155):

> It is true that any composition for four parts, *Canto, Alto, Tenore,* & *Basso* is made up of two *Tuoni* namely an authentic [mode] and its plagal [mode], or a plagal [mode] and its authentic [mode]. The *Canto* corresponds to the *Tenore* and the *Alto* to the *Basso.*

Bononcini appears to have been the first theorist to regard as "*regolare*" an imitation whose intervals are varied for the sake of tonal clarity.[62] After a demonstration of various types of imitation and "fughe" where he describes as "*regolare*" those which duplicate intervals, he says:

> There are in addition other *Fughe composte* [*composte* = figured and with syncopations] which, although they do not observe the same [arrangement of] tones and semitones, are none the less regular and perfect because they embrace all the tones of the octave of which a *Tuono* is formed, as are others *incomposte* which are *regolare* and perfect, for the same reasons.[63]

He then gives examples in which the upper tetrachord is answered by the lower pentachord, the tonic by the dominant, the dominant by the tonic, etc.

In the *sonate da chiesa* Bononcini uses these materials quite consistently as the basis of the thematic and formal structure of contrapuntal (especially "A") movements. Themes in authentic modes lie above the final and move easily by way of the fifth into the upper tetrachord and are answered by the corresponding lower fourth of the plagal mode. Plagal and authentic elements are balanced. Both authentic and plagal cadences are used. Elaborate and uncompromising plagal cadences (possibly of liturgical significance) are appended to BI: 2,3,4,5,7,11. Also, in the cadences of such movements as are actually in plagal modes (BI: 6, last 3 bars), although the final cadential step is dominant-tonic, the subdominant harmonies figure very largely and are the point of departure for the cadential phrase.

The most used modes are the eleventh and twelfth, the C modes, which

62. A. Mann, *A Study of the Fugue* (New Brunswick, N. J., 1958), p. 44.
63. *Op. cit.,* p. 83.

correspond to the major scale. They account for more than a third (13) of the thirty *sonate da chiesa*. The G modes, seventh and eighth, which are, after the C modes, the closest to the major scale are used in five sonatas. The d modes, first and second (with the constantly lowered sixth, b♭, and occasionally raised seventh, c♯, so that the effect is virtually that of d minor), are used in eight sonatas, and the a modes, ninth and tenth, *in situ* or transposed, in three.

To sum up Bononcini's attitude to tonality it may be said that he felt the need of the stability of tonal imitation in fugue exposition but was unwilling or unconstrained to relinquish the variety and character of the more stable modes (d,a,G,C) in the construction of his thematic material.

The modal details which tinge the melodic materials in these movements (and which in turn determine the tonal designations, as in BVI) may perhaps be most easily observed in the comparison of "profiles" (based on incidence and duration in the first violin part) of the several tones of the most used scales. (In actual compositions they are somewhat more appreciable than their proportions here might suggest because of other features, contour, etc.)

C mode (transposed), BVI:3, bars 13-38

High incidence of III because of 3rds in cadences. ♯IV for *transient* cadences on V only.

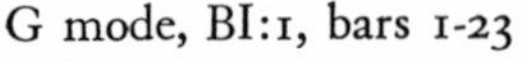

G mode, BI:1, bars 1-23

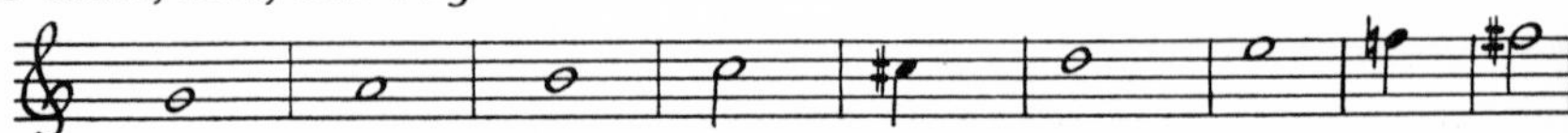

N.B. ♭VII, used in direct contradiction of ♯VII, bars 11 & 8, 17 & 18. High incidence of II & V & IV♯. Low incidence of IV; tendency to "bright side."

d mode, BI:6, bars 29-54

♯III entirely accounted for by *tierce de Picardie* at final cadence.

a mode (transposed), BVI:6, bars 1-26

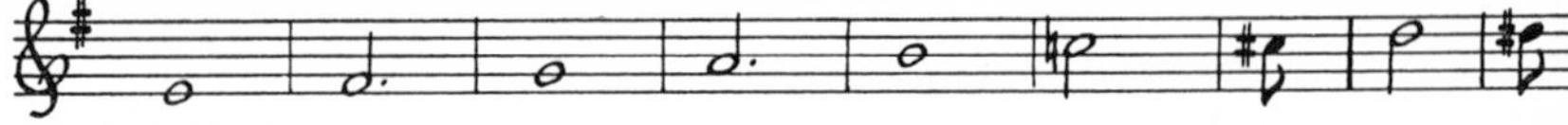

iii. *Harmony*

The contrapuntal fabric of Bononcini's *sonate da chiesa* is supported and given tonal definition by the usual harmonic matrix of the Basso Continuo, presumably for the organ.[64] This is in BI and BVI, an independent, non-imitative bass which shows some modal tendencies but is more tonal in effect than the upper parts because of a higher incidence of tonic, dominant and subdominant tones. (Compare p. 154 *supra*).[65]

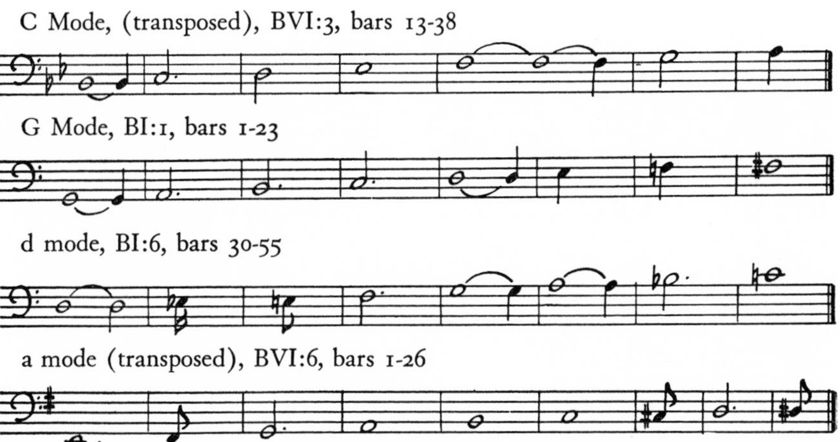

In op. IX, where a separate, string bass part which participates in the imitation is provided, the keyboard part has the appearance of a reduction to harmonic essentials of the imitating part. These together form a heterophonic texture. However, given the evolution of the style, it might with equal propriety be observed that the florid part is formed by the diminution of the harmonic bass.

If the idiomatic melodic substance of the *canzona* movements of the *sonata da chiesa* can be traced to the systematic diminution technique of the sixteenth century, the supporting, functional bass can be referred to the harmonic (as distinct from contrapuntal) materials to which this technique

64. We have no specific information regarding Bononcini's preferences in respect to the realization of the Continuo beyond the actual figures he generally (but by no means always) supplies. He does not discuss the matter in *Il Music Prattico,* which is devoted to elements and contrapuntal theory. Failing his own recommendations, perhaps the suggestions of Bononcini's fellow academician, Lorenzo Penna (*Li Primi Albori Musicali* . . . di . . . Lorenzo Penna [Bologna, 1672]), which are closest to Bononcini in both points of time and locality, may be considered applicable. A resumé of these is to be found in F. T. Arnold, *The Art of Accompaniment from a Thorough Bass* (London, 1931).

65. In BI: 6, bar 85, Bononcini uses a key signature, one flat, in the bass only, making it what we would call D minor, and none in the violin parts, which are presumably considered to be in D modes. The discrepancy appears to be intentional, since in the succeeding movement (bar 112) he removes the flat from the bass key signature.

was applied. Chief among these are, of course, the traditional *ostinato,* "improvisation" basses derived from recitation formulae and dances, the *romanesca, ruggiero, passamezzo antico, passamezzo moderno, bergamasca, ciaccona,* and *folía.*[66] In these the integrating force of harmonic organization is applied to instrumental as well as vocal forms. Diego Ortiz gives examples of such basses which he says the Italians called *tenores.*[67]

These traditional *ostinato* basses are of two general kinds:

1. Those based on the tonally integrating and cadential effect of the contrast of the tonic and two dominant harmonies. These, such as the *ruggiero, bergamasca,* and *passamezzo antico, passamezzo moderno,* and *folía,*[68] are characterized by wide intervals (4ths and 5ths). Their most conspicuous feature is the presence of the elements of the most powerful tonal formula we have, the "perfect cadence": I,IV,I,V,I.
2. Those based on the tonal effect of the scale and scale segments (tetrachords and hexachords). These, the *ciaccona*[69] and related types,[70] are characterized by conjunct intervals (usually descending) or scalewise sequences of larger intervals (such as the *ciaccona*: g,d, e,b, c,d, g—a particularly dynamic formula).

These harmonic formulae or basses,[71] with the melodic vocabulary they support, formed the stock-in-trade of the seventeenth-century Italian composers[72] whose enormously dexterous treatment literally "rings the changes" on simple basic materials in a way that can only be compared with the similar fertility in the realm of graphic design, where Italian artists show a seemingly inexhaustible invention based on a few *motifs.*

Although not yet the subject of systematic theory, by Bononcini's time the properties of these tonal formulae had been empirically explored, and, while more characteristic of less severe forms (*capricci, partite,* etc.), had been

66. Alfred Einstein, "Die Aria di Ruggiero," SIMG, XIII, 444; "Ancora sull' Aria di Ruggiero," RMI, XLI (1937), 163; Hugo Riemann, "Der Basso Ostinato und die Anfänge der Kantate," SIMG, XIII, 531.

67. *Tratado de glosas sobre clausulas* (Rome, 1553); new ed. by M. Schneider (Kassel, 1936), pp. 106 ff.

68. Cf. Bukofzer, *MBE,* p. 41.

69. *Ibid.,* p. 42.

70. Which may include traditional, scalewise *obbligi* such as *Ut, Re, Mi, Fa, Sol, La* used as the basis of contrapuntal compositions. Cf. G. Frescobaldi, *Il primo libro di Capricci, Canzone Francese . . . Fatti Sopra Diversi Soggetti et Arie . . .* (Venice, 1626), cited in Sartori, BMI, p. 313.

71. They were still in use as dance music in Modena in Bononcini's time as the MS. of *Balli per Basso Solo* in the Estense library in Colombi's hand, which begins with the *Bergamasca* bass, shows. The designation *per Basso Solo* is puzzling, as the contents are merely undecorated basses.

72. See examples of Colonna in Supplement.

assimilated by the *canzona* in both strict variation form[73] and in a synthesis of elements[74] in the free bass necessary to the construction of cumulative

73. Cf. Tarquino Merula, *Canzon Ruggiero,* 1637, in H. Riemann, *Old Chamber Music* (London, n.d.); Giolamo Frescobaldi, *Canzon prima sopra Rugier, canzon seconda, sopra Romanesca,* 1634, Sartori, BMI, p. 343; G. Salvatore, *Canzona Francese . . . sopra . . . la Bergamasca, ibid.,* p. 377.

74. H. Riemann, "*Basso Ostinato* and *Basso quasi ostinato,*" in *Lilienkron Festschrift* (Leipzig, 1910).

fugal movements of the *sonata da chiesa*. In this synthesis the dynamic effect of the wide intervals of the *ruggiero* and *passamezzo* types are combined and contrasted in sequences with the integrating, centripetal force of the scale of the *ciaccona* types. (Not infrequently when stepwise motion prevails in the bass, the propelling force of the ascending fourth is confided to an upper part).

When the scale patterns and alternate fourths and fifths are combined in the bass the result is the so-called cycle of fifths. This is the most powerful tonal resource of the Baroque composer. Its conquest is the history of the longer seventeenth-century instrumental forms.

Bononcini's work, like that of the period in general, tends toward a more plastic use of the elements contained in the traditional formulae. A tendency toward bass repetition is of course imposed by the imitations, repetitions, and exchanges of the upper parts as in BI: 1, bars 1-8 and 8 ff., BI: 12, bars 1-12, *Sonata* from the *Scelta* of *Silvani,* bars 1-4, 5-8, and *passim*. However the repetitive, static arcs of the *ruggiero, passamezzo*-like basses[75] of BI: 1, bars 1-23, BI: 3, bars 39 ff., BI: 4, bars 1-15 and 69-75, are mingled with other, more plastic treatments, containing scalewise, cumulative sequential elements in BVI: 4, bars 1-49, BVI: 11, bars 1-36, BIX: 3, bars 1-29, etc.

A clear and characteristic example of the sequential use of root movements of fifths is to be found at BVI: 4, bars 43-45, where all the tones of the (diatonic) octave are employed. The tonal advantage is, however, not pressed; the diminished fifth does not appear, the actual cadence is delayed by static harmonies and the "centripetal force" of the sequence somewhat dissipated. Although the tool is at hand, its full potential is not yet exploited—yet another generation will hone its edge and lengthen its stroke in the search for more and more affective tonal devices.

In addition to the cyclic use of fifths, Bononcini characteristically exploits the milder but colorful juxtaposition of chords related by root or bass movement of thirds combined with the tonal ambivalence of 6 and $^{6}_{5}$ chords. A remarkable instance of the systematic use of the cycle of thirds is found in BI: 3, bars 74 ff. Here, after four repetitions of a *ruggiero*-like pattern, the bass proceeds in a sequence of no fewer than thirty-eight falling thirds or rising sixths, in seven repetitions of a cycle of (diatonic) thirds. The ultimate effect is that of a cycle of fifths much mitigated by the slower unfolding and by the intervening succession of triads with two common tones. Modal-

75. It should be noted that BI: 1 and BI: 3 are in the traditional tonality of the *ruggiero* and *passamezzo* formula—the G modes.

tonal equilibrium is maintained (G modes), and the undesirable effect of the diminished triad formed by the succession of f♮, d, b is neutralized, by the execption, ♯VII $\substack{5 \\ 3}$, V $^{\sharp 3}$, which contains and integrates the "cross-relations" f♮-f♯ germane to the (G) mode. He shows his realization of the inconclusive, non-cumulative nature of the cycle of thirds by appending a closing passage which has as its bass the complete descending scale (G mode; a-A), whose last tone (A) initiates the cadential formula II,I,V,^{4} ^{3}I. (See also BI: 6, bar 112 to end, BVI: 11, bars 13-21.)

The cycle of thirds, the cycle of fifths, and the (ascending) scale are combined in BI: 5, bars 11-16, in a sequence of falling thirds and rising fourths (with the characteristic athematic hocket-like dovetailing of the same intervals in the upper parts, which suggests that the scale is the generic part of the passage). The propelling force of this vigorous formula derives from the direct succession of a triad and its "substitute" a third lower. The ear (in *Allegro*) willingly associates these as the components of an implied seventh chord whose immediate resolution is the chord whose root lies a fourth above its lowest tone. The effect is that of a scale sequence of mutual dominants, alternately weak (3^{d}) and strong (4th).

The passage BI: 1, bar 16, which is a rising scale $G^{5\ 6}$ $A^{5\ 6}$ $B^{5\ 6}$ $C^{5\ 6}$ $D^{5\ 6}$ $E^{5\ 6}$, where each tone begins as a root and becomes the third (bass of $\substack{6 \\ 3}$ chord), is, in terms of root progression, a variant of the same thing.

A similar sequence, based on the combined cycles of thirds and fifths and the scale, is the pattern of descending fourths and rising thirds found at BVI: 4, bar 109.

Closely associated with the "substitution effect" of the root movement by descending thirds is that of the replacement of the ascending fourth by the ascending second as found in "deceptive" or evaded cadences, where the expected chord is directly supplanted by one whose root lies a third lower. These devices in combination, as a descending scale of rising seconds and falling thirds, permit a slow unfolding of tonality and provide opportunities for the use of colorful secondary harmonies of which Bononcini makes capital.

A characteristic diatonic example is found at BI: 8, bar 6. Many step-wise bass passages, e.g., BVI: 3, bars 42 ff., BVI: 5, bars 85 ff., bear the figures 5-6 or 7-6. These are but variants of the falling third, rising second pattern, which their *root* movements describe. The effect is heightened when the rising second is made from a $\begin{smallmatrix}6\\3\end{smallmatrix}$ chord so that the actual root progression is cyclic by upward fourths and falling fifths, as at BVI: 8, bars 12-15.

These basses, then, may be described as tonal arrangements of modal materials. They, with the upper parts, delimit a single tonality, generally touching upon the neighboring tonalities, especially the dominant, V, and the third related keys, VI and III. They characteristically cadence in these tonalities but do not modulate *into* them in the sense of stabilizing a new tonality and repeating significant materials in it. "Since, in such matters," says Bononcini, *Il Musico Prattico,* p. 138, "examples are more effective than words," examples of his treatment of the bass and its tonal-harmonic import may be appropriate here. They show vigor and refinement. The refinement is due to the observance of good vocal and melodic principles. The vigor is the result of the surprisingly high incidence of combinations which permit contruction as "first class" root progression, i.e., by fourths and fifths, varied by the root or bass movement by seconds and thirds ("substitutions") and their substitution effects.

Plate VII

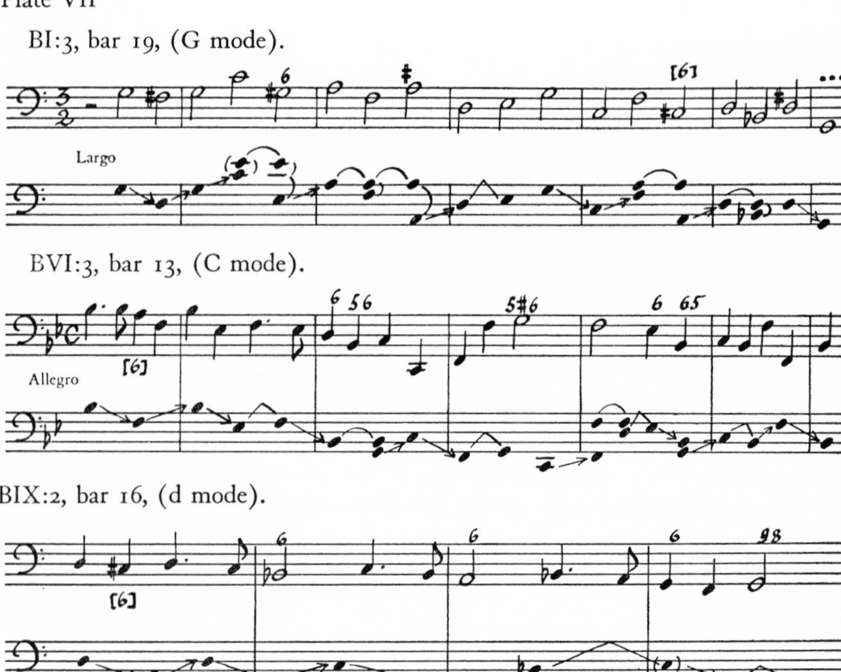

It has been observed that the fugue is in music what the dome (a feature of many Baroque buildings[76]) is in architecture—the greatest volume enclosed by the least material and most science. We may extend the analogy and describe the homophonic ("x") movements and full cadences of Bononcini's *sonate da chiesa* as the musical equivalents of the devices, i.e., the heavily ornamented entries, porticos, lanterns, pediments, staircases, and colonnades with which Baroque architects intensified and articulated the elevations and volumes of their buildings. Like their ceiling and wall paintings in forced perspective, these architectural details were also often designed to create false or exaggerated perspective.[77]

76. Viz. St. Peter's, 1564; St. Paul's, 1675-1710; *Les Invalides,* 1670-1706; *S. M. della Salute,* 1632.

77. Bernini's colonnade before St. Peter's in Rome and his famous staircase, the *Scala Reggia* in the Vatican, are notable and monumental examples. See H. Wölfflin, *Principles of Art History,* pp. 116-118 and 121. One instance of the direct association of graphic representation of such architectural features and printed music (i.e., in parts intended for performance,

As musical "entries," "elevations," and "exits" Bononcini's homophonic *intrada* and *elevazione* movements are intended to be overtly impressive and affective. They contain his most audacious writing and show the taste for colorful, intense chromaticism, which had been a distinguishing feature of the Italian style for a century or more.

His predilection for original and pungent effects shows itself early and continues late. In BI: 1 at bars 64, 65; sequential 7-6 suspensions (in a canon at the second), secondary harmonies, dissonant changing tones and *echappées,* cross relations and three pairs of parallel fifths combined in a close texture result in a surface of much character. At bars 74 and 75 the same passage in an open texture transposed a tone higher by an abrupt, if dexterous, shift in tonality (C, E), gives the effect of a tonal "parenthesis." Its close, in a, is the point of departure for a normal cadence structure (in G) $\underset{\text{a}}{\text{II}}$, $\underset{\text{D}}{\text{V}}$, $\underset{\text{G}}{\text{I}}$. At BI: 5, bars 42, 43, there are suspension-like formations which bluntly contradict the "classical" practice, reversing the rhythmic position of consonance and dissonance. A very remarkable passage is found in the *sonata da camera à 4,* BIII: 16, bar 35, where the keys of A♭, G♭, D♭ are touched upon in a chromatic sequence. This *sonata da camera* (not in dance forms) is without keyboard, so that the limitations of the prevailing meantone temperament need not apply. A telling passage or bit of *musica reservata* in the sonata (Bononcini's last?) in Silvani's collection, bars 77-78, apparently touches the keys of B flat and E flat minor in a manner that must have puzzled others beside the printer and delighted the *cognoscenti.*[78]

This quality of calculated audacity which is a feature of the early Baroque—it could be called part of its experimental, "scientific" phase—is strong in Gesualdo, Frescobaldi, and Monteverde and disappears from the later "classic" style, e.g., Corelli.

The musical means comparable to the architect's and painter's false or intensified perspective and foreshortening is the manipulation of harmony—the juxtaposition and alteration of functional harmonic combinations to in-

---

as distinct from title pages, etc., or incidental representations of music in painting, marquetry, etc.) is to be seen in the *Sonate per Camera a Violino è Violoncello di vari antori* engraved and published by Carolo Buffagnotti. Here the music is framed by designs which employ violent contrasts of light and shadow, foreshortenings (which affect the music as well, and are no aid to the reader), long and near perspective, monumental fragments, and heraldic devices. The Sonatas, although *Sonate da camera,* make specific use of the tonal devices we are considering.

78. The sonata was published after Bononcini's death, and, without his insistence the printer may well have hesitated to print the g♭ necessary in the first violin part and the two flats (e♭ and g♭) in the bass; or, the d♭ in bar 77 may be an error. The immediately succeeding bars are also corrupt, the only instance in Bononcini's printed works.

rease their effect. While by no means confined to it, the situation where this an be most effectively exploited is of course at the cadence—the junction f structural elements. In the affective Baroque style this moment is char- cteristically treated by intensifying (by harmony) the desire for, while at the ame time delaying, the close (by suspensions, etc.).

In "minor modes" Bononcini's practice makes capital of the low sixth nd of the artificially raised seventh degrees, as does our current "harmonic ninor" scale and its harmonies.

In "major" modes the inherent contrast of the two dominants and their elationship to the tonic is heightened by (similarly) lowering the sixth legree, the third of the subdominant function, stressing its downward tend- ncies, which then contrast the more strongly with the upward tendency f the leading tone in the dominant chord. This device is an earmark of he late seventeenth-century Italian style which Purcell mentions ("a flatt ixth before a close") in the *Preface* of his *Sonnatas* 1683). It is frequent vith Bononcini, e.g., BI: 6, last three bars, BVI: 8, bar 67. Likewise, the hird of a tonic chord preceding a cadential dominant chord may be lowered, ending it a degree of subdominant quality and offering contrast to the najor tonic chord to follow (I♭, V, I♯), as at BI: 9, bar 35.

The doubly altered (diminished seventh) chord formed by the raised ourth degree, the tonic, and the lowered third is a yet stronger contrast, vhose three leading tones create a strong desire for the dominant and its esolution, e.g., BI: 6, bar 26, BVI: 8, bar 31, and in the sonata of Silvani's ollection, bar 31. See also Cazzati, op. XVIII, *La Rossetta,* bar 9. Here he analogy to the false perspective is complete: the chord contains the liminished fifth, the musical equivalent of the draughtsman's "vanishing oint." The raised fourth degree functions as a "forced" upward leading tone o the fifth degree, the root of the cadencing dominant chord, while the ther tones are in the relationship of subdominant (downward leading ones) to it, so that the cadential dominant chord, V, has been approached rom both directions at once. A similar "converging" upon the dominant s to be seen in BIX: 2, bars 49-53, where, in the part writing, the raised ourth and lowered sixth follow in close succession.

The last vestige of the Phrygian or third and fourth (e) modes to sur- vive the seventeenth-century transition to tonality is the so-called Phrygian adence or half cadence. Bononcini discusses the cadences of this mode (which he otherwise rejects in *stile concertato* as imperfect) in *Il Musico Prattico,* pp. 136, 137. He seems to give precedence to the harmonic, tonal

3 5 I 5 8 ♯3
formes 8 4-3 I and ♯3-8 5 8 using the former as the first of two three-par
E,B, E; 5 3 5
E, A, E;

6 8
examples (with the modal form 3 ♯3 : as the second) and the latter as th
F, E

final cadence of a four-part example which also contains the modal form

In his actual practice he uses the modal formula as a half cadence (♭II, I in e = ♭VI, V; in a) in which the bass of the dominant chord is approache by a semitone from above, another use of the lowered sixth to intensify th contrast of subdominant and dominant. The effect is sententious an pathetic, a "monumental fragment" (as in BIII: 16, bars 25-29), analogou to the broken contours and intense effects of light and shadow of Baroqu façades.

At BI: 6, bars 89-90, the dominant chord (A) is followed, after a rhetorical rest, by the chord of the mediant (F); and the theatrical, "spatial," effec of the cross-relation (C♮, C♯) is added to the chromaticism of the cadenc itself (see also B:I, 5 bars 84-86). At BIII: 16, bars 25-29, and BIX: 5, bar 3 the tonic succeeds the caesura.[79]

The "spatial" processional *intrada* quality of these movements is als often emphasized by ending or beginning with another aspect of the tonality than the tonic, most frequently the dominant. However, as in VI: 5, bar 57,

♯3
the relationship by third, with cross-relations (here A, F♯), or without (i.e., the "relative minor") is also used. Their asymmetry is assured; if they begin in the tonic (of the whole sonata) they end elsewhere (III or V), and vice versa.

Another device for intensifying the cadential moment is the exaggerated tonal perspective of a protracted pedal on a fixed tone,[80] such as that on the dominant found in BI: 8, bar 50. The reverse, the "walking" eighth-note bass which moves consistently at twice the speed of the other parts, creating a constantly shifting play of "light and shade," consonance and dissonance, breaking up the surface with many harmonic details, is found at BVI: 11, bar 70. This is a variant of the *tremolo* "elevation" movement which figures so largely in this category.

79. The device is of course not new with Bononcini; cf. Cazzati, *La Rosetta,* bar 3, and *Messa Concertata,* where it is used to give an imposing first impression or "façade" to the eight-part mass.

80. See H. Wölfflin, *op. cit.,* re the obelisk in the square before St. Peter's.

Direct chromaticism, where successive chromatic tones in the same part ‘spell out" the harmonic intensification, is found at the close of BI: 8. This s used to intensify a cyclic sequential bass movement of thirds and fifths in 3VI: 6, bar 21, and BVI: 8, bars 34 ff., forming the "receding, intersecting ›lanes" of an incomplete cycle of secondary dominants.[81]

The introduction of these chromatic elements, or the combination of :haracteristics of other modes which appear in these homophonic "frame" novements, spells, of course, the destruction of any modal consistency. As he persistent intensification of the dominant function by alteration of the ubdominant and tonic elements shows, these ("x") movements are strongly onal, although not systematically so. Their materials, although more 'arious, are, like those of the fugal movements the highly tonal arrangement ınd selection of empirically ratified formulae. These operate within a imited tonal scheme in which modal derivations are still visible.

81. *Ibid.*, pp. 119-120.

CHAPTER XIII. THE CANONS

Bononcini's works in the form of canon stem from his own delight in the traditions and transcendent virtuosity of his craft as a composer and the cultivation of his public, for whom the proper sign of the professional composer was his skill in counterpoint. (It is the only manifestation of of the virtuoso element visible in his work; he ignores ostentatious instrumental dexterity.) In Modena the aristocratic *dilletanti* such as Francesco II, and in Bologna the *virtuosi* of the Accademia Filarmonica provided him with an audience for these demonstrations of skill.

This is, of course, everywhere apparent and permeates the fabric of the sonatas themselves. In one case (BI: 6) a (*tripla*) movement is actually marked "In Canon."

The location of Bononcini's instrumental canons[1] is op. III, nos. 20-30.

20 *Sonata a due Violini in Canon all'Unissono, col suo Basso Continuo.*[2]

21 *Canon a quattro Soprani, ò Contralti all'Unissono.*

22 *Canon a 8. Voci all'Unissono, & all'ottaua bassa, dopo un sospiro dall'una all'altra.*

23 *Canon a 12. Voci all'Unisono.*

24 *Sonata a due Violini in Canon alla terza bassa per mouimenti contrarij col suo Basso Continuo.*

25 *Canon a due Voci alla quinta bassa, con l'osseruazione de gli effetti del Punto.*

26, 27 *Canoni a due Voci all'Unissono, sotto diuersi segni.*

28 *Canon a 3. Voci, sotto varij segni, "Qui potest capere capiat."*

29 *Sonata a due Violini in Canon alla riuersa, mà naturalmente, col suo Basso Continuo.*

30 *Sonata a due Violini in contrapunto doppio all'ottaua bassa, col suo Basso Continuo.*[3]

These constitute abstract contrapuntal propositions rather than developed functional works—cabinet curiosities, scientific and archeological specimens an aspect of the "scientific mannerism" we have mentioned earlier (see pp. 84-85 *supra*). They are comparable to the by-products of mathematical speculation: "magic number" squares, triangles, etc.

The whole quasi-scientific atmosphere which surrounds this genre is per

1. Vocal canons are prefaced to other works. See chap. v.

2. The items with basso continuo do not really require this "solvent," as the parts in canon adhere perfectly independently to the principles laid down in Bononcini's *Il Musico Prattico* Part II.

3. Sartori, *BMI*, p. 456.

ceptible in Bononcini's gentle "spoofing" in a canon which prefaces op. III (frontispiece), which also affords us as a pleasant sidelight on Bononcini's sense of humor. The canon is of the type called "perpetual," blown up to Protean dimensions and for a fantastic number of voices. The canon, the same as BIII: 22 (see supplement), reads:

> Canon for 2592 Voices; separated by an eighth rest [and] divided into 648 choirs, and should you wish to go beyond Musical rule—that is to make the *Maxima* larger than that which has its limits in Music, we may proceed to infinity.[4]

The canon itself consists of a descending d-minor triad (A F D) written in *Maximae* in "tempo perfetto," "prolazione perfetta," and "modo maggior" (see supplement), and being merely a triad can, indeed, be extended "into infinity" without breaking any contrapuntal precept.

However, the vogue for musical "curiosities" and his natural disposition for contrapuntal virtuosity quite apart, Bononcini's interest in the canon may be traced directly to his teachers. In the work of Marco Uccellini a number of canons are to be found which have direct relationship to some of those produced by Bononcini. Gustav Beckmann describes a puzzle canon in Uccellini's op. III (?) of 1642.[5] The "sonata" (♯12) is prescribed "for three violins," but only two parts are provided. The third part is derived from the first by extracting only the whole notes.[6]

Bononcini's "puzzle" canon of the Al Lettore of the Violin I part of op. III (see Plate I) may be regarded as a descendant of Uccellini's. Bononcini's puzzle, intended as a jibe at his enemies, bears the motto *Caecus non iudicat de colore,* which is (in true mannerist fashion) a veiled hint to its solution. The solution consists of extracting the notes by their several values (*color temporis*), each of which makes up one of the four parts of the *cantilena.* The entire text, before resolution, is, of course, a meaningless jumble, not a consecutive part as in Uccellini's canon.

Uccellini's "Communis est via," op. IX (see supplement), is provided with the key to its solution.

> Canon, *Communis est via* for two violins. [In] this canon one [violin] plays all the notes on the lines below the middle, the other plays all the notes

4. "Canon a 2592 Voci dopo un mezzo sospiro dell'una all'altra divise in 648 chori, e volendo uscir fuori dell'ordine Musicale, cioè di far valer le Massima più di quello, che nelle Musica ha il suo termine, si puo procedere in infinito." See also Vitali, *Artificii Musicale* op. XIII, ♯44, ♯45.

5. Gustav Beckmann, *Das Violinspiel in Deutschland vor 1700* (Leipzig, 1918), p. 27.

6. This is very reminiscent of the devices of the Netherlanders, especially Obrecht, who, in his *Missa Graecorum,* derives parts by similar means.

on lines above the middle, be advised that all the notes on the middle line must be played by both Parts, from which it is called *Communis est via.*[7]

Uccellini's op. IX also contains a *Secondo Canon á due Violini* where one player begins at the beginning and the other at the end, in reverse. Another such is Uccellini's canon, op. V, no. 12.[8] These devices and variants are the basis of several canons of Bononcini's op. III, as the list we have given shows.

The items among Bononcini's canons which are truly remarkable for the period are the mensuration canons (nos. 26, 27, and 28) written in the archaic way, with the old signs of proportion and mensuration. They are part and parcel of Bononcini's theoretical bent and taste for "classicizing" continuity and the traditions of his craft. The principles—mensural-proportional—to which they are referring are given in his treatise, *Il Musico Prattico,* along with the modern principles of notation toward which Bononcini's ordinary practice persistently leans.

G. B. Vitali, Bononcini's contemporary and successor at Modena, continues the tradition of the canon in his op. XIII,[9] which has every appearance of being prompted by the atmosphere of Modena, since no such items appear in his work before his removal there. However, Vitali's *Artificii* make no use of the mensural-proportional signs, although the frontispiece does provide a *Cantilena á quattro* in mannered notation (a "circle" canon).

We have already had occasion (see p. 22 *supra*) to describe Bononcini's relationship to his teacher of counterpoint, Bendinelli, and its consequences. Chief among these would seem to be Bononcini's skill in the sequential type of canon which plays so large a part in his work, especially in the *sonate da chiesa.*

The respect with which Bononcini was regarded as a contrapuntist and theorist and which kept his laurels green into the eighteenth century is shown in the canon of his teacher Bendinelli, which prefaces *Il Musico Prattico.* It (Plate VIII) makes an appropriate close to our study.

7. "Canon *Communis est via,* á due violini, questo sudetto Canon, uno sonarà tutte le note delle righe di mezzo in sù l'altro sonarà tutte le note delle righe di mezzo [*sic*] in giù, avertando, che tutte le note che sono nelle righa di mezo, tutte due le Parti sono obligate a sonar le, che per tale estetto viene chiamato *Canon Communis est via.*"

8. Gustav Beckmann, *op. cit.,* p. 27.

9. Sartori, *BMI,* p. 553. New ed. Smith College Archives, Number XIV (Northampton, Mass., 1959).

Plate VIII

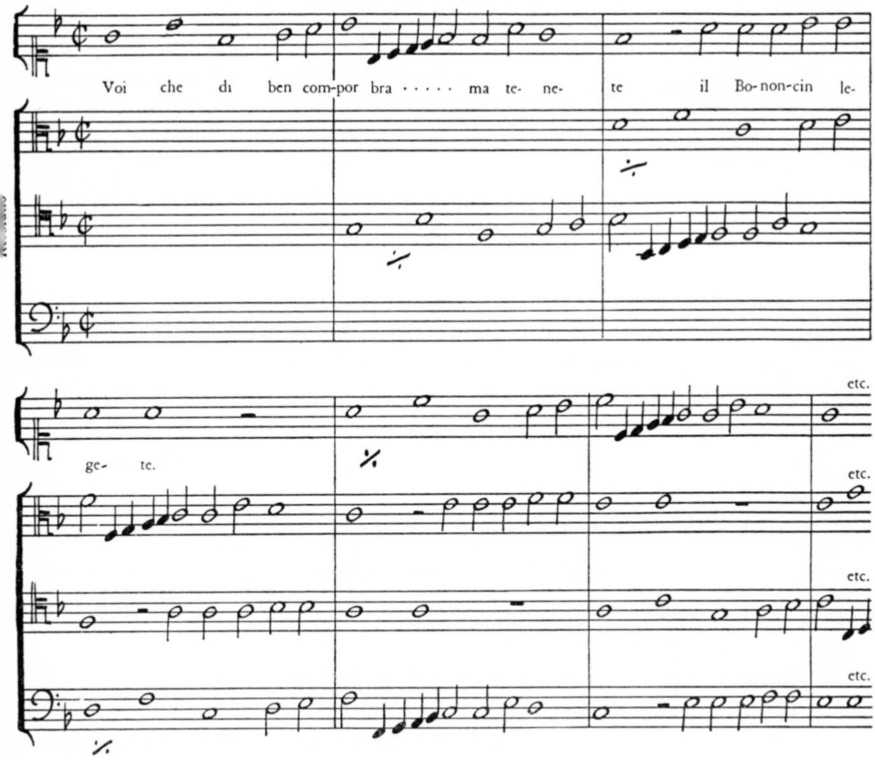

Voi che di ben com-por bra · · · · · ma te- ne- te il Bo-non-cin le- ge- te.

etc.

IN LODE DELL' AUTORE [G. M. Bononcini]
ALLI STUDIOSI DI MUSICA

Canone à Quattro voci *del Padre D. Agostino Bendinelli, canonico Regolare Lateranense.*

Il Tenore entra in decima col Canto.

L'Alto entra in Terza col Tenore.

Il Basso entra in decima col Alto.

Avertino i Cantori nel tornar da Capo di principiare nella voce che Lasciano; Cantino poi Quanto vogliono, è postone.

Chapter XIV. CONCLUSIONS

In the person of G. M. Bononcini the circumstances which result in a local tradition or "school" of instrumental music in late seventeenth-century Modena have their most complete reflection and highest exponent. This tradition takes its rise from the removal of the cultivated family d'Este (long known as patrons of the arts, especially music) from Ferrara to Modena at the end of the sixteenth century. Its direction and vitality become apparent at mid-century with the arrival of Marco Uccellini, one of the best violinists of the day, who was brought to Modena to the Este court and the Duomo in 1641.

This event is comparable in significance to the arrival at San Petronio in Bologna of Maurizio Cazzati in 1657, from which date the rise of the Bolognese instrumental school is usually reckoned. Thus it is clear that the Modenese violin school really antedates by some fifteen years that of Bologna, of which the Modenese tradition is generally considered a subsidiary branch. Moreover, the social fabric of Modena, a feudal hierarchical duchy was, in terms of the total structure of the Baroque social order (Counter-Reformation absolutism) more complete. It embraced the secular elements of the Este court as well as the ecclesiastical component of its Cathedral, whereas in the Bolognese circumstances the ecclesiastical element was (in a Papal fief) predominant. To provide a professional *ambiance* comparable to that provided by aristocratic patronage at Modena, Bolognese were impelled to form the Accademia Filarmonica, which, however, originally accepted as members (*Compositori*) only active church musicians.

The standing of the musical establishment of the Este Court was sufficient to attract significant artists (Vitali, Gabrielli, Bassani) from the Bolognese milieu, artists whose style and characteristic production were affected by their removal to Modena.

As the most gifted and technically endowed representative of the Modenese tradition, the native G. M. Bononcini, despite a tragically short life, gave to the current instrumental forms (*sonata da camera, sonate da chiesa*) a definite character which is the result of the formation of his personal gifts within the specific atmosphere of the combination of the Este Court and the Cathedral, where he was *Maestro di Cappella* from 1673 until his death in 1678. The specific and principal contributions of Bononcini to these forms include:

1. A strongly increased component of contrapuntal stringency and development. This is visible not only in the *sonata da chiesa,* where it is historically germane and results in the expansion of that form, but also in the *sonata da camera,* where it gives functional dance music a new dimension as chamber music of sufficient refinement and interest to hold the attention of player and listener. In the *sonata da chiesa,* Bononcini's interest in the canon has the specific effect of expanding the fugal movements by sequential development. His strong contrapuntal bent and theoretical rationalizing of problems of tonality have the result of regularizing fugal exposition.

2. The assimilation of current French and international dance forms and styles and their refinement in the *sonata da camera.* This is to be seen not only in the works labeled "in the French style," but in the amalgamation of French and Italian elements in all the dance and ballet forms, the *courante* most particularly, but also in the *aria, balletto, allemanda, sarabanda,* and *giga.* Bononcini's work is thus a repository for and a means of transmission to the Italian *sonata da camera* of the intellectual and formal expression of *maitres à danser* and *maitres de ballet* (with whom he may have worked directly), whose highly esteemed achievements are (given their ephemeral character and our unsympathetic age) otherwise beyond recall. Bononcini's dance forms are at the dividing line of functional and abstract music. They could, and from direct and circumstantial evidence doubtless did, serve as well for actual dancing as for chamber music. They must, therefore, be regarded as the peak of the development of these forms before the division between dance music and chamber music becomes complete, as it is in the work of Corelli (1681).

Bononcini's influence in both secular and church styles was not restricted to Italy, where his music was published and republished, but extended to England, where his works were published and reprinted by J. Walsh in several editions up to 1720. There is little reason to doubt that Bononcini was known in England before this time. An important member of the Este family, Maria Beatrice, had married James, the Duke of York, in 1673, and it seems altogether probable that she would have brought with her the printed works of Bononcini, as well as the taste for the serious Italian *sonata* which could have had as their direct result the "Sonnatas" of Henry Purcell (1683), modeled on those of "the most famed Italian Masters."

In addition to his output of music for court, church, and chamber, Bononcini entered the realm of theory with his treatise *Il Musico Prattico.* A practical manual of counterpoint, it was a standard text until the appearance of Fux's *Gradus ad Parnassum.* In several editions, Italian and German, it established and maintained Bononcini's reputation as a contrapuntist into the eighteenth century.

Last but not least, Bononcini was the father of two sons whose reputations exceed and obscure his own. Dying young, he could not oversee their education, but Giovanni and Antonio, continuing in the tradition to which he had contributed, gained the competency which carried them to highest posts in the capitals of Europe.

APPENDIX A

Discorso musicale sopra una composizione a 3, datagli per aggiungerui il Basso; et in difesa della 3ª sua opera uscita gia dalle stampe non di lui, *ma* tolta *e* rubata *in buona parte da altri autori*

Sono alcuni giorni che un mio benignissimo Signore e Padrone datami l'annessa composizione a 3, benche segnata a 4, mi comandò di farui il Basso, dicendo di hauerlo smarrito; et io, più che volontieri, e per l'ambizione, e soddisfazione sicome di chiunque da lui dipende, accettai a promisi servirlo. Poche ore passarono, che io diei piglio alla penna per aggiungere alle tre parti il sodetto basso, ma pòstole in partitura conobbi non esservi bisogno di altro fondamento, seruendo ordinariamente, per chè in alcuni luoghi le parti si cambiano tra di loro, e ciò per l'obbligazione del *suggetto,* per l'unione dell'*armonia* e per l'eleganza delle modulazioni. Dopo havere attentamente bene considerata l'accenata composizione, e trouatavi molto aggiustata e studiosa quell'armonia, che a tre voci si ricerca, supposi (e mi dò a credere di non hauere errato) che per altro non foss'io stato richiesti a farmi la 4 parte se non per mettere in chiaro la mia debole capacità e per appagare insieme la saggia curiosità di qual che accreditato professore dell'arte. Nulladimeno, posta da parte ogni riflessione, e per seruire, como ho detto il prefato mio padrone, e per compiacere a chi altro si sia, non solo ho aggiunto il Basso alle tre parti sudette, ma due, tre, e quattro in diversi modi, con una e due altra parti, come si puo uedere; protestandomi di poterui fare molt'altri Bassi con molt'altri obbligazione, e aggiungerui di vantaggio più di tre parti ancora. E ben però uero che qualunque parte aggiunta non puo imitare in tutto e per tutto il suggetto principale con figure del medisimo ualore, per esser egli unito, e molto obbligato; sicome non ponno tutti i Bassi esser totalmente varianti perchè in molti luoghi e di necessità che si trouino in una stessa corda, per ischivare diversi inconvenienti; nè tampoco può il Basso sempre modulare, secondo il suo proprio, facendo le parte principali molti mouimente che a lui si appartengono e finalmente non piro qualsivoglia parte aggiunta procedere in tutto e per tutto regolarmente, essendo altra cosa il comporre sciolto, e l'altra l'obbligato come sanno gl'intendenti. Insomma conchiudo che per fare una cantilena, se à poche come a molte uoci e ben purgata dagli errori, conuiene che il contrappuntista sia libero; che habbia perfetta cognizione di tutte quelle cose che concorrono alla composizione de i canti; degli elementi del contrappunto, della natura delle consonanze e dissonanze; delle regole e precetti generali del contrappunto, del proprio passagio di ciascuna consonanza, del legare e risolvere le dissonanze; di molti osseruazione particolari; del contrappunto semplice e del composto; de' contrappunti de' cànoni, delle fughe, et imitazione, dei dodici tuoni del canto figurato, delle cadenze e di molt'altre cose, che tralasciò per altra occasione. Quanto poi al canone unito alla composizione come sopra datami, e col motto "*caecus non iudicat*", per anche e maggiormente sperimentare con questo la mia insufficienza, sebbene trattandosi d'indouinare il pensiere d'un altro, che è un atto riservato al sommo sapere, haverei senz'alcun mio scapito potuto esimermi de tale fatica, per hauere di già colla 3ª mia opera esposta alla luce et al giudicio di ognuno pubblicato anche lo studio da me fatto, e applicatamente in simile materia di cànoni, ho però ciò non ostante uoluto aggiungere sotto la parte del soprano la resoluzione al Come sopra presentatomi; a la quale è in *subdiapente* cominciando il *conseguente* nello stesso tempo che principia la *guida* e tenendo la *figure* al doppio del suo valore. E piochè hora mi è venuto in taglio, per mia buona sorte, di poter disingannare che, censurata essa mia opera tosto che fu uscita dalle stampe, si lasciò fuggir di bocca che non era fattura di mio braccio, ma usurpata di qua e di là (ancorchè dalla tessitura tutta dell'opera medesima si potesse e possa arguire quanto sia fallace e lontano dal vero cosi fatta opinione) parmi di non douer più tacere et anzi essere stimolato a dire, che non basta solo il discorre al vento, o chiacchierare a capriccio per scredito dalle altrui composizione, ma che conuenga e sia parte e debito di veramente virtuoso il porre in chiara, cioè il nero in bianco, onde appariscono le ragioni, se i fondamenti per i quali habbiano a costitursi difettose o bastarde le stesse composizioni. E quando pure ciò non ualesse, per battere l'opinione sodetta doueva bene in ogno caso la mia tenue habilità essere e scusata, e compatita, se, camminando al pari degli anni, trascorre in forsi troppa arditezza e temerità propria della gioventù, a dichiararsi et esibirsi pronta sempre à un virtuoso cimento, sedendo con pace e quiete al tauolino, non con altro oggetto mai, che di appunto illuminare, mediante l'altrui sapere et ualore, la mia cecità, rimproveratami, m'immagino di sopra col "*caecus non iudicat di colore*" quale è scritto similmente nella prementovata mia opera sopra un *obbligo* a 4 ch'è fuori, secondo me, delle capacità di chi non è instrutto nell'arte, e di cui fu, et è costume appunto lo sempre censurare e biasimare ciò, che non intende, ben mi sono auueduto essere stato da questi solamente interpretato con senso di uanaglori e superbia, per ferire forsi nell'humile mia condizione la bassezza del mio ingegno, quasi che, non conoscendo io me stesso, habbia preteso a uoluto sourapormi à tanti eccellenti virtuosi, che hoggidi sono, à qualí in specie, si come à tutti in generale gli amatori della virtù hauerò sempre per mia somma gloria e uentura di potere con gli effetti dimostrarmi, secondo che hora per mezzo di questo foglio mi protesto e dedico divotissimamente e reverentissimo servitore.

APPENDIX B

Adriano Banchieri, *Conclusioni nel suono dell'organo*

NONA CONCLUSIONE DILUCIDATA

Delle Messe Cantabili nell'Organo in alternitava di canto fermo. Trovandosi questo segno . . . s'intende Cerimoniale. Romana cap. 28.

In tutte le feste, & Domeniche dell'anno, suonasi l'Organo nelle Chiese . . . & quivi trattaremo quello, che deve l'Organista suonare nelle Messe di Canto fermo ordinatamente.

Nelle Domeniche di tutto l'anno, finita terza si canta una Antiphona, in guise d'Introito, che comincia Asperges me Domine & è finita, & di nuovo reiterata, cantasi l'Introito, al quale cantato il versetto Sicut erat si suona un ripieno il quale serve per reiteratione dell'Introito alternando al Choro cinque risposte à gli Kirie, & Christe brevemente.

Intonata la Gloria dal Sacerdote à quella s'alterna brevemente.

Cantata l'Epistola suonasi un ripieno, overo fugha, à discrettione.

Cantato l'alleluia, & versi rispondesi per il secondo alleluia.

Sopra il Credo se ne tratterà più sotto in altro occasiô.

Cantato dal Sacerdote Oremus suonasi sino all'orate fra.

Suonasi dui fiate brevemente à gli Sanctus.

Suonasi all'levatione con gravità, che rendi devotione.

Suonasi dopo il Pax Domini una fiata All'Agnus Dei.

Replicato il secondo Agnus Dei in Choro suonasi una francese, overo aria Musicale.

RICORDO PARTICOLARE.

Il Giovedi Santo intuonata la Gloria in excelsis, insieme con le campane suonasi un ripieno allegro.

Il Sabbato Santo, intonata la Gloria s'alterna come di sopra non si suona dopò l'Epistola, ne si canta il Credo.

All'Offertorio, & Sanctus suonasi come gi à s'è detto, & similmente alla levatione (non occorrono *Agnus Dei*).

Dopo il Pax Domini si suona sin tanto, che il sacerdote e communicato.

Dopo in Choro si canta il vespro annèsso alla Messa, & suonasi dopò il salmo Laudate Dominus omnes gentes.

Suonasi al cantico Magnificat l'ottavo tuono alternativamente, & nel fine una francesina allegra, & Ita Missa est.

Il Credo nelle Messe devesi cantate tutto in choro à maggiore devotione degli fedeli . . . s'alterna però con l'Organo ogni volta, che l'Organo, & Organista risponda con voci musicali overo dove fossero poco in numero di religiosi al choro, però mentre suona l'Organo un Chierico con voce intelligible legga il versetto; Avertendo, che al l'Et incarnatus est tochi al choro a cantarlo, per la genuflessione.

BIBLIOGRAPHY

ADDISON, J. *Spectator,* No. 135 [London], Saturday, August 4, 1711.

APEL, WILLI. *The Notation of Polyphonic Music 900-1600.* Cambridge, Mass.: The Mediaeval Academy of America, 1942.

ARNOLD, F. T. *The Art of Accompaniment from a Thorough Bass.* London: Oxford University Press, 1931.

ASSOCIAZIONE DEI MUSICOLOGI ITALIANI, Pubblicazione. *Catalogo delle Opera Musicali . . . esistenti nelle Biblioteche e negli Archivi Pubblici e Privati d'Italia. Serie II: Città di Bologna; Archivio e Museo della Basilica di S. Petronio.* (Comp. A. Bonara.) Parma: Officina Grafica Fresching.

———. *Serie II: Città di Bologna; Bibl. Avv. Raimondo Ambrosini.* Parma: Officina Grafica Fresching.

———. *Serie VIII: Città di Modena; R. Biblioteca Estense.* (Comp. Pio Lodi.) Parma: Officina Grafica Fresching.

BABITZ, SOL. "A Problem of Rhythm in Baroque Music," *The Musical Quarterly,* XXXVIII, Oct., 1952, 533 ff.

Ballet du Roy dansé a Fontainbleau. Lyons: Ballard, 1664.

BANCHIERI, ADRIANO. *Conclusioni nel suono dell'Organo.* Bologna: Heredi di Gio. Rossi, 1609.

———. "La Sampogna Musicale," *Il Virtuoso Ritrovo Academico,* op. 49. Venice: Magni, 1626.

BECKMANN, GUSTAV. *Das Violinspiel in Deutschland vor 1700.* Leipzig: N. Simrock, 1918.

BLUME, FRIEDERICH, ed. *Die Musik in Geschichte und Gegenwart; allgemeine Enzyklopädie der Musik.* 6 vols. (to date). Kassel und Basel: Bärenreiter-Verlag, 1949.

BONONCINI, GIOVANNI. *Sinfonie A 5, 6, 7 e 8,* op. III. Bologna: Giacomo Monti, 1685.

———. See Chapter V, *Editions.*

BOYDEN, DAVID. "The Violin and Its Technique in the Eighteenth Century," *The Musical Quarterly,* XXXVI, Jan., 1950, 9 ff.

BUKOFZER, MANFRED. *Music in the Baroque Era.* New York: W. W. Norton and Company, Inc., 1947.

BYROM, JOHN. "Epigram on the Feuds Between Handel and Bononcini," *Miscellaneous Poems.* Manchester, 1773.

CAROSO, FABRITIO. *Nobiltà di dame del S^r. Fabritio Caroso da Sermoneta, libro altra volta, chiamato Il ballarino Nuouamente dal proprio auttore corretto ampliato di nuoui balli, di belle regole & alla perfetta Theorica ridotto: con le creante necessarie à caualieri, e dame. Aggiontovi il basso, & il Soprano della musica: & con l'intauolatura del liuto à ciascun ballo-ornato di vaghe & bellissime figure in rame. . . .* Venetia: Presso il Muschio, 1605.

CAZZATI, MAURIZIO. *Messa, e Salmi a tre voce, Alto, Tenore, e Basso con violin & Ripieni a Bene placito,* op. XXIV. Bologna: Antonio Pisarri, 1660.

———. *Risposta alle Oppositioni fatte del Signor Giulio Cesare Arresti.* Bologna: Heredi del Dozza, 1663.

———. *Sonate à due, trè, quattro, e cinque, con alcune per Tromba,* op. XXXV. Bologna: Marino Silvani, 1665.

———. *Trattenimenti Per Camera D'Arie, Correnti, E Balletti, A' Due Violini, E Violone, Se Piace,* op. XXII. Bologna: Antonio Pisarri, 1660.

———. *Varii, E Diversi Capricci Per Camera, e per Chiesa, da sonare con diuersi Instromenti. A Uno, Due E Tre,* op. L. Bologna, 1669.

COLOMBI, GIUSEPPE. *Balletti, Correnti, Gighe, Sarabande A due Violini, e Violone, ò Spinetta,* op. III. Bologna: Giacomo Monti, 1674.

———. *Delle Sinfonie Da Camera Brandi, E Corrente Alla Francese, Con Corrente, & Arie da Camera, e Suonate per suonare à due, à trè, & à quattro,* op. I. Bologna: [Monti?], 1668.

———. *La Lira Armonica, Sinfonie a due Violini, col suo Basso continuo,* op. II. Bologna: Giacomo Monti, 1673.

———. *Sonate A Due Violini Con un Bassetto Viola se piace,* op. IV. Bologna: Giacomo Monti, 1676.

———. *Sonate Da Camera A Tre Strumenti, Due Violini, e Violone, ò Cimbalo,* op. V. Bologna: Pietro Maria Monti, 1689.

COLONNA, G. P. *Missa Prima a 8, due cori e stromenti.* MS., Biblioteca Conservatorio Cherubini, Florence.

———. *Motetti sacri a voce sola con due violini,* op. II. Bologna: Giacomo Monti, 1681.

DAVIES, SIR JOHN. *Orchestra, or a Poem of Dancing.* Ed. E. M. W. Tillyard. London: Chatto and Windus, 1947.

DE LAUZE, F. *Apologie de la Danse* (1623). Translated by Joan Wildeblood. London: Frederick Muller, Ltd., 1952.

ECORCHEVILLE, JULES. *Vingt Suites d'Orchestre du XVII Siècle.* 2 vols. Paris: L. Marcel Fortin, 1906.

EINSTEIN, ALFRED. "Ancora sull'Aria di Ruggiero," RMI, XLI, p. 163. "Die Aria di Ruggiero," SIMG, XIII, p. 444. *The Italian Madrigal.* 3 vols. Princeton: University Press, 1949.

EITNER, ROBERT. *Biographisch-Bibliographisches Quellen-Lexicon der Musiker und Musikgelehrten.* 10 vols. Leipzig: Breitkopf und Haertel, 1900-1904.

FOCILLON, HENRI. *Vie des Formes.* Paris: Presses Universitaires, 1947.

FRESCOBALDI, G. *Il primo libro di Capricci, Canzone Francese . . . Fatti Sopra Diversi Soggetti et Arie. . . .* Venice, 1626.

GANASSI, SYLVESTRO. *Opera Intitulata Fontegara Laquale insegna a sonare di flauto con tutta l'arte opportuna a esso instrumento massime il diminuire il quale sara utile ad ogni instrumento di fiato et corde: et ancora a chi si dileta di canto. . . .* Venice, 1535. New ed. by Hildemarie Peter. Berlin, 1956.

GEMINIANI. *The Art of Playing the Violin.* London, 1751. Facsimile ed. D. Boyden. London: Oxford University Press, 1951.

GIEGLING, FRANZ. *Guiseppe Torelli.* Basel: Bärenreiter-Verlag, 1949.

HAAS, ROBERT M. *Die Musik des Barocks. Handbuch der Musikwissenschaft.*

Ernst Bücken, ed. vol. 3. Wildpark-Potsdam: Akademische verlagsgesellschaft, 1928.

Hayes, Gerald R. *Musical Instruments and Their Music 1500-1750.* 2 vols. Oxford University Press. London: Humphrey Milford, 1928-30.

Iselin, D. J. *Biago Marini.* Basel: Bärenreiter-Verlag, 1930.

Klenz, William. "Les Origines du Violoncelle Instrument Soliste," *Le Conservatoire: Bulletin du Conservatoire Nationale de Paris,* November, 1952.

Leggi Presentate dall'Accademia de Filarmonici. Bologna: Lelio dalla Volpe, 1773.

Lipsius, Marie [pseud. La Mara]. *Musikerbriefe aus fünf Jahrhunderten, Erster Band.* Leipzig: Breitkopf und Hartel, 1886.

Luin, Elisabetta J. *Repertorio dei Libri Musicali di S. A. S. Francesco II d'Este nell'Archivio di Stato di Modena.* Florence: Leo S. Olschki, 1936.

Mann, A. *A Study of the Fugue.* New Brunswick, N. J.: Rutgers, 1958.

Maylender, Michele. *Storia delle Accademie d'Italia.* Vol. VI. Bologna: L. Capelli, 1926.

Menestrier, Père Claude Francois. *Des Ballets Anciens et Modernes Selon Les Regles du Theatre.* Paris: René Guignard, 1672.

Mersenne, Marin. *Harmonie Universelle contenant la théorie et la pratique de la musique où il est traité de la Nature de Sons & des Movvemens, des Consonances, des Dissonances, des Genres, des Modes, de la Composition, de la Voix, des Chants, & de toutes sortes d'Instruments Harmoniques.* Par F. Marin Mersenne de l'Ordre des Minimes. Paris: Chez Sebastian Cramoisy, 1636.

Mompellio, Federico. *Sigismondo d'India.* Milan: Ricordi, 1957.

Morini, Nestore. *La R. Accademia Filarmonica di Bologna.* Bologna: L. Capelli, 1930.

Nettl, Paul. *Story of Dance Music.* New York: Philosophical Library, 1947.

North, Roger. *The Musicall Grammarian.* Edited by Hilda Andrews. London: Oxford University Press, 1925.

The Universal Dictionary of the English Language. Oxford: Clarendon Press, 1955.

Paget, Violet [Vernon Lee]. *Studies in the 18th Century in Italy.* 2d ed. London: Unwin, 1907.

Palestrina, Giovanni Pierluigi da. Opere Complete. Ed. Casimiri. Rome: Fratelli Scalera, 1939.

Pancaldi, Evarista. *Atti e memorie di R. Deputazione di Storia Patria per le provincie modenesi.* Vol. VI, *Su la Famiglia dei Bononcini.* Modena, 1929.

——— and Roncaglia, Gino. *Studie Documenti della Reale Deputazione di Storia Patria per l'Emilia e Romagna* ("Maestri del Duomo di Modena"): Vol. III, *D. Marco Uccellini* and *Padre Mario Agatea;* Vol. IV, *G. M. Bononcini;* Vol. V, *Giuseppe Colombi.* Modena, 1939-1941.

Penna, P. F. Lorenzo. *Li Primi Albori Musicali.* Bologna: Giacomo Monti, 1684.

Playford, John. *An Introduction to the Skill of Musik: in three books.* London: Printed by W. Pearson for J. Sprint, 1713.

PULVER, JEFFREY. "The Ancient Dance Forms," *Proceedings of the Musical Association*. London: Novello and Co., Limited, 1913-1914.

RAMEAU, P. *The Dancing Master* (1725). Translated by Cyril W. Beaumont. London: C. W. Beaumont, 1931.

Ricordi per li Signori Compositori dell'Accademia di Signori Filarmonici. Bologna: Eredi d'Antonio Pisarri, 1689.

RIEMANN, HUGO. "Der Basso Ostinato und die Anfänge der Kantate," SIMG, XIII, p. 531.

———. *Old Chamber Music.* 4 vols. London: Augener n. d.

RINALDI, MARIO. *Arcangelo Corelli.* Milan: Edizioni Curci, 1935.

RONCAGLIA, GINO. *Atti e memorie della Accademia di Scienze, Lettore e Arti di Modena.* Vol. X, *Guiseppe Colombi e la vita Musicale Modenese durante il Regno Francesco II d'Este.* Modena, 1952.

———. *Atti e memorie di R. Deputazione di Storia patria per le provincie modenesi.* Ser. VII, Vol. VI, *Di Insigni musicisti modenesi.* Modena, 1929.

———. *La Cappella Musicale del Duomo di Modena.* Vol. V, *Historiae Musicae Cultores Biblioteca.* Florence: Olschki, 1957.

SACHS, CURT. *World History of the Dance.* New York: W. W. Norton, 1937.

SARTORI, CLAUDIO. *Bibliografia della Musica Strumentale Italiana Stampata in Italia fino al 1700.* Biblioteca di Bibliografia Italiana XXIII. Florence: Leo S. Olschki, 1952.

———. "Une pratique des musiciens lombards (1582-1639), l'hommage des chansons instrumentales aux familles d'une ville," *La Musique Instrumentale de la Renaissance.* Edited by J. Jaquot. Paris: Centre national de la recherche scientifique, 1955.

SCHENK, ERIC, ed. *Die Italienische Trio Sonate.* Cologne: Arno Verlag, 1954.

———. "Osservazioni sulla Scuola instrumentale modenese nel Seicento," *Atti e Memorie della Accademia di Scienze, Lettere e Arti di Modena,* Series V, Vol. X, Modena, 1952.

SCHERING, ARNOLD. *Geschichte der Musik in Beispielen.* Leipzig: Breitkopf und Härtel, 1931.

SMITH, WILLIAM C. *A Bibliography of the Musical Works Published by John Walsh during the years 1695-1720.* London: Printed for the Bibliographical Society at the University Press, Oxford, 1948.

SOLERTI, ANGELO. *Musica, Ballo e Drammatica.* Firenzi: R. Bemporad & Figlio, Editori, 1905.

SQUIRE, W. BARCLAY. *Catalogue of Printed Music Published between 1487 and 1800 Now in the British Museum.* London: Printed by Order of the Trustees, 1912.

———. *Purcell as Theorist.* Sammelbände der Internationalen Musikgesellschaft. Vol. VI. Leipzig: Breitkopf & Härtel, 1904-1905.

TABOUROT, JEHAN [pseud., THOINOT ARBEAU]. *Orchesography, A Treatise in the Form of a Dialogue Whereby all manner of persons may easily acquire and practice the honourable exercise of dancing.* Translated by Cyril W. Beaumont. London: C. W. Beaumont, 1925.

TORCHI, LUIGI, ed. *L'Arte Musicale in Italia.* 7 vols. Milan: G. Ricordi e C., 1897.

TOSI, G. F. *Observations on the Florid Song.* London, 1743.

Tratado de glosas sobre clausulas, Rome, 1553. New ed. by M. Schneider. Kassel, 1936.

UCCELLINI, D. MARCO. *Sinfonici Concerti, Brieui, è facili, à uno, à due, à tre, & à quatro strumenti; Ogni cosa, con il suo Basso Continuo, Per Chiesa, è Per Camera. Con Brandi, è Corenti alla Francese, e Balletti al Italiana, giusta l'uso aprouatissimo della Corte di Parma,* op. IX. Venetia: Francesco Magni detto Gardano, 1667.

URSPRUNG, OTTO. *Handbuch der Musikwissenschaft.* Ernst Bücken, ed. Vol. IX, *Die Katholische Kirchenmusik.* New York: Musurgia Publishers, 1931. Wildpark-Potsdam: Akademische verlagsgesellschaft.

VALDRIGHI, LUIGI FRANCESCO. *Musurgiana No. 8, I Bononcini da Modena.* Modena: G. T. Vicenzi e Nipoti, 1882.

———. *Musurgiana No. 19, Capelle, Concerti e Musiche di Casa d'Este.* Modena: G. T. Vincenzi e Nipoti, 1884.

VATIELLI, FRANCESCO. *Arte e Vita Musicale a Bologna.* Vol. I. Bologna: Nicola Zanichelli, 1927.

VITALI, G. B. *Artificii Musicali Ne Quali Si Contengono Canoni in Diverse Maniere, Contrapunti Dopii, Inuentionj Curiose, Capritii, E Sonate,* op. XIII. Modena: Eredi Cassiani Stampatori Episcopali, 1689. New ed. Louise Rood and Gertrude Smith. Northampton, Mass., 1959.

———. *Balletti, Correnti alla Francese, Gagliarde, e Brando per Ballare. Balletti, Correnti, e Sinfonie da Camera à quattro Stromenti,* op. I. Bologna: Giacomo Monti, 1667.

———. *Balletti, Correnti e Capricci Per Camera,* op. VIII. Modena: Gasparo Ferri, 1683.

———. *Salmi Concertati a due, tre, quattro e cinque Voci,* op. VI. Bologna: Giacomo Monti, 1686.

———. *Sonate Da Camera A Trè, Due Violini, E Violone,* op. XIV. Modena: Christoforo Canobi, 1692.

WAGNER, PETER. "Die Konzertierende Messe in Bologna," *Festschrift . . . H. Kretschmar.* Leipzig: Breitkopf und Härtel, 1918.

———. *Geschichte der Messe* (I Teil, bis 1600). Kleine Handbucher der Musikgeschichte nach Gattungen. Vol. XI, 1. Leipzig: Breitkopf und Härtel, 1913.

WALTHER, JOHANN GOTTFRIED. *Musikalisches Lexicon oder Musikalische Bibliothek,* 1732. Documenta Musicologica, Erste Reine: Druckschriften-Faksimiles III. Kassel und Basel: Bärenreiter, 1953.

WASIELEWSKI, J. W. VON, ed. *Instrumentalsätze vom Ende des XVI. bis Ende des XVII. Jahrhunderts.* Berlin: Leo Liepmannssohn. [1874].

WILSON, J., ed. *Roger North on Music.* London: Novello, 1959.

WIND, EDGAR. *The Feast of the Gods.* Cambridge, Mass.: Harvard, 1948.

INDEX

SUPPLEMENT

SELECTIONS FROM THE WORKS OF G. M. BONONCINI *ET AL.*

FOREWORD TO SUPPLEMENT

Since no significant body of Bononcini's work is accessible, it has been thought worthwhile to provide a sizable body of complete works, rather than inevitably unsatisfactory fragmentary examples.

What is at hand is to all intents and purposes the text of the surviving documents. The works have been scored directly from the original parts, either MS or printed editions. Of the two the MS parts, although often less complete than the printed editions, are the easier to read, since their style kept pace with new requirements, (beams for 8^{ths}, and 16^{ths}, long slurs, etc.). The style of the printed parts is perforce that of the (older) movable type from which they were printed.

A few—very few—obvious errors have been corrected without comment by collation between MS and printed parts, between which discrepancies are remarkably few.

In general the habits, together with amenities, asperities, peculiarities, and some apparent inconsistencies of 17th century notation have been retained. This principally for the same reasons as they were adopted in the first place—they convey the most information with the fewest symbols. In particular anything which could indicate a special way of performance (accentuation or ornamentation etc.—as for example the hemiola) has been left in its original form.

The reader should be warned that accidentals *usually, but by no means always* apply only to the note they prefix and its immediate repetition. A number (by no means exhaustive or necessarily binding) of editorial suggestions in regard to alterations have been made. These and others must be decided on their own merits nor is an entirly consistent procedure essential or desirable.

The "extra" accidentals which appear in the Basso Continuo part apply of course to the structure of the chord. The sharp, ♯ and flat, ♭ are used as mutual contradictions, although the natural, ♮ is not unknown.

Bar lines, used very irregularly in the parts, have been supplied according to the precepts and examples given by Bononcini in *Il Musico Prattico,* op. VIII, and in his only published work in score, the Madrigals of op. XII. This corresponds to general usage of the period which explains one facet of meaning of the term *spartire*—partitura, i.e. "score" in the sense of "mark with lines." In the interests of a rational score *fermate,* tempo indications, and some dynamic marks have been regularized in location and spelling.

CONTENTS

G. M. Bononcini

Op. I

Op. II

Op. III

[, Sonata I

13
6
56
56
56
56
56
56
6
19
6
56
6
5
6
6

6
Adagio
43
60
6
5

73
Allegro
79

85
5b6 6 6b5
6 6b5
91
6 5b 65 65
[#]
56 56 56

)p. I, Sonata 2

6
5
6
5
6
6
2
6
4 3
6
6
6
4 #

28
5
34
6
7 6 #
6
4 3

52
58

[♯]
4
4 ♯
6
6
5
[♯]
6
6
5

Op. I, Sonata 3

7
6
6
5
10
6
6
5
6♯
6
[♯]
6
6
6♯
16
6
♯6
6
6♯

Largo
19
25
6

iola maggiore ●●● = ◆◆◆ = ○○○ , cf. text p. 119.

55
6
5
6
61
6

, Sonata 4

Allegro

6 6/5 6 6/5 6

6 6 5 6

6/5 6

6 6/5 6 6/5 6/5

po
po
f
13
19

Adagio, tremolo

61
67
[Allegro]
Allegro

Op. I, Sonata 5

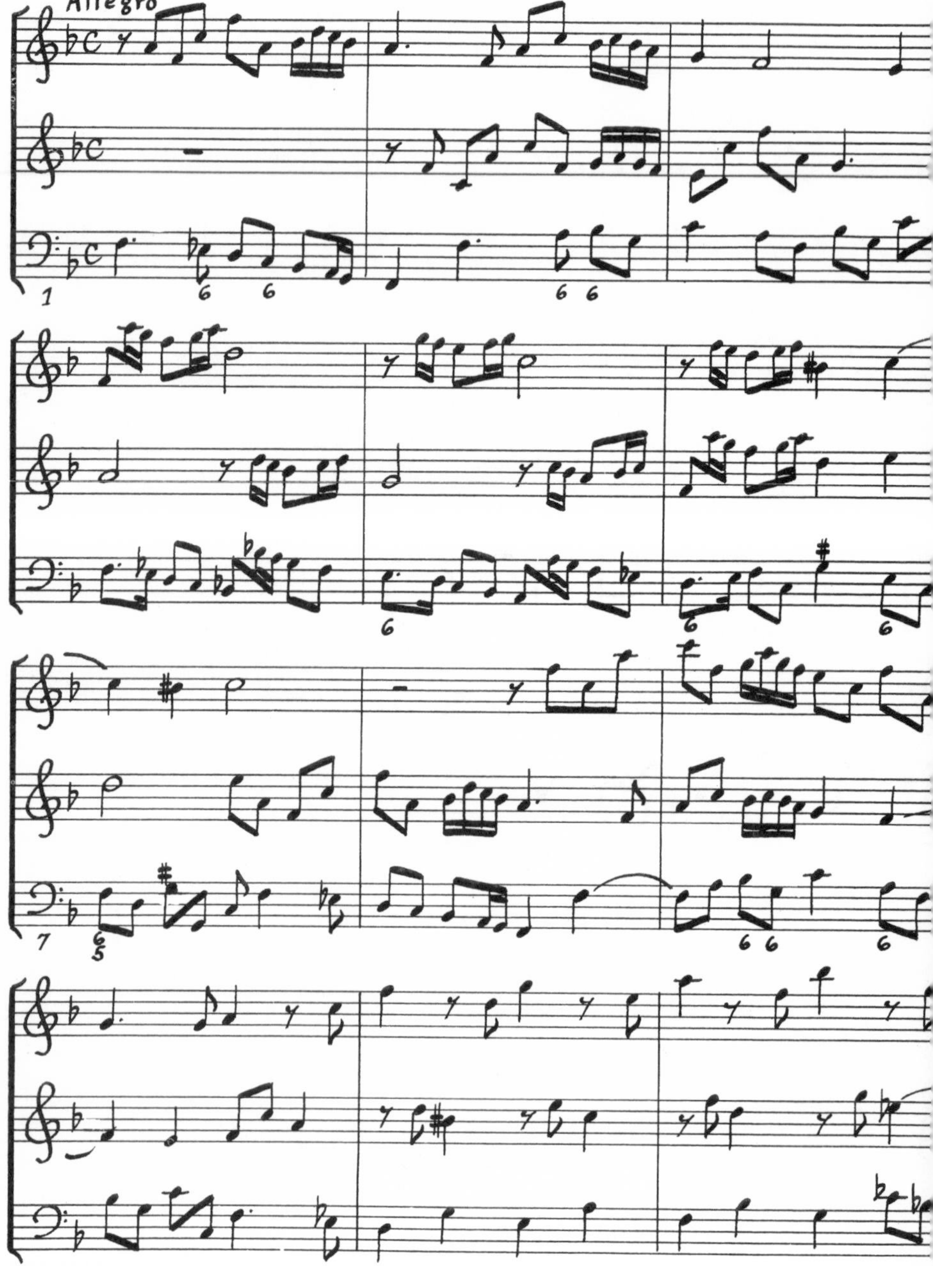

25
6
Grave
6 ♭5
8 ♭7
32
9♭ 8
56
56
7
5 ♭7
43
6 ♭5

50
4#
6
56
3 4 3
6

4#
6
6
6
6
4#
8
6
6
6

74
5
6
6
80
6
7 6
Adagio
83
6
5
6
7 6

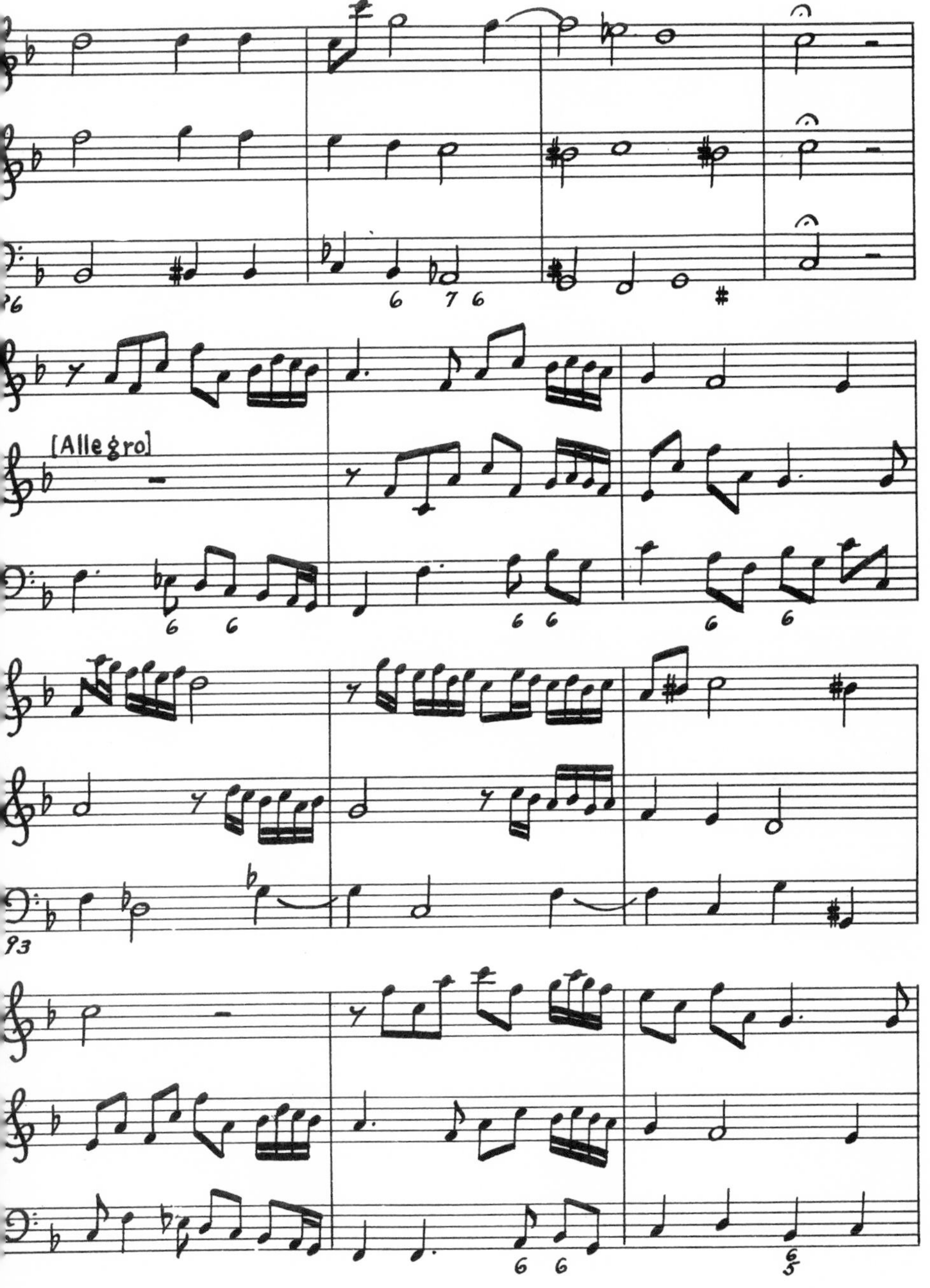

[Allegro]

Op. I, Sonata 6

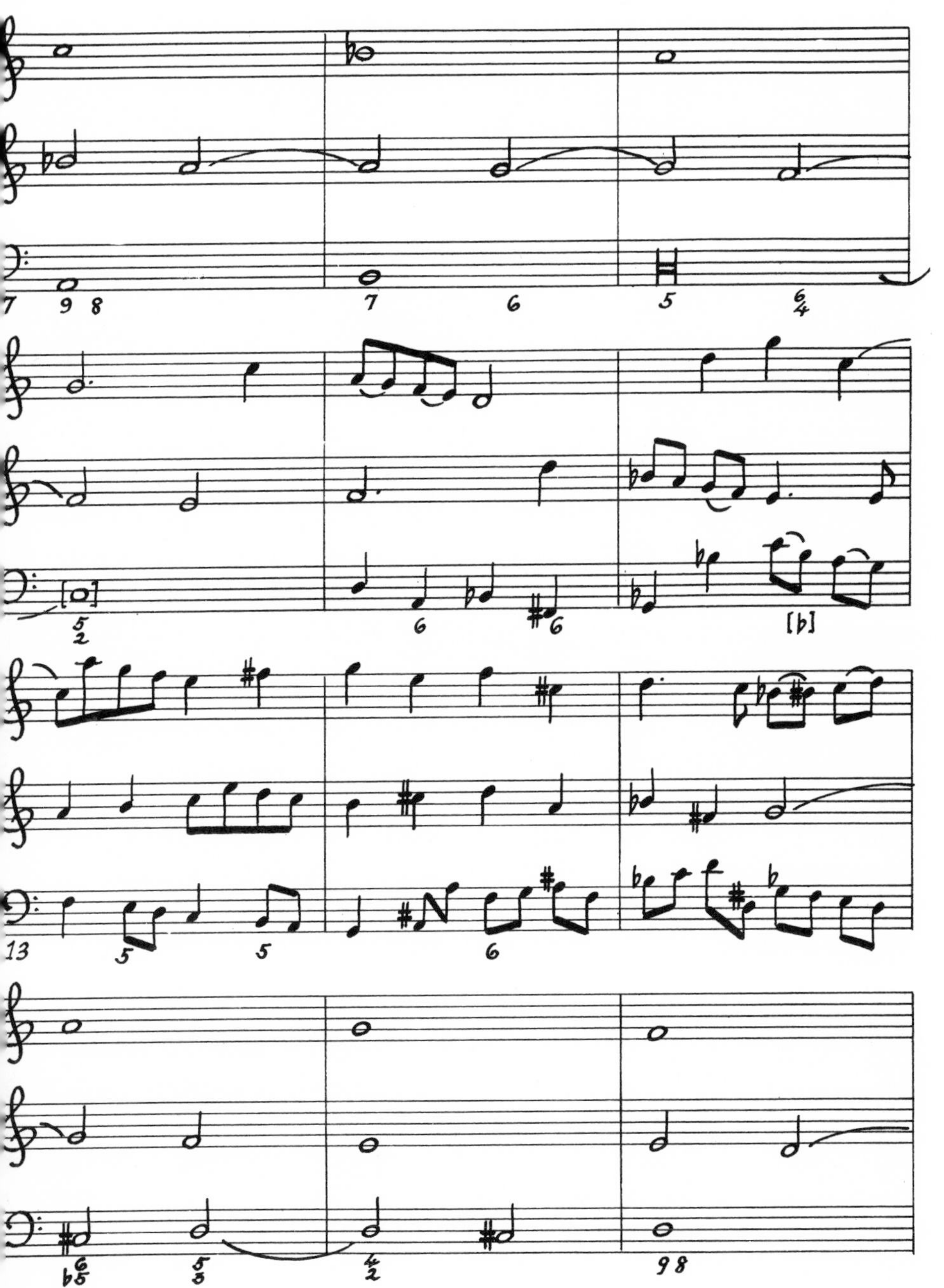

Allegro

Adagio

In Canon
56
4 3
4 3
6
6
4 3
♭4 3
[♭]
62
4 3
6 5
6 5
4 3

[#]
68
43
4
6
65
43
74
65
43
65
43
6

Grave
86

[All°]

122
128
Adagio

I, Sonata 7

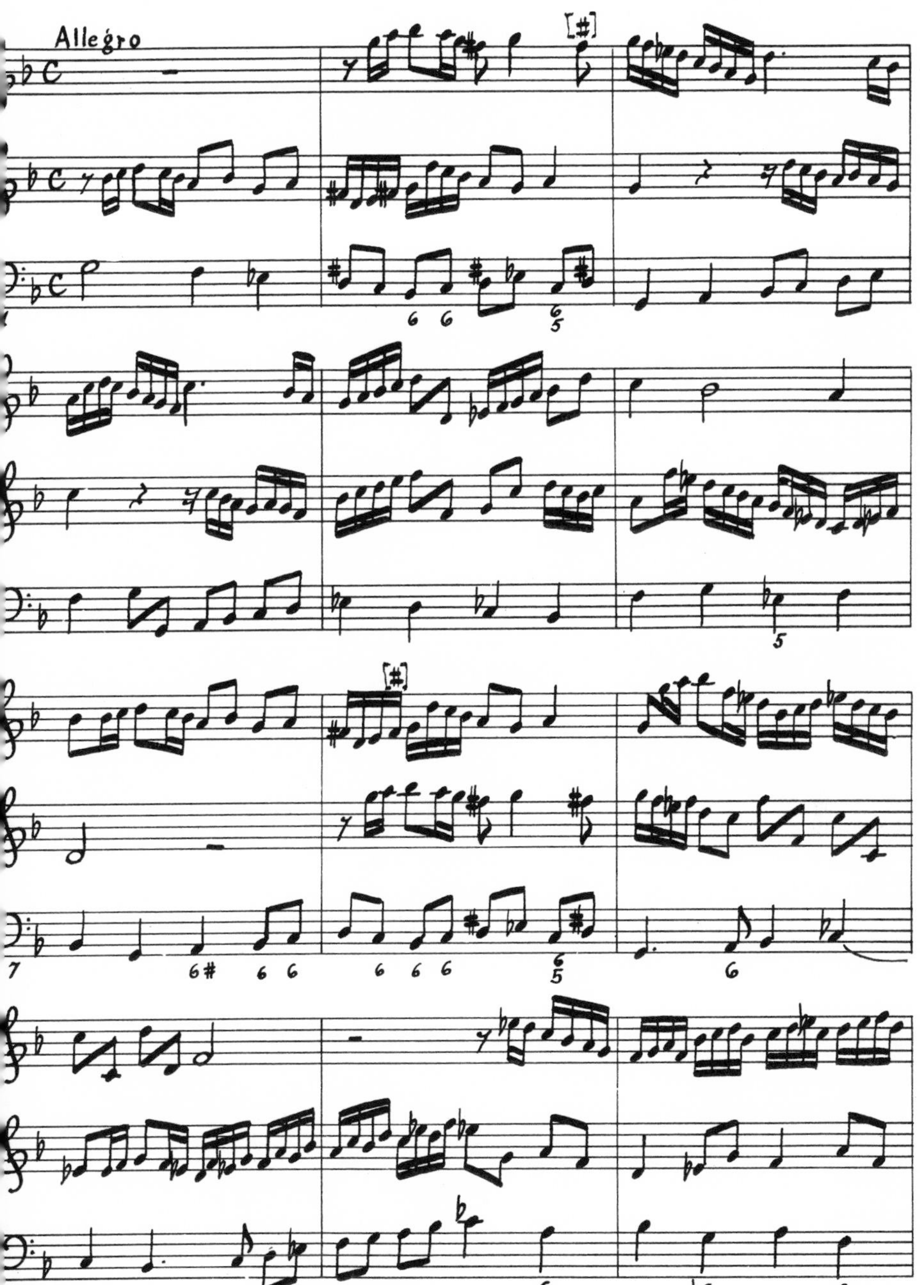

13
2
6
7 6
6 6
4#
6♭
6
[♭]
19
43
6
43
Adagio
9
8
7
6

26
[6]
6
6
6
6 5
4♯
34
6
6♯
6
Presto
6 5
4 3

42
Grave
48

Allegro
67
73

Adagio
6
5 #6

Op. I, Sonata 8

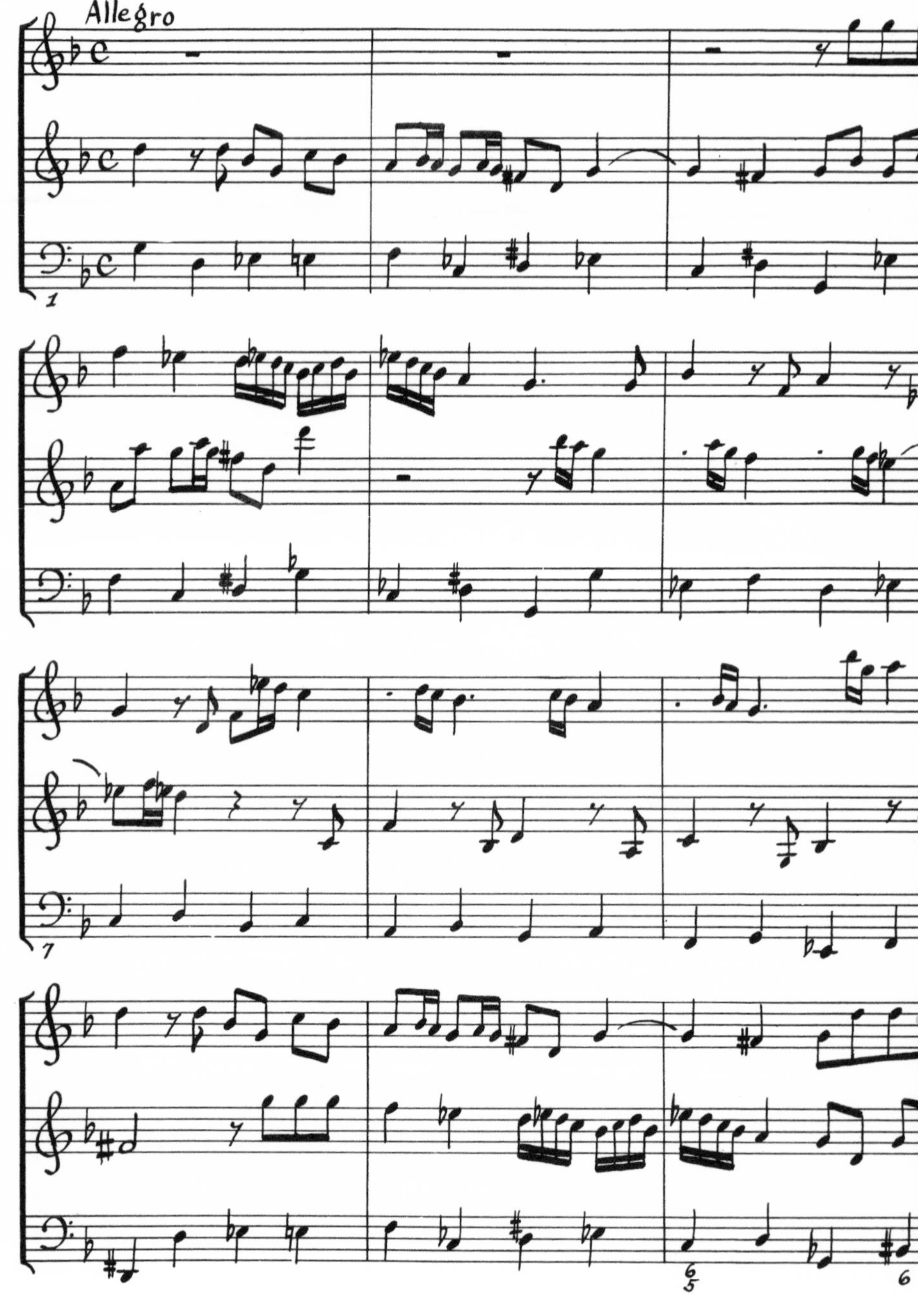

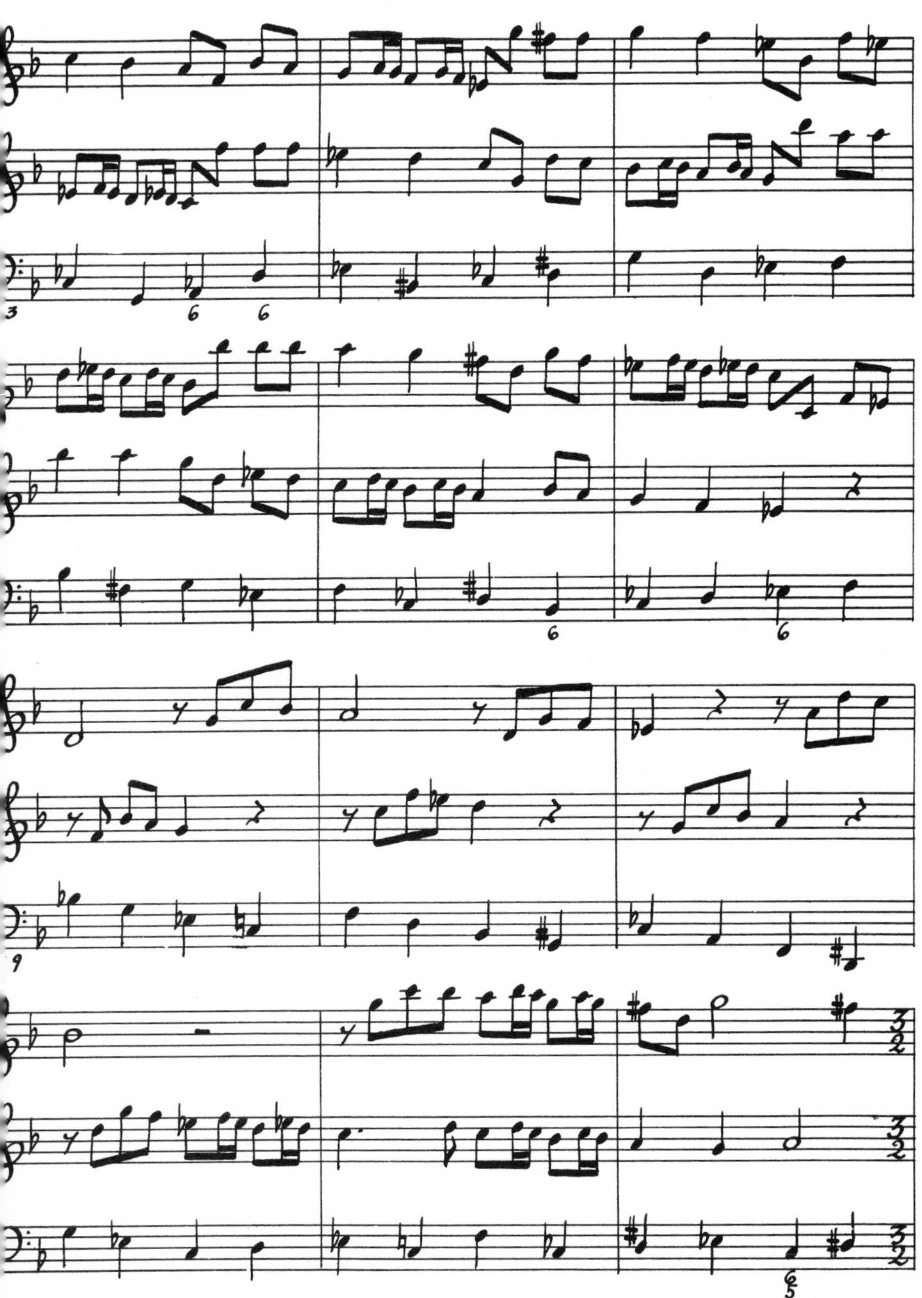

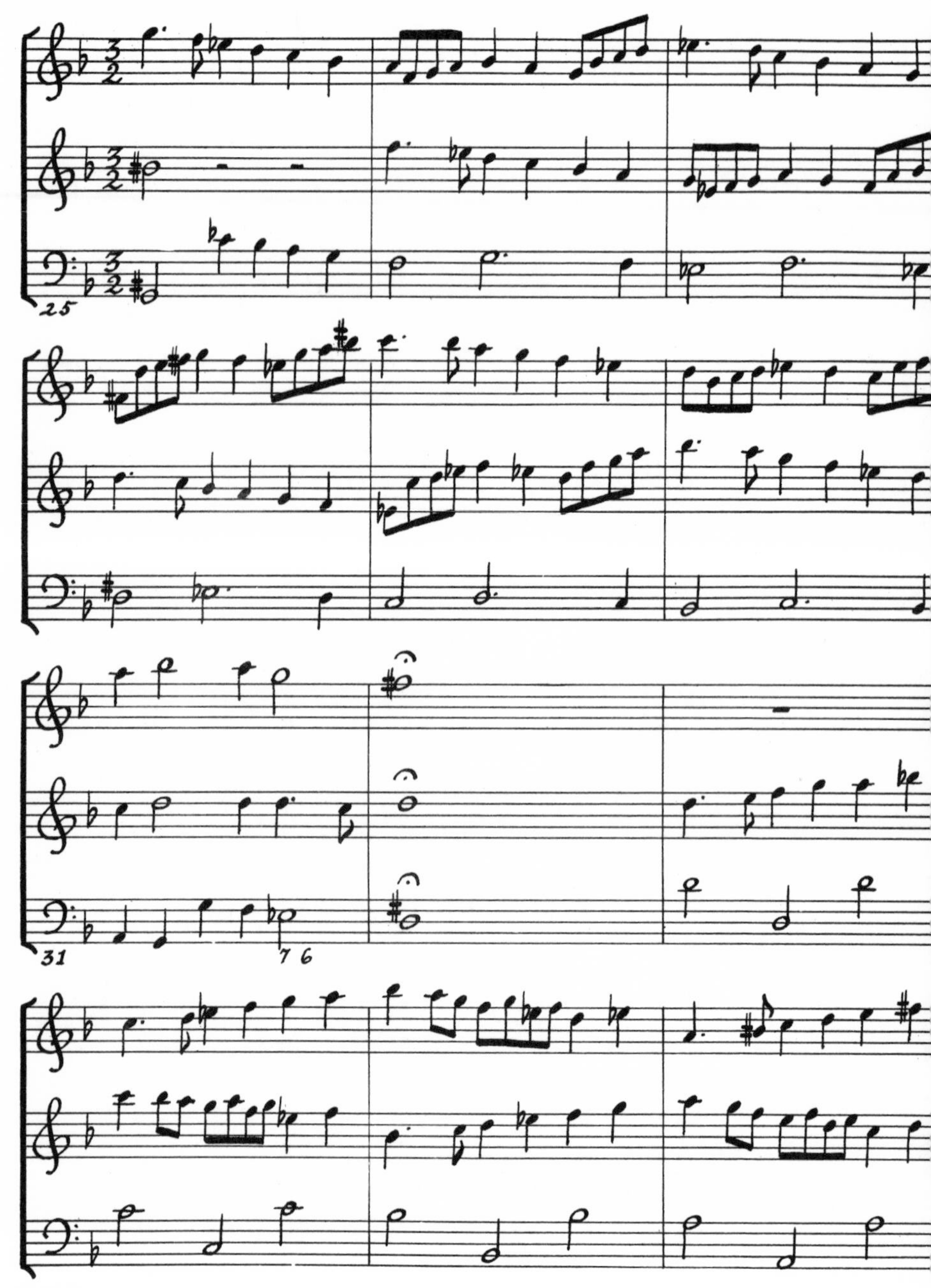
25
31
7 6

Adagio
p:
f
p:

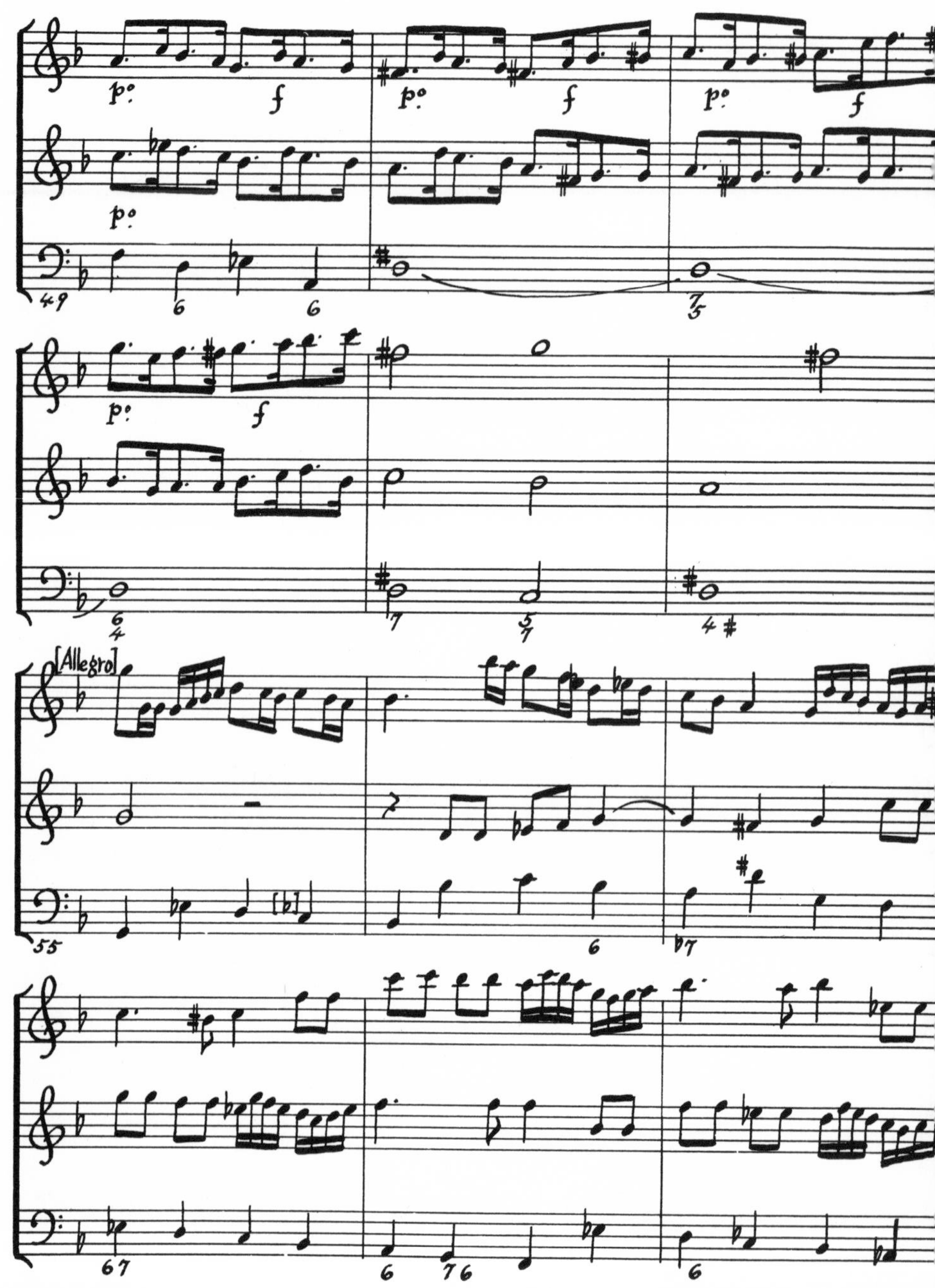

49
[Allegro]
55

[6]
[6]
5 6
4
5 6
3 4
6
5 6
6
5
4 3

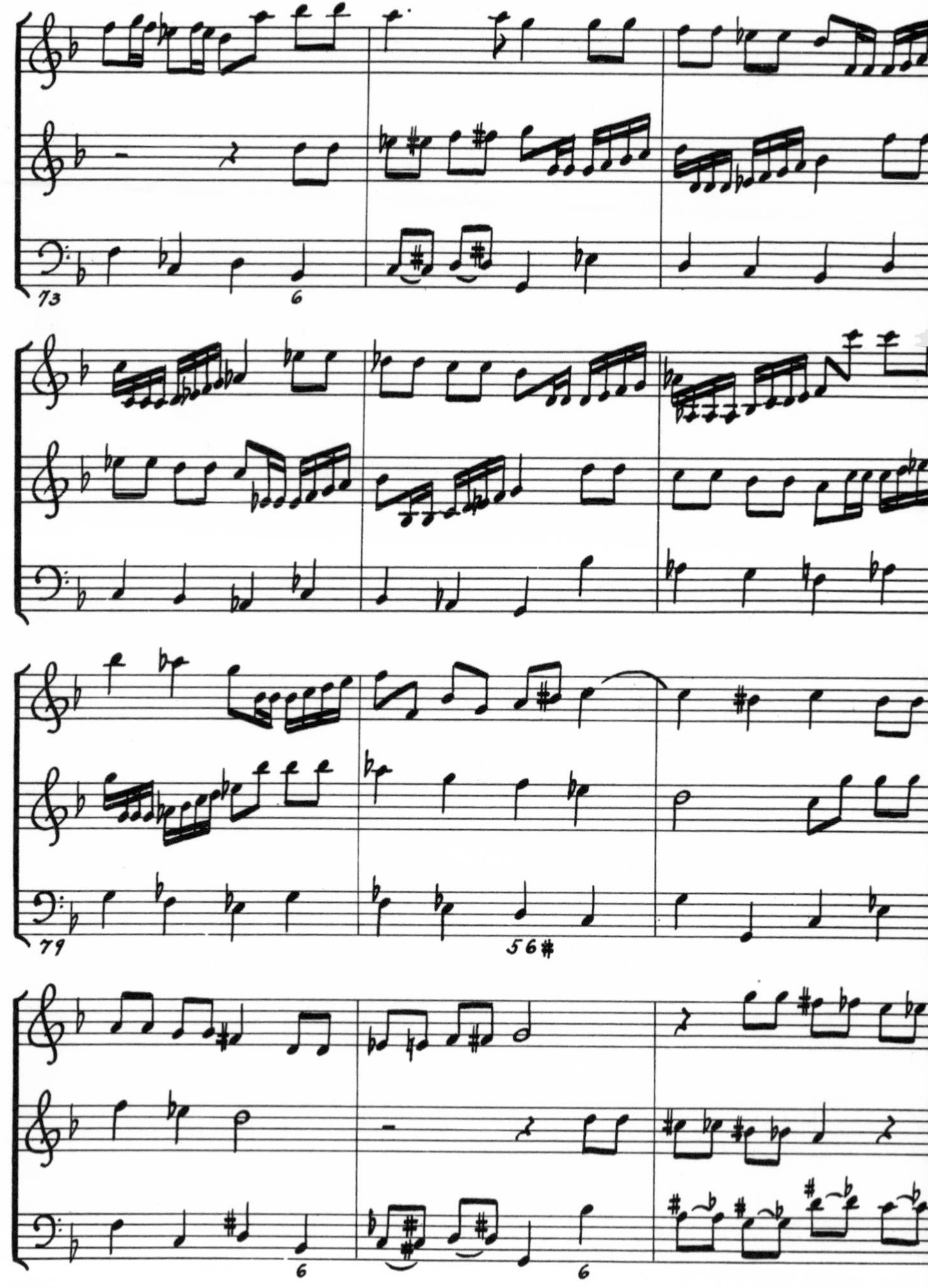
73
79

I, Sonata 9

31
6
Adagio
37
9 8
7 6 6 5
Tremolo
6

[Allegro]

55
6
6
4
5#
61
6
76
43

p. I, Sonata 12

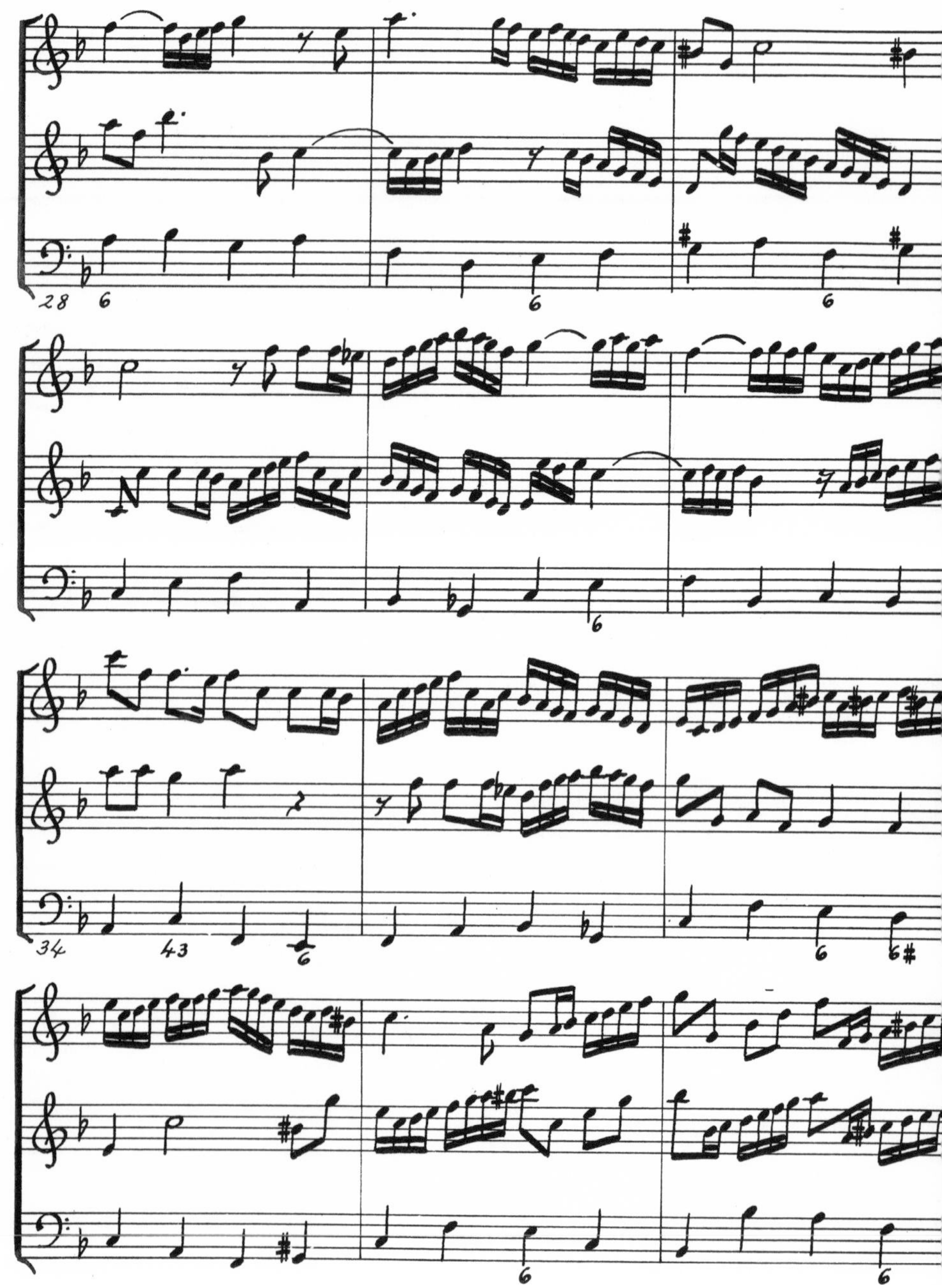

Grave

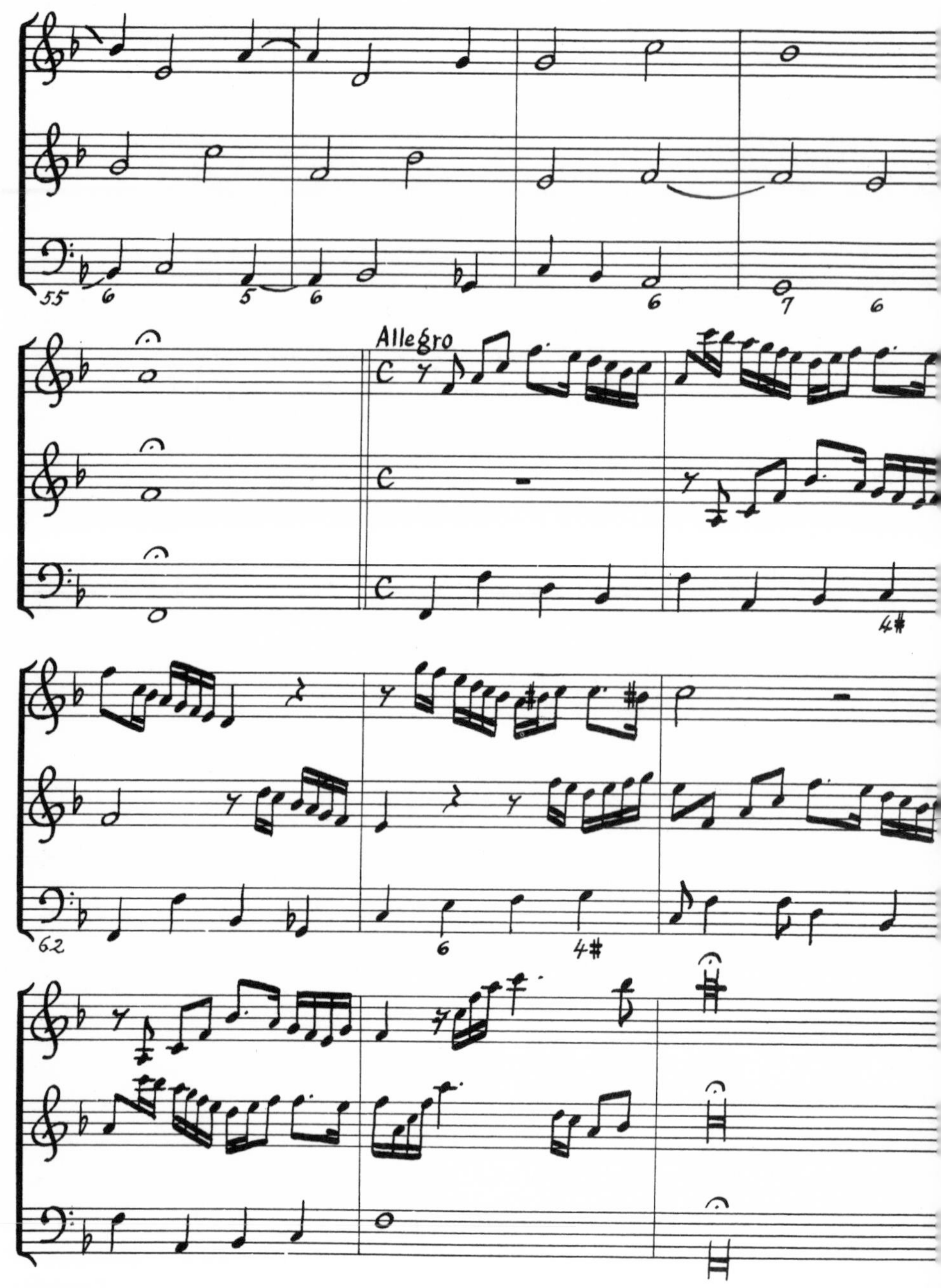
Allegro

. I, [13.] Brando I*ma* Parte

5
76
6
3
5
6
6
9
4#
[14.] Brando IIda Parte
6
76
17
76

[15.] Brando IIIa Parte

38
6
S.
S.
46

16.] Gavotta
[17.] Sua Corrente (cf. Brando Ima Parte [13])

Op. II, 3. Gigha

3
Op. II, 4. Gigha

7
Op. II, 6. Gigha
6
18

Op. II, 7. Gigha

Op. II, 11. Balletto

[#]
p
16
[#]
Op. II, 25. Corrente
4

24
32

. II, 37. Aria, *Discordia Concors* à 4*

*The Modena MS (of which this a scoring) affords only the three parts ven. The printed edition, which is "à 4" is currently (1959) untraceable.

13
19
Op. II, [38.] Sua Corrente

Op. III, 5. Gigha à 4

4
6
56
6

7

10
6
43
56
43

13
6
#6
5
6

16
#4 #
6
6 6 # 4#

[♩.?]
19

III, 7. Gigha à 4*

*This *Gigha,* in the French style, is, like other parts of this opus, without so Continuo. On page 7 of the BC part, Monti edition, "7, Gigha à 4 cet." On p. 14 "16, Sonata da Camera à 4 Tacet" and on p. 15 "18, e 19 ndo e Corrente in stil Francese à quattro Tacet."

. III, 8. Allemanda à 4

7
6
34
3

10
#4

13
6
6

16
6
43

Op. III, 10. Allemanda a 4

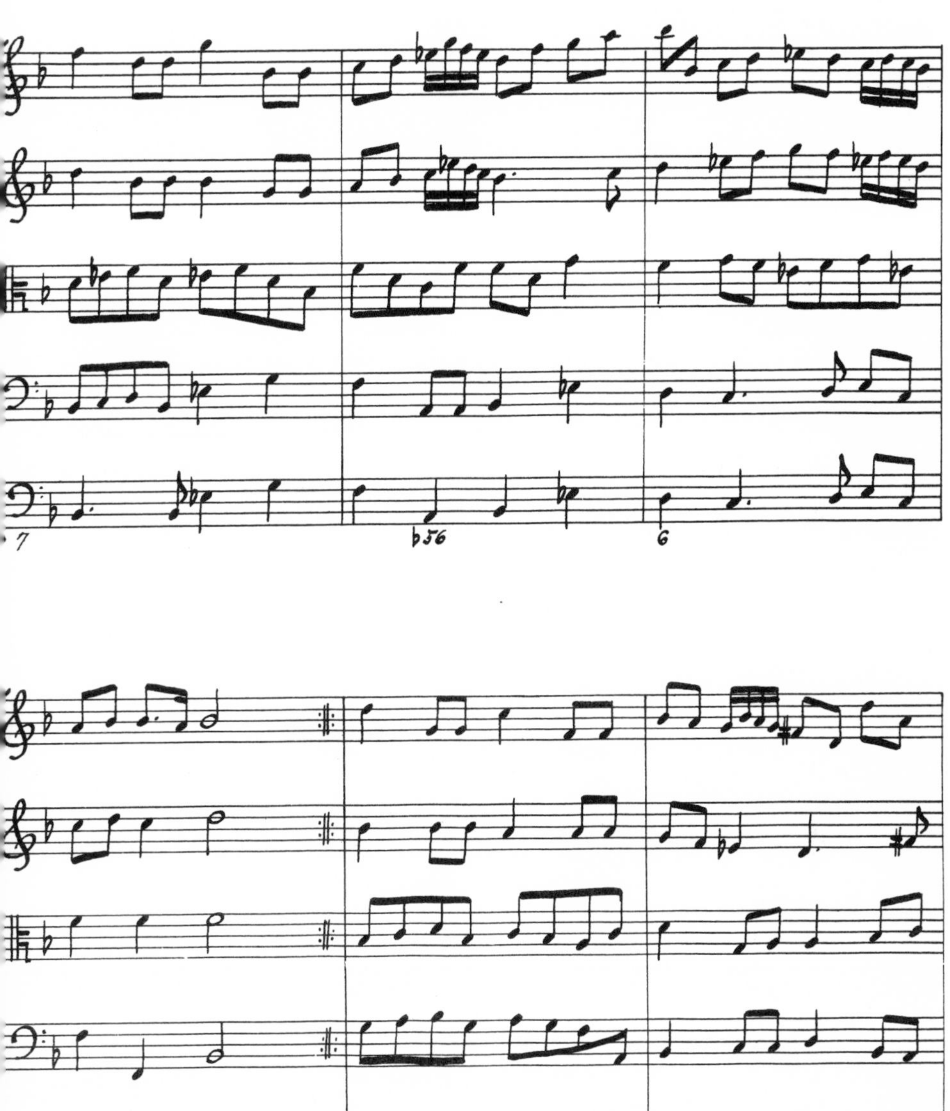
7
♭56
6
10
43
56
♯6

13
#4
#

16
6
5

. III, 12. Allemanda à 4

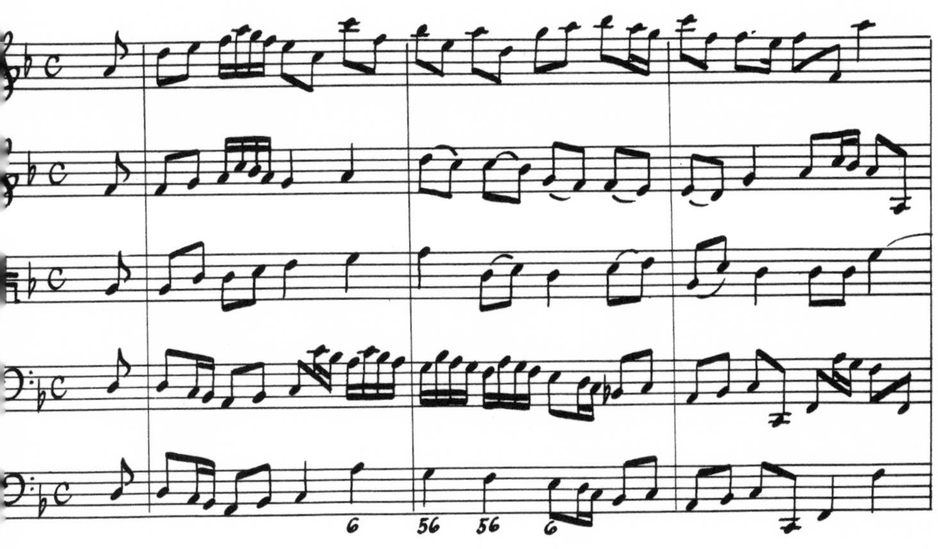

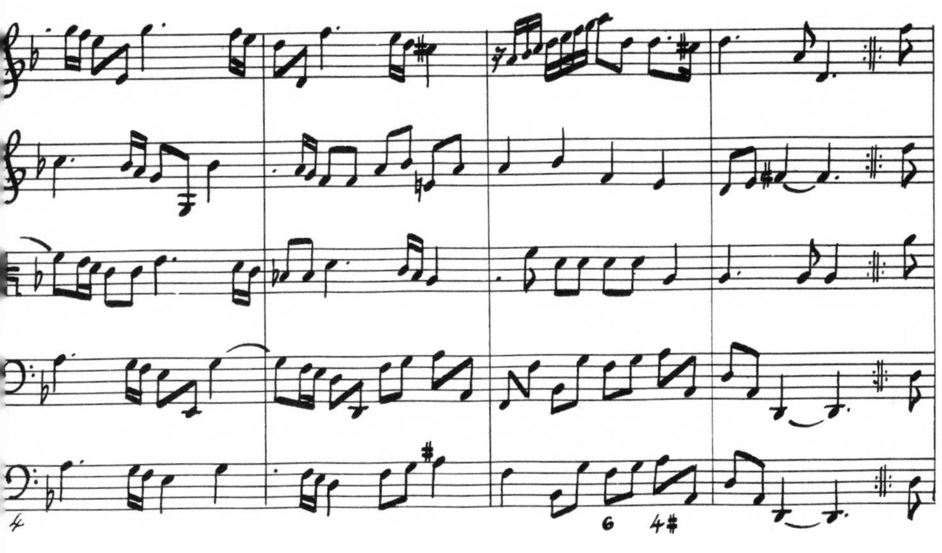

8
6
♯4

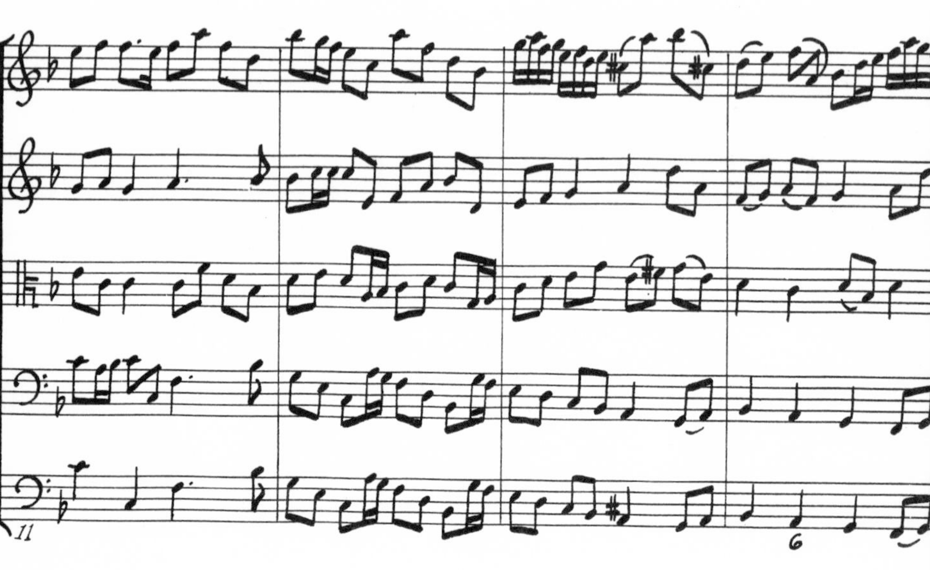
11
6

III, 16. Sonata da Camera à 4

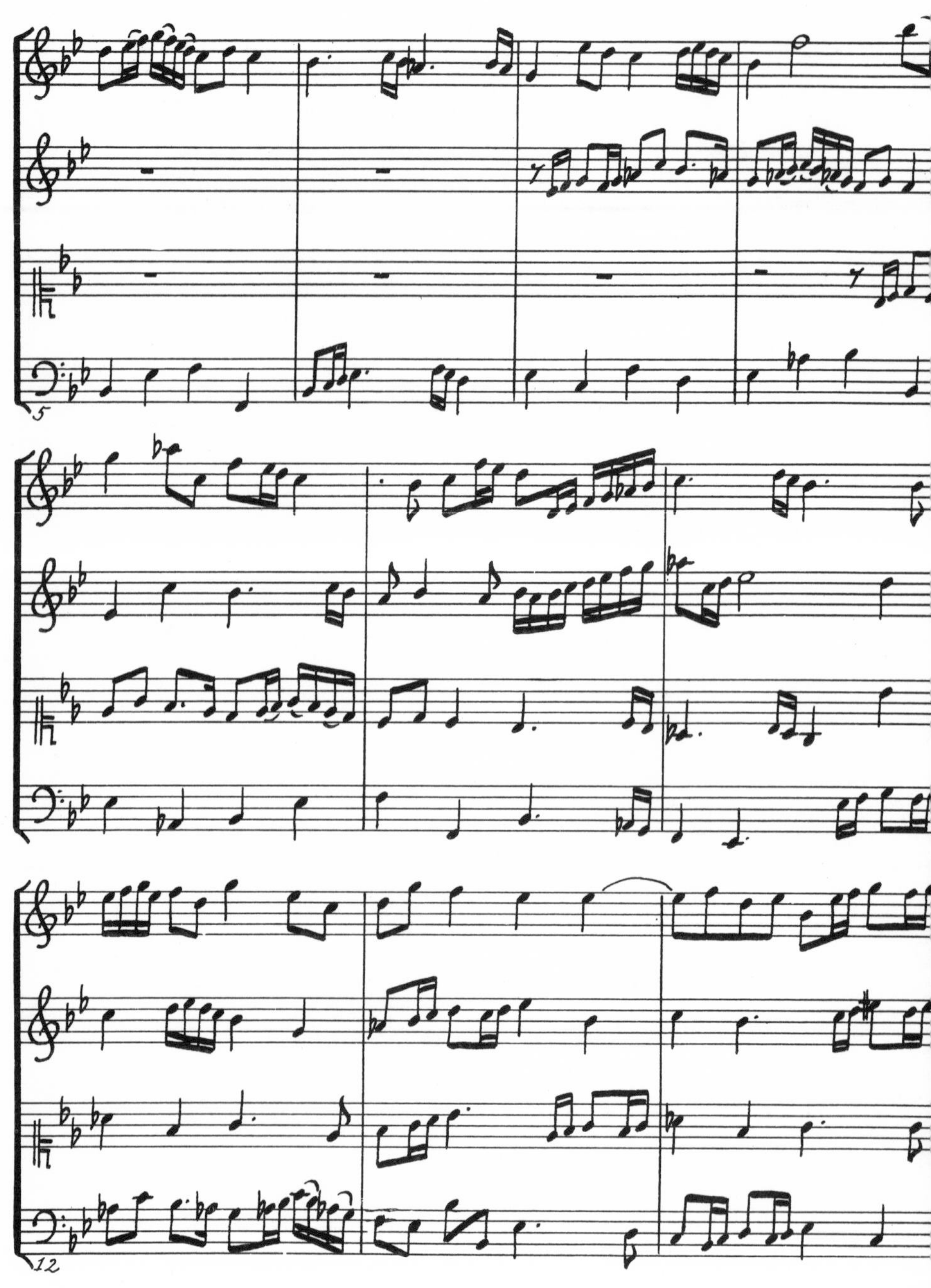
5
12

15
[♭]
Adagio, e tremolo
[♭]
[♭]
[♮]
21
[sic]

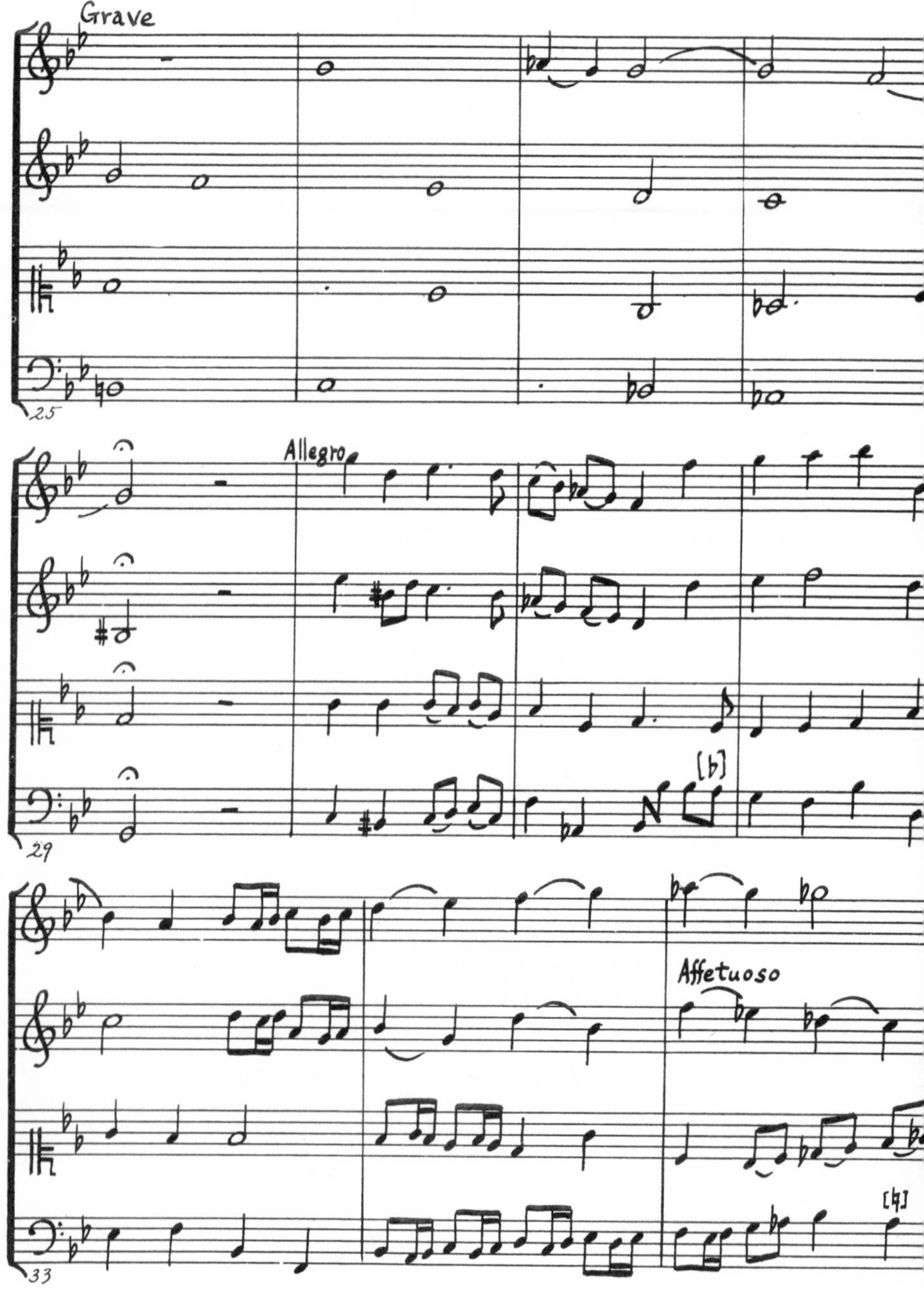
Grave
25
Allegro
[♭]
29
Affetuoso
[♮]
33

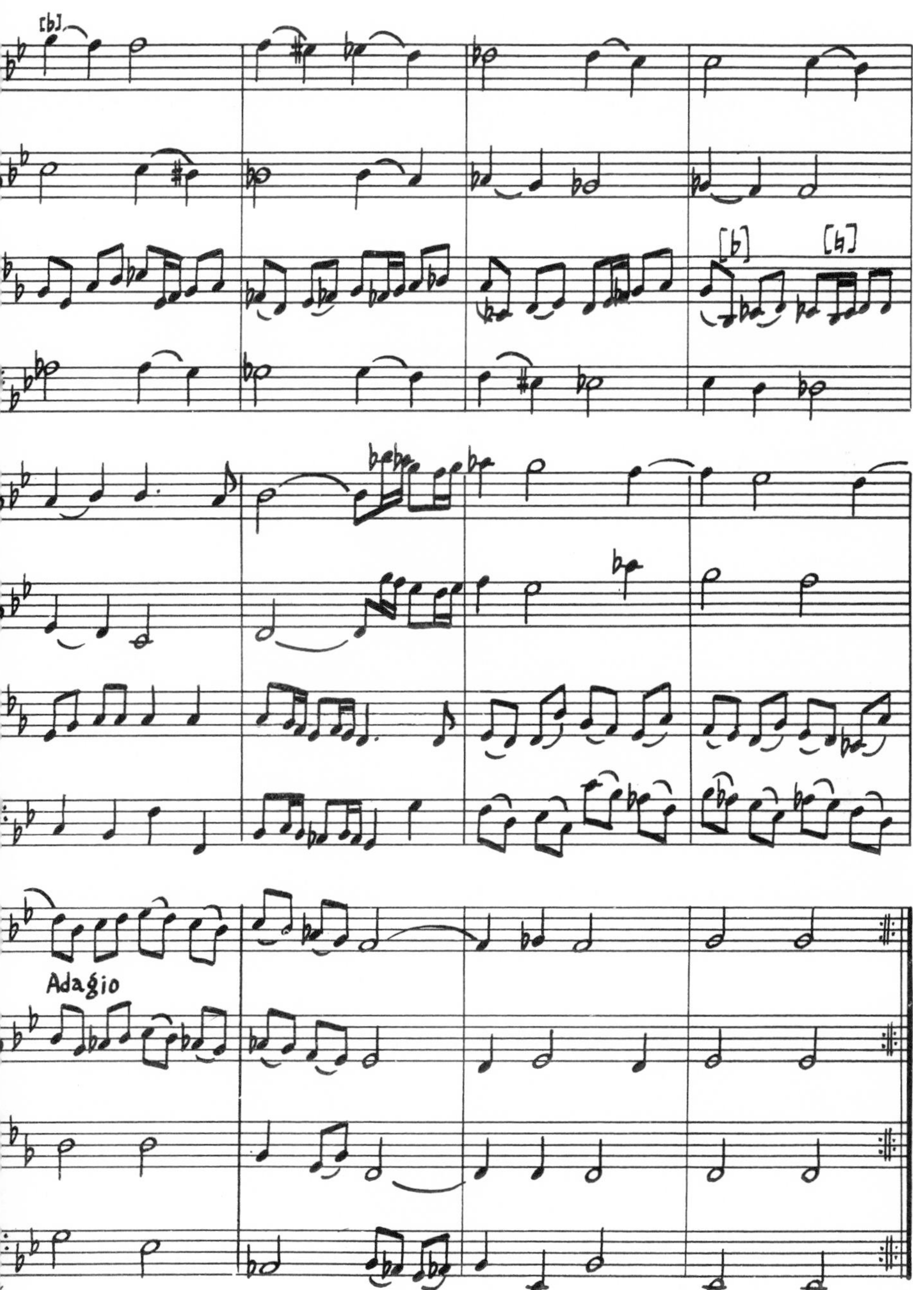
Adagio

Op. III, 17. Sonata da Camera à 3

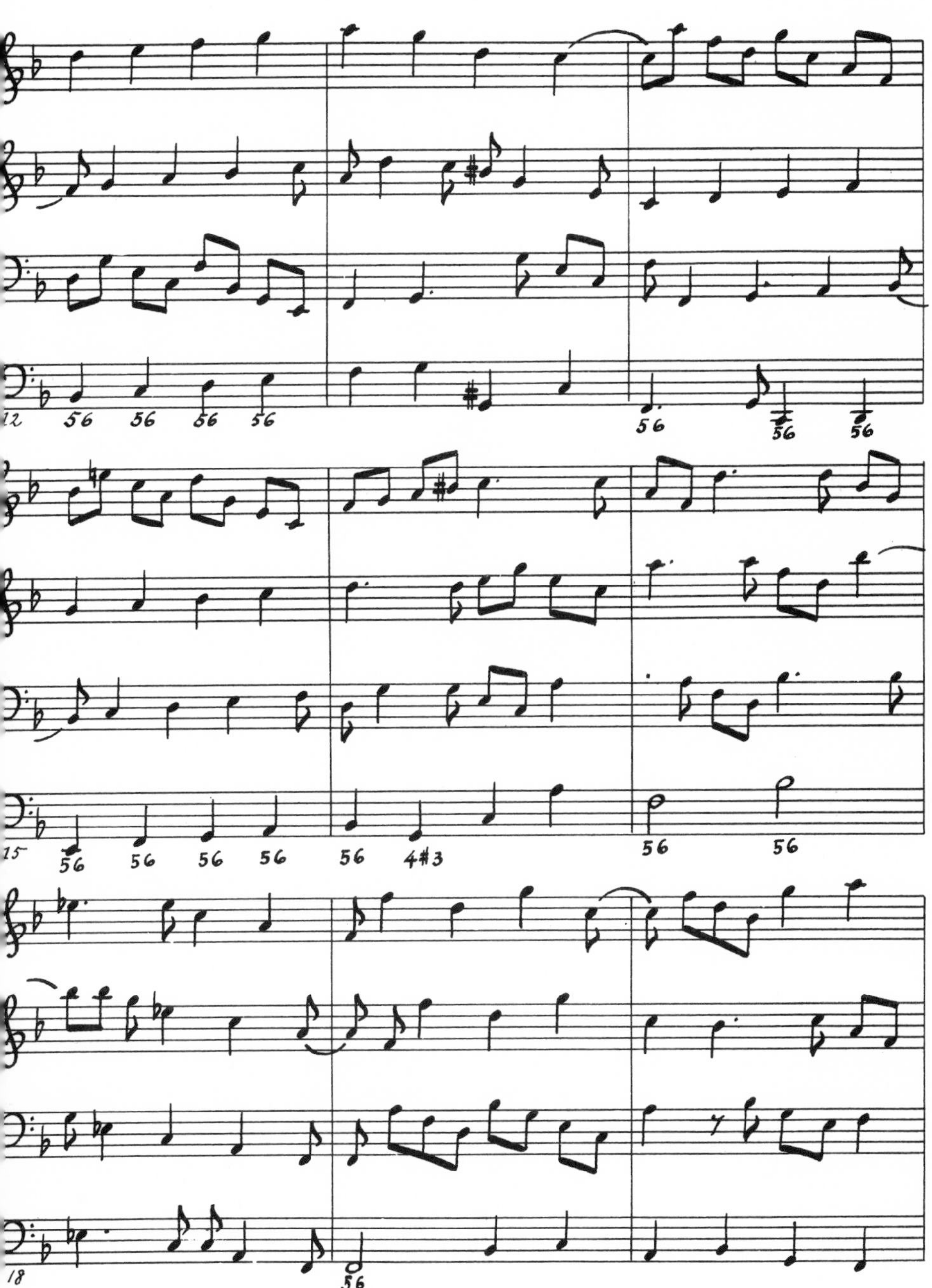
12
56 56 56 56
56 56 56
15
56 56 56 56 56 4#3 56 56
18
56

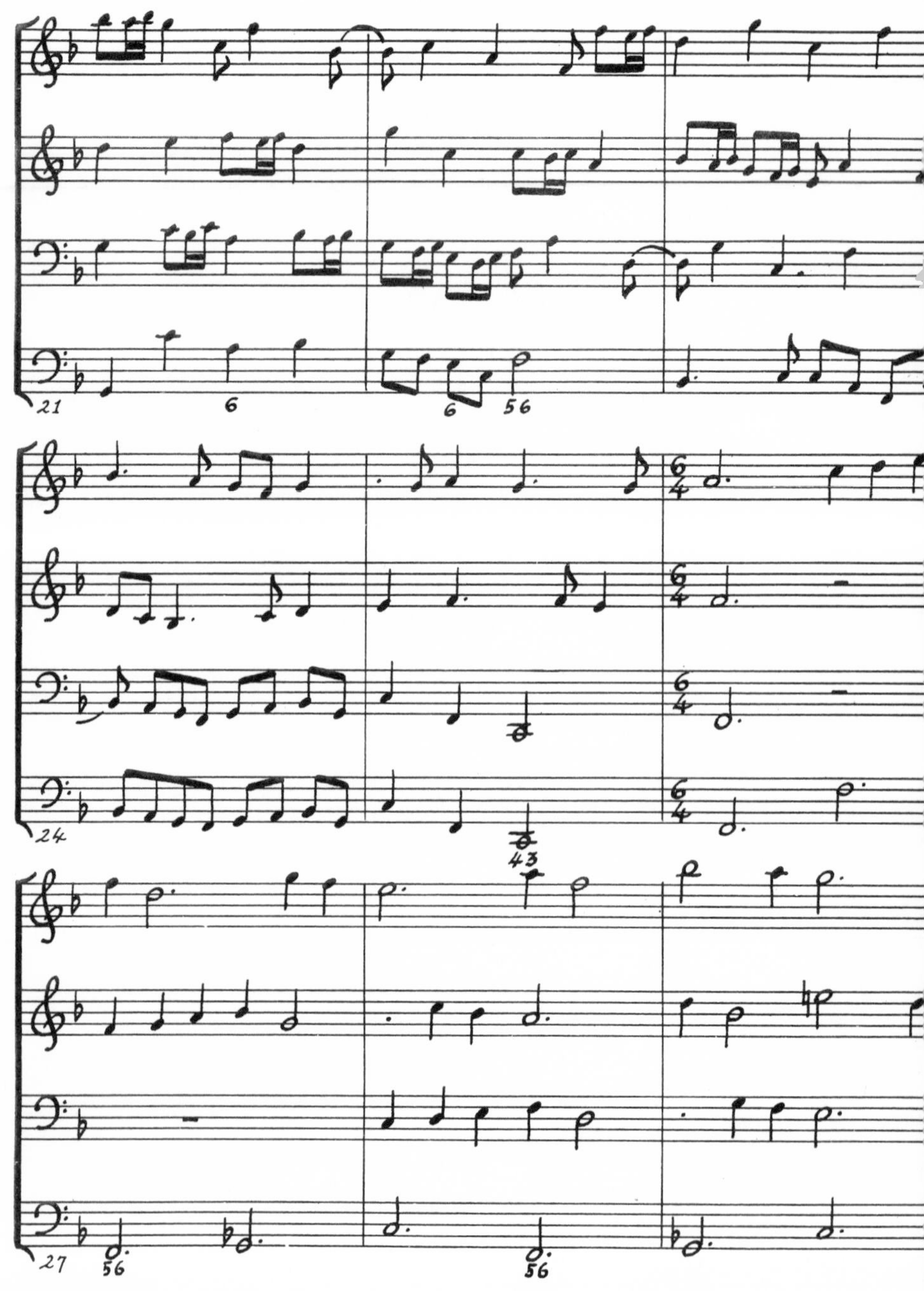
21
24
27

56
6♯
76
7♯6
4♯
56
56
56
6
56
5
6
5♯6
6
6
6

Op. III, 21. Canon à 4 Soprani ó Contralti all' unisono

III, 22. Canon à 8 voci all'unisono & all'ottava bassa doppo sospiro dall'una all'altra *

. III, 24. Sonata à due Violini in canon alla terza bassa per ovimenti contrarii, col suo Basso Continuo

This is a version of the same canon which appears on the title page of Op. as "Canon à 2592 voci . . . divisi in 648 Chori. . . ."

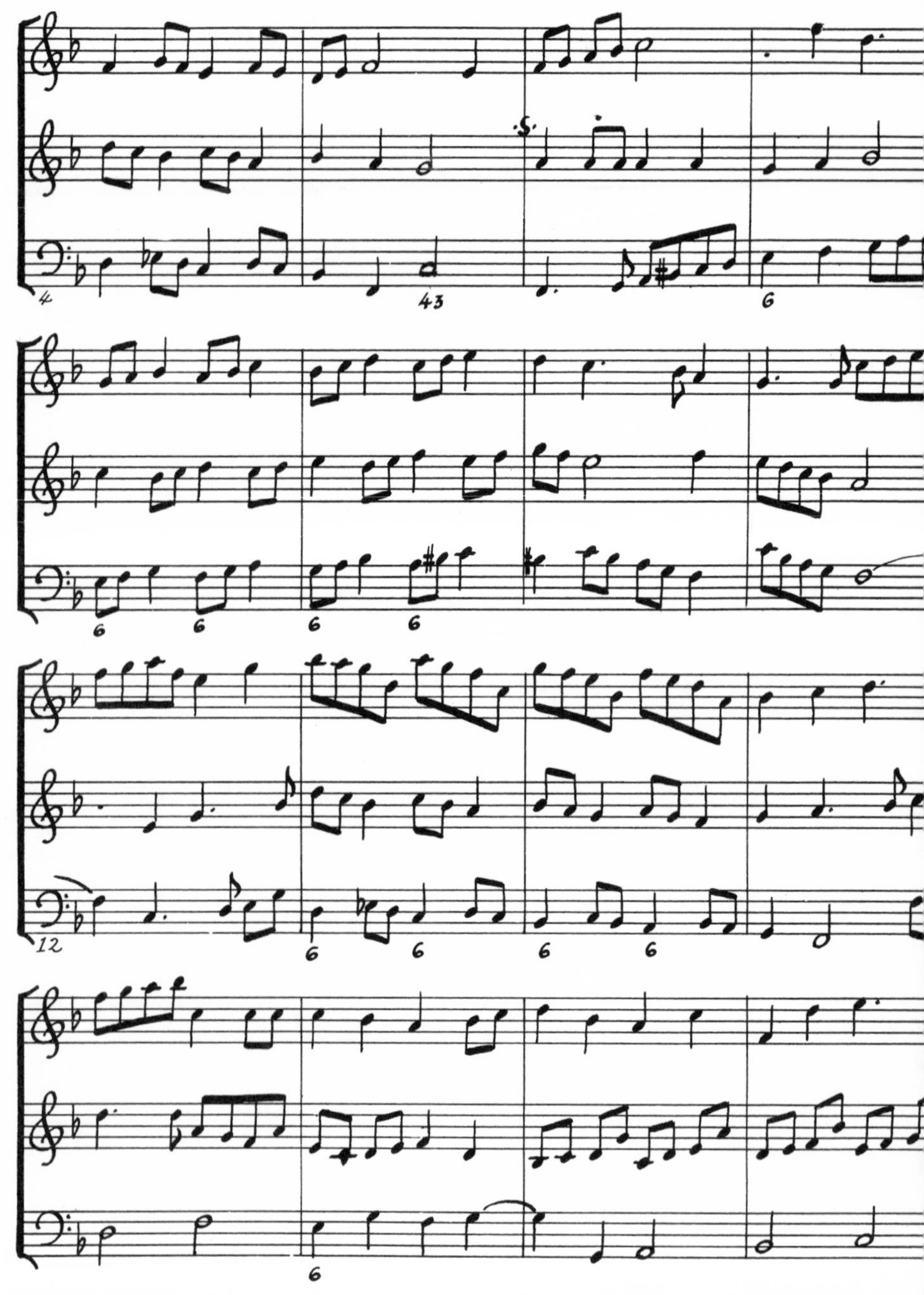

II, 27. Canon à due voci all'unisono

Op. III, 28. Canon à tre voci, *Qui Potest Capere Capiat*

Op. IV, 3. Aria in stil Francese, *La Palavicina*

. IV, 4. Corrente in stil Francese, *La Strozza*

Op. IV, 5. Sarabanda in stil Francese

*NB the diminished fourth, an item of French taste. These three pieces (3, 4, 5) are linked by melodic materials.

IV, 7. Aria, *La Pozza*

Op. IV, 8. Corrente, *La Montanara*

IV, 9. Sarabanda

Op. IV, 13. Gigha, *La Cimicella*

). IV, 15. Corrente, *La Buffalina*

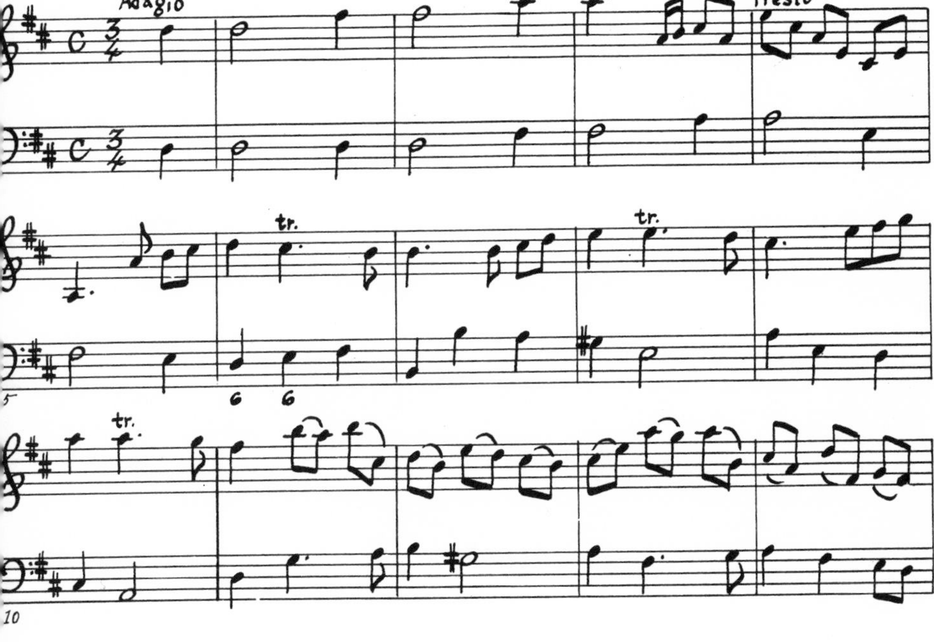

Adagio
Presto

IV, 20. Corrente, *La Pegolotta*

Op. IV, 22. Sarabanda

V, 6. Corrente à 5

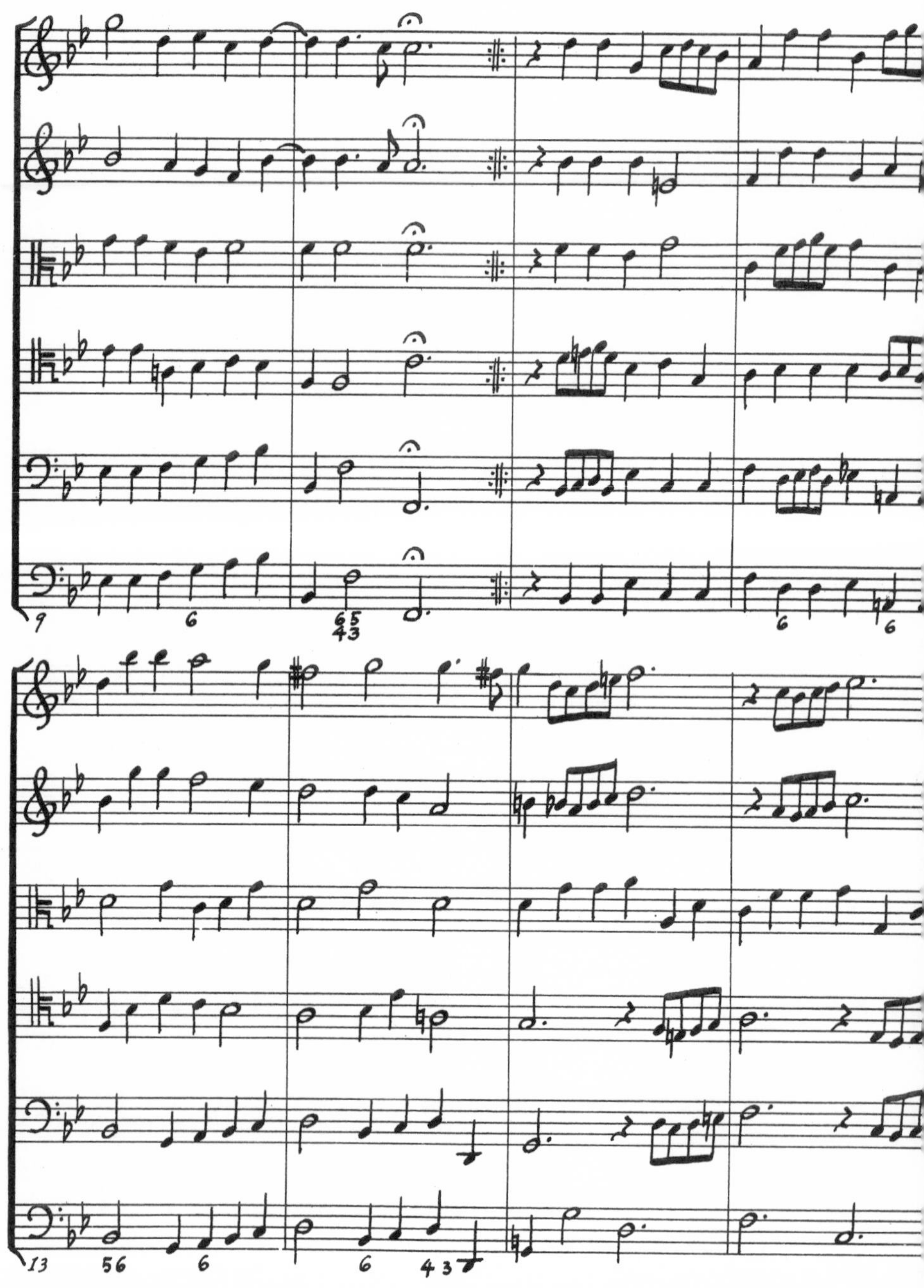

Op. V, 12. Corrente à 5

5
6 5
4 3
10
6
6
4 3

5
♭6 5
6
5 6
20
6
4 3
6
7

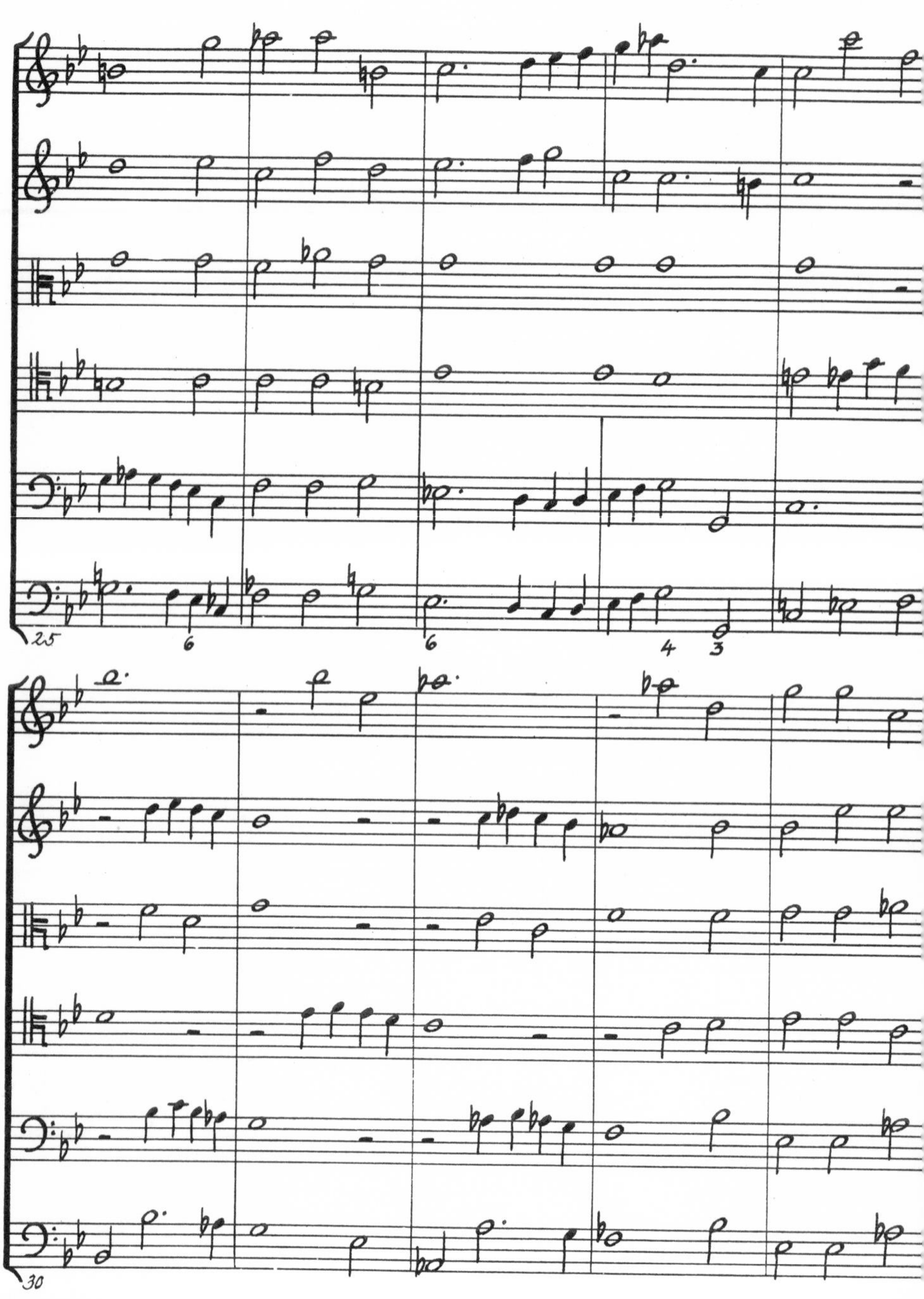
25
6
6
4
3
30

35
6
43
40
6♭5
65

Op. V, 17. Sarabanda à 5

Op. V, 20. Sarabanda à 5

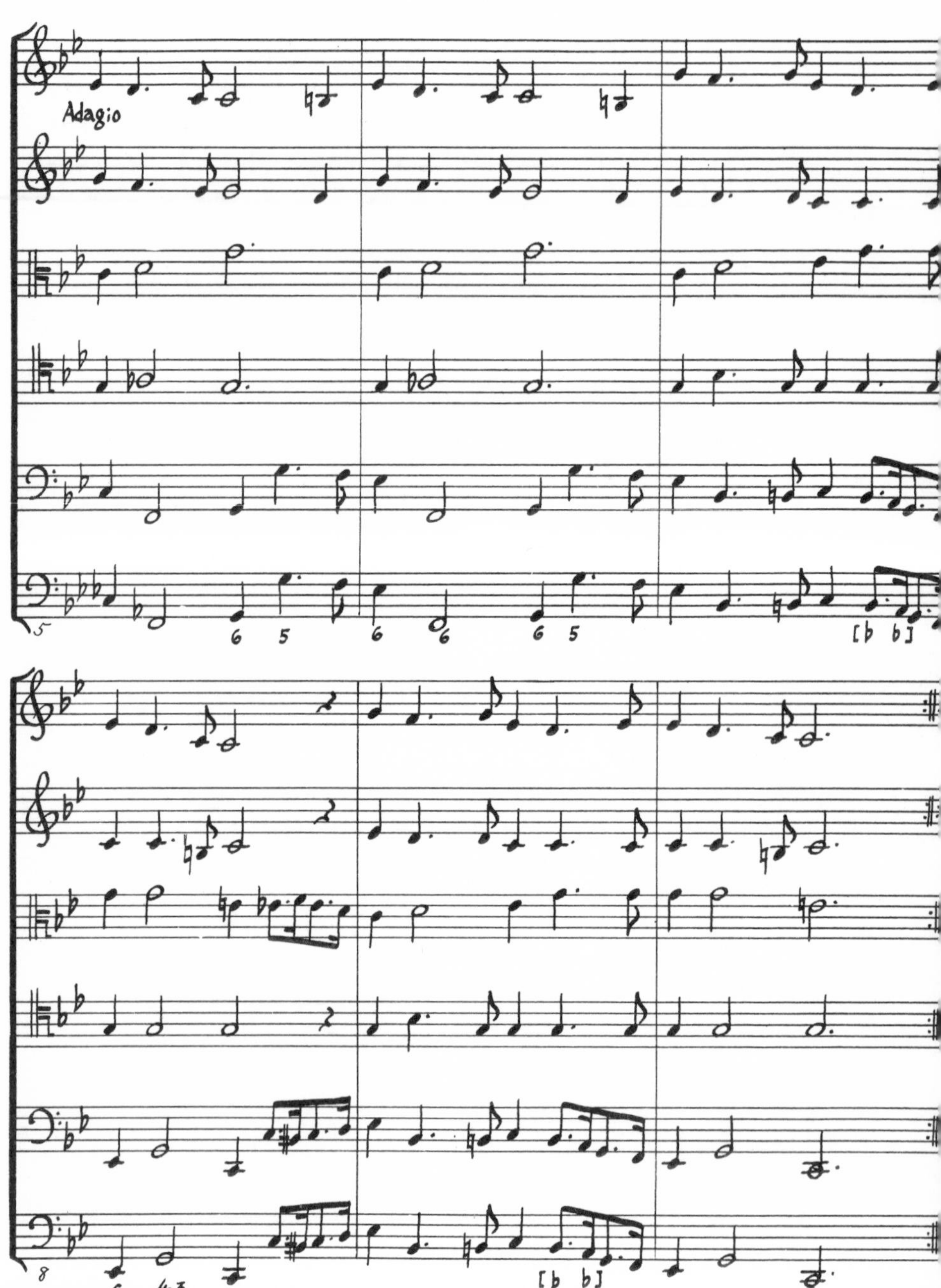
Adagio

p. V, 25. Corrente à 6

*This part is in the soprano clef in the Monti edition, printed in the *Alto* *iola* part.

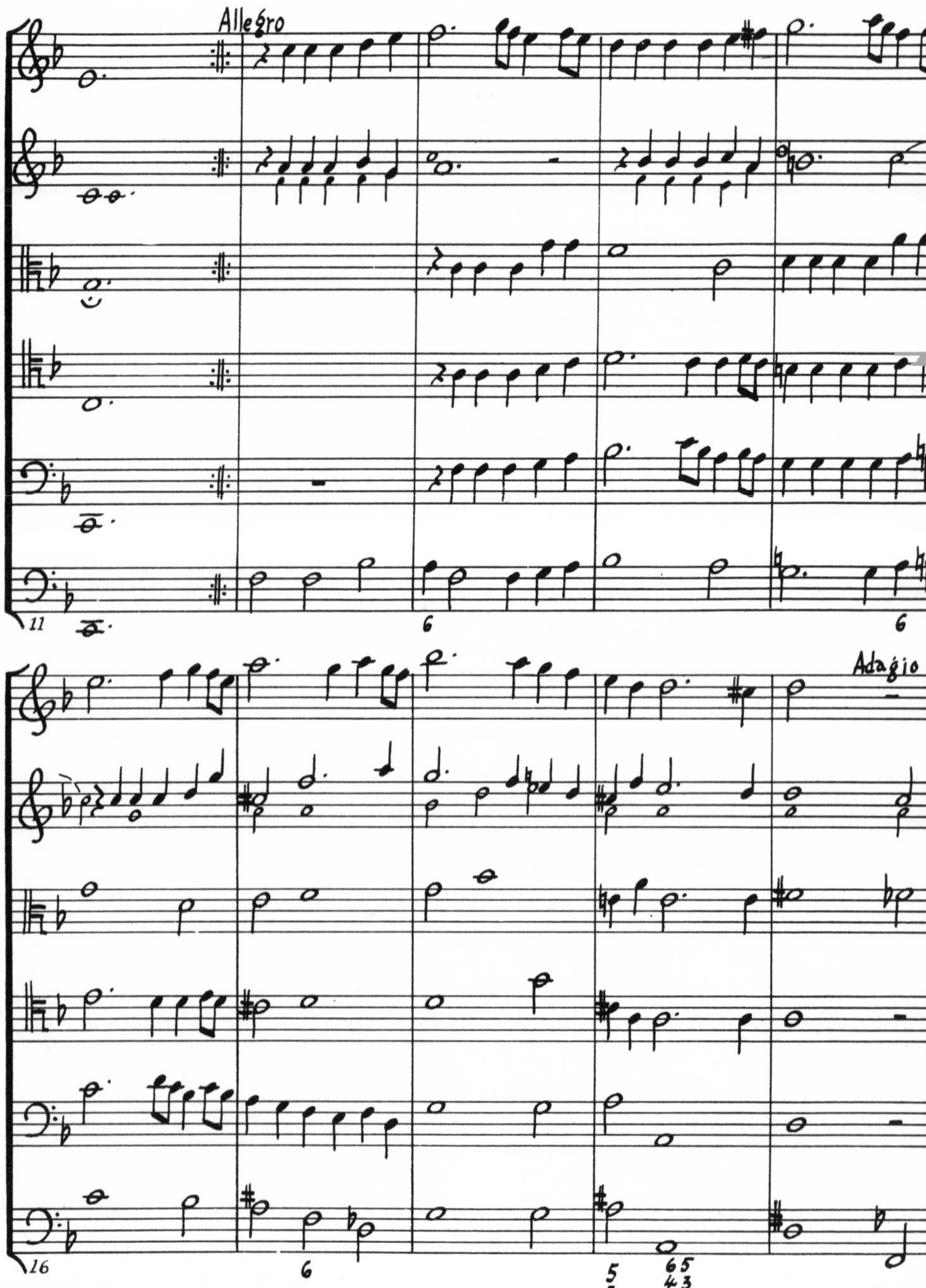
Allegro
11
6
6
Adagio
16
6
5
3
65
43

Op. V, 26. Sarabanda à 6

Op. VI, 3. Dell' undecimo Tuono un tuono più basso

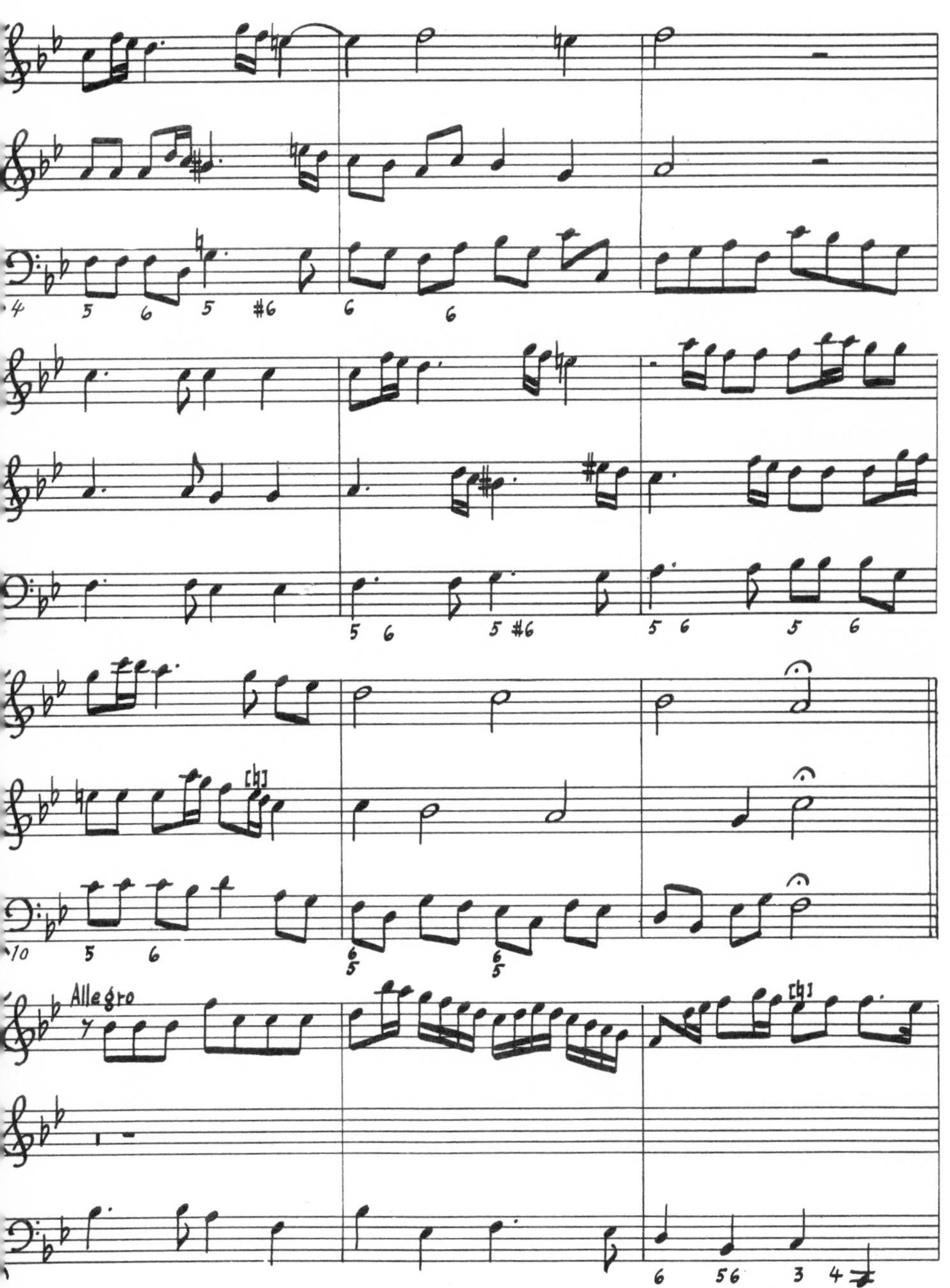
Allegro

16
22

Adagio

63
Adagio
69
Adagio

Allegro
6
♯6
2
6
6
5
♭5

88
6
5
94
6
6
6
6

. VI, 4. Dell' undecimo Tuono un tuono più alto

9
6
5
6

31
6
6
5
65
6
5
65
5
37

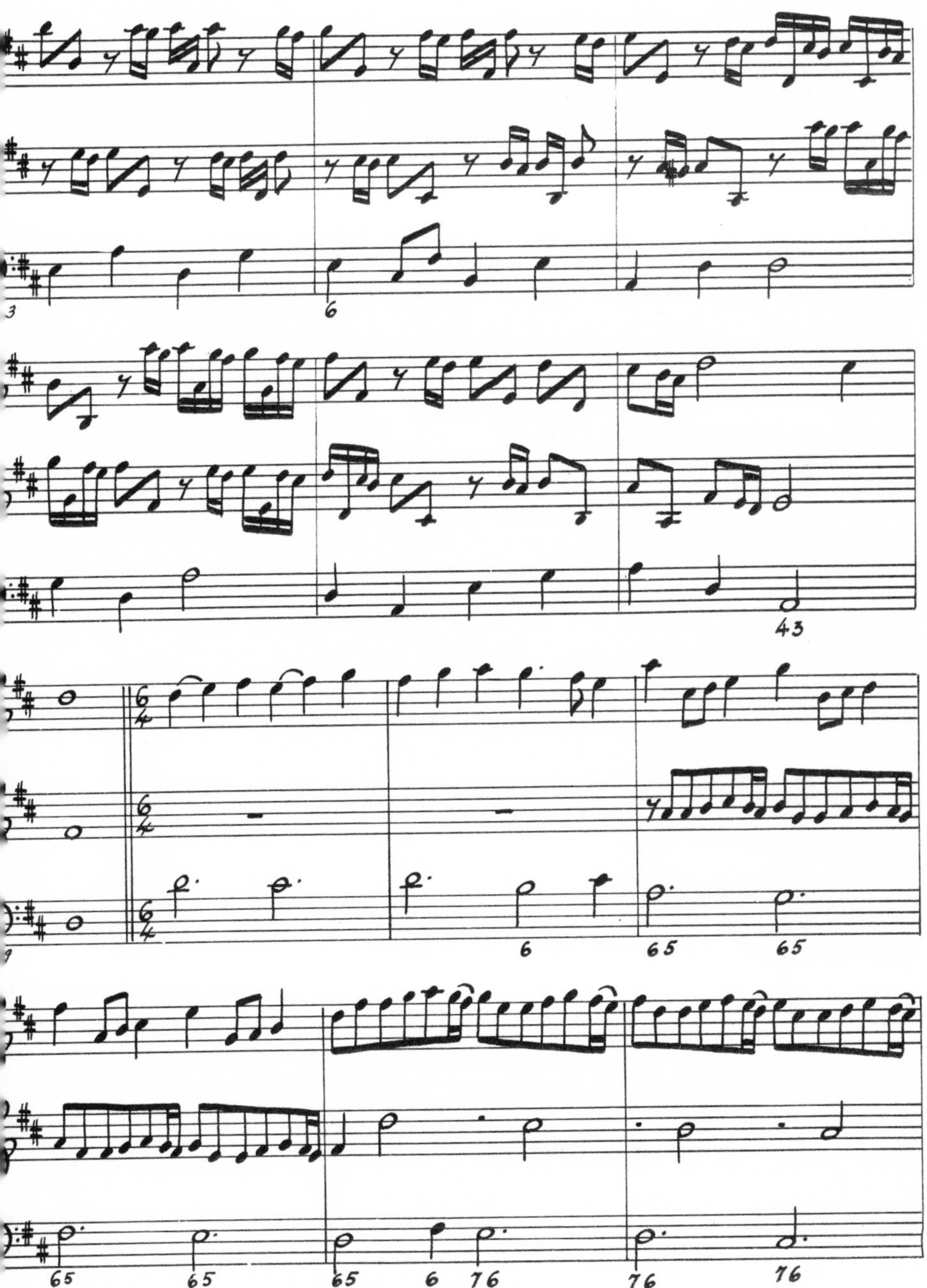

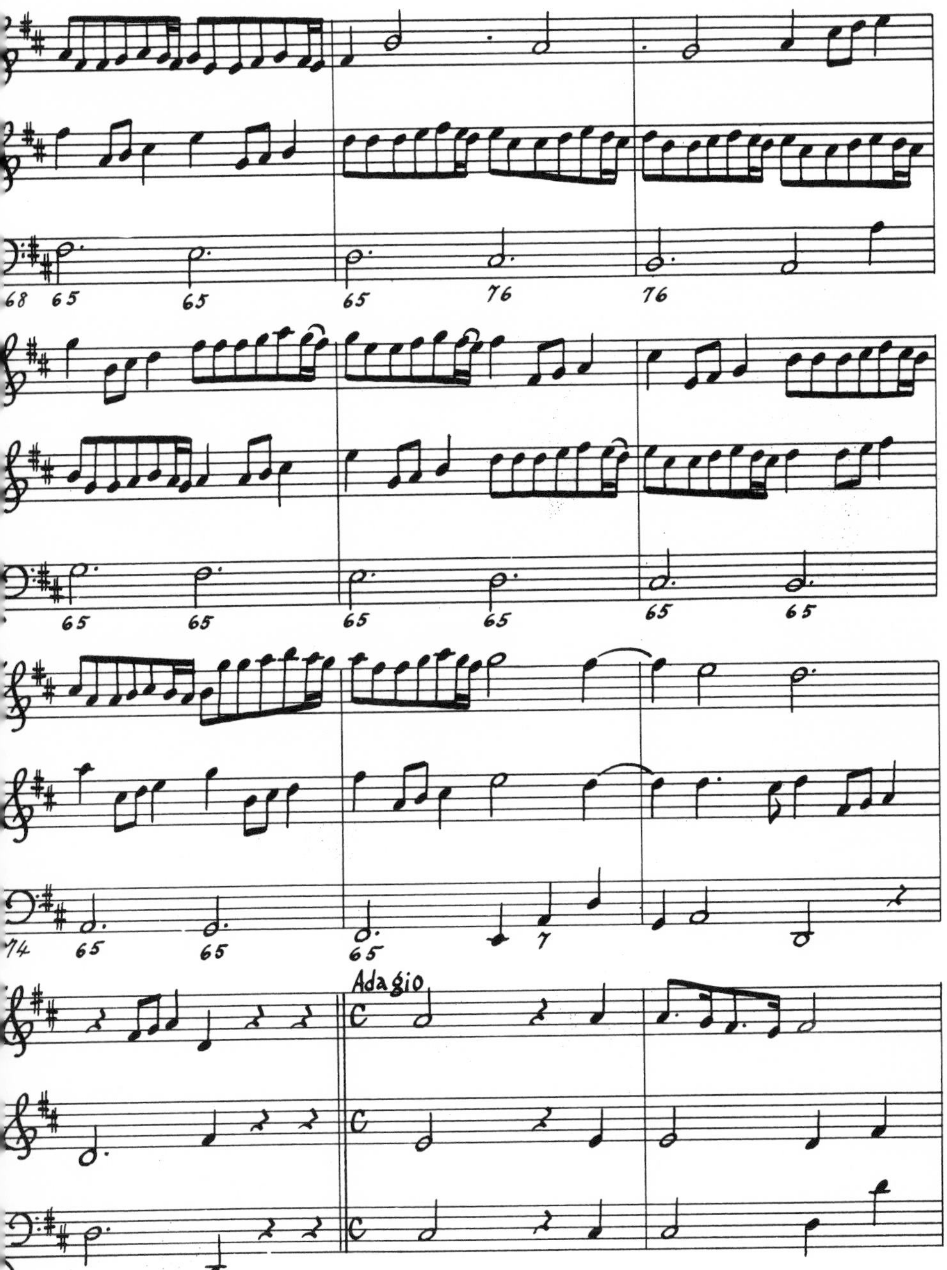
68 65 65 65 76 76
65 65 65 65 65 65
74 65 65 65 7
Adagio

80
86

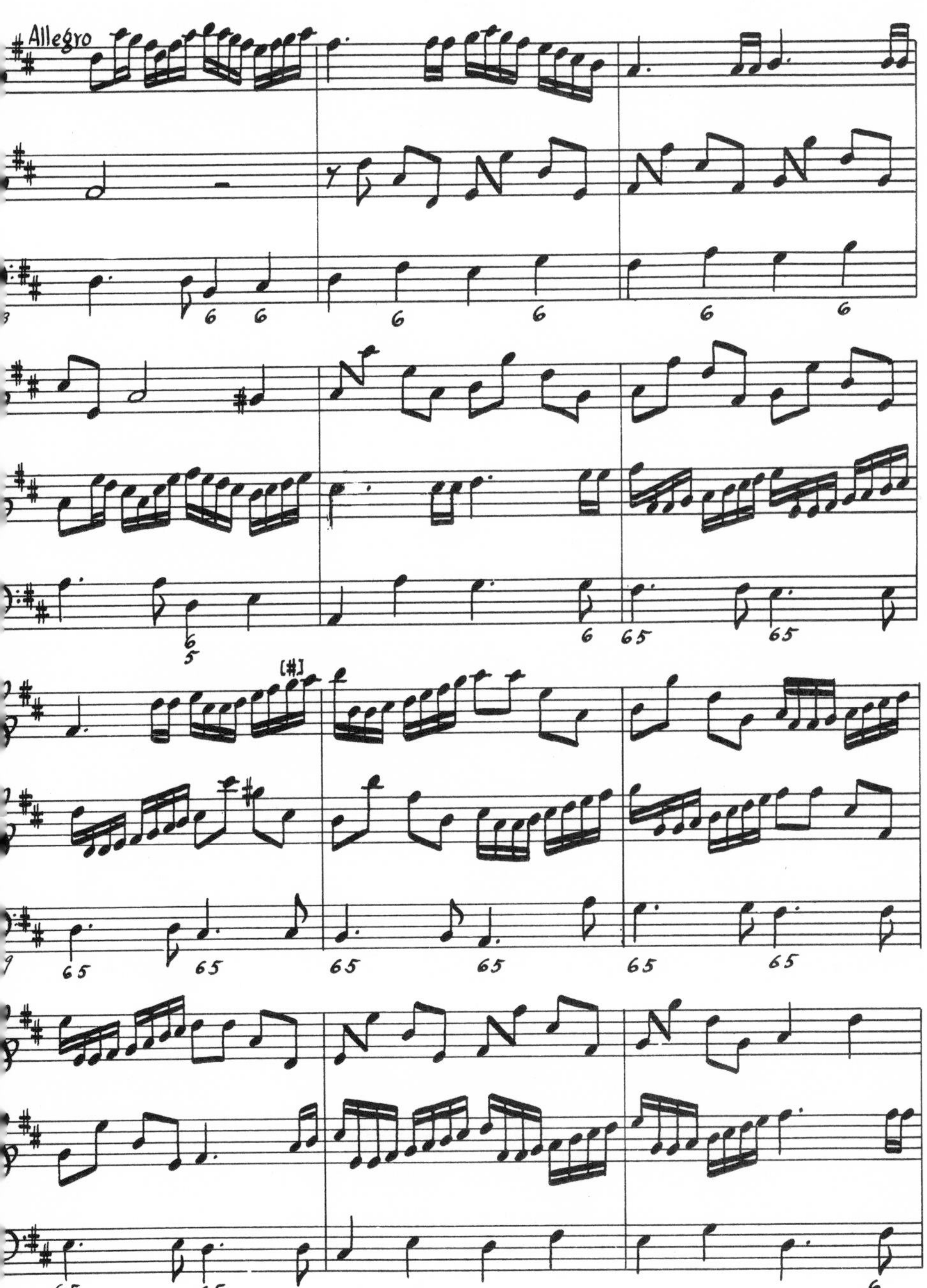
Allegro

105
111

p. VI, 5. Dell' ottavo Tuono un tuono più alto

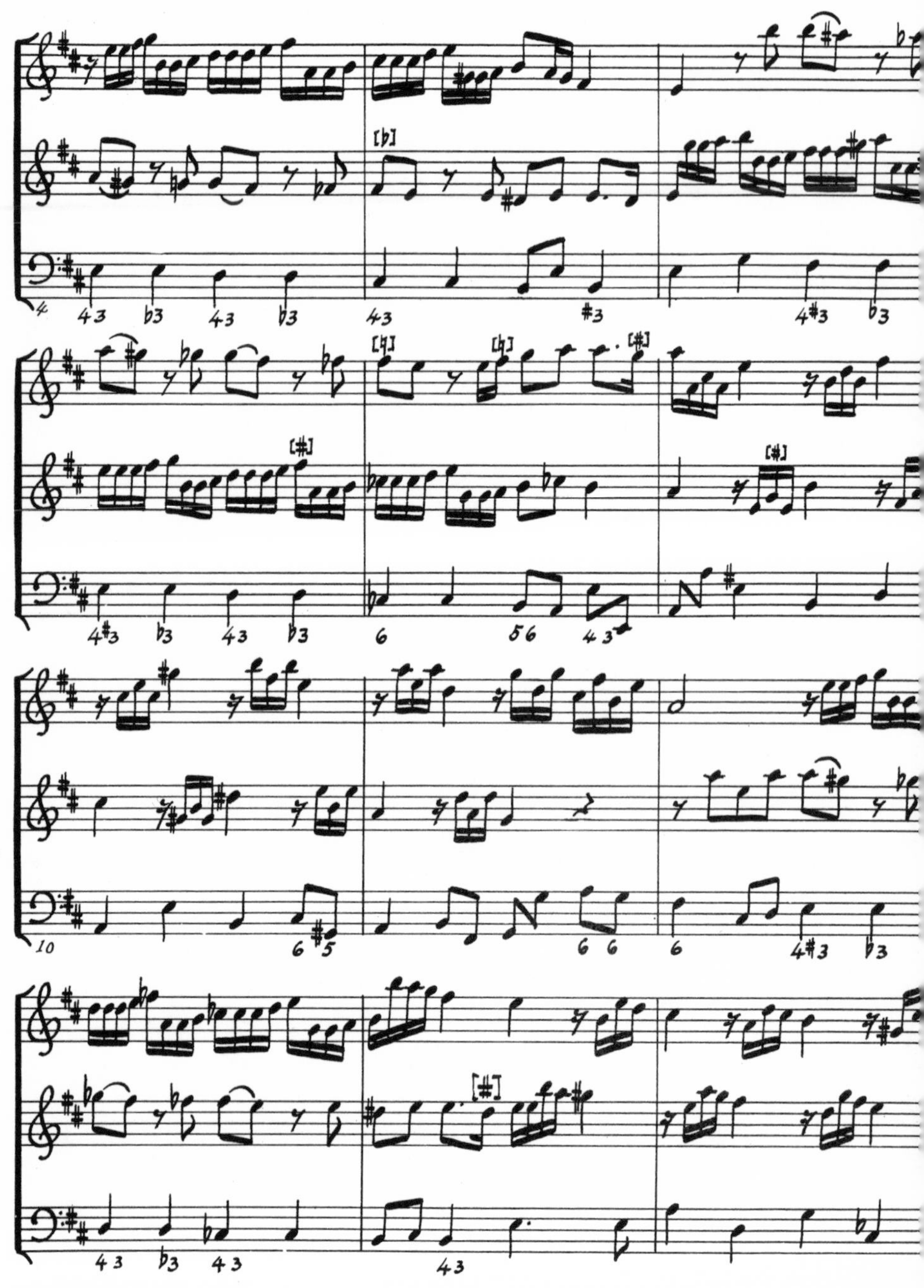

40
6
[6]
6
[6]
65
[6]
65
6
46
6
5
6
65
6
[#]

Adagio
[Adagio]

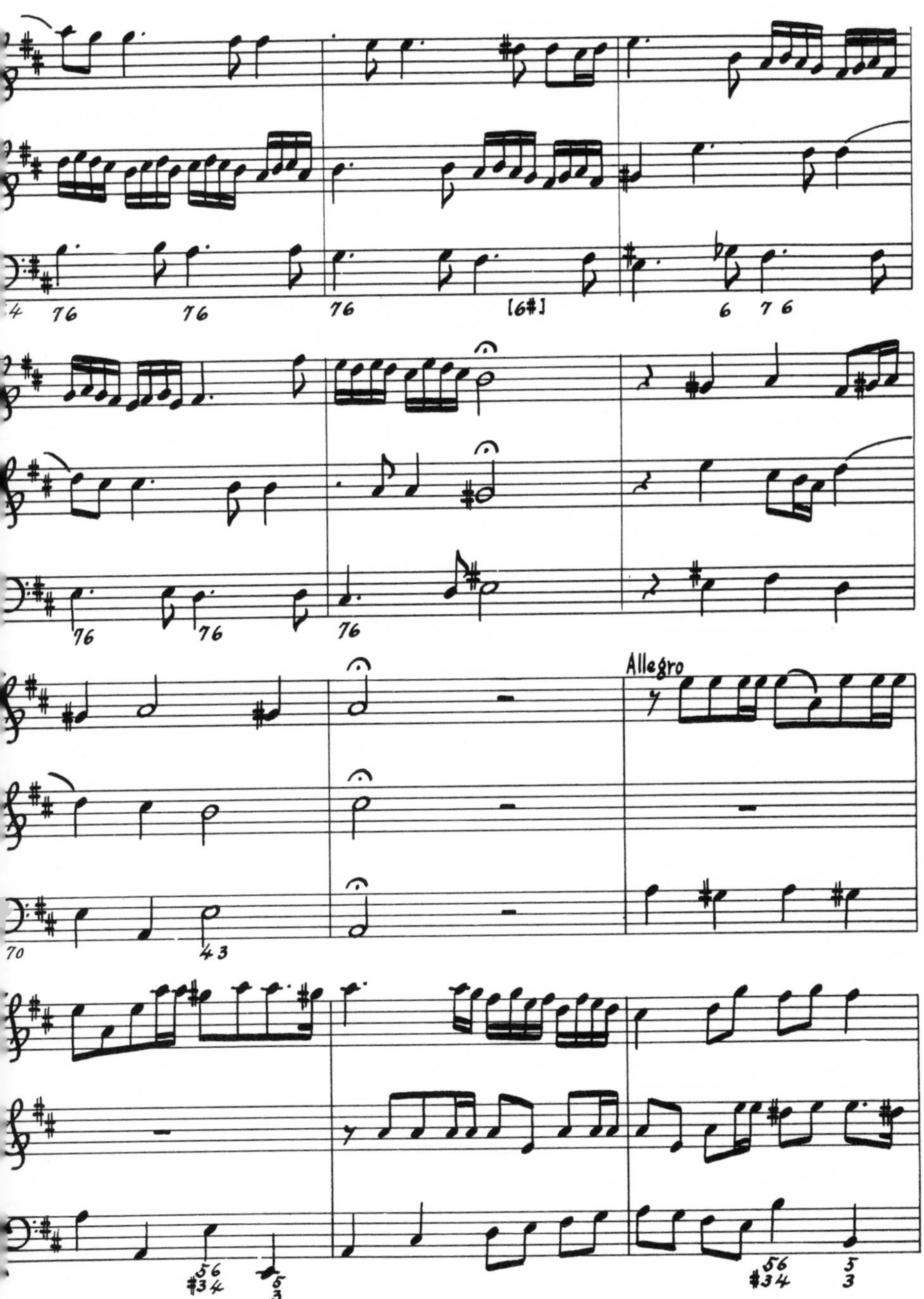
Allegro

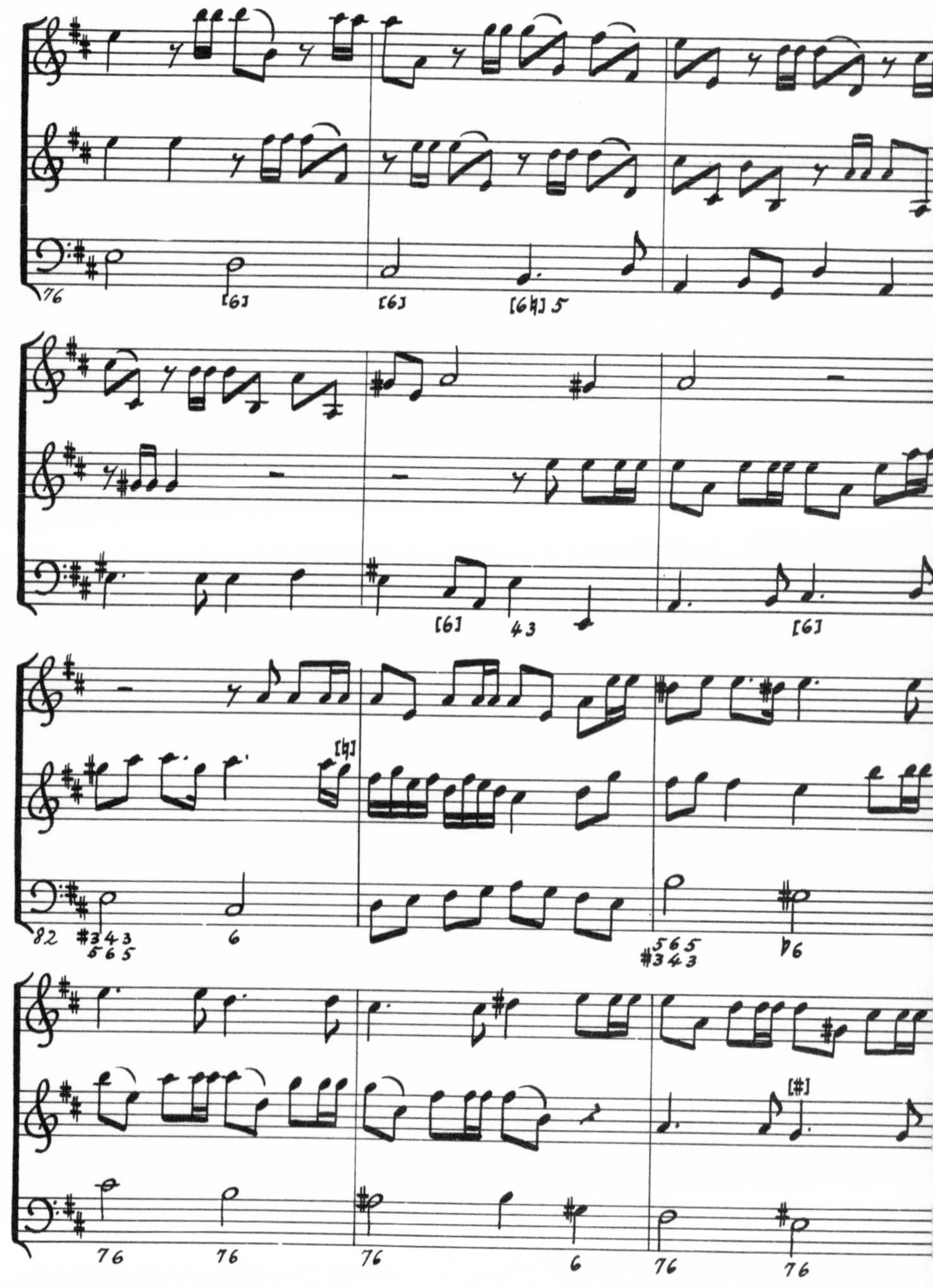
76
82

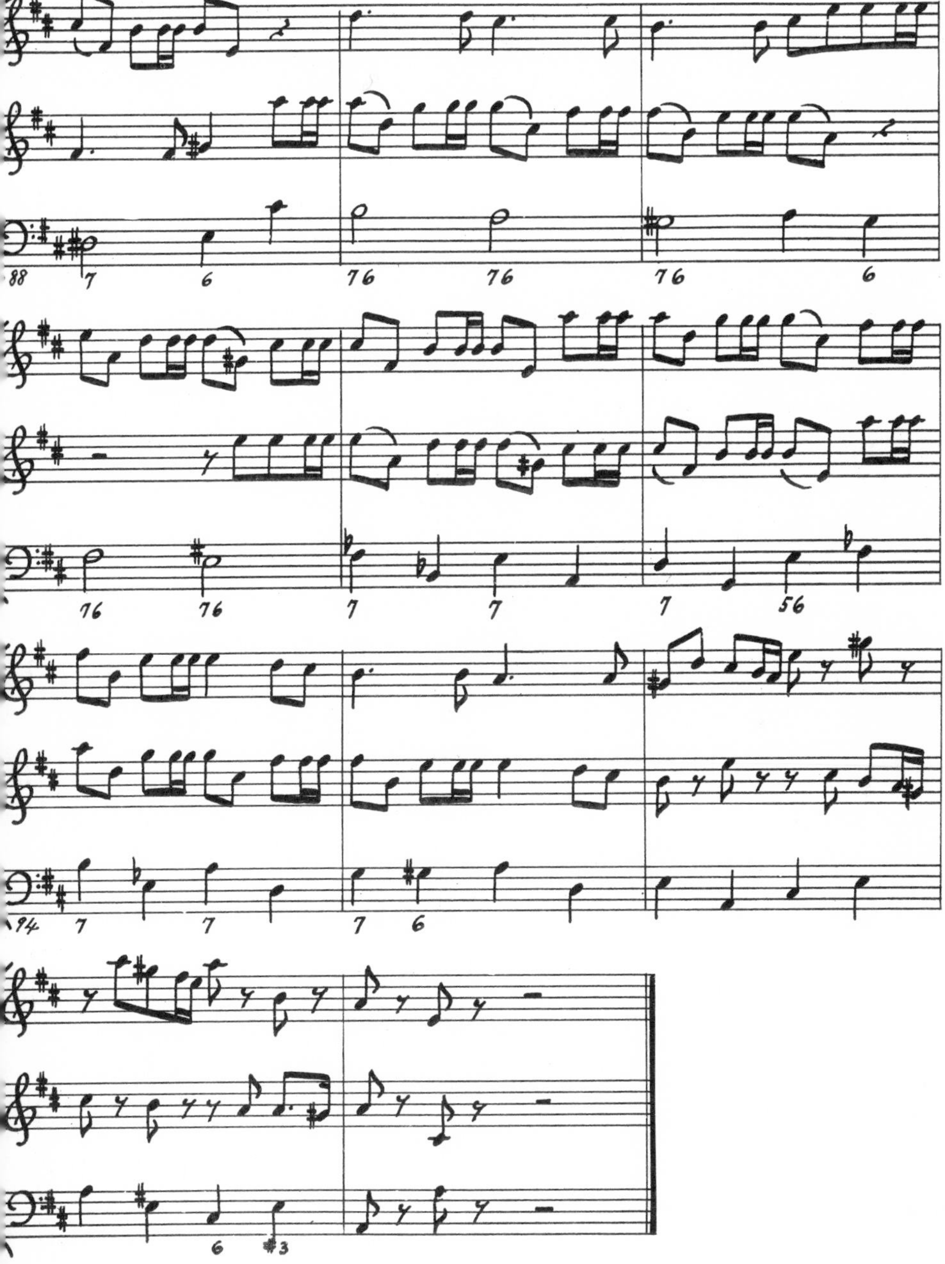
88
7
6
76
76
76
6
76
76
7
7
7
56
94
7
7
7
6
6
♯3

Op. VI, 6. Del decimo Tuono una quarta bassa

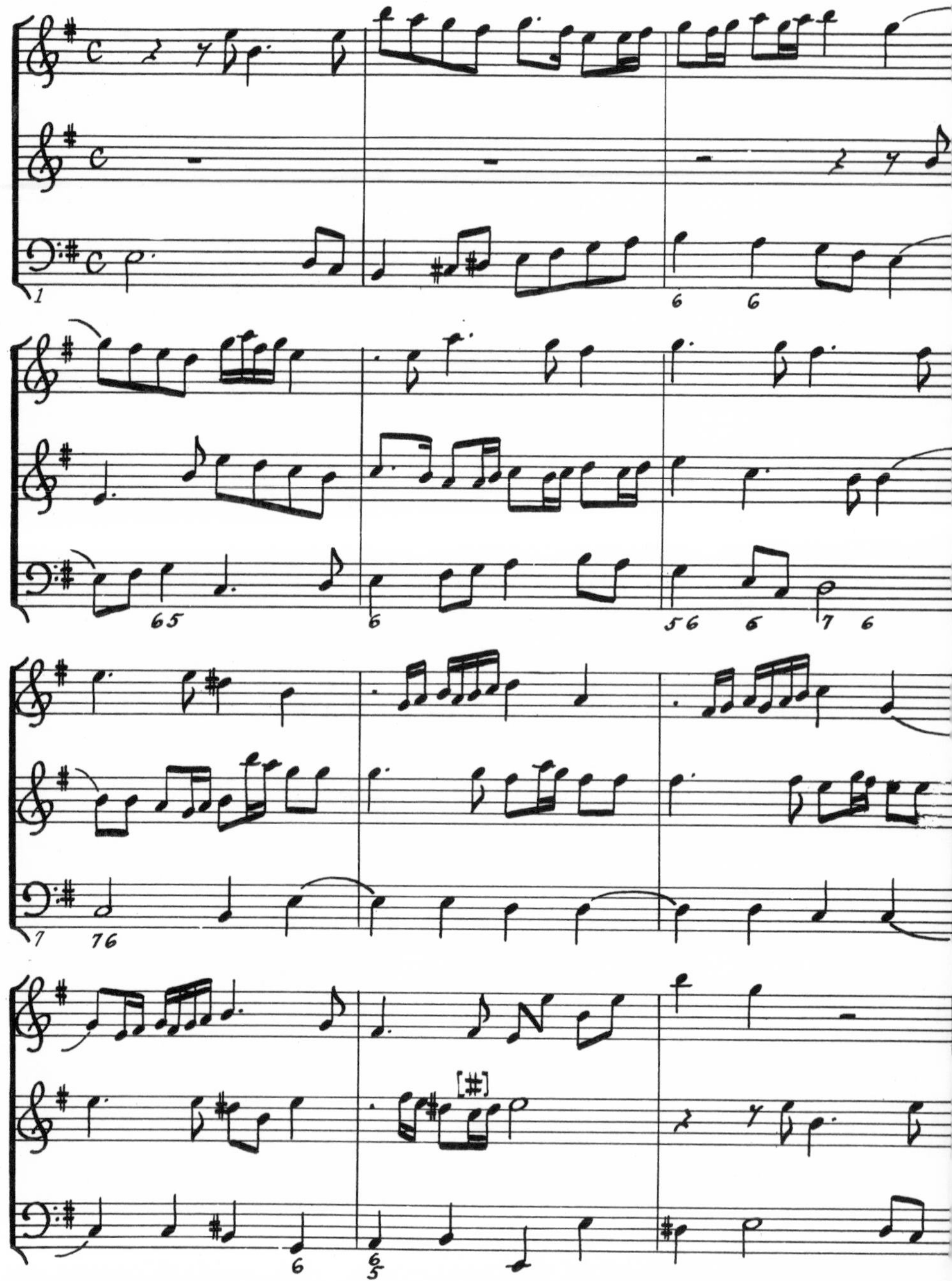

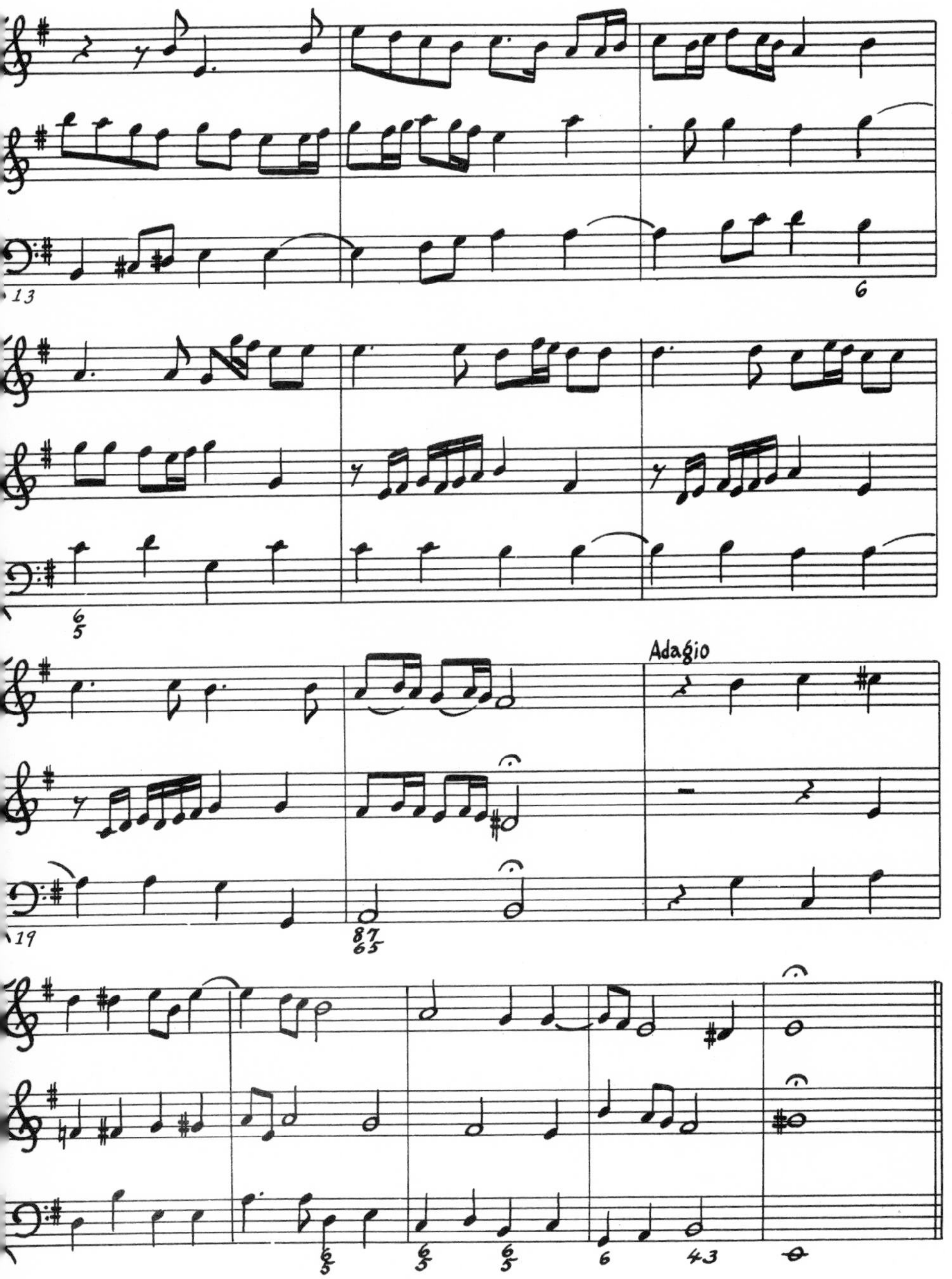
13
6
6
5
Adagio
19
8 7
6 5
6
5
6
5
6
5
6
4 3

Largo
27
38

Adagio

Allegro
66
72

78
84

Op. VI, 8. Dell' ottavo Tuono nelle sue corde naturale

4
6
5
6
6
5
5
3
6
6
5
10
6
6
6
43
♭6
6
5
6
6
6
6
5

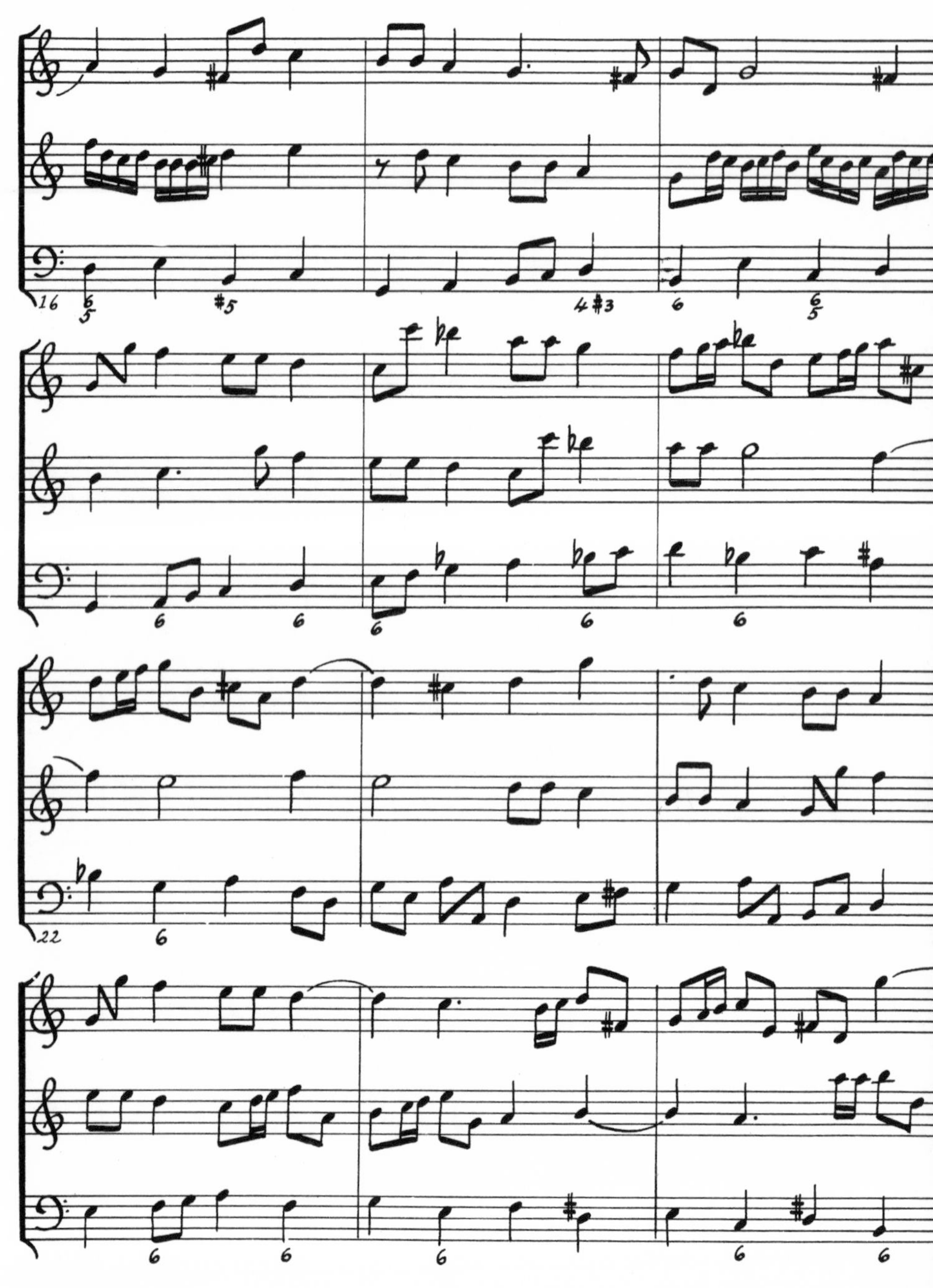
16
22

* ⊙ $\frac{3}{1}$ in Monti; 1677, $\frac{3}{4}$ in MS.

p
p
p
[#]
[#]
[#]
[#]
Adagio
7
6
5
9 8
7 6

Allegro

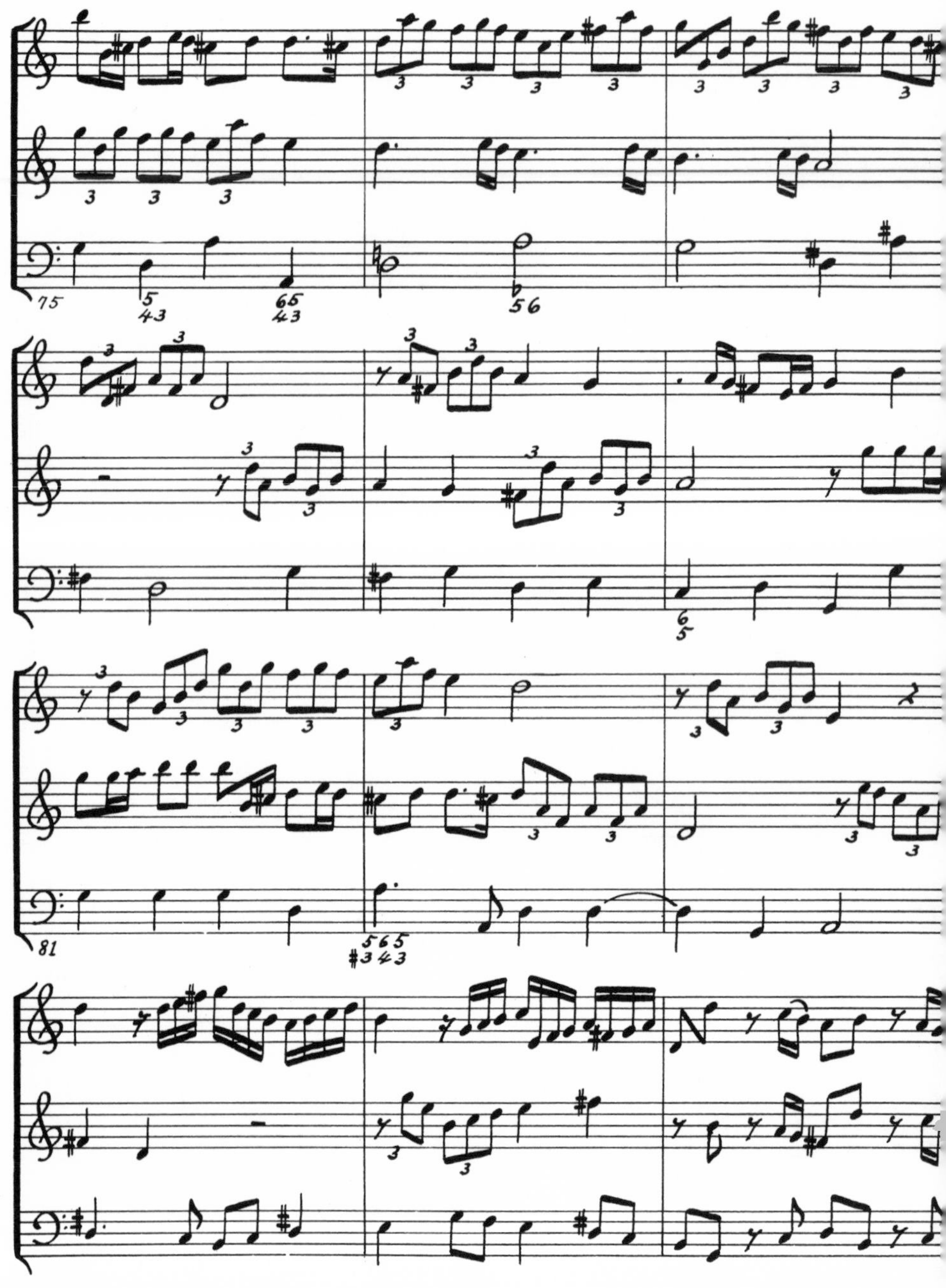

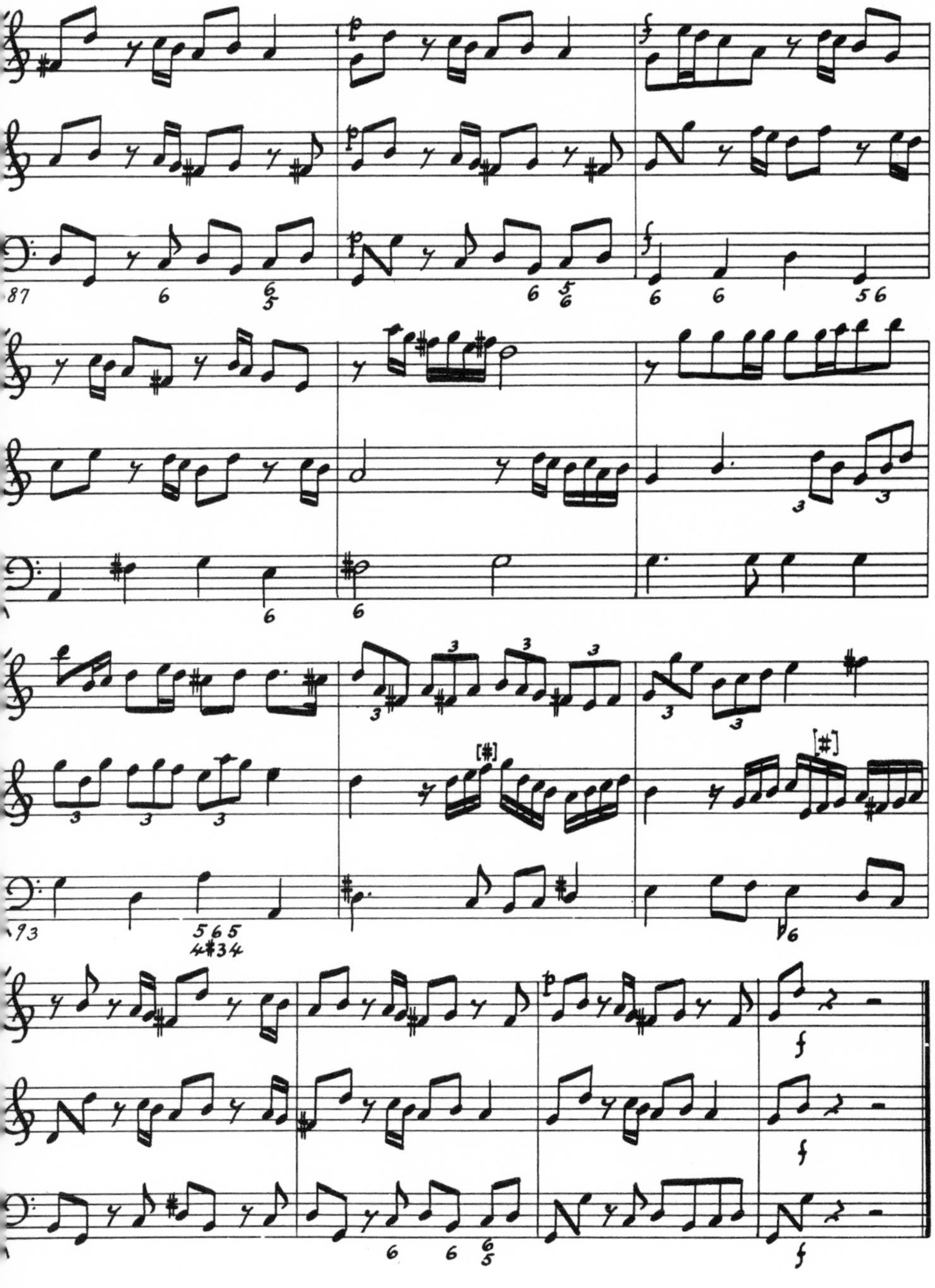

Op. VI, 11. Del secondo Tuono una quarta più alto

25
31

Adagio
37
6
76
34
6
♭6
3
6
4
5
3
Adagio
44
76
43
98
76
♭6
5

52
4 3
♭♯
♭♯
59
4 3
♭♯
♭♯
4 ♯3

[d] [o]
Largo
[d. d]
67
43
6
6
6
6
[b]
6
74
6
5 7 5
#3 5 4 3
6

80
[6]
6
4 3
Presto
[♭]
86
5 6

92
98

104
110

Op. VI, 12. Del duodecimo Tuono una terza più alto

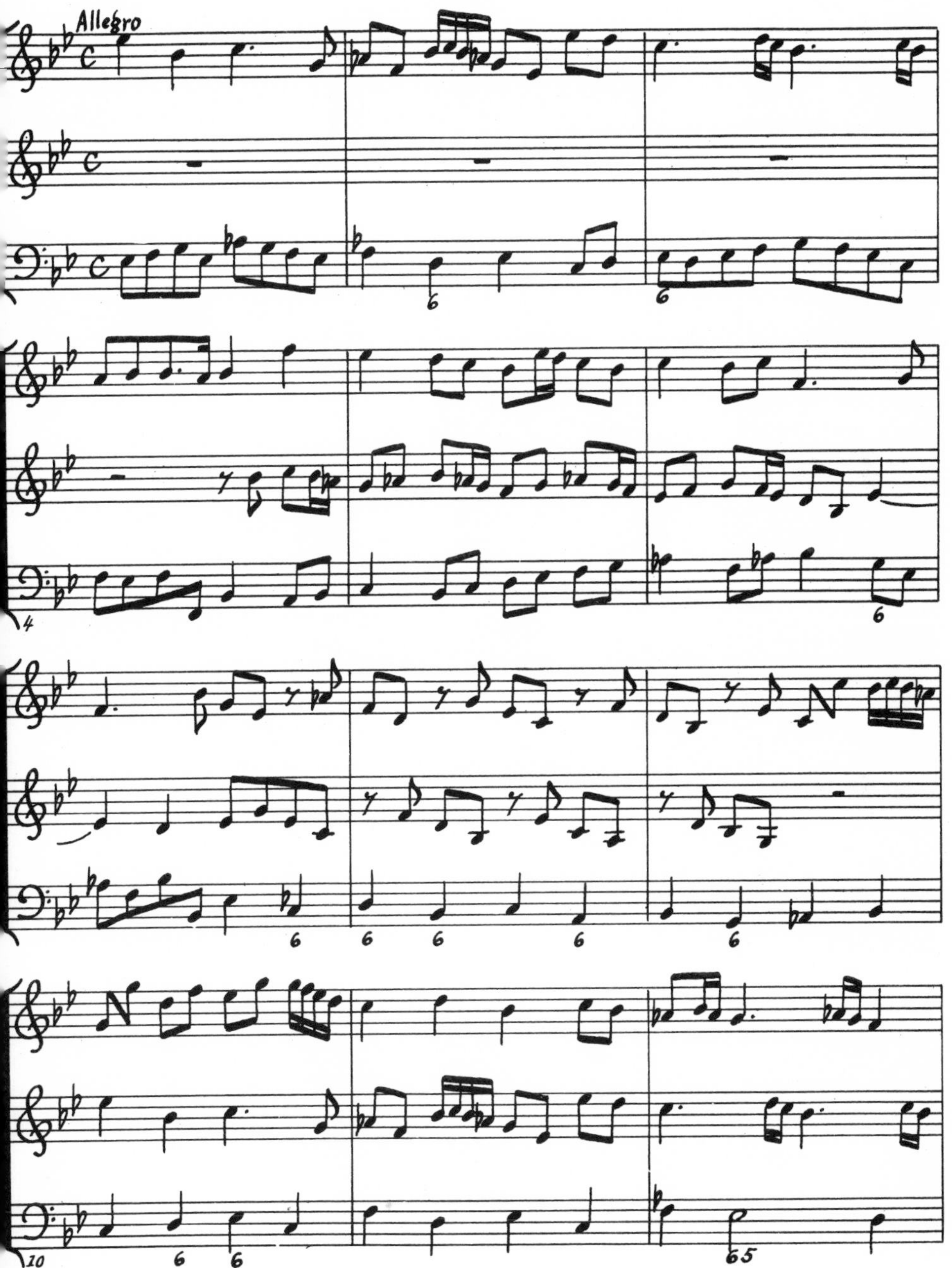

[♭]
13
6
4 3
65
[♮]
[♮]
19
6
5
6

Adagio
Largo

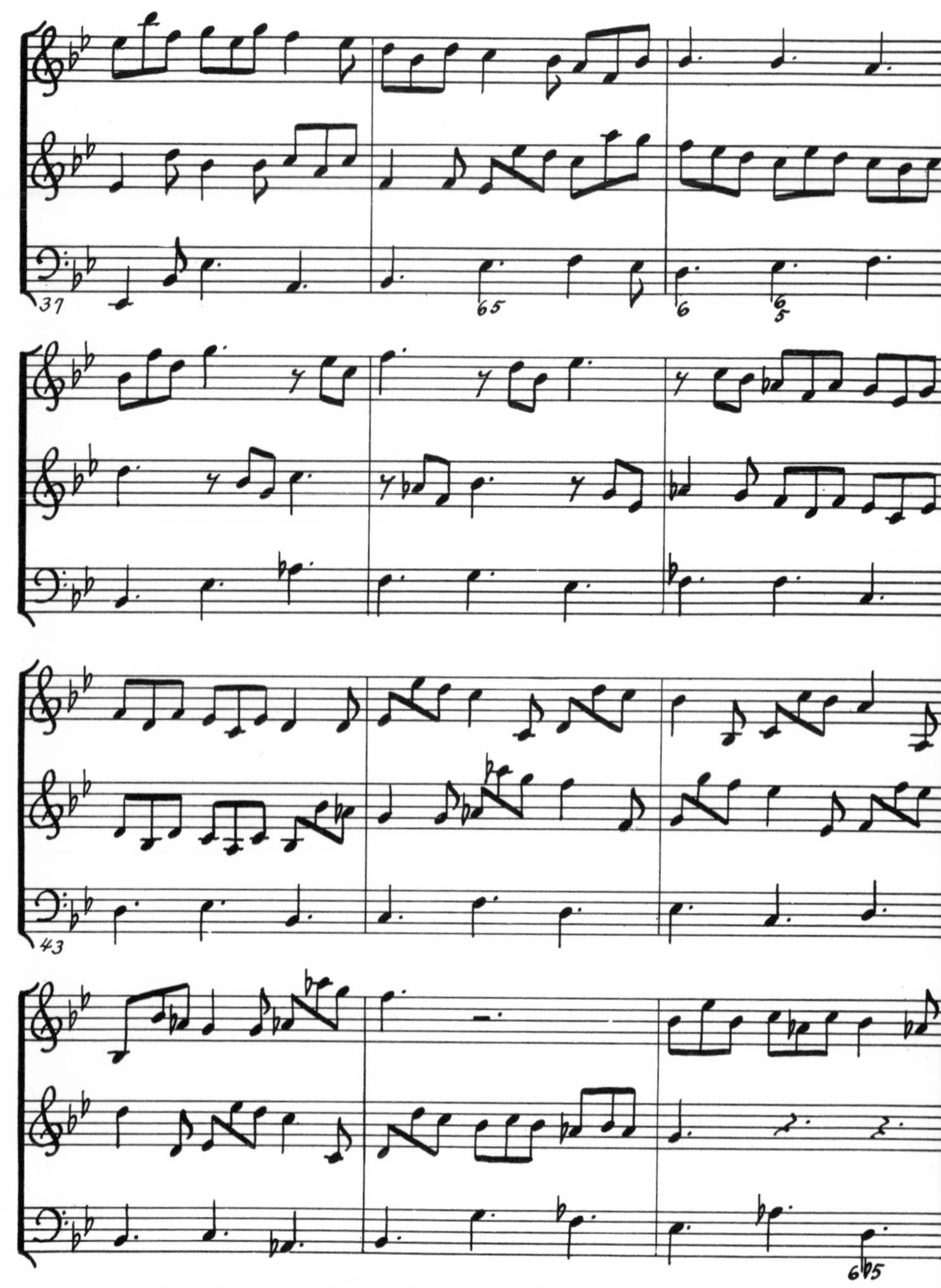
37
43

49
55

[♭]
61
Tremolo Largo
etc....
67

73
Presto
tremolo Presto
80
[etc]

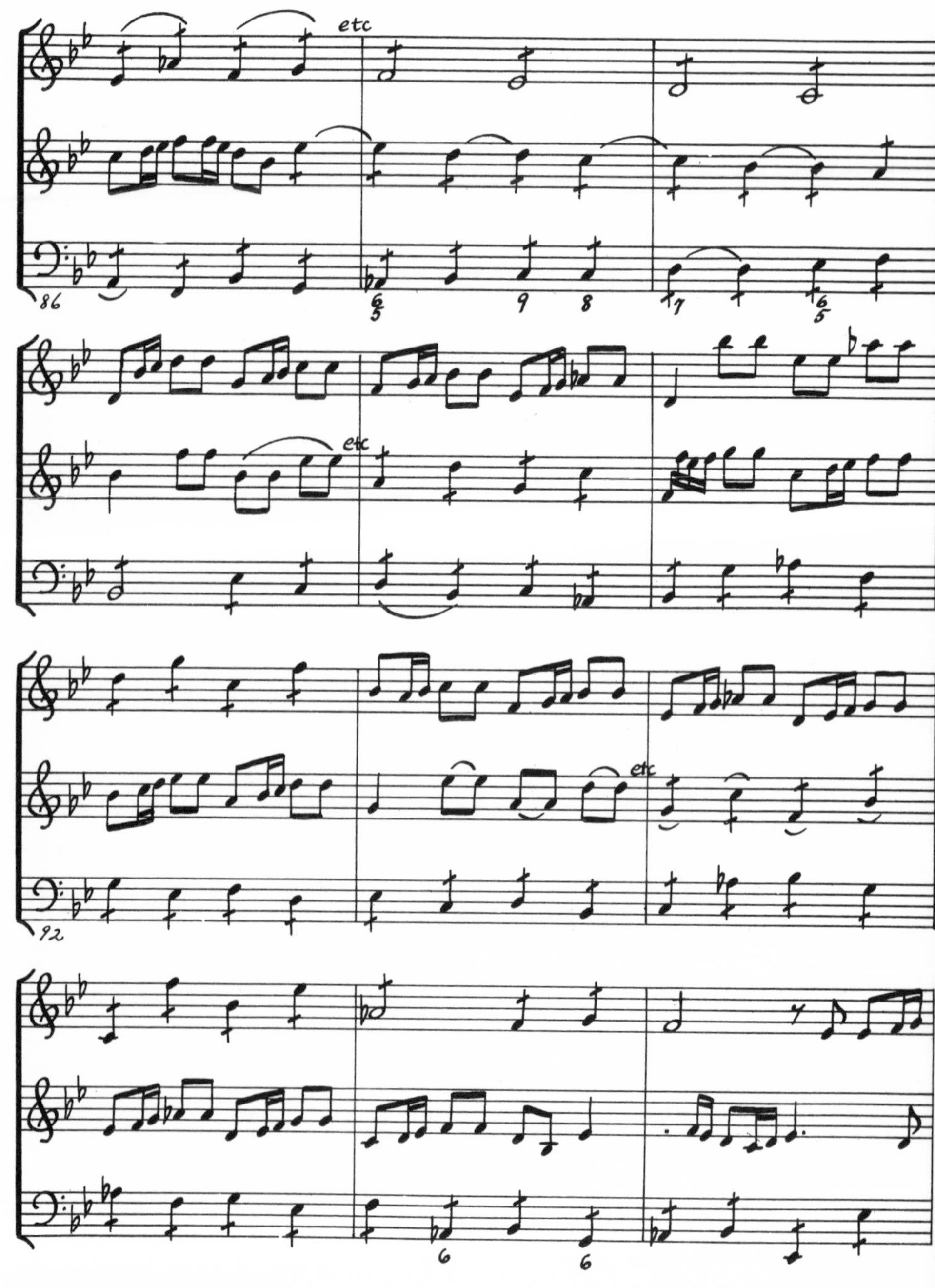
etc
etc
etc
86
92

98
6
6
5
7
6
5
98
7
[♭]
104
4
3
7
43
43
43
43
43
43
43
43
6

Op. VII, 1. Aria*

V1

V2

Alto Viola

Violone o Spinetta

*"Arietta" in Gardano edition

f
p

Op. VII, 2. Corrente

p
15 6 43
76
567
6
22 76
43
6
26 6 6
#6
43
6 #6

Op. VII, 18. Corrente

VII, 23. Aria

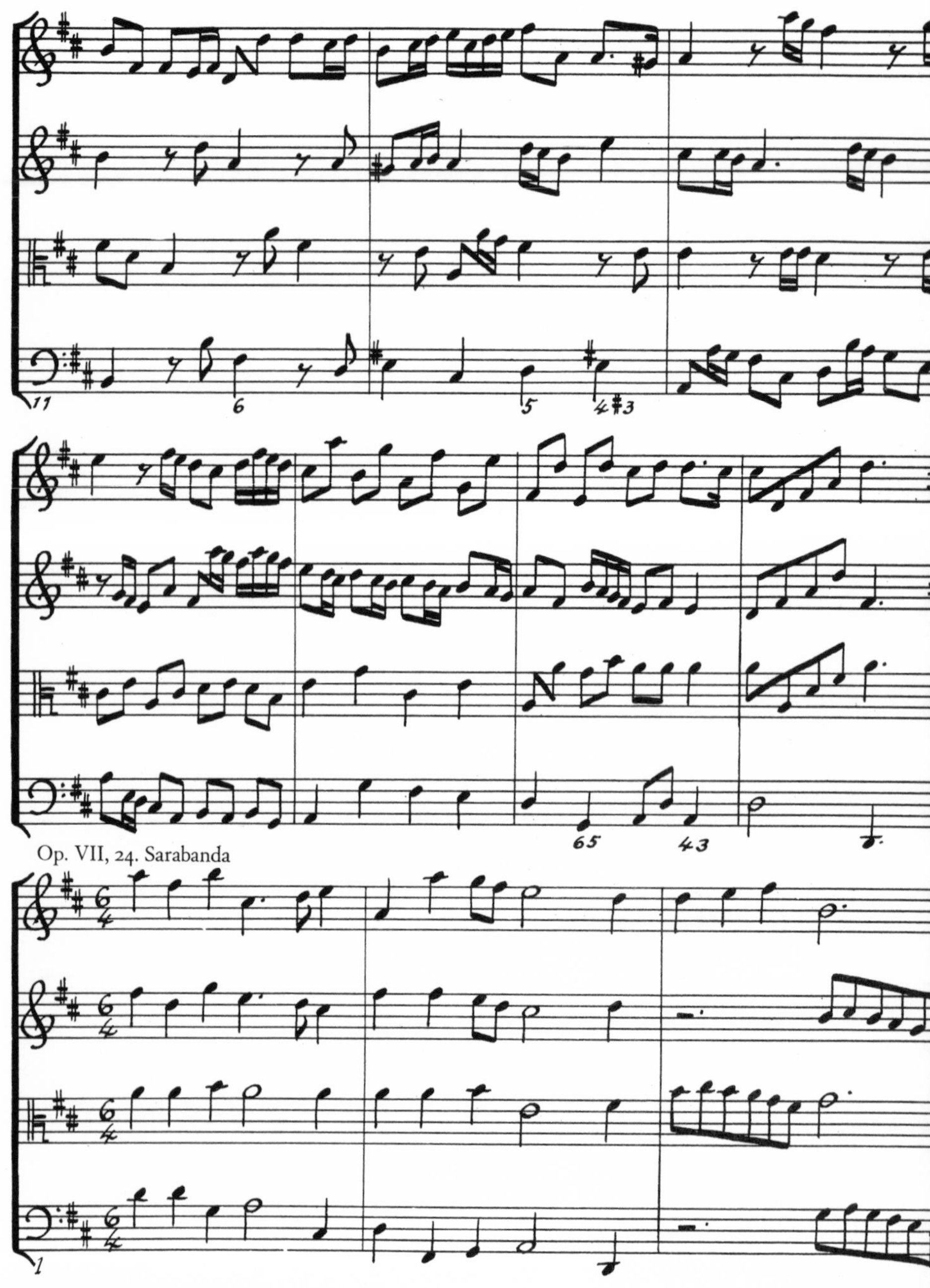
11
6
5
4♯3
65
43
Op. VII, 24. Sarabanda
1

6
fine

Op. VII, 25. Corrente, *La Castelvetra*

* The Modena MS (in what appears to be Colombi's hand) gives only the upper part in normal notation, suggesting that it was also played so, i.e., with normal tuning and no (or optional) double stops.

IX, 1

VI
Adagio
VII
Violone
B.C.
6 9 8 7 6
7 6 7 6 7 6 6 5 6 5 6 6 6 6 6
Allegro
7 4 3 6

13
56
21

[♮]
6

37
4 3
4♯3
Adagio
4 3
45

4♯3
6
43
Allegro
♯3 7
7 5
43

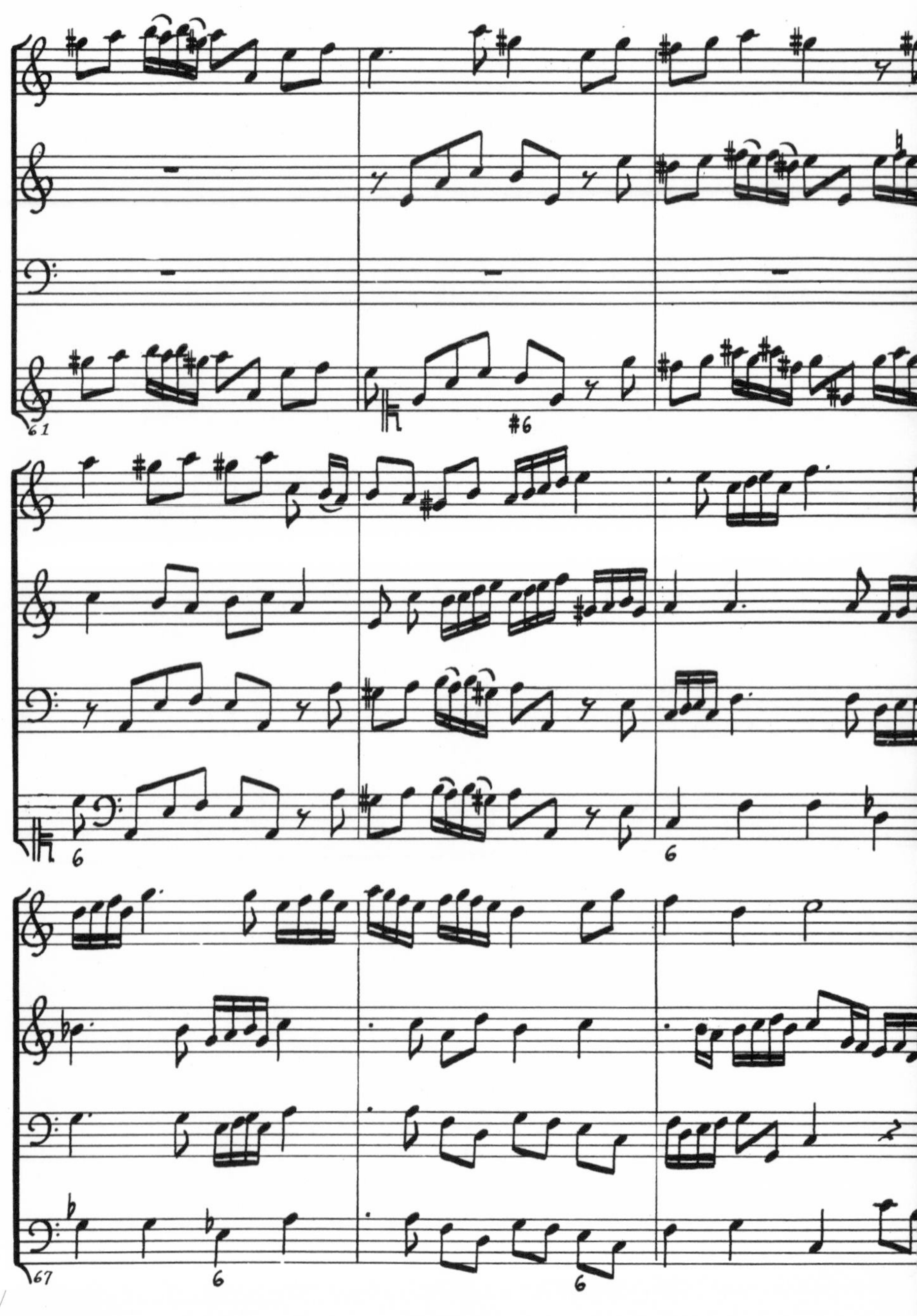
61
67

70
76

Adagio
e tremolo
79
98
76
#3
7
7
5
7
5
43

Op. IX, 2

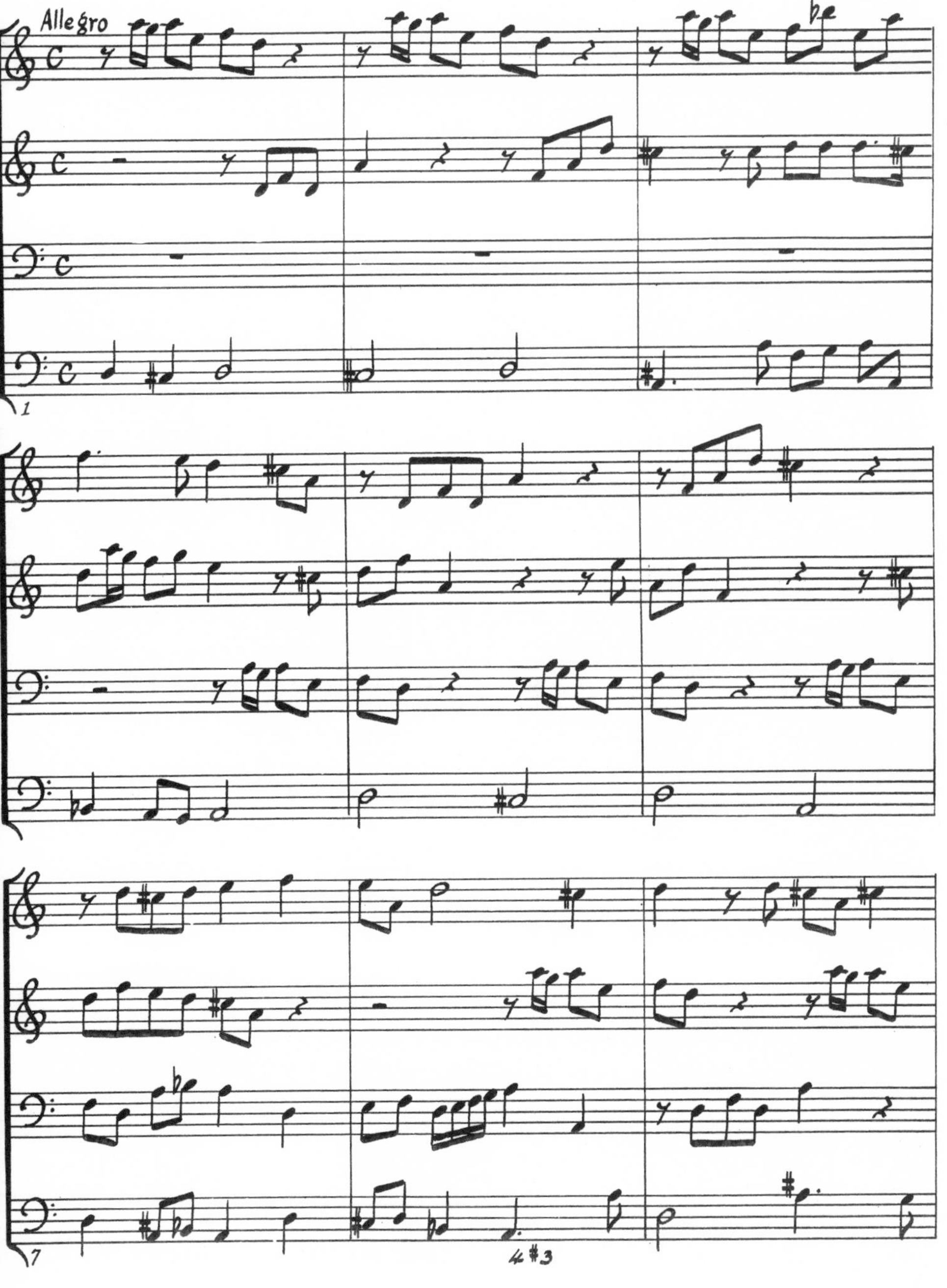

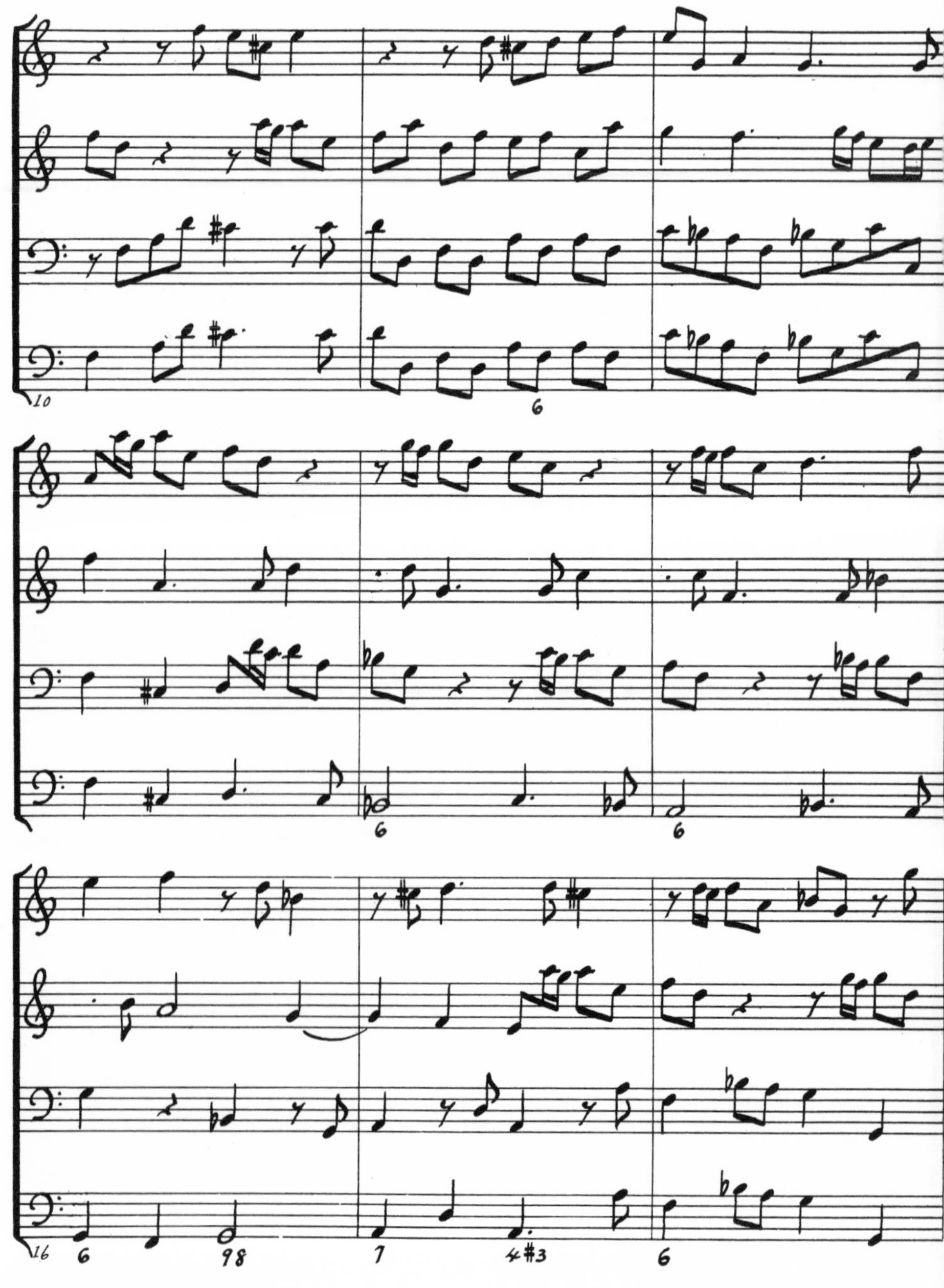
10
6
6
6
16 6
98
7
4#3
6

19
43
43
Allegro
6
76
76
76
76
25
76
76
76
65

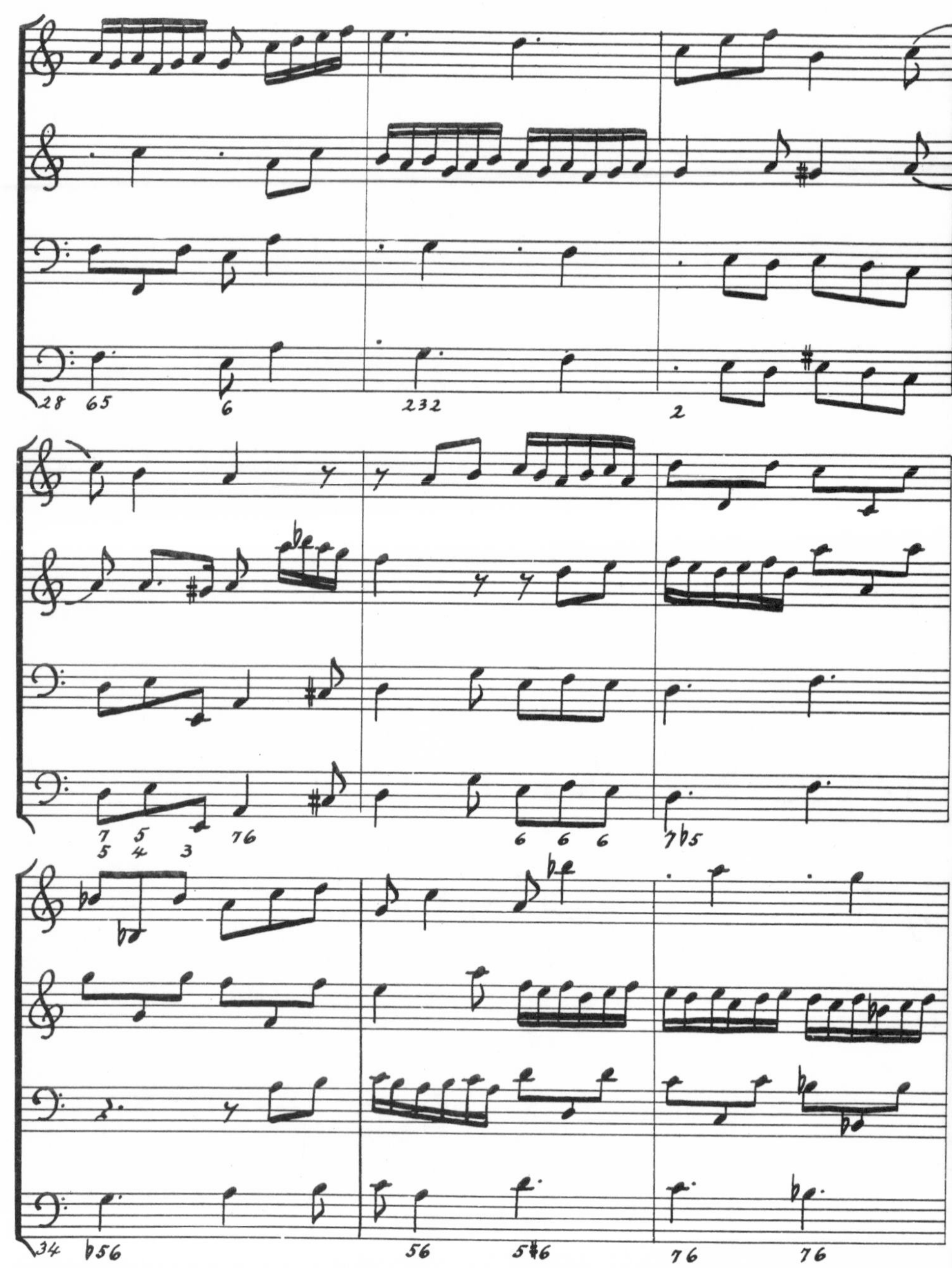
28 65 6 232 2
7 5 5 4 3 76 6 6 6 7♭5
34 ♭56 56 5♯6 76 76

37
76
♭76
76
76
76
[♮]
[sic]
40
76
♯6
7
7 5
5 4 ♯3
Adagio
43
6
7
5
4 3
♯6

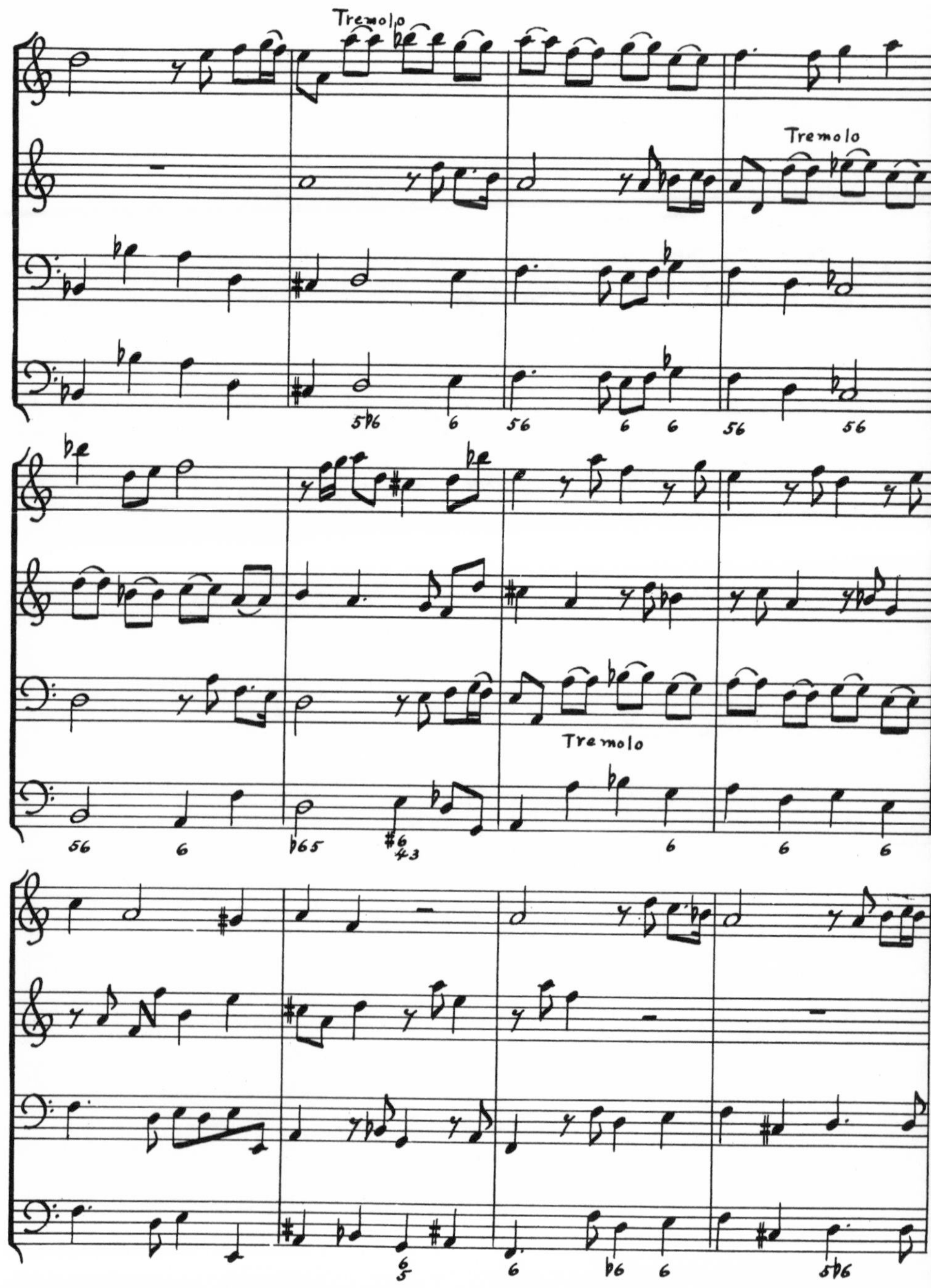
Tremolo
Tremolo
Tremolo

Allegro

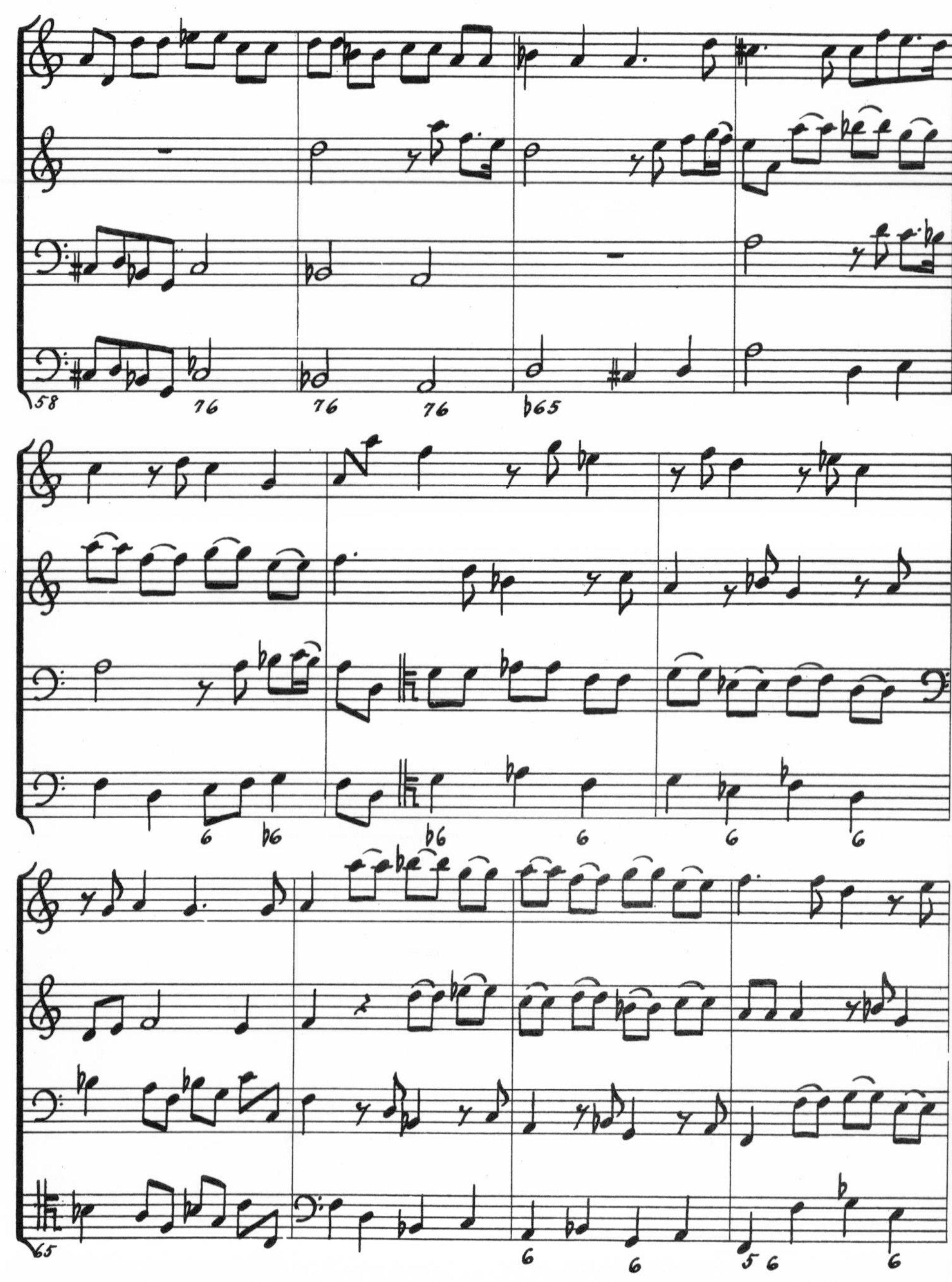

Op. IX, 3
Allegro

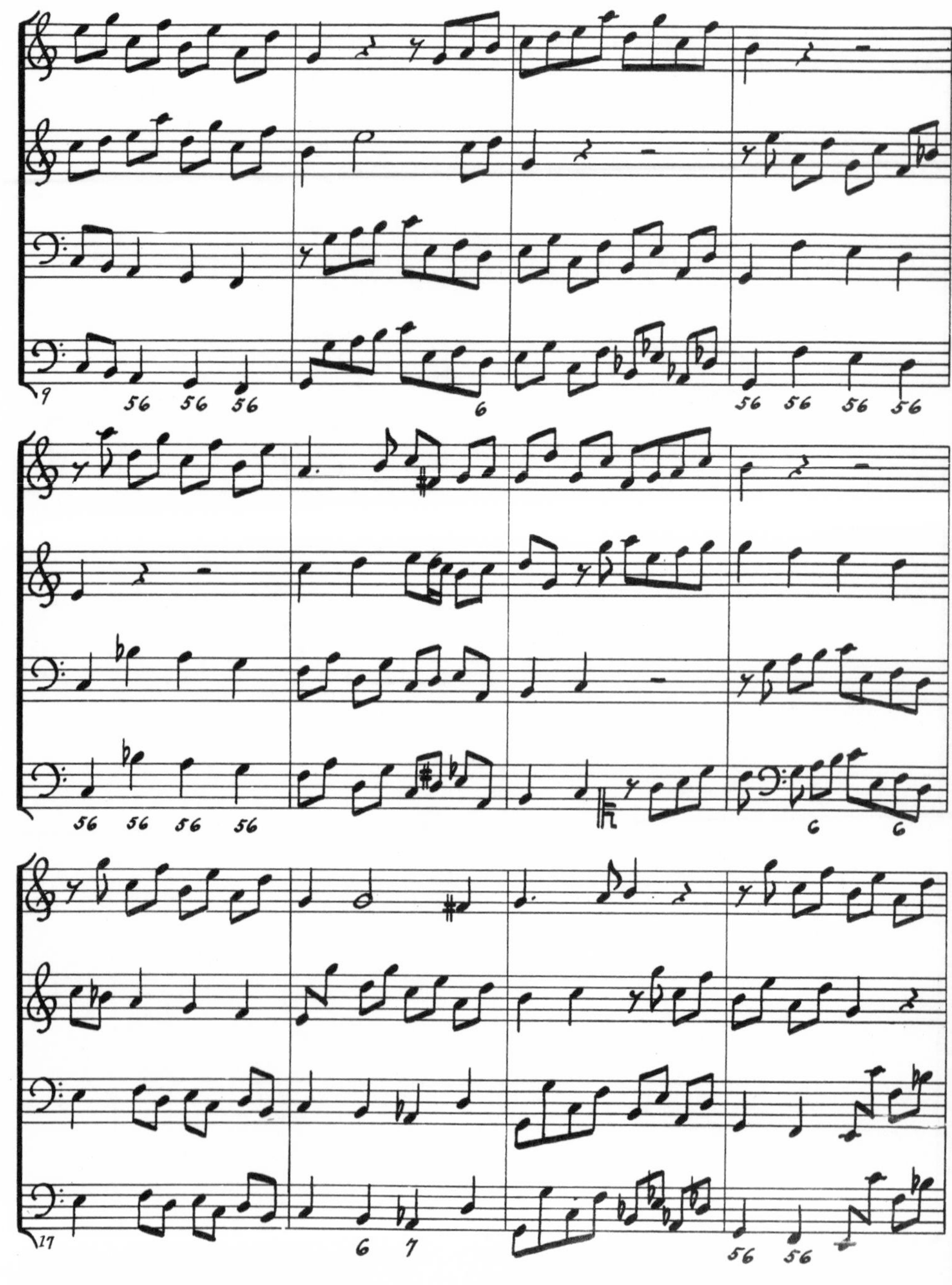

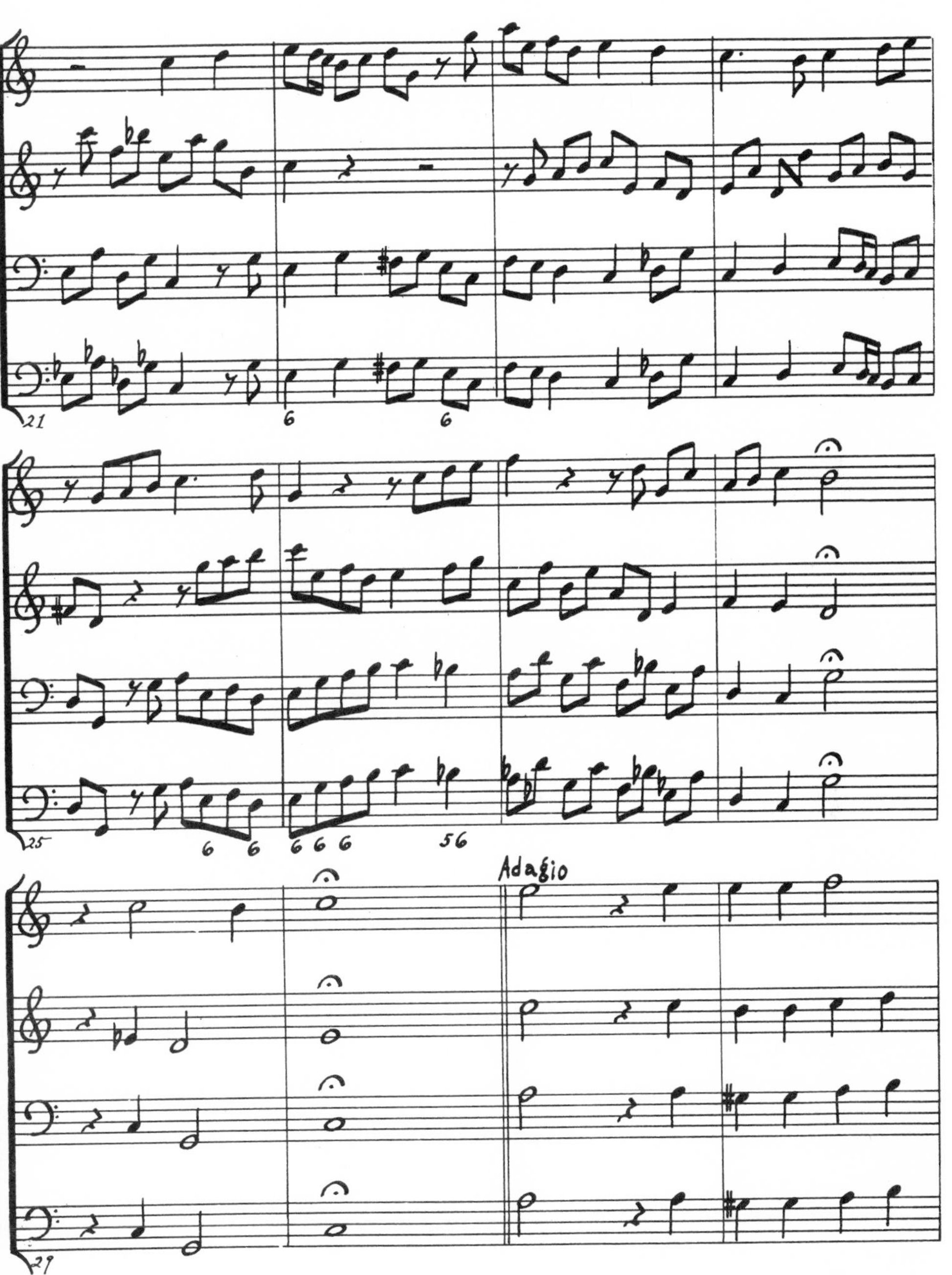
21
25
Adagio
29

33
65 65 6 6
98 76 34 6 4♭3
[♮]
41
43 ♯3 5 56 43 43

Largo

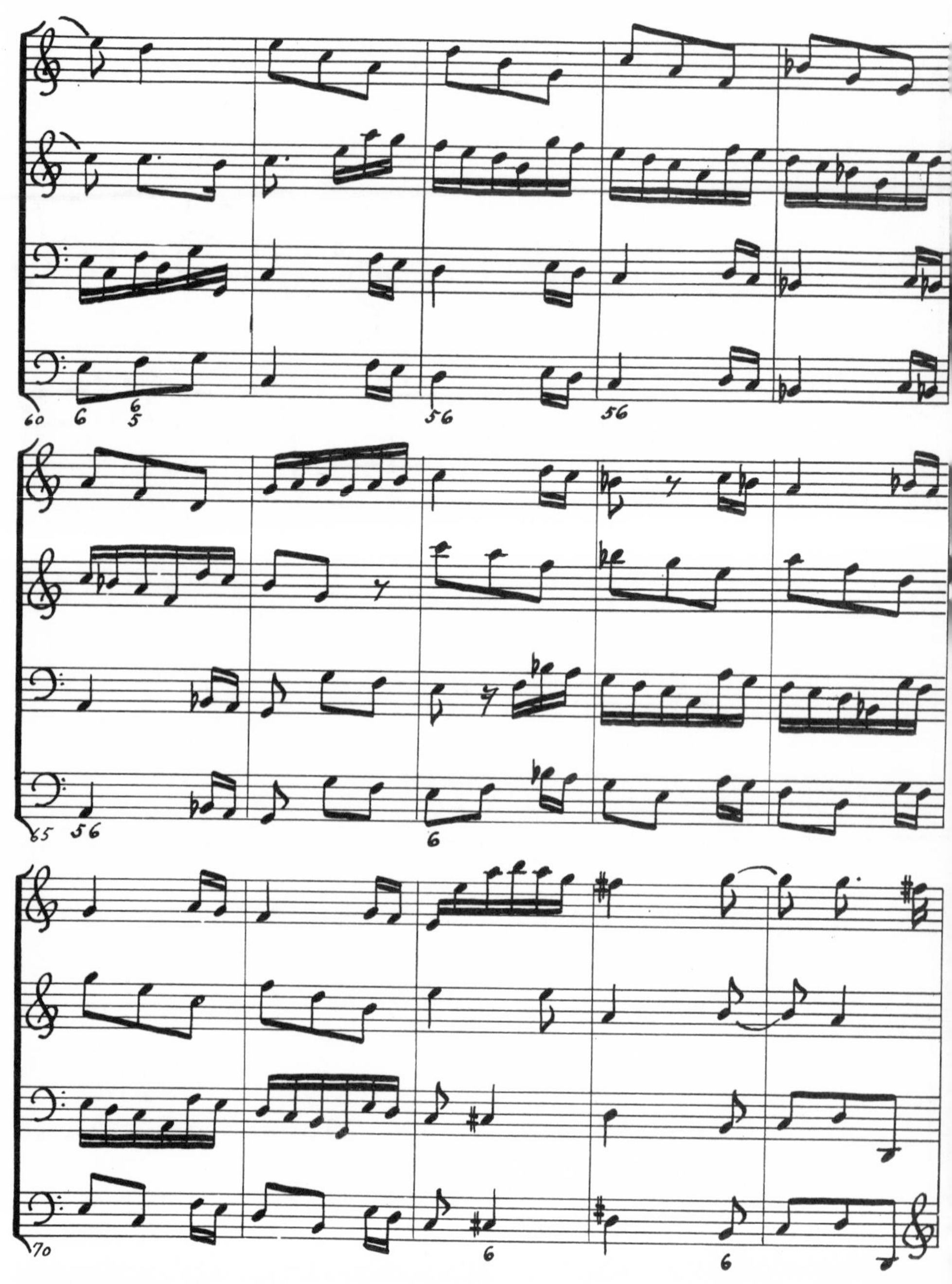

Op. IX, 5

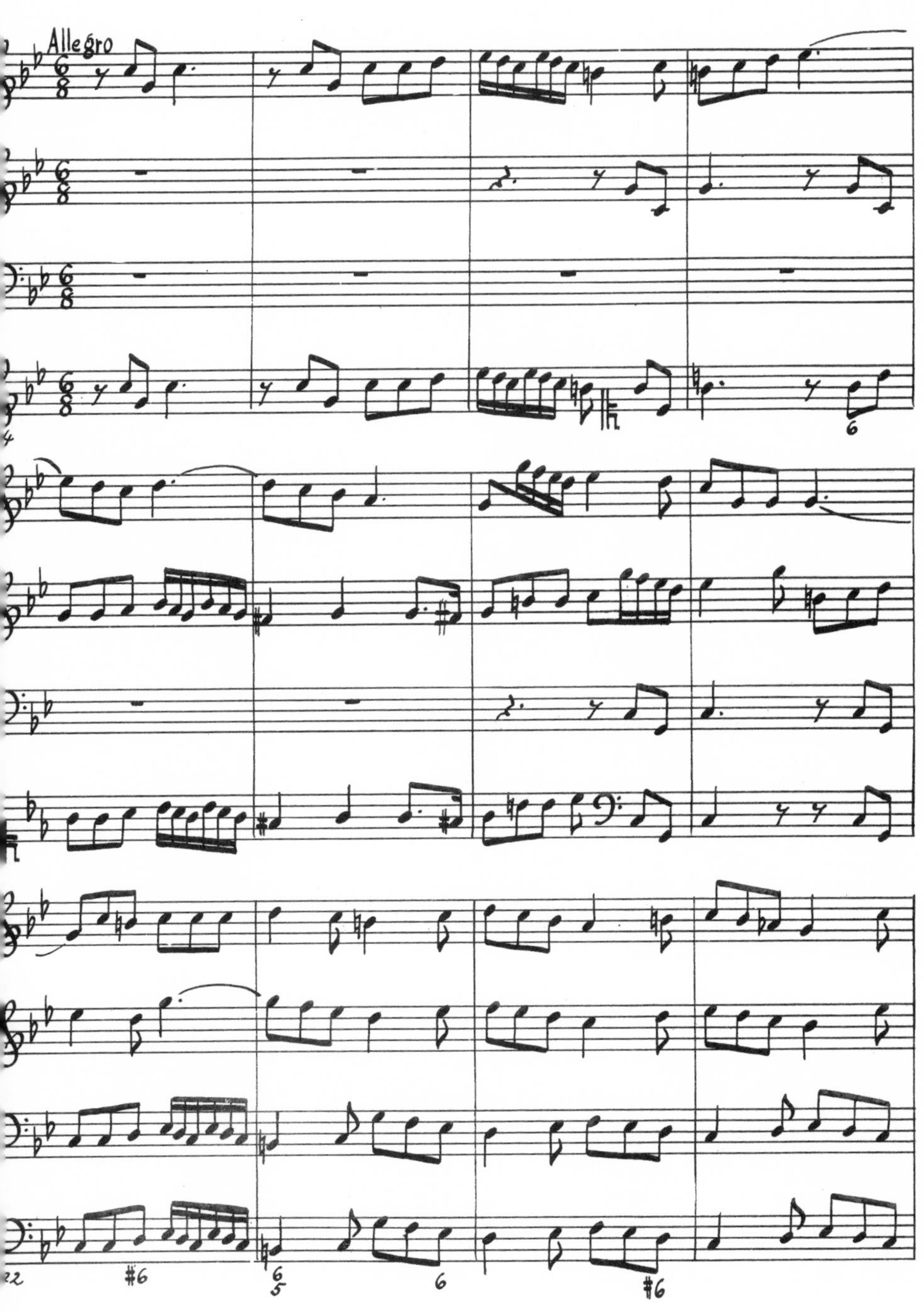
Allegro

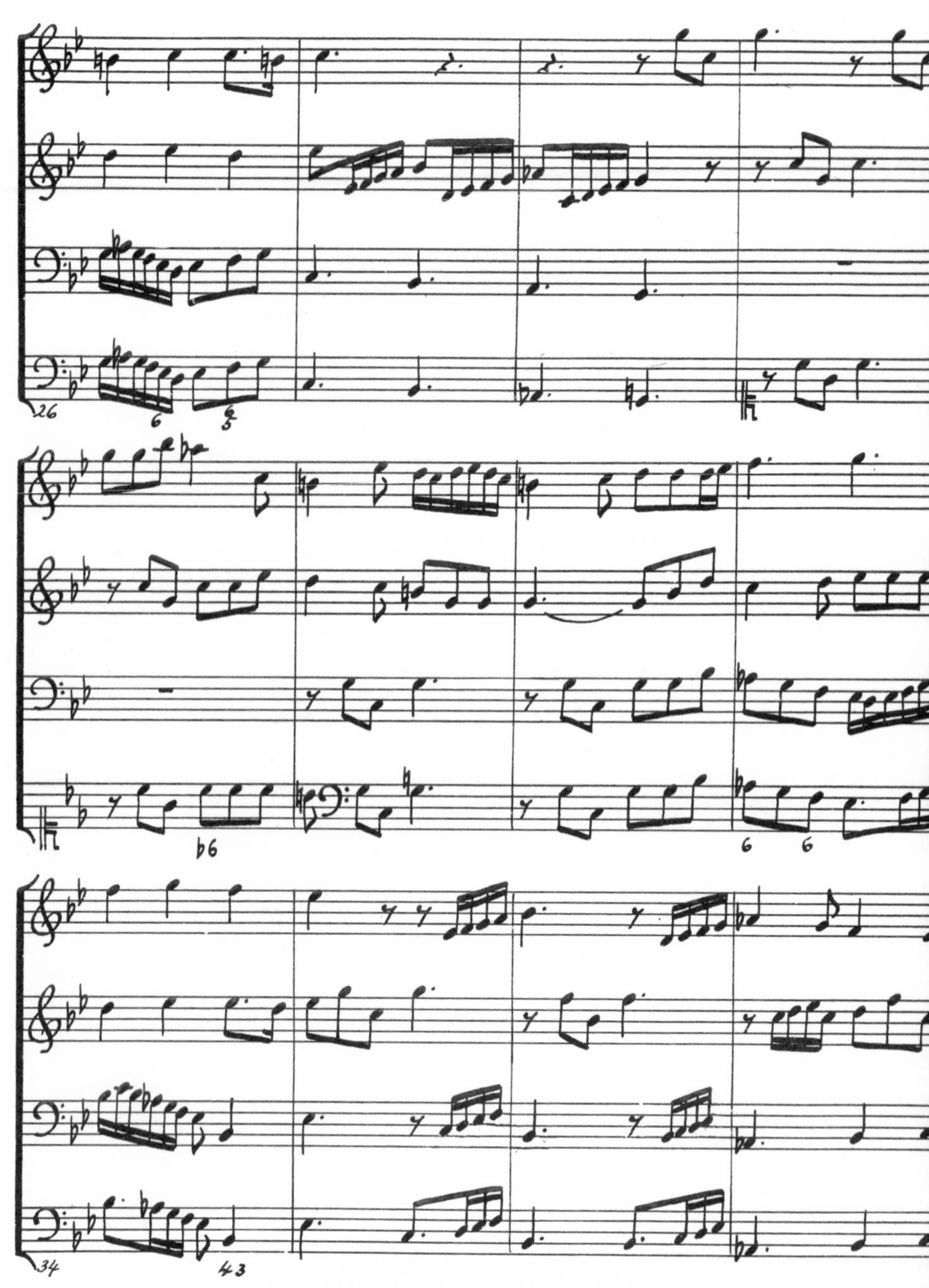
26
6
6
5
b6
6
6
34
43

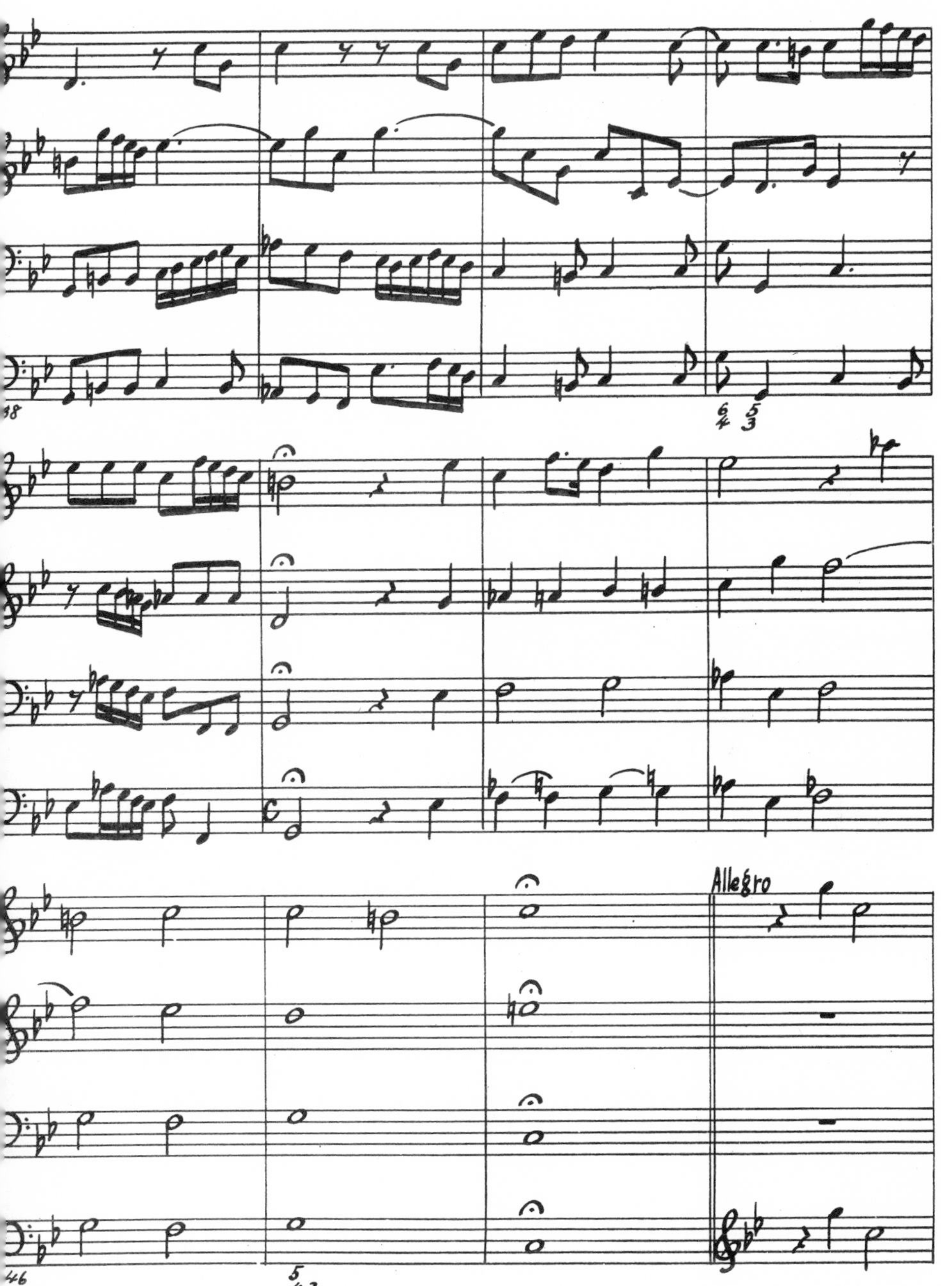
38
6
4
5
3
Allegro
46
5
4 3

50
58

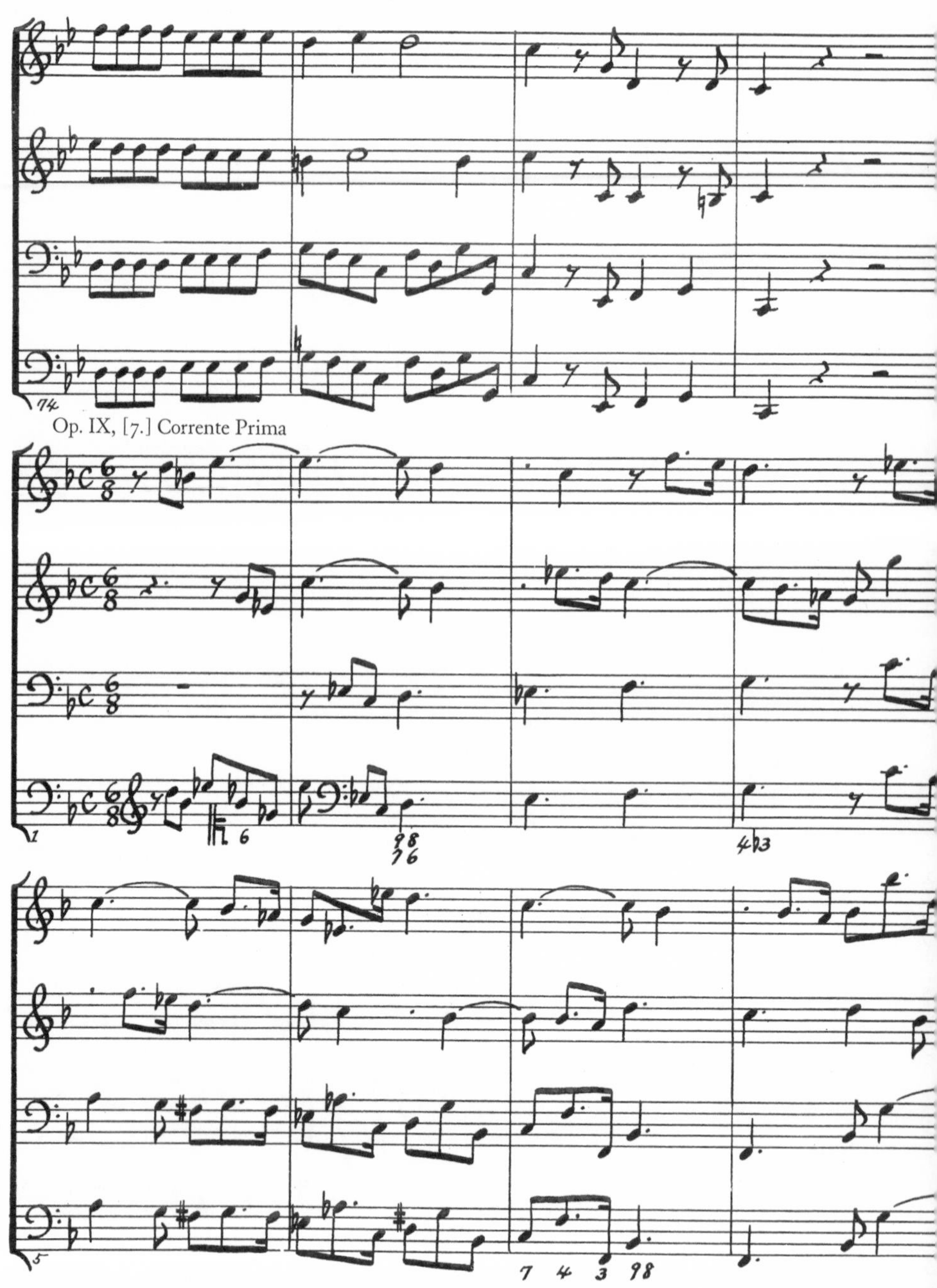
74
Op. IX, [7.] Corrente Prima
1
5

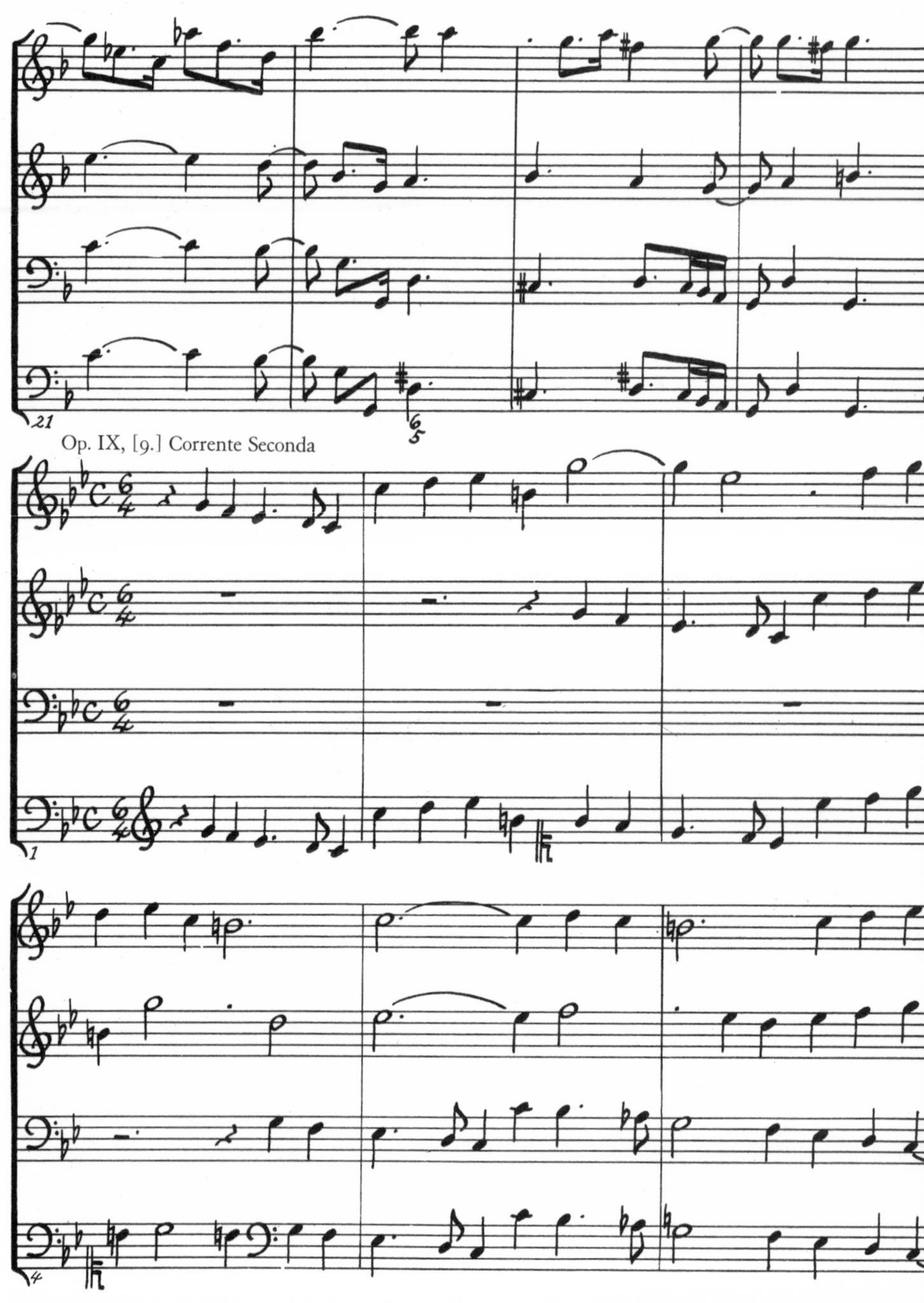
21
Op. IX, [9.] Corrente Seconda
1
4

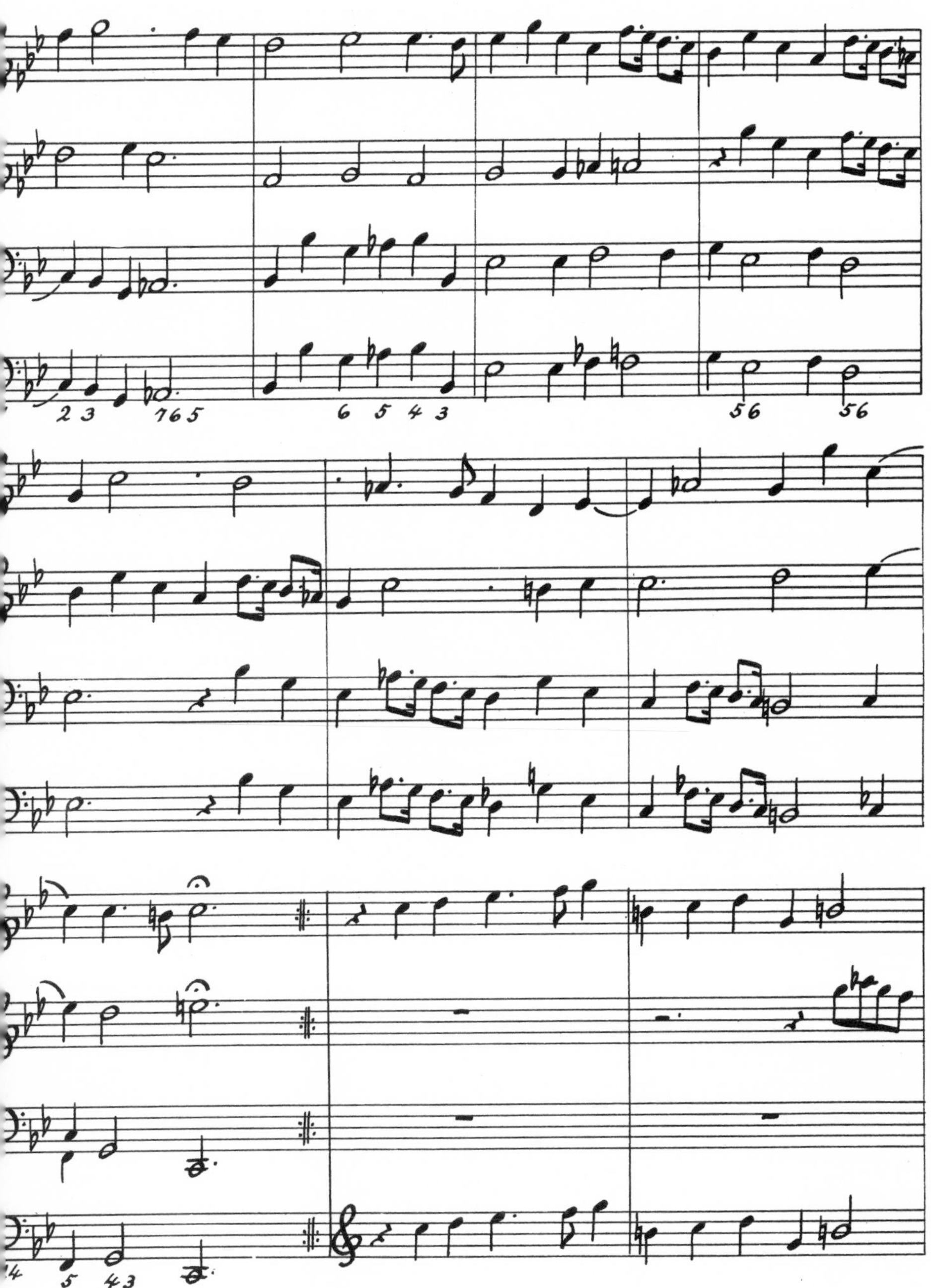

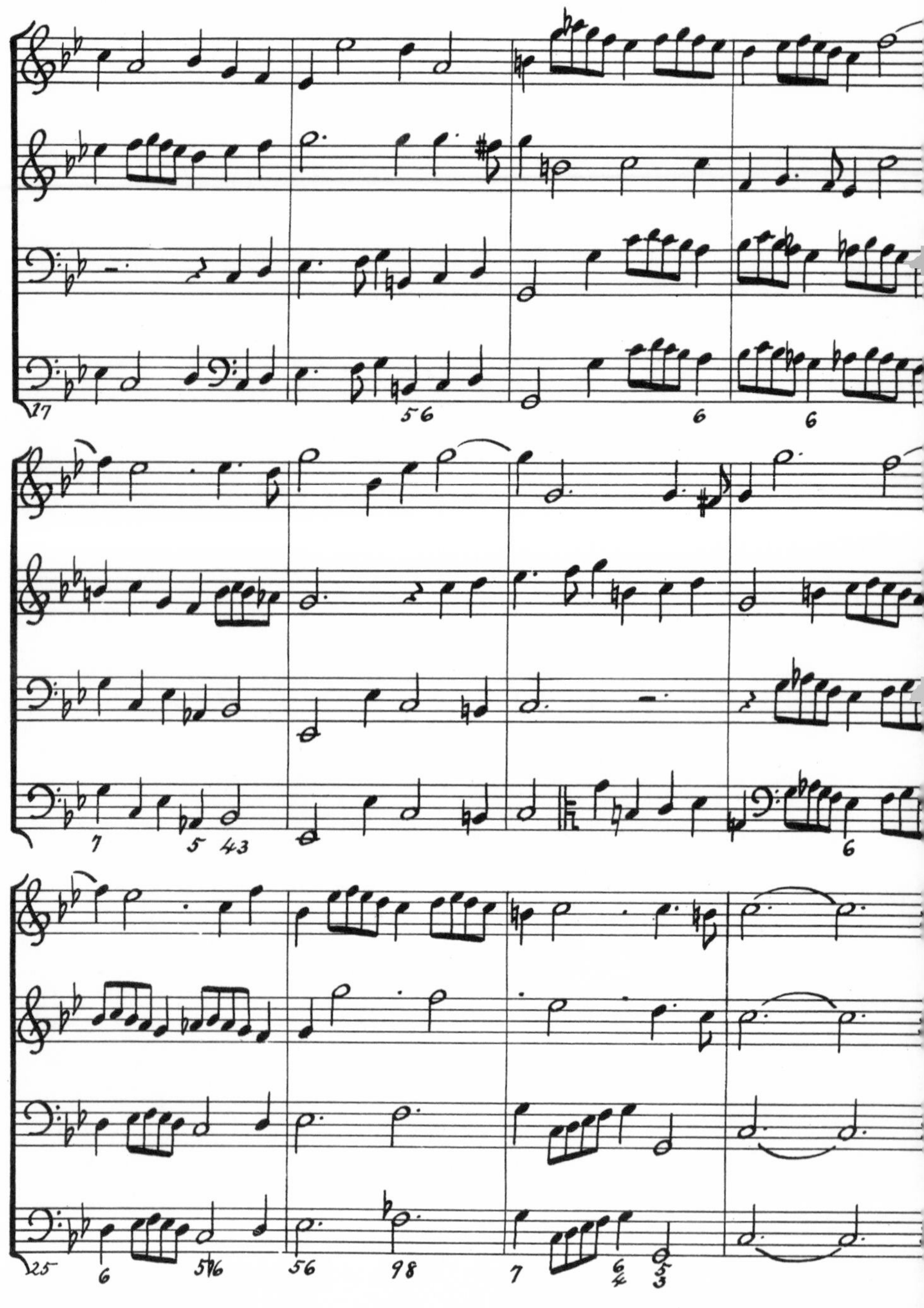

. IX, [12.] Allemanda Quarta

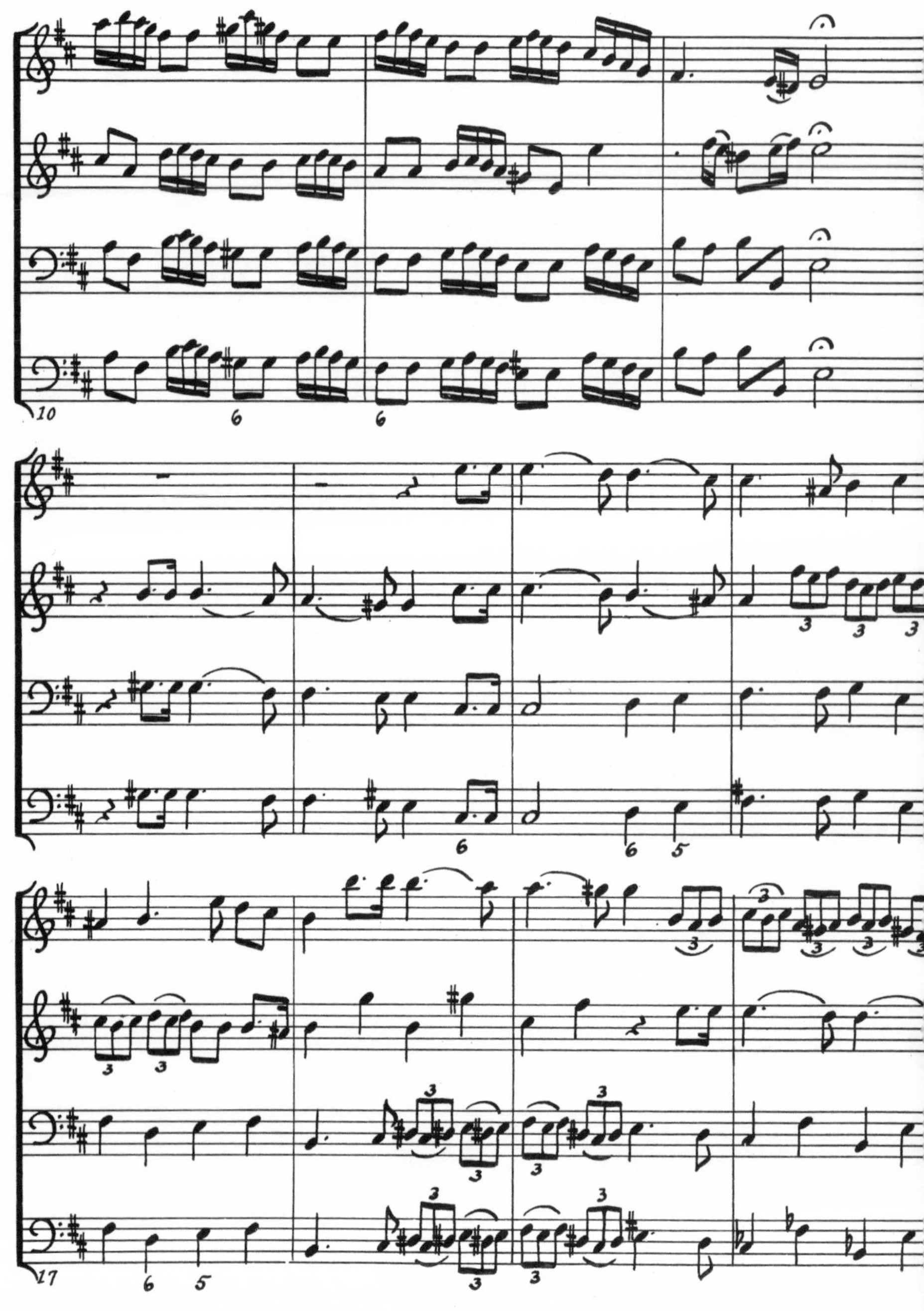
10
17

. IX, Sonata da Camera à Quattro in stil Francese

*As with other pieces in the "French style," there is no Basso Continuo, but "extra" inner part. The parts of the original edition (Monti) lack bar lines rely.

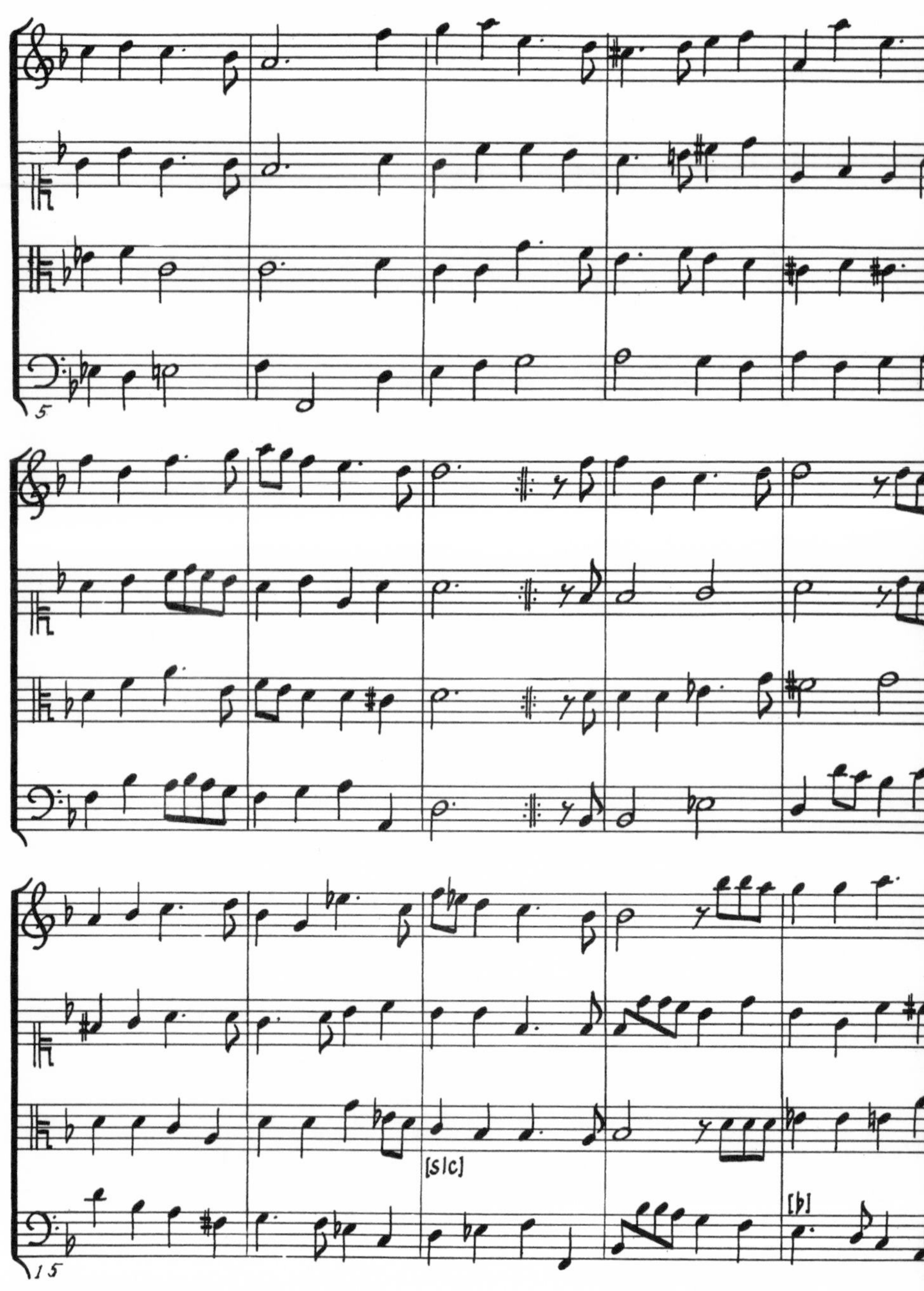
[SIC]
[♭]

Op. IX, [20.] Gagliarda*

*No bar lines in the original. The heavy bars indicate the grouping in 2, the real rhythm. See text *re* Galliard, p. 111.

Op. XII, 10. Corrente

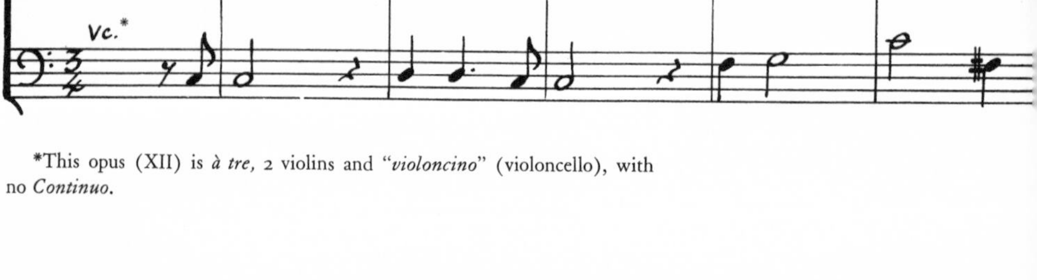

*This opus (XII) is *à tre,* 2 violins and "*violoncino*" (violoncello), with no *Continuo.*

6
18

Op. XII, 16. Corrente

12
Op. XII, 24. Correntе
5

9
17

Scelta Marino Silvani, 1680
Sonata Settima del Sig. Gio. M. Bononcini

14
6
6
5
♭7
5
20
6
5
6
6
[♭?]
6
6

Adagio
26
5
6
98
43
6
5
♭7
43
34
[♭]
6

42
50

58
6
6
Grave
[♭]
6
43
76
4♯
tremolo
67
4♭3
9
8
76
5
[♭]
tremolo

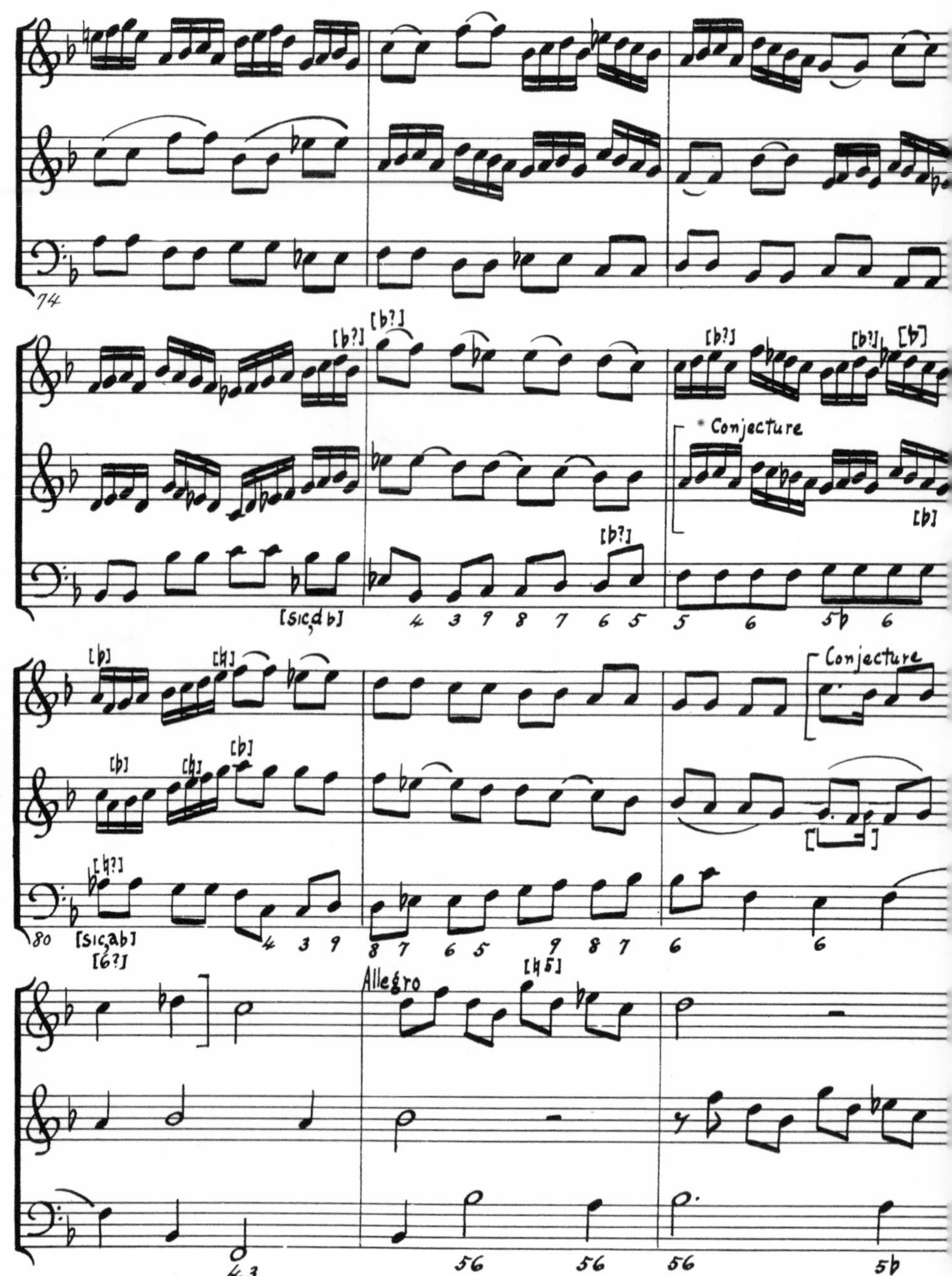

*The text of the violin parts is incomplete, being shorter than the bass. Since this was published after Bononcini's death it may be an unfinished work, exploited by the enterprising Marini.

*Original barring and notation, showing cross-rhythms.

M. Cazzatti Op. VIII
Canzona Prima, *La Vertua*

Allegro

21
27

*redundant accidentals omitted.

Conjecture

Grave

Allegro
90
6 5 4 3
6
5
#5
97

M. Cazzatti
Op. XVIII Sonata Settima, *La Rosella*

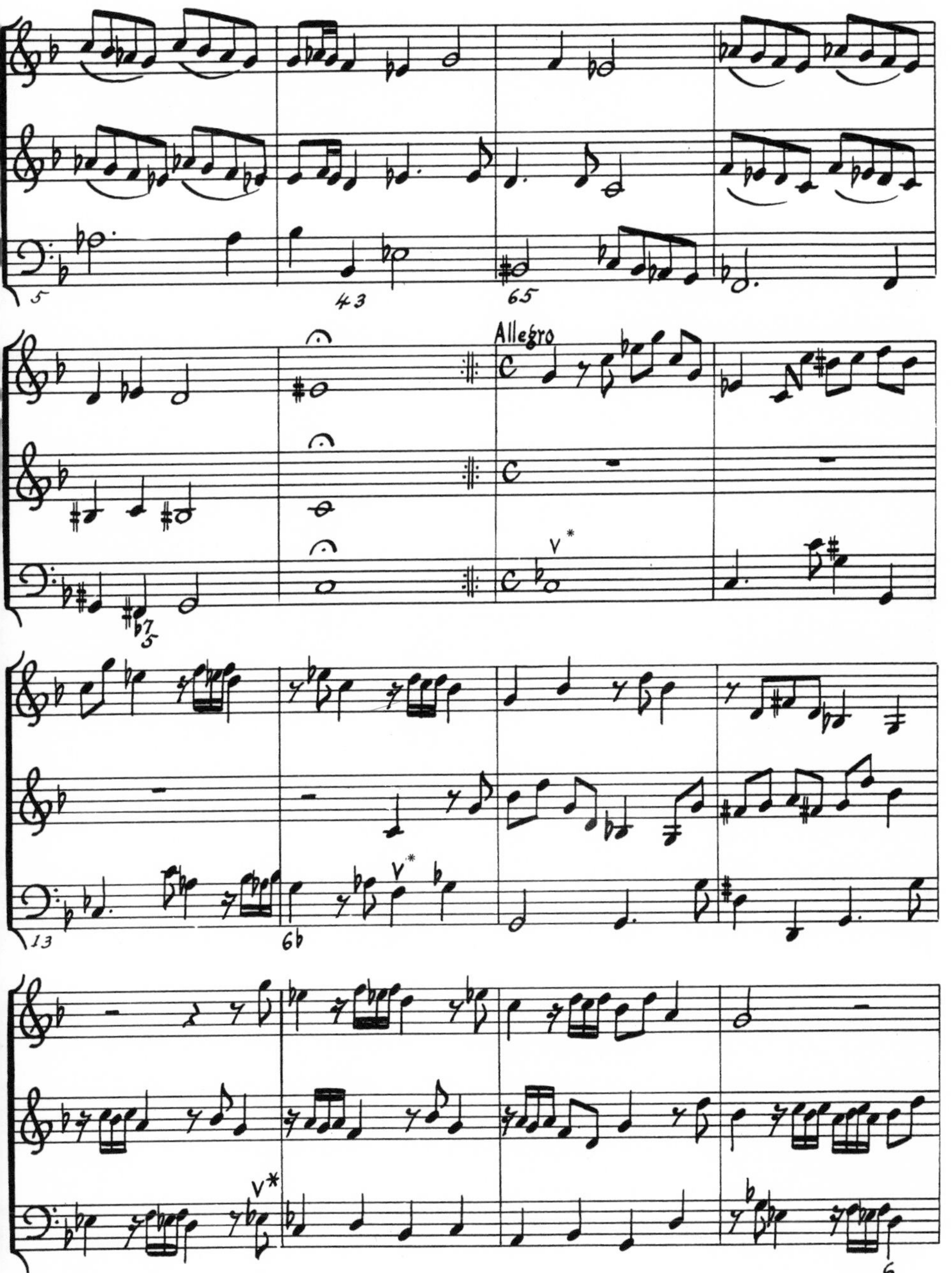

*These "V's" of course mark the entrance of a violin part. Useful to the Continuo player, with only the bass before him, they are redundant in a score and will not be included beyond this point.

21
6
65
6
6
piano
Presto
piano
29
piano
6
37

45
6
76
43
53
Grave
61
67

M. Cazzatti Op. XXIV, Messa Concertata, *Sinfonia*

V1, 2
Canto
Ky - ri - e e - le - i - son
Alto
Alto Ripieno
Tenore
Tenore Rip.
Basso
Basso Ripieno
B.C.

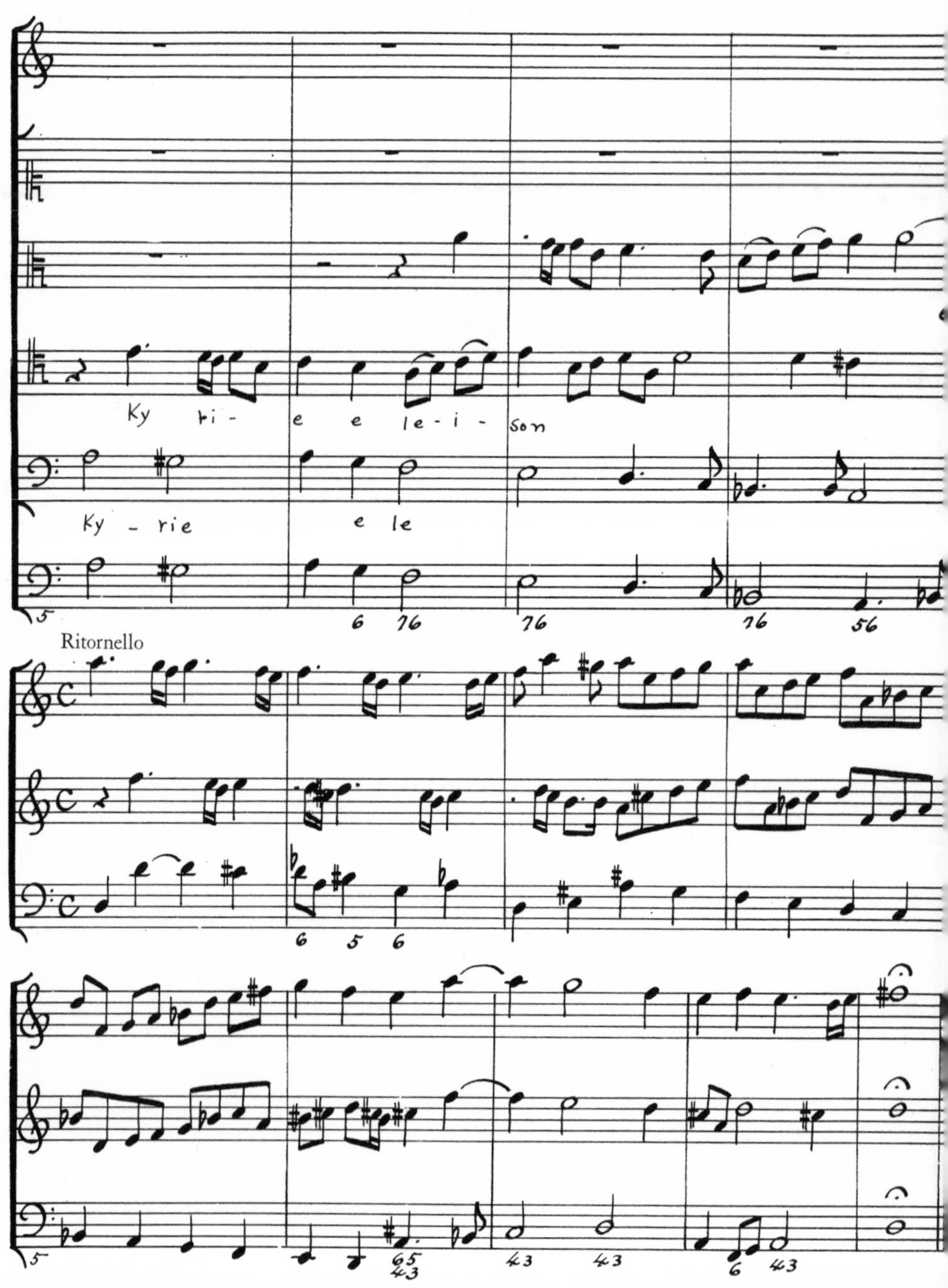
Ky ri - e e le - i - son
Ky - rie e le
Ritornello

Christe e - le - i - son - - -
etc
(W. Tacet)

V1
V2
Et incarnatus est de spiritu sanctu ex Maria Virgine et ho - mo factus est
76
56
765

M. Cazzatti
Op. XXXV, *La Casala*

f
p
f
f
p
19
25

* The concerto is already at hand. NB the *concertante* manner of the *Allegro,* and the *solos* of the *Grave* (which should be heavily ornamented).

Tremolo etc
etc, Col, B, C.
43
55

Largo
61
[G?]
71

76
Col, B.C.
86

Vivace
91
97

100
106

M. Cazzatti
Op. XXXV, *La Malvasia,* à 4: due Violini, Alto e Basso

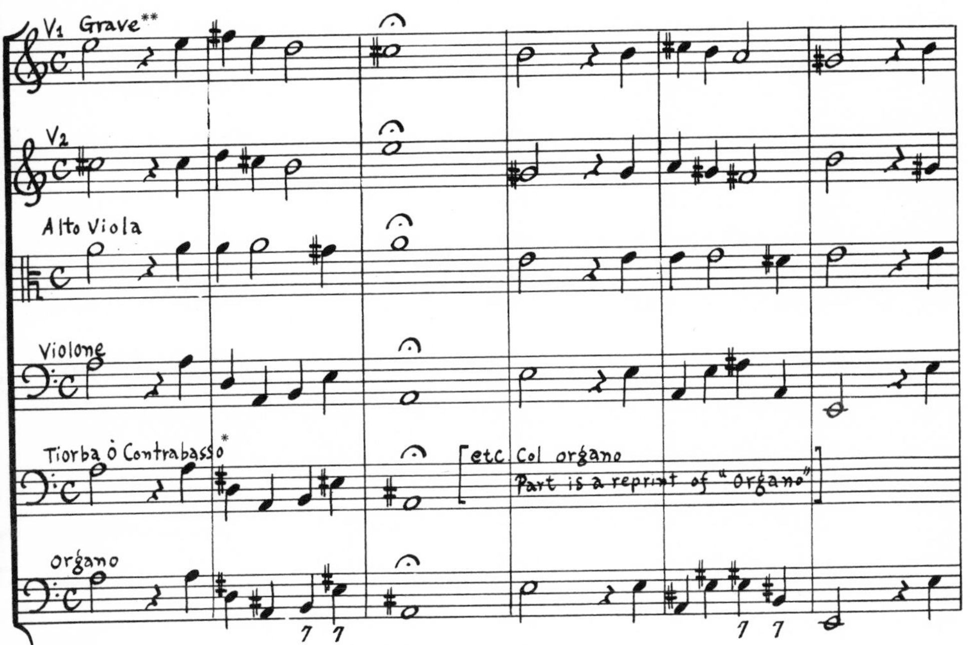

*The heavy instrumentation of the bass suggests that the upper parts were doubled, concerto fashion, which was probably necessary for large functions at S. Petronio

**cf. *Sinfonia* of Cazzatti, Mass, Op. XXIV.

[Violone]
[Tiorba c. Basso e organo]

Alegro[!]

18
6#

22

26

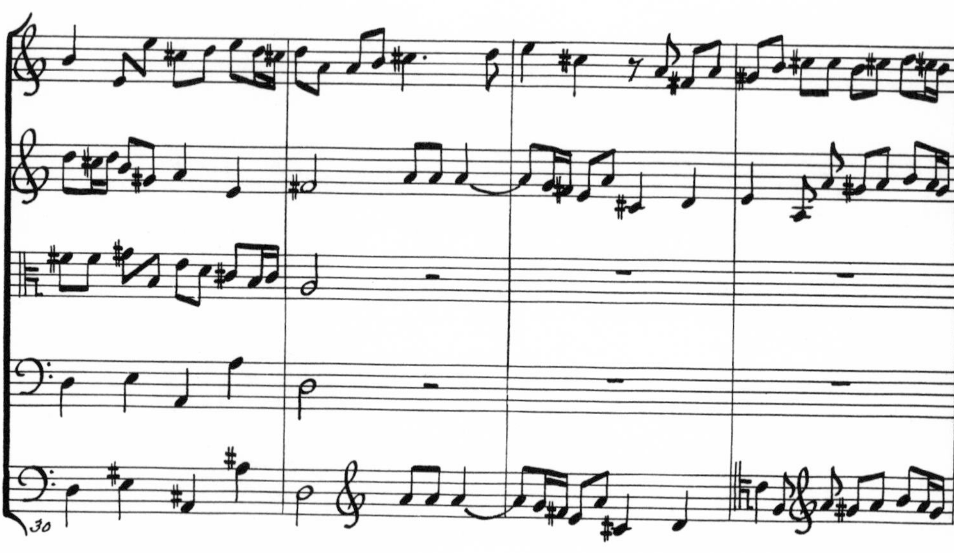
30

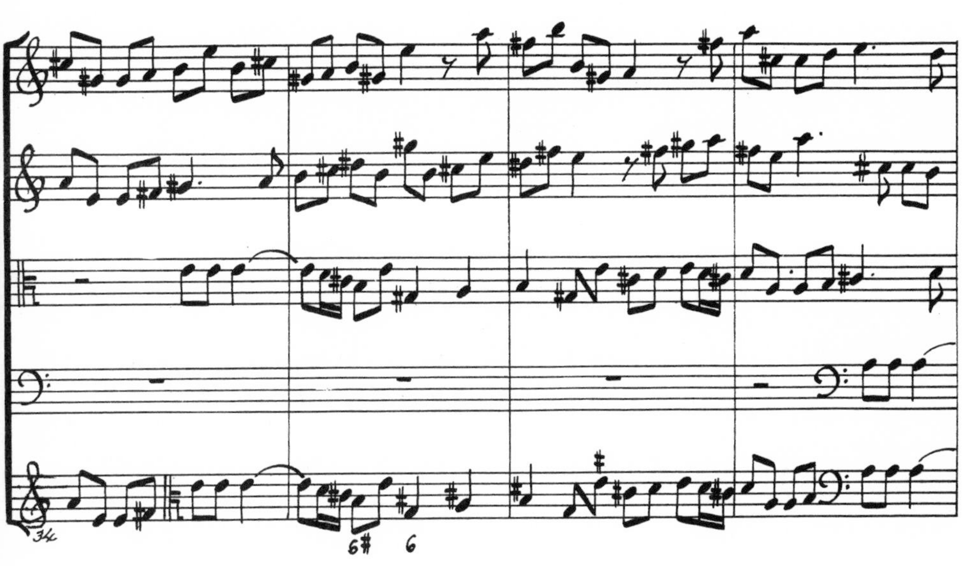

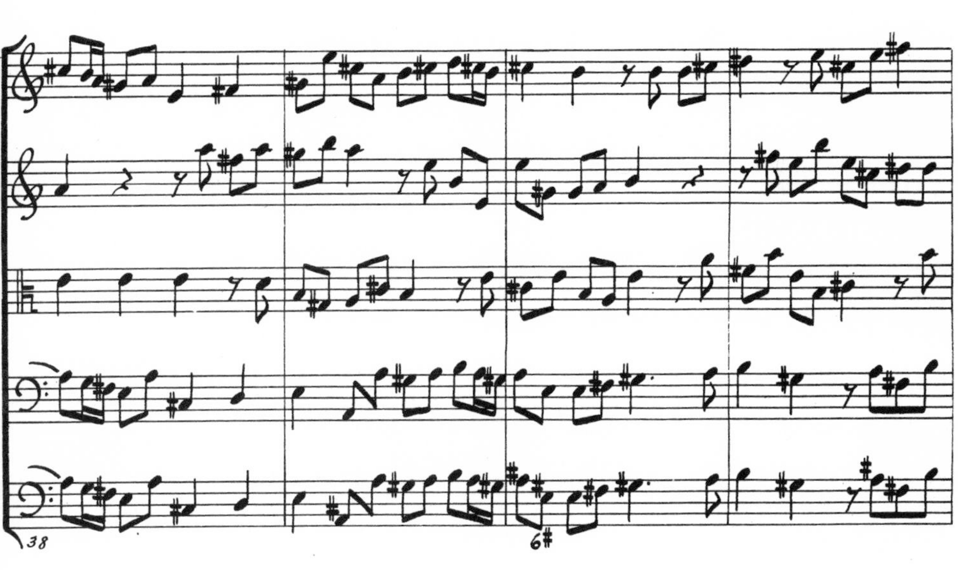

42

Grave
46

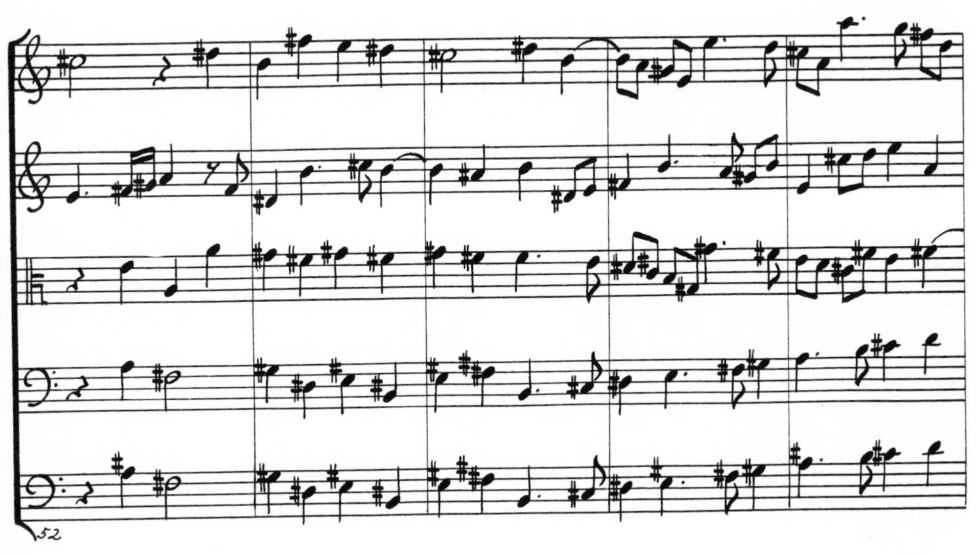
52

Vivace
Vp
Vs
57
765

Presto Presto

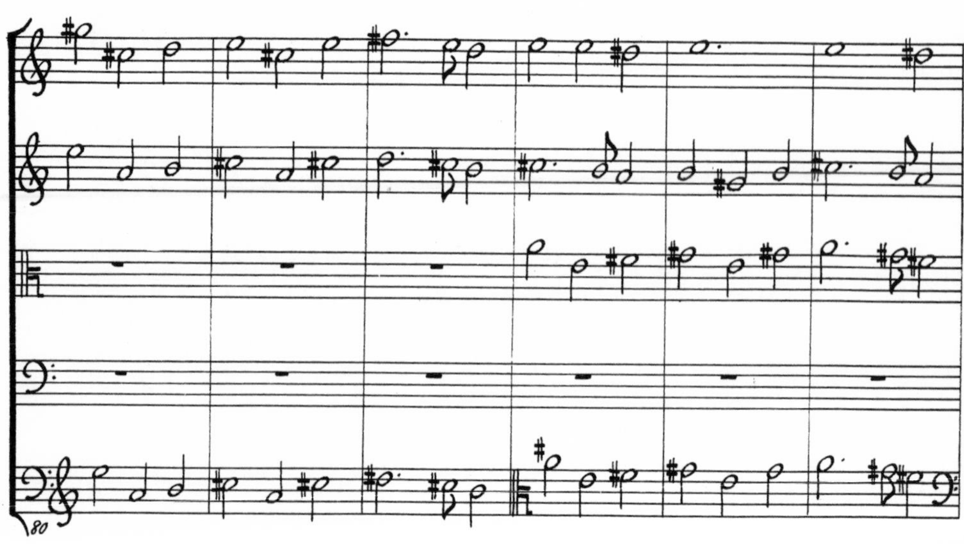
80

86

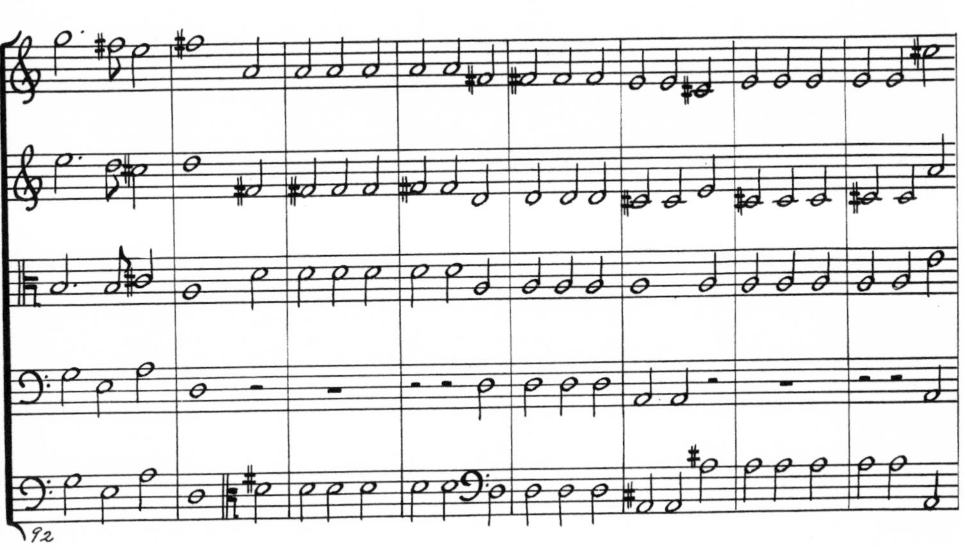
92

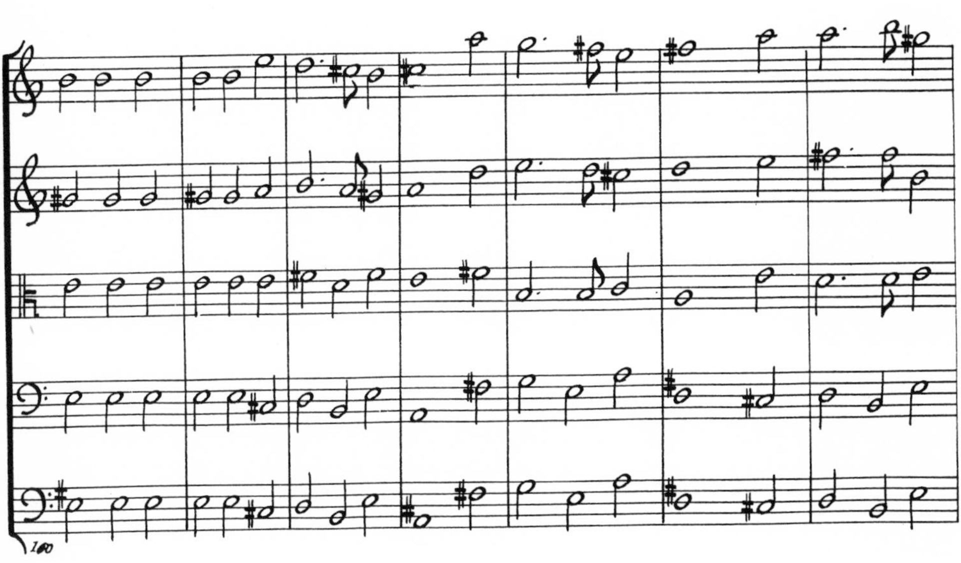
100

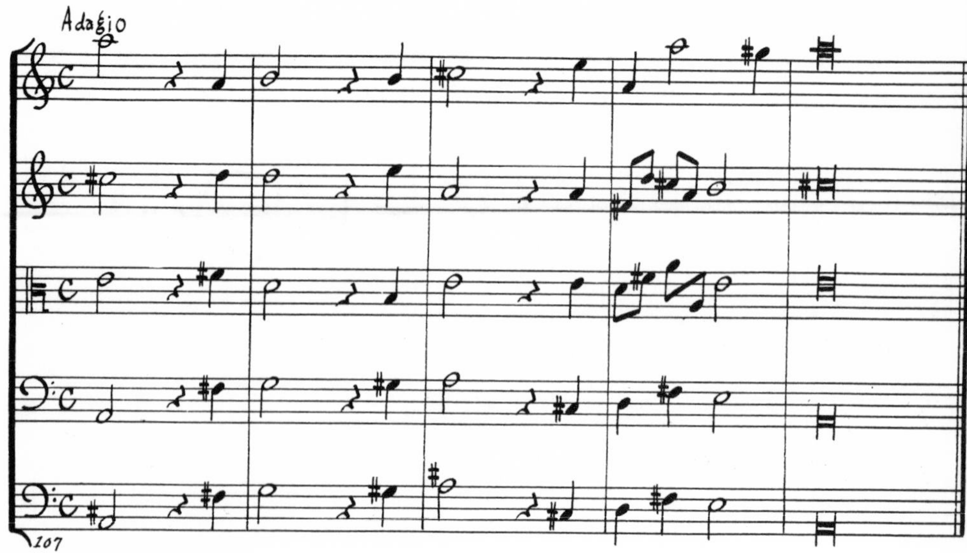
Adagio
107

Gio. P. Colonna
Missa Prima à 8, con Violini ad libitum

etc ...
Christe Christe elei son
etc ...
Christe
Et Incarnatus est de Spiritu Sancto ex Maria Virgine et Homo factus est

Gio. P. Colonna
Motet, *Ad novum coeli jubar*

-ta
25
te mortales exul-ta
33
te
Segue il Ritornello
[V1]
[V2]
[B.C]
5
... recit

Adagio
Is ta mundi Per er ro res - nostre micat - stel la va ti —
etc
Ritornello
Alle lu ia Al — — — — — — le lu -

ia
Alle luia Al – – – –
6
le lu ia
%
%
Al – –
– – le lu ia
%
18

Gio. P. Colonna
Motet, *O Sidera*

D. Marco Uccellini
Op. IX, Sinfonia Prima à Violino Solo.

30
38
50
5
♭ 4♯

* Probably refers to the way of performing the passage, i.e. by exaggerating the contrast of long and short notes.

D. Marco Uccellini
Op. IX, Sinfonia Decima à due Violini e Violone

etc
5
[b]
13
[b]

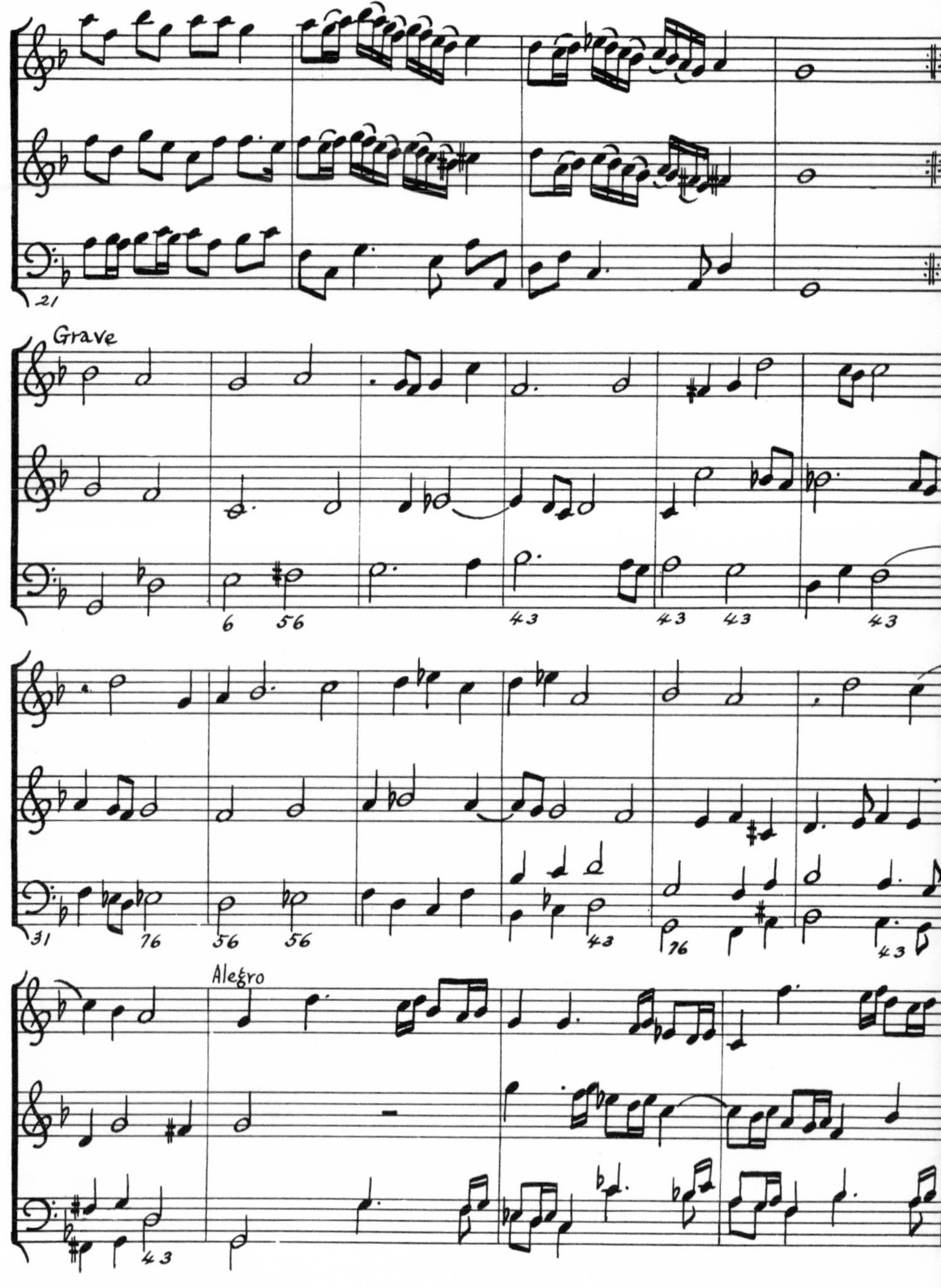
21
Grave
6 56
43
43 43
43
31
76
56 56
43
76
43
Alegro
43

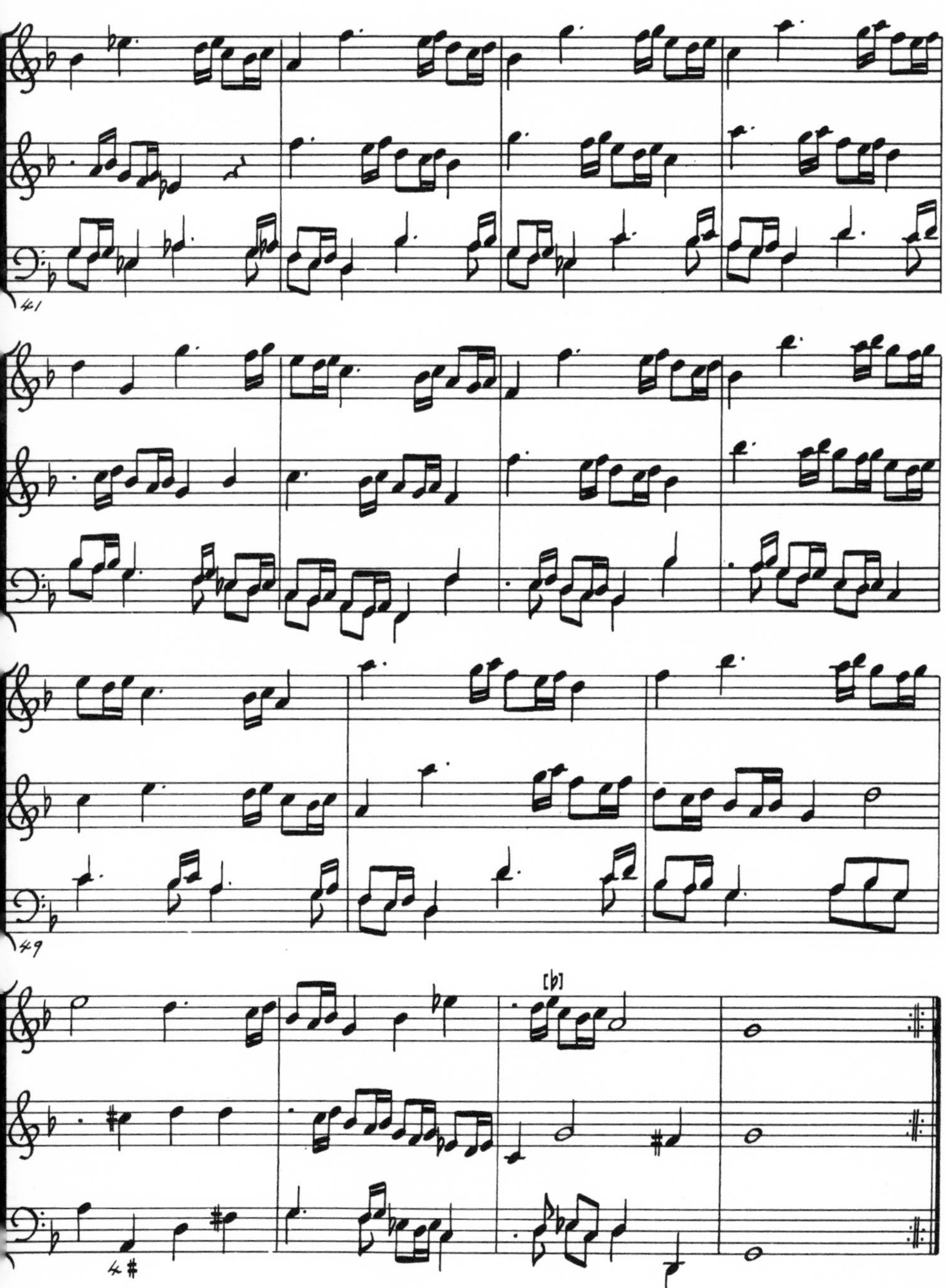
41
49
[♭]
4 ♯

Solo
V1
V2
B.C.
tr.
Solo
[♭]
tr.

D. Marco Uccellini
Op. IX, Canon, *Communis est via,* a 2 VV.

Resolutio

G. M. Bononcini, Op. III (frontispiece)

Canon a 2592 voci dopo un mezzo sospiro dall' una all' altra divise in 648 chori, e volendo uscir fuori dell ordine Musicale cioe di far valer le Massina piu di quello, che nella Musica ha suo termine, si puo procedere in infinito.

Seguo del tempo perfetto, della prolazione perfetta, e del modo maggior perfetto.

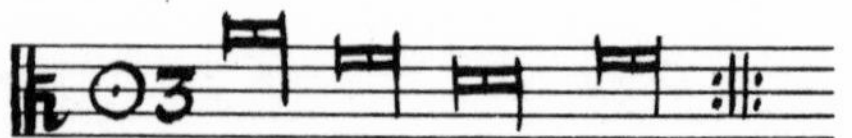